DATE DUE

INTERNATIONAL REGULATION
OF BANKING

INTERNATIONAL REGULATION OF BANKING

Basel II: Capital and Risk Requirements

Simon Gleeson

OXFORD

UNIVERSITY PRESS

OXFORD

UNIVERSITY PRESS

Great Clarendon Street, Oxford OX2 6DP

Oxford University Press is a department of the University of Oxford.
It furthers the University's objective of excellence in research, scholarship,
and education by publishing worldwide in

Oxford New York

Auckland Cape Town Dar es Salaam Hong Kong Karachi
Kuala Lumpur Madrid Melbourne Mexico City Nairobi
New Delhi Shanghai Taipei Toronto

With offices in

Argentina Austria Brazil Chile Czech Republic France Greece
Guatemala Hungary Italy Japan Poland Portugal Singapore
South Korea Switzerland Thailand Turkey Ukraine Vietnam

Oxford is a registered trade mark of Oxford University Press
in the UK and in certain other countries

Published in the United States
by Oxford University Press Inc., New York

© Simon Gleeson 2010

British Library Cataloguing in Publication Data
Data available

Library of Congress Cataloging-in-Publication Data

Gleeson, Simon.
International regulation of banking: Basel II, capital and risk requirements /
Simon Gleeson.
    p. cm.
Includes bibliographical references and index.
ISBN 978–0–19–921534–8 (hardback : alk. paper) 1. Banks and banking,
International—Law and legislation. 2. Asset–liability management—Law and
legislation. 3. Risk management—Law and legislation. 4. Banks and banking,
International—Management. 5. Basel II (2004) I. Title.
    K1066.G58 2010
    332.1—dc22

                                                          2009050894

Typeset by Glyph International, Bangalore, India
Printed in Great Britain by CPI Antony Rowe, Chippenham, Wiltshire

ISBN 978–0–19–921534–8

1 3 5 7 9 10 8 6 4 2

To Maxim and Josephine

PREFACE

Bank regulation is primarily about the quantification and restriction of the level of risk which banks are permitted to take. However, it has for some time been an unfairly neglected area of law, since those who understand law are uncomfortable with the quantitative aspects of risk calculation, and those who understand risk quantification are not generally lawyers. This situation was tolerable in the 1980s and 1990s, when bank capital regulation existed as a separate discipline broadly outside the main body of regulatory law. However, today bank capital regulation is as much a part of mainstream law as the rules relating to market abuse or authorization, and lawyers must be able to find their way around it.

The current work is an attempt to provide a topographical map of the regulatory landscape. Its aim is to describe and explain the concepts involved in bank capital regulation, to set out how they fit together, and to show how they contribute to the ultimate aim of regulating risk. It is not intended to be a 'how to' manual setting out how to perform risk capital calculations—for that there are other and better sources. It is, however, intended to enable lawyers who are called upon to construe the concepts in the context of legal requirements to understand the purpose and the aim of the provisions which they are being called upon to interpret.

This book was finalized in the summer of 2009, a period when bank regulation was changing rapidly. The explanation for this apparently curious timing is that an author on this topic who had decided in 1999 to wait for the regime to be finalized before commencing work would not yet have put pen to paper, and would see no prospect of doing so for at least the next four or five years. It is, however, necessary to flag that some sections of this book may be out of date when it is published. Nonetheless, even if the substantive content may be in need of constant updating, the fundamental conceptual material which is its primary purpose should remain intact.

The conceptual nature of the content makes it slightly difficult to anchor the work in any particular legal system. The basic concepts which surround bank risk regulation are still determined by the Basel Committee on Banking Supervision. These are elaborated at the European level in directives, elaborated further by the EU Committee for European Banking Supervision, and finally implemented (with—at least in the case of the UK—further clarificatory material) by national bank supervisors. In theory at least, none of this clarification alters the fundamental concept. However, it is an open (and unresolveable) question as to what extent guidance given at one tier is useful or relevant at a higher tier. Non-UK readers, in particular, may take the view that too much emphasis is placed herein on the views of the UK Financial Services Authority on contentious issues. However, this can be defended on the basis that the FSA is, in this area, one of the primary intellectual powerhouses of the global public sector, and even where other regulators take the view that the FSA view should not be followed, it is unlikely that any regulator would take the view that the FSA view should be disregarded. An apology may also be ventured for the relative disregard of US regulatory concepts in this area. At the time of writing the US was teetering on the brink of embracing the Basel regime for banks (but admittedly had been so teetering for some years) and the disregard seemed legitimate for a non-US work. Events may prove this wrong.

I should record two debts of gratitude. One is to OUP, and in particular Rachel Mullaly and Anna Krzyzanowska, who have put up with 'the dog ate my manuscript' excuses from me for longer than any human being should be expected to tolerate. The other is to my children, who have put up with the writing process for the same period, and to my wife, whose continued tolerance passes all understanding. Thank you.

Simon Gleeson
September 2009

Extracts from the Basel Accord and from the publications of other Basel committees are reproduced with the permission of the Bank of International Settlements. All of these documents are available free on their website: <http://www.bis.org/bcbs/index.htm>.

CONTENTS—SUMMARY

IV OTHER RISKS

V BANK GROUP SUPERVISION

CONTENTS

V BANK GROUP SUPERVISION

Contents

TABLES OF LEGISLATION

Note: In this table, 'Banking Co-ordination' and 'Banking Consolidation' Directives have been merged into one entry under 'Banking Consolidation Directives'.

LIST OF ABBREVIATIONS

ABCP	asset backed commercial paper
AIRB	Advanced IRB
AMA	Advanced Measurement Approach
ASRF	Asymptotic Single Risk Factor
BCBS	Basel Committee on Banking Supervision
BCD	EU Banking Consolidation Directive
BIPRU	the UK FSA's Prudential Sourcebook for Banks, Building Societies and Investment Firms
BIS	Bank for International Settlements
CAD	EU Capital Adequacy Directive
CCF	credit conversion factor
CCR	counterparty credit risk
CEBS	Committee of European Banking Supervisors
CESR	Committee of European Securities Regulators
CF	Commodities Finance
CFP	contingency funding plan
CIU	Collective Investment Undertakings
CLN	credit linked note
CNCOM	concentration risk capital component
CRD	EU capital requirements directives (the BCD and the CAD)
CRR	counterparty credit risk requirement
DSCR	debt service coverage ratio
DVP	delivery against payment
EAD	exposure at default
ECAI	External Credit Assessment Institution
EE	effective exposure level
EEA	European Economic Area
EL	expected loss
ELBE	estimate of expected loss
EPE	effective positive exposure
EU	European Union
EUL	Expected and unexpected loss
FRA	forward rate agreement
FSA	Financial Services Authority
GENPRU	the UK FSA's General Prudential Sourcebook
HVCRE	High-volatility Commercial Real Estate
IAA	internal assessment approach

IPRE	income-producing real estate
IRB	internal ratings based
KRI	Key Risk Indicators
LE	large exposure
LGD	loss given default
LTV	Loan to Value
MDB	multilateral development bank
MiFID	Markets in Financial Instruments Directive
OECD	Organisation for Economic Co-operation and Development
OF	Object Finance
PD	probability of default
PF	Project Finance
PFCE	potential future credit exposure
PFE	potential future exposure
PRA	Position Risk Adjustment
PRR	Position Risk Requirement
PSE	public sector entity
QRRE	Qualifying Revolving Retail Exposures
RBA	Ratings Based Approach
RDS	Reference Data Set
repo	repurchase agreement
RWA	risk-weighted assets
SL	specialized lending
SPV/SPE	special purpose vehicle/special purpose entity
UKIG	UK Integrated Group
UL	unexpected loss
VaR	value at risk
WIG	Wider Integrated Group

PART I

THE ELEMENTS OF BANK FINANCIAL SUPERVISION

1

INTRODUCTION TO BANKS
AND BANKING

In order to understand bank regulation, it is first necessary to understand what a **1.01** bank is. Everyone knows that a bank is an institution which takes deposits from the public and lends the monies thus raised, but even the simplest bank is more complex than this. Bank balance sheets include a range of types of exposures to a range of types of counterparties, and even where these exposures are as simple as fixed rate, fixed term bullet repayment loans, the interaction of those loans with other parts of the balance sheet may itself give rise to risks.

This highlights the point that there are two ways of looking at banks. An econo- **1.02** mist, for example, may see a bank primarily as a monetary phenomenon—a conduit for passing and creating credit. On this analysis a bank is simply a mechanism by which money is borrowed from the future and lent in the present.[1] This approach, however, is useful for those trying to describe and quantify the financial system, but not for those trying to control it. Viewed from the perspective of a bank board or a bank regulator, a bank is a mechanism for taking risks. Banks take risks for the same reasons that all commercial entities take risks—to obtain rewards. The nature of these risks and these rewards deserves a word of explanation.

---

[1] A process rather grandly referred to as 'intertemporal resource allocation'.

3

A. Banks Considered as Risk Takers

1.03 A bank takes in money from one group of people (depositors) and lends it to another (borrowers). It is (almost) certain that it will have to repay depositors; it is not certain that it will be repaid by borrowers. This means that there must be a gross profit margin made from loans advanced which can be set against borrower defaults. The business of lending is the same as any other business, in that increased profit comes at the expense of increased risk. Thus a bank may lend either at very high rates to very risky borrowers and hope that the default rate is sufficiently low to leave it in profit, or at very low rates to creditworthy borrowers and hope that the profit margin is sufficient to cover any loss which does occur. The key point here is that the riskiness of the strategy is not the same as the riskiness of the borrowers. A strategy of making large loans to high quality borrowers may be a very high risk strategy, since the margin on such loans may be very low, and even one default may destroy the entire institution. Conversely, a portfolio containing a very large number of small loans to relatively uncreditworthy borrowers at very high rates may be a relatively low-risk strategy, since the gross margin on the portfolio may be sufficient to cover likely losses many times over. This explains why institutions which are constrained in their lending to particular types of assets viewed as 'safe' (for example UK Building Societies and US Thrifts) have not in general proved particularly more stable than other deposit taking businesses.

1.04 Most banks, of course, diversify their lending across a number of different strategies, and seek to minimize their risk exposures by diversifying across a number of different types of business. However, the basic risk versus reward model is common to all areas of business, as it is to all businesses. Thus both managers and regulators of banks have a task which in principle is relatively straightforward. First, they must understand exactly which risks the bank is in fact exposed to (this is not as simple as it sounds). Second, they must—to the extent possible—quantify those risks. Third, they must assess the returns which may be obtained through the taking of those risks, in order to satisfy themselves that the risks are justified. Fourth, they must assess the degree to which the risks to which they are exposed are correlated to each other, in order to establish the total risk which is faced by the institution as a whole. In doing this they will be guided by the well-known principle that the generation of commercial returns necessitates the taking of risks, but the taking of risks by no means necessarily results in the generation of any returns.

B. A Prototypical Bank

1.05 In order to understand how this process may work in practice, we begin with a representative example of a bank. This particular example is not intended to resemble any bank living or dead, but was constructed in November 2001 by the Joint Forum[2] as a comparator for a cross-industry exercise.[3]

Assets		Liabilities	
Asset class	**%**	**Liability class**	**%**
Cash and cash equivalents	0.8	Inter-bank borrowing (deposits) (1)	10.1
Inter-bank lending (1)	12.4	Customer deposits (5)	60.4
Securities (2)	8.5	Debt securities (6)	10.9
Loans and advances to customers		Other liabilities	4.6
Gross loan amounts	69.0		
Loan loss reserves	(0.8)		
Loans net of reserves (3)	68.2		
Prepayments and accrued income (4)	1.9	Accruals and deferred income (4)	2.8
Tangible and intangible fixed assets	3.4	Loss reserves (provisions) for liabilities and charges (7)	1.2
Other assets (5)	4.8	Subordinated debt (8)	4.5
		Total shareholder equity	5.5
Total Assets	**100**	**Total Liabilities**	**100**

Notes to stylized balance sheet

(1) Inter-bank lending and borrowing generally occur through deposits and/or money market instruments. These are short-term securities issued or bought by the bank. In effect, when held to maturity, they are the equivalent of a traditional inter-bank time deposit.

(2) Securities: this corresponds to securities bought and held by the bank either for trading purposes (market-making or proprietary trading) or for investment purposes (buy-and-hold). Fixed income securities are held to maturity at cost value. Securities held by banks are in most cases essentially made up of fixed income instruments.

(3) Loans and advances to customers are comprised of all types of credits extended to customers, including overdrafts. This item also presents loan loss reserves as a negative (contra) asset item, consistent with its presentation in a number of countries.

(4) Prepayments and accrued/deferred income is related to all balance sheet items that are accounting for at cost and whose income is accrued. This is the case in particular for loans and advances to customers and customer deposits but can also be the case for a large proportion of inter-bank borrowing and lending.

(5) Customer deposits are the aggregated total of all outstanding deposits and cash balances of all customers' accounts.

(6) Debt securities include all securities issued by the bank, regardless of maturity. In addition to bonds and medium-term notes, this might also include deposit certificates although, in some jurisdictions, such certificates are aggregates either with inter-bank borrowing or with customer deposits, depending on the nature of the investor.

(7) Loss reserves for liabilities and charges: this can encompass, in some jurisdictions, loss reserves and/or provisions calculated on a statistical basis for specific events such as staff pensions. It also includes provisions for deferred tax. The proportion of such reserves for a bank is dependent on the taxation regime of its jurisdiction of incorporation.[4]

(8) Subordinated debt is made up of dated and undated subordinated securities qualifying for regulatory capital purposes (tier two capital).

---

[2] *The Joint Forum—Risk Management Practices and Regulatory Capital—Cross Sector Comparison* published by the Basel Committee on Banking Supervision November 2001. Much of what follows in this section is based on the description set out in that document.

[3] The paper also contains a typical securities firm, a typical life insurer, and a typical life and non-life insurance company.

[4] In jurisdictions which permit provisions to be deducted from taxable profits, loan loss reserves are generally higher.

Business summary

1.06 Banks primarily engage in granting loans and extending credits, although market activities have become more important. Assets are mainly funded by deposits collected from customers and from other banks (inter-bank deposits). Hence, these two classes represent the bulk of respectively, assets and liabilities in the stylized balance sheet of a bank. Proportions can, however, be as low as 40 per cent of assets for loans and 40 per cent of liabilities for customer deposits, depending on the bank's reliance on market operations and inter-bank funding.

1.07 The reliance on inter-bank funding and proportion of inter-bank lending varies widely between banks. This proportion increases if the bank is active in the derivative markets, since these are generally inter-bank transactions. More importantly, banks which raise money in the repo markets are likely to have a significantly higher proportion of inter-bank funding.

1.08 Customers range from retail customers to commercial and industrial entities to other financial institutions and governments. In some banks a substantial part of a bank's assets can be made up of securities held for trading or investment purposes, although this is clearly not the case in the example referenced above. Likewise, part of a bank's liabilities can take the form of bonds or other securities.

1.09 Off balance, traditional transactions are the undrawn credit facilities granted, and guarantees and collateral given or received. The bulk of off-balance sheet items, however, are likely to be derivatives contracts. The aggregated nominal amounts outstanding for derivatives contracts are often a multiple of the balance sheet total. The issue of netting of derivative exposures varies—in the US, for example, derivatives contracts are more easily netted than in Europe—but this figure does not generally give any particularly useful information as to the level of market risk to which the bank is actually exposed.

1.10 The interest margin on the traditional banking activity still constitutes the bulk of many banks' income, but diversification strategies have increased reliance on fees and commissions earned on all kinds of financial services provided by the banking sector (asset management, payment and settlement services, custody, proprietary trading, investment banking).

Risk analysis

1.11 Having seen what a bank looks like, we now turn to the risks which it faces.

1.12 Credit risk arising out of lending business is the dominant risk for banks. In the stylized example given above, loans make up approximately two-thirds of the assets, and this is a relatively representative figure. For most banks, loans will make up between 25 per cent and 75 per cent of total assets, although there are some exceptions.

No bank expects its lending to be entirely risk-free, and in general all banks will   **1.13**
provide against at least some of their loans. The circumstances in which provisions
may be taken on the balance sheet of a bank are explained below (see para 4.68).
In the example above loan loss reserves are shown on the stylized balance sheet as
a contra-asset item, reflecting their treatment in a number of jurisdictions. Such
reserves can range from less than one per cent of loans outstanding to much larger
amounts in some cases.

A major source of credit risk for banks does not appear on the balance sheet of   **1.14**
the bank at all. This is the agreed but undrawn lines of credit and other forms of
lending commitments which the bank will have entered into. There are many
ways in which a bank can give customers a promise to lend money at a future time,
ranging from the grant of committed borrowing facilities through to guarantees
and standby letters of credit. None of these appear as accounting items (although
they are sometimes disclosed in the notes to the accounts). They are, however, a
real source of credit risk, since in general a bank which has entered into a commitment to lend will not be able to refuse to make the advance when called upon to
do so. For many banks, total undrawn loan commitments are half again as large as
their total assets, although naturally there is a wide range of variation across banks.

Interbank activities, securities holdings, and other traded assets tend to make up   **1.15**
the bulk of a bank's assets not devoted to customer loans. These assets may be held
either as part of the bank's own treasury operations, or may be employed in proprietary securities trading business. Depending on the size and scale of these activities, banks are exposed to market risks and other risks associated with holding
traded securities.

Similarly, banks have in many cases become significant users of derivative instru-   **1.16**
ments. The notional value of derivatives entered into is now very large for most
banks. However, there are two aspects of this which require more detailed thought.
One is that in general the relevant figure for the bank is not the notional value of
the derivatives which it has entered into, but the 'mark to market' figure, being
(loosely) the amount of money which the bank would have to either pay or receive
in order to be released from the contract. This figure will be shown in the accounts
as a receivable (or an amount payable), and is likely to be a very small fraction of
the total nominal value of the derivatives concerned. Thus banks frequently have
very large nominal exposures to assets through the derivatives markets, but show
a relatively small exposure in their accounts.

Finally, the bank will be exposed to risks such as foreign exchange risk and interest   **1.17**
rate risk which may arise across its entire portfolio. In general, foreign exchange
risk arises wherever a bank enters into any transaction where the amounts receivable are calculated by reference to a currency other than the currency in which the
bank accounts, and interest rate risk arises in any circumstance where the bank's

obligations to pay interest on an asset are not precisely matched by an equivalent interest stream. Interest rate risk generally arises as a result of reinvestment risk.

1.18 On the liability side, customer deposits remain the largest source of bank funding for almost all banks (although there have been some notable exceptions in the recent past—Northern Rock springs to mind). Interbank liabilities and other forms of short-term wholesale funding are also important, particularly for banks active in trading activities. Importantly, the structure of bank's liabilities relative to its assets can give rise to both funding liquidity risks and to interest rate risk if the underlying maturity of a bank's assets and liabilities do not match.

1.19 Capital issued by the bank tends to be between 5 and 15 per cent of assets depending on the bank and on how capital is defined. For example, for the bank shown on the stylized balance sheet, equity capital is equal to 5.5 per cent of assets, while subordinated debt eligible for regulatory capital makes up another 4.5 per cent. In general, the total ratio of bank capital to total assets is unlikely to exceed 5 per cent—or, put another way, at least 95 per cent of a bank's assets will be funded out of borrowings.

Credit risk

1.20 Credit risk is the risk that a counterparty will fail to perform fully its financial obligations. It includes the risk of default on a loan or bond obligation, as well as the risk of a guarantor or derivative counterparty failing to meet its obligations. This risk is present to some extent in all businesses—including non-financial businesses. The management of credit risk is the most highly developed area of any bank's activities. In general modern banks will employ credit personnel who will establish abstract criteria for the taking on of any credit exposure. These criteria will include borrower qualifications and credit limits, the incorporation of appropriate risk premiums in pricing, and the establishment of loan loss reserves. The credit unit will operate independently of the business areas charged with originating business for the bank.

1.21 When a new business proposal is brought in, the process by which it will be evaluated is generally very formal. For large credits a specialized unit will analyse the risks inherent in the relevant product and geographical sectors as well as the particular borrower itself. The process by which credits are approved is a source of some concern to bank management. The issue is generally that for any substantial credit, the individual or individuals within the bank who originated the proposal are likely to feel some degree of 'fatherhood' for it, and even if the bank's remuneration structure does not specifically incentivize them.

1.22 In general credit exposure is managed through a process of imposing exposure limits, to individual borrower, to counterparties and groups of connected counterparties, to particular economic sectors, geographic regions and specific products.

Such limits are generally based at least in part on an internal credit grading scale. Banks price credits in such a way as to cover all of the embedded costs and compensate them for the risks incurred—however, the approach used to price credit is by no means always the same as the approach used to assess the exposure of the bank. Finally, in general banks assess the profitability of particular business areas by charging them the cost of their use of capital—ie by adjusting their apparent profitability to reflect the amount of risk and risk capital which they absorb. Thus a business which generates high margin loans to high-risk borrowers can be compared with a business which generates lower margin loans to higher quality borrowers (see below, para 1.40).

Most banks have now developed systematic internal models for the quantification **1.23** of credit risk, which operate as internal rating systems. These models assess portfolios of credit risks as well as individual credits, and provide estimates for default probabilities, exposures at default and potential losses given default. This modelling activity is used to estimate the amount of economic capital needed to support banks' activities that involve credit risk. The economic capital for credit risk is determined so that the estimated probability of unexpected credit loss exhausting economic capital is less than some target confidence level. In practice, this target confidence level is often chosen to be consistent with the bank's desired credit rating.

Banks may also seek to reduce their risk exposures by using risk mitigants—col- **1.24** lateral, guarantees, and credit derivatives. These techniques can be used not only to reduce absolute levels of risk, but also to restructure portfolios of risk in order to obtain diversification benefits. The increase in the use of portfolio models within banks appears to have driven the rapid development of credit derivatives. Credit risk mitigation techniques used by banks for their market operations, especially in their trading books, are similar to those used by securities firms in that they rely heavily on collateral.

In the trading book, banks expose themselves to credit risk through many of their **1.25** activities such as making margin loans to customers, entering into derivatives contracts, borrowing or lending securities, executing repurchase/reverse repurchase agreements, and occasionally extending accommodation loans in connection with pending transactions. In general credit risk arising out of trading activities is managed by the taking of highly liquid securities as collateral. These arrangements are generally subject to daily re-margining. In addition, banks seek to minimize the levels of such obligations by entering into master netting and collateral arrangements with counterparties where there are multiple exposures across different business lines.

Market and asset liquidity risks

Market risk refers to the potential for losses arising from changes in the value or **1.26** price of an asset, and asset liquidity risk refers to the risk that there will be no liquid market for the asset when it is to be sold. It is important to understand that although these are separate risks, they are both encountered as regards securities holdings. To take a simple example, imagine that a bank has one million shares in a particular company with a market price of £1. The bank is exposed to the risk of the market price falling. However, if the normal market size is only a few thousand shares per day, the fact is that if the bank decided the following morning that it wanted to sell the entire holding it would likely receive considerably less than the ordinary market price for each share.

1.27 Market risk can be subdivided into specific and general risk. Specific risk is the risk that the value of a particular security will change for reasons connected to that specific security—for example, the issuer of a bond suffers a rating downgrade. Specific risks generally affect no other security. General risks, however, affect all of the securities of a particular type—for example, if interest rates change, all of the bonds in a particular portfolio of debt securities will move in value simultaneously. General risk may arise from fluctuations in interest rates, currency exchange rates, or commodity prices.

1.28 Most securities firms and banks, together with insurance companies running significant trading positions, use statistical models to calculate how the prices and values of assets are potentially impacted by the various market risk factors. These models generate a 'value at risk' ('VaR') estimate of the largest potential loss the firm could incur, given its current portfolio of financial instruments. More precisely, the VaR number is an estimate of maximum potential loss to be expected over a given period a certain percentage of the time.

1.29 For example, a firm may use a VaR model with a 10-day holding period and a 99-percentile criterion to calculate that its $100 million portfolio of financial instruments has a potential loss of $150,000. In other words, the VaR model has forecasted that with this portfolio the firm may lose more than $150,000 during a 10-day period only once every 100 10-day periods. Most VaR models depend on statistical analyses of past price movements that determine returns on the assets. The VaR approach evaluates how prices and price volatility behaved in the past to determine the range of price movements or risks that might occur in the future. VaR models are commonly back-tested to evaluate the accuracy of the assumptions by comparing predictions with actual trading results. In practice, while VaR models provide a convenient methodology for quantifying market risks and are helpful in monitoring and limiting market risk, there are limitations to their ability to predict the size of potential losses.

1.30 Firms use stress tests and scenario analyses to supplement and to help validate VaR models. Stress tests measure the potential impact of various large market movements on the value of a firm's portfolio. These tests can identify market risk exposures that appear to be small in the current environment but may grow disproportionately under certain circumstances.

Scenario analysis focuses on the potential impact of particular market events on the value of the portfolio. Frequently, large and disruptive events from the past (eg major stock and bond market crashes) are used as potential scenarios. The main way to mitigate market risk, once assumed, is by taking positions in securities and derivatives whose price behaviour is negatively correlated to the issue or instrument whose risk is to be mitigated. **1.31**

Asset liquidity is increasingly taken into account in marking instruments and in interpreting VaR results based on short holding horizons. Banks take account of the difficulty in liquidating some assets at or near market value by discounting such market values, for instance when the securities are thinly traded or when the firm holds a large position in a specific security. **1.32**

Funding liquidity risk

Funding liquidity risk is the risk that a bank cannot obtain the necessary funds to meet its obligations as they fall due. In general, banks cannot know what the calls on their liquidity will be, since the vast majority of their liabilities (for example retail deposits) could in theory all be withdrawn tomorrow. They are therefore obliged to rely on forecasts of customer behaviour in modelling the likely outflow of liquidity, and must ensure that they maintain sufficient liquidity to meet that outflow. Contingency plans and stress testing are particularly important in this regard. In general, liquidity risks are dealt with through a combination of maintaining a poll of highly liquid assets which can be called upon within the relevant timescales, and diversification of funding sources in order to ensure that if one source fails there are others available. **1.33**

Banks are particularly vulnerable to funding liquidity risk because they finance many illiquid long-term assets, mainly loans, with shorter-term liabilities, largely customer and inter-bank funding deposits, that are vulnerable to a 'run' in the event of a drop in confidence. **1.34**

Interest rate risk

Interest rate risk is the exposure of a bank's financial condition to adverse movements to interest rates. Commercial banks, which tend to have large portfolios of long-term fixed rate loans funded by shorter-term floating rate deposits, are particularly exposed to this risk. Mitigation is accomplished to some degree by interest rate swaps, repackaging, and asset securitization, and banks seek to manage this exposure on a whole-bank basis using asset-liability management techniques. Callable debt and derivative products can also be helpful in managing the **1.35** contingent nature of interest rate risks linked to mortgages with prepayment options.

Operational risk

1.36 Operational risk can be defined in a variety of ways. For example, the Basel Committee has defined operational risk as the risk of loss resulting from inadequate or failed internal processes, people and systems or from external events (see below, Chapter 17). This definition generally excludes such risks as the strategic risk associated with business decisions. However, it does include some elements of reputational risk as well as legal and compliance-related risks. Most firms address legal and reputational risks by seeking to have well-developed compliance programmes and by focusing on the need for adequate legal documentation of transactions.

1.37 Other types of operational risks arise when a firm is exposed to loss because of employee error, the failure of an automated system, or the failure of a communications network. As banks have increased their reliance on technology and automated systems, the management of these operations-related risks has taken on higher priority. The increasing prevalence of outsourcing of technology-related services is another contributing factor to the emphasis on such risks.

Risk consolidation

1.38 Many banks are increasingly seeking to take a consolidated, enterprise-wide view of risk management. Their motivation comes from competitive forces to increase risk-adjusted returns on equity, in part by making more efficient use and allocation of capital, as well as from other current trends, such as globalization, expansion across sector lines, and increasing involvement with products that entail multiple types of risk. Further, financial firms are increasingly managing their risks in structurally complex ways. For example, many firms use inter-affiliate transactions to transfer risks from different legal entities into a common vehicle where the risk can be managed and hedged on a more aggregate basis.

1.39 The need to consolidate or aggregate measures of risk can arise at several different levels within an organization. Within a business line, individual risk types (eg market risk or credit risk) may be aggregated across the various activities and positions. Consolidation at this level typically makes use of the relevant risk measurement methodology for the particular risk under consideration. This allows offsetting exposures to identical risk factors to be fully netted out and allows for diversification benefits across similar risk factors to be considered. Some firms take this approach a step further and attempt to perform firm-wide aggregation of particular risk types. For example, it is common for firms employing VaR techniques for market risk measurement to attempt to aggregate all market risks related to trading positions throughout the firm into a single aggregate VaR calculation for the entire firm. This produces a consolidated measure of market risk for the entire firm.

Economic capital

Banks conventionally use 'economic capital' as the internal currency for risk across **1.40** risk types and across business units. Firms using economic capital models calculate the amount of economic capital needed to support a given risk at a given level of confidence. Many firms set the confidence level for the measurement of risk so that it matches the default probability associated with a particular external credit rating. In this way, firms are calculating the amount of economic capital required to obtain a given rating for a firm taking on the underlying amount of risk on a stand-alone basis. As well as being performed at the business level, economic capital calculations are often performed at the business line level for a given risk type, and may be performed on a business line by business line basis.

In this regard economic capital—or, more precisely, the allocation of economic **1.41** capital—becomes the primary management tool for bank management. Individual business lines within the bank may be given a certain amount of economic capital, and told to manage their overall business within that 'budget'. Business lines which generate what they believe to be unusually profitable business opportunities which require capital above their allocation may be allowed to 'bid' for capital internally against other business lines. The aim of this mechanism is to improve the overall risk/return ratio within the bank by ensuring that capital is used for the most profitable business.

2

WHY ARE BANKS SUPERVISED?

The starting point for a discussion of bank regulation is to ask why banks should **2.01** be regulated to any greater extent than, say, car manufacturers. It would be reasonable (although cowardly) to avoid this issue altogether, and to begin from the proposition that they just *are*. However, it is helpful in understanding some of the issues which arise in the context of bank regulation to have a clear idea of what it is that the banking regulatory system is ostensibly trying to achieve.

A. Basis of Bank Supervision—the Basel Principles

The locus classicus of bank supervision is the statement of the Basel Committee as **2.02** to the Core Principles for Effective Banking Supervision, produced by the Basel Committee in September 1997 and reissued in a revised version in October 2006. It is helpful to consider these here, since they set out in a short but comprehensive fashion the elements which may be found in the banking supervisory regimes of all major jurisdictions.

Principle 1—Objectives, independence, powers, transparency, and cooperation. **2.03** An effective system of banking supervision will have clear responsibilities and objectives for each authority involved in the supervision of banks. Each such authority should possess operational independence, transparent processes, sound governance and adequate resources, and be accountable for the discharge of its duties. A suitable legal framework for banking supervision is also necessary, including provisions relating to authorization of banking establishments and their ongoing supervision; powers to address compliance with laws as well as safety and soundness concerns; and legal protection for supervisors. Arrangements for sharing information between supervisors and protecting the confidentiality of such information should be in place.

2.04 **Principle 2—Permissible activities.** The permissible activities of institutions that are licensed and subject to supervision as banks must be clearly defined and the use of the word 'bank' in names should be controlled as far as possible.

2.05 **Principle 3—Licensing criteria.** The licensing authority must have the power to set criteria and reject applications for establishments that do not meet the standards set. The licensing process, at a minimum, should consist of an assessment of the ownership structure and governance of the bank and its wider group, including the fitness and propriety of Board members and senior management, its strategic and operating plan, internal controls and risk management, and its projected financial condition, including its capital base. Where the proposed owner or parent organization is a foreign bank, the prior consent of its home country supervisor should be obtained.

2.06 **Principle 4—Transfer of significant ownership.** The supervisor has the power to review and reject any proposals to transfer significant ownership or controlling interests held directly or indirectly in existing banks to other parties.

2.07 **Principle 5—Major acquisitions.** The supervisor has the power to review major acquisitions or investments by a bank, against prescribed criteria, including the establishment of cross-border operations, and confirming that corporate affiliations or structures do not expose the bank to undue risks or hinder effective supervision.

2.08 **Principle 6—Capital adequacy.** Supervisors must set prudent and appropriate minimum capital adequacy requirements for banks that reflect the risks that the bank undertakes, and must define the components of capital, bearing in mind its ability to absorb losses. At least for internationally active banks, these requirements must not be less than those established in the applicable Basel requirement.

2.09 **Principle 7—Risk management process.** Supervisors must be satisfied that banks and banking groups have in place a comprehensive risk management process (including Board and senior management oversight) to identify, evaluate, monitor and control or mitigate all material risks and to assess their overall capital adequacy in relation to their risk profile. These processes should be commensurate with the size and complexity of the institution.

Principle 8—Credit risk.   Supervisors must be satisfied that banks have a credit   **2.10**
risk management process that takes into account the risk profile of the institution,
with prudent policies and processes to identify, measure, monitor and control
credit risk (including counterparty risk). This would include the granting of loans
and making of investments, the evaluation of the quality of such loans and investments, and the ongoing management of the loan and investment portfolios.

Principle 9—Problem assets, provisions, and reserves.   Supervisors must be   **2.11**
satisfied that banks establish and adhere to adequate policies and processes for
managing problem assets and evaluating the adequacy of provisions and reserves.

Principle 10—Large exposure limits.   Supervisors must be satisfied that banks   **2.12**
have policies and processes that enable management to identify and manage
concentrations within the portfolio, and supervisors must set prudential limits to
restrict bank exposures to single counterparties or groups of connected
counterparties.

Principle 11—Exposures to related parties.   In order to prevent abuses arising   **2.13**
from exposures (both on balance sheet and off balance sheet) to related parties and
to address conflict of interest, supervisors must have in place requirements that
banks extend exposures to related companies and individuals on an arm's length
basis; these exposures are effectively monitored; appropriate steps are taken to
control or mitigate the risks; and write-offs of such exposures are made according
to standard policies and processes.

Principle 12—Country and transfer risks.   Supervisors must be satisfied that   **2.14**
banks have adequate policies and processes for identifying, measuring, monitoring and controlling country risk and transfer risk in their international lending
and investment activities, and for maintaining adequate provisions and reserves
against such risks.

Principle 13—Market risks.   Supervisors must be satisfied that banks have in   **2.15**
place policies and processes that accurately identify, measure, monitor and control market risks; supervisors should have powers to impose specific limits and/or
a specific capital charge on market risk exposures, if warranted.

Principle 14—Liquidity risk.   Supervisors must be satisfied that banks have a   **2.16**
liquidity management strategy that takes into account the risk profile of the institution, with prudent policies and processes to identify, measure, monitor and
control liquidity risk, and to manage liquidity on a day-to-day basis. Supervisors
require banks to have contingency plans for handling liquidity problems.

Principle 15—Operational risk.   Supervisors must be satisfied that banks have   **2.17**
in place risk management policies and processes to identify, assess, monitor, and
control/mitigate operational risk. These policies and processes should be commensurate with the size and complexity of the bank.

2.18 **Principle 16—Interest rate risk in the banking book.** Supervisors must be satisfied that banks have effective systems in place to identify, measure, monitor and control interest rate risk in the banking book, including a well-defined strategy that has been approved by the Board and implemented by senior management; these should be appropriate to the size and complexity of such risk.

2.19 **Principle 17—Internal control and audit.** Supervisors must be satisfied that banks have in place internal controls that are adequate for the size and complexity of their business. These should include clear arrangements for delegating authority and responsibility; separation of the functions that involve committing the bank, paying away its funds, and accounting for its assets and liabilities; reconciliation of these processes; safeguarding the bank's assets; and appropriate independent internal audit and compliance functions to test adherence to these controls as well as applicable laws and regulations.

2.20 **Principle 18—Abuse of financial services.** Supervisors must be satisfied that banks have adequate policies and processes in place, including strict 'know-your-customer' rules, that promote high ethical and professional standards in the financial sector and prevent the bank from being used, intentionally or unintentionally, for criminal activities.

2.21 **Principle 19—Supervisory approach.** An effective banking supervisory system requires that supervisors develop and maintain a thorough understanding of the operations of individual banks and banking groups, and also of the banking system as a whole, focusing on safety and soundness, and the stability of the banking system.

2.22 **Principle 20—Supervisory techniques.** An effective banking supervisory system should consist of on-site and off-site supervision and regular contacts with bank management.

2.23 **Principle 21—Supervisory reporting.** Supervisors must have a means of collecting, reviewing, and analysing prudential reports and statistical returns from banks on both a solo and a consolidated basis, and a means of independent verification of these reports, through either on-site examinations or use of external experts.

2.24 **Principle 22—Accounting and disclosure.** Supervisors must be satisfied that each bank maintains adequate records drawn up in accordance with accounting policies and practices that are widely accepted internationally, and publishes, on a regular basis, information that fairly reflects its financial condition and profitability.

2.25 **Principle 23—Corrective and remedial powers of supervisors.** Supervisors must have at their disposal an adequate range of supervisory tools to bring about timely corrective actions. This includes the ability, where appropriate, to revoke the banking licence or to recommend its revocation.

Principle 24—Consolidated supervision. An essential element of banking **2.26** supervision is that supervisors supervise the banking group on a consolidated basis, adequately monitoring and, as appropriate, applying prudential norms to all aspects of the business conducted by the group worldwide.

Principle 25—Home-host relationships. Cross-border consolidated supervi- **2.27** sion requires cooperation and information exchange between home supervisors and the various other supervisors involved, primarily host banking supervisors. Banking supervisors must require the local operations of foreign banks to be con-ducted to the same standards as those required of domestic institutions.

B. Capital Regulation

These principles set out the general objectives which a bank supervisor should **2.28** seek to achieve as regards its supervision of the management of the undertaking of each of its banks. However, although these objectives are all correct and desirable, they are all indications of general direction rather than statements of specific limits. Possibly more importantly, all of these principles would also be the objec-tives of the board and senior management of any well-run bank. Once the regula-tor has satisfied itself that the bank has systems in place to achieve these objectives, and that those systems are reasonably effective and in line with best industry practice, it is tempting for the bank regulator to assume that he has done all that he can.

This is not, however, the practice of bank regulators. The reason for this is that for **2.29** the reasons set out below in paras 2.33 to 2.38, bank regulators seek to reduce the overall risk exposure of the banking system to a level below that which the direc-tors of the bank would otherwise maintain. This is done by requiring the mainte-nance of a specified amount of regulatory capital.

It should be noted that the requirement by a regulator that a bank maintain a **2.30** specific amount of capital relative to the risk which it runs is exactly the same mechanism as that which bank management employ within the institution when they impose economic capital limits on individual businesses (see above, paras 1.40 to 1.41). In both cases the specification of a limited amount of capital is imposed as a proxy for the imposition of a risk limit—however, rather than the regulator specifying in detail the amount of each type of risk which the bank may run, the regulator in practice gives the bank a 'risk budget' by specifying the amount of capital which can be recognized and the mechanism by which capital may be allocated to risk. A bank which perceives itself as having access to particularly advantageous business is free to raise more capital, but until it has done so the regulator will not allow it to engage in that business unless it simultaneously decreases its risk exposure by reducing or exiting other businesses.

2.31 This approach makes capital requirements the primary tool of bank regulation. The idea that capital regulation is the proper study of bank regulators is deeply embedded within regulators, and many senior bank regulators quietly believe (*pace* Rutherford) that bank regulation can be divided into quantitative supervision and stamp collecting. It is fair to say that the usefulness of regulatory capital requirements is frequently rejected amongst academic commentators,[1] who object that there is no academically validated proof to show that capital regulation has in fact reduced risk. Put simply, the argument is that the level of capital maintained by a particular bank is not necessarily a good guide to how likely it is to survive a financial crisis and, in particular, it is clearly not the case that banks with capital levels substantially above the regulatory minima will necessarily survive financial turbulence. Banks with low capital but good risk controls are more likely to survive a period of financial turbulence than banks with high capital levels but poor risk controls.

2.32 It should be noted, however, that it does not follow from the fact that capital requirements are justified that capital regulation in the form in which it has existed has always been useful. Most importantly, a regulatory capital regime which sets a requirement lower than that which the bank would otherwise maintain is a bureaucratic burden which is of no value. Secondly, an insufficiently risk-sensitive capital requirement is likely to create perverse incentives which outweigh any benefit which it may create (arguably the position of Basel I from about 2001 onwards). Thus we cannot simply say that capital regulation is a good thing per se—it is necessary to explain what the objectives of such regulation should be.

C. The Constraints on Bank Capital Regulation

2.33 We begin with the drivers of bank capital. In reality, a bank's decision as to how much capital it needs will be driven by the question of how to maximize its returns by minimizing its costs of borrowing. Put simply, if a bank has too little capital, lenders will demand an increased interest rate for lending to it. However, it is also possible for a bank to have too much capital—beyond a certain level, the decrease in borrowing costs will no longer be sufficient to compensate for the dilution of

---

[1] See eg Ed Scott, *Capital Adequacy Beyond Basel* (OUP, 2005), Barth Caprio and Levine, *Rethinking Banking Regulation* (Cambridge University Press, 2006), and Tarullo, *Banking on Basel* (Petersen Institute, 2008).

return on equity.[2] Consequently for any given bank, ordinary business analysis will produce an optimum level of capital which maximizes return on equity, and that is the capital level to which the bank will naturally gravitate. The question for regulators is as to why they should seek to require a bank to maintain more capital than this.

The primary reason for this is known as the 'asymmetry' problem. This is the fact **2.34** that bank profits accrue to private shareholders but bank losses in practice fall (in at least some cases) on the public purse (and therefore on the public). There are a number of explanations for this, but the simplest (and the most convincing) is that although managers and directors of banks are highly incentivized to avoid their bank failing, they are not particularly incentivized to differentiate between small and large failures—a bank manager will be unemployed whether his bank fails owing £1 or £1bn. This results in the odd situation that the individuals within a bank are incentivized not to fail, but, if they do fail, to fail big.

This phenomenon is not, however, unique to banks, and is to some extent present **2.35** in all corporations. However, unlike most other forms of commercial firms, banks perform a public as well as a private function—the transmission of money and credit around the economy is a function which is similar in some ways to that which is performed by sewerage or electricity companies. If an electricity transmission company were to fail, government would take measures to ensure that it continued operating (analogous in our case to implementing a special resolution regime), and this is comparable to the steps which are taken in practice on a bank failure to ensure the continued operation of the payment and deposit-taking functions of the bank. In reality, government has little choice but to act to keep these operating come what may, since the maintenance of these services is part of the irreducible minimum of services which electors regard governments as created and elected to ensure. However, if an electricity company were to fail, there is no obvious reason why government should support its ordinary commercial creditors. Why should banks be any different? The answer is that creditors of banks are, in this regard, generally other banks. To allow one bank to fail in this way would create a knock-on impact for other banks, which would be likely to result in further failures and the necessity for further intervention. Further, since banks are the mechanism by which credit is supplied to the economy, the collapse of even one substantial bank would imperil short-term economic prospects, and the collapse of multiple banks would be *a fortiori* in this regard. Thus governments act to save troubled banks (and therefore support their existing creditors) not because they choose to but because there is no acceptable policy of choosing not to.

---

[2] The Capital Asset Pricing Model states that in pure theory a bank should be indifferent to this, since (again in pure theory) the two should balance each other out. This is not, however, the experience of most banks in the real credit markets.

2.36 The issue, therefore, is as to how to reduce to an acceptable minimum the chance that government may be obliged to commit public resources to support failing banks, and the amount of public resources that may have to be committed in such a case. The primary technique must necessarily be to restrict the risks taken by a bank relative to its resources, and this is the task which capital regulation performs (another important part of the process of minimizing impact on the public purse is the establishment of 'resolution regimes'—specialized insolvency regimes which permit government to intervene early and effectively in the affairs of a failing institution in order to minimize the harm resulting from its demise. These are considered below at paras 2.53 to 2.61).

2.37 The aim of bank capital regulation is therefore not to increase bank capital per se, but to limit risk exposures relative to the bank's capital. Since risk and reward are two sides to the same coin, if a bank is to be limited in the level of risk which it takes on for a given amount of capital, it is also necessarily limited in the return which it can make on that capital. Since banks ultimately compete for capital with other corporations, the perception is therefore that regulators are limited in their powers to restrict bank capital, since if a bank's permitted return on capital is restricted below that of other types of business, no capital will be invested in the banking sector and the sector itself will disappear. However, this is not quite correct. Banks can be required to maintain any level of capital that the regulator chooses and may remain profitable (even super-profitable) provided that they have a sufficient degree of monopoly over at least one of the services which they provide. Banks do in practice have a statutory monopoly in almost all jurisdictions on the acceptance of deposits, but in general do not have such a monopoly on lending.[3] Regulators have the option of imposing almost any level of capital requirement which they choose on banks, provided they are prepared to co-operate in ensuring that banks are able to charge their customers sufficient to enable them to raise that capital. Thus the idea of meaningful capital requirements is inextricably connected with the idea of a protected statutory monopoly.

2.38 This monopoly must, however, be a regulated monopoly. It could be argued that we could dispense with the detail of financial regulation and simply permit the financial services markets to be dominated by a small, closed cartel. The cartel would act in its own best interests by restricting its rate of increase of risk in good times in order to avoid suffering losses in bad times. There are two objections to this, one theoretical and one practical. The theoretical objection is that conventional economic theory tells us that such a cartel would act in its own interests, and would require regulatory intervention to require it to act in the best interests of its customers. The practical objection is that in reality the position in the banking

---

[3] Except in a few countries—notably France.

market is exactly the opposite of this—the market is highly fragmented and highly competitive and produces low costs to users. In such a market, even assuming that bank managers were individually convinced of the merits of holding higher capital levels, they could not do so voluntarily—if one bank were to do so it would be competed out of business, and if banks were to agree collectively to do so this would almost certainly constitute illegal anti-competitive behaviour. As a result the cumulative private interests of market participants fall short of an outcome which is optimal for the market as a whole. Thus in order to promote the social benefit which arises from an efficiently functioning market, it is necessary to impose regulation to require the market as a whole to preserve itself.

D. The Quantum of Bank Capital Requirements

If this is the justification for bank capital requirements, the next issue for regula- **2.39**
tors is as to the level of those requirements. The issue may be regarded as an insurance problem—would the public prefer to pay for future bank crises up front in the form of higher bank charges or after the event in the form of bank rescues leading eventually to higher taxes? The problem for the regulator is nothing more than to set the insurance premium level correctly. The remainder of this book is devoted to a detailed consideration of the technical and scientific rules which are used to carry out this calculation. However, it must be accepted that there is no technical or scientific technique which can answer the basic question as to how high these levels should be. The initial Basel 8 per cent requirement was famously set because '7 per cent sounded too low and 9 per cent too high', but it must be accepted that the determination of the 'right' regulatory capital level comes down, in the end, to guesswork.

E. Did Risk Capital-based Regulation Fail in 2007–8?

If prudential supervision is a good thing, then the immediate question to ask is as **2.40**
to why it seems to have failed so spectacularly in 2007–8. In order to answer this question we need to do two things. One is to understand what the cause of the 2008 crisis actually was, and the second is to understand how bank regulatory capital requirements interacted with that cause.

Quantitative risk modelling and the crash

Bank failure can broadly be divided into general and idiosyncratic failures. An idi- **2.41**
osyncratic failure is a failure which results from factors which are unique to a single bank (or a group of banks). Idiosyncratic failure can have systemic consequences if the bank concerned is large enough. However, in most cases of idiosyncratic

failure the failure is of risk control within the individual institution. A general failure, by contrast, occurs where there is a failure of part of the intellectual underpinning of the market. An example of this is the Dutch tulip mania of the seventeenth century. Whilst the market proceeded on the common belief that tulip bulbs had a particular value, stability was assured. However when this belief evaporated, the consequent collapse in values affected a large number of industry participants simultaneously. Similar events can be discerned in some other historic systemic crises—the 1929 Wall St Crash is an instance. Sometimes such events are entirely external to the financial markets, and the impact on banks is simply an instance of the impact of such developments on businesses generally. However, from time to time it is the internal mechanism of banks themselves which fail. The typical instance of one of these latter episodes is a general conviction amongst bankers that a particular asset class is highly valuable—railway stocks in the nineteenth century, sovereign debt in the 1980s, commercial real estate in the 1970s, and dot-com shares during the 1990s are all examples. In these cases an analytical error becomes a collective error, and after a while begins to derive its validity from the fact that it is collective—'it must be so because all the other banks think it so'. The asset class which occupied the position of most overvalued asset in 2007–8 was the residential mortgage—in particular the US sub-prime residential mortgage—and it was the collapse in the valuations of this asset class which led to some of the most significant write-downs in bank balance sheets. However, the reason that the crisis appeared at the time to be different from those which had preceded it was that the problem was not simply a collective misapprehension of the value of a particular asset class. What appeared in the early stages to have been uncovered was a flaw in the entire market's fundamental approach to risk and risk quantification, a flaw which could potentially have invalidated almost every risk control paradigm used in every financial institution. For the second half of 2008, the primary concern of the market was whether any bank could ever be trusted again.

2.42 The technique which had apparently failed so spectacularly was statistical risk modelling. The use of risk modelling to assess and control bank exposures has been a fast developing field for the last 20 years, and the significant advances made in financial mathematics enabled very sophisticated statistical techniques to be applied to portfolios of financial assets. Eventually these techniques graduated from being used by banks to assess their risk exposure to being used by structured product engineers to create securities with defined risk characteristics. In effect these structures reversed the ordinary process of risk analysis—instead of starting with a portfolio of risks and assessing its riskiness, they started with a target level of riskiness and structured the portfolio to deliver it. The result was the creation of a deep and liquid market in securities whose pricing was in effect determined by the output of risk models. These securities were—reasonably enough—treated as interchangeable with ordinary securities—thus a AAA bond issued by a corpo-ration was regarded as broadly similar to a AAA bond issued by a structured vehicle.[4]

The difficult with this was—as we now know—that the output of the risk models **2.43** was wrong, and significantly understated the riskiness of these structured securi-ties. This discovery had a devastating impact not only on the market for securities based on risk structures, but also on the balance sheets of those who owned large proportions of these securities—a group which included the banks. Lead had been sold as gold, and once this was realized the balance sheets of financial institu-tions suffered badly from the write-downs. Even worse, the institutions which believed that they had found the way to turn lead into gold had made the cardinal error of keeping that apparent gold on their own balance sheets and borrowing against it—as was frequently pointed out, the problem with the 'originate to dis-tribute' model was that it had become an 'originate to not distribute' model. Banks had in effect become so enamoured of the high-return low-risk securities which they believed that they were creating that they could see no reason not to keep those returns for themselves.

It is worth examining at this stage why the output of the models turned out to be **2.44** so wrong. Statistical risk modelling was in many ways a victim of its own success, in that the more work was done in the field, the more robust the models appeared, until eventually it became impossible to doubt that which had been so clearly demonstrated by so many able mathematicians. This created a self-reinforcing cycle of confidence, such that—as explained in the Senior Supervisors Group report[5]—in some financial institutions the output of the statistical risk model became the sole guide for the making of trading and investment decisions through-out the bank. The problem, of course, was that the validity of a statistical model is an entirely separate issue from the validity of the output of the model. A model must be mathematically valid to be of any use at all—no useful output will be produced by a flawed model. However, the output of a model is only as good as the inputs to that model, and in the context of financial mathematics the data-set of historical information about markets and prices is surprisingly weak. The rea-sons for this weakness are multifarious, but one of the most important is that if one goes back more than 10 years in most institutions the bulk of the available data will be on paper in filing cabinets (if it has been retained at all). Even where such data can be recovered and turned into usable electronic form, it is unlikely to

---

[4] In fact market prices tended to show a significant spread in the yield of such bonds over the 'true' AAA rate, suggesting that the market maintained a degree of scepticism as to the value of such bonds. However this level of scepticism proved insufficient.

[5] *Observations on Risk Management Practices during the Recent Market Turbulence*, 6 March 2008, available on the BIS website <http://www.bis.org>.

pass any very stringent test of formal validity—for example, the exact definition of 'default' used may not be clear from the record, the extent of the exposure at default may not be clear, and amount ultimately recovered may not be capable of being established. In many cases the inclusion of such data in the default database would have created serious validation problems for institutions seeking to demonstrate to their regulators that their systems were internally consistent and data was subject to rigorous review before being used in the models.

2.45 Aggregate market index numbers are available for an extended historical period spanning several severe economic downturns. However, specific pricing information about securities in electronic form, and even more importantly default and loss data about loans and recoveries in electronic form, is rare, and what is in existence is relatively recent. At this point it is important to remember that the name for the period of 10 years to 2007 amongst economists is 'the "NICE" decade' (non-inflationary, constant expansion), and that this period is generally reckoned to have been one of the most benign economic environments of the preceding century. In other words, the data which the models had to work on was not only incomplete, but was in fact drawn almost exclusively from a period in which default and crisis was notably absent.

2.46 The point here is, of course, that a statistician is only as good as his data. In the absence of hard historical data it is impossible to just make up some more. Manful efforts were made to take the data that was available and 'flex' it to reflect harder economic times. However, although it is possible in this way to project trends, it is very difficult to construct a statistical mechanism which reflects the prospect that the data on which it operates is wholly unrepresentative—not least because beyond a certain point the output would lose the primary merit that a statistical analysis has; that it is based on facts.

2.47 The point which many argue ought to have alerted the banks to the fact that they were basing decisions and products on unacceptably rosy scenarios was the level of returns which they were making on this business. A system which produced apparently AAA bonds with yields far above the equivalent yields paid on ordinary AAA bonds should have sent a clear warning signal that something was wrong. This became particularly clear when repackaging was taken into consideration—if your model is underpricing risk, if you then put the output of that model back into it you will end up with a greater underpricing and so on. This phenomenon, and the proliferation of 'squared' and 'cubed' products which it generated, led to repackaging of structured paper being almost a licence to print money. These developments did raise alarm. However, by that stage no-one was prepared to take the view that the output of the statistical risk models on which these securities were based was anything less than perfect—not least because, as seen above, the models themselves could be exhaustively validated mathematically.

The defaults which occurred within structured vehicles in 2008 constituted a very **2.48** public demonstration that something was wrong with the architectural theory on which these constructs had been based. The crisis of confidence which this created had the effect of closing many of the financial markets almost completely, on the—quite reasonable—basis that investors knew that something was wrong but did not know what, and as a result avoided anything which might be tainted with the structured finance tar brush. The resulting market panic resulted in massive falls in the market price of apparently safe assets, and it was the consequences of these falls—and their impacts on bank balance sheets—which provided the links in the chain to the meltdown of late 2008.

F. Market Crisis and Regulation

This brings us neatly to the interplay between the market crisis and regulation. **2.49** As will be seen from the above, the market meltdown was in fact nothing more than a particular instance of an asset price bubble, with the distinguishing feature (there is always a distinguishing feature in every asset bubble) being that the very high levels of confidence which banks had in their models translating into very high levels of confidence in their outputs, and as a result into very high levels of confidence in the valuation of securities based on those outputs. The revaluation of these assets, when it came, was therefore particularly severe and particularly unexpected.

Now any sufficiently severe asset revaluation will break a bank. Banks are typically **2.50** at least 25 times geared (ie their total liabilities equal 96 per cent of their equity capital), and consequently even a relatively small move in aggregate values is sufficient to wipe out that capital. However, what the regulatory system does is to assess (roughly) the riskiness of assets, and to arrange that relatively little capital need be held against high-quality assets (such as government and AAA bonds), whilst larger amounts are held against more volatile assets. The problem in 2007–8 was that the regulatory system had accepted the banks' models own assessment of the value of structured bonds, and had accepted that, being low risk, these should require relatively small amounts of capital. Thus, when these bonds started to suffer substantial liquidity and valuation impacts, the amount of capital held against those positions was rapidly consumed, and the shortfalls radiated out across the banking system as a whole.

It may be argued that this proves that the Basel II system—which is itself based on **2.51** statistical modelling—must also be fundamentally flawed. However, this is to confuse the method and the application. The fact that statistical models, applied to the wrong data, give the wrong results, does not demonstrate that the technique of statistical modelling is itself invalid. It remains the case that there is a substantial difference in risk profile between a US government bond and an equity interest in a start-up, and a system which disregards this difference is unlikely to be an improvement on one which does. It remains the case that the regulatory system is likely to be at its most effective where it is based on an assessment of actual risk exposure. In retrospect, it is not surprising that regulators should have based their work on approaches which were accepted across the industry and across academe—and indeed it is positively desirable in general terms that they should do so. In many respects all that this proves is that where everyone in a particular market suffers from a common error, the regulator in that market is almost certain to suffer in the same way from the same error. The error has now been corrected (at least within the regulatory system), but there will of course be others. Nonetheless, if capital requirements are necessary for society (and it does appear that they are), then even a failure of the system to assess risk correctly can justify the adoption of a system which rejects risk analysis completely. If we are to have capital regulation then we must have risk-based capital regulation, and if we are to have risk-based capital regulation then we must accept that the analysis of risk within the regulatory system is likely to follow the same lines as the analysis of risk in the market which the regulator regulates. If the whole industry is wrong then the regulator will be wrong too, but even so it is better for the regulator to be occasionally wrong in line with the industry than invariably wrong by refusing to adopt sensible risk-based criteria to regulation.

2.52   However, what does follow from this is that it is arguable that the regulator's focus on the use and output of risk-based models, although it followed the industry's own best practice, may have been to some extent flawed in the same way. Quantitative risk regulation may be essential, but it is not sufficient, and regulators must follow bank management into a position where a broader overview may be taken of the risk and reward profile of the bank as a whole. This may in some cases be presented as a retreat from an over-reliance on quantitative modelling, and there may be something in this position. However, it should not be presented (or considered) as an abandonment of risk-based regulation, any more than any bank management team should be permitted to cease to attempt to quantify risk for internal purposes.

G. Protecting the Public from the Consequences of Bank Failure

2.53   Given that bank failures are inevitable in any system, it is also important for the public sector to take steps to mitigate the impact on the public purse of bank failure. When a bank is in danger, or fails, in principle it should be subject to the ordinary insolvency regime of the jurisdiction in which it is established. However, it may be necessary for the public sector to intervene. This is because—as noted above—bank failure has social consequences above and beyond the immediate impact on creditors of the bank, and the application of ordinary insolvency procedures may lead to sub-optimal outcomes for society as a whole. Such intervention is often necessary and sometimes socially desirable even though technically unnecessary. Consequently governments should ensure that they have the necessary legislative, administrative and legal powers in place to enable themselves to conduct such interventions in a swift and effective fashion, and in particular should ensure that they have in place all of the relevant powers and authorities identified in the IMF/World Bank *Overview of the Legal, Institutional, and Regulatory Framework for Bank Insolvency*.[6]

It is universally accepted that government intervention in the affairs of particular **2.54** businesses is most effective if it satisfies the criteria of being:

(a) rapid—there should be no significant period of uncertainty between the announcement of intervention and the intervention itself;

(b) transparent—creditors and counterparties of the institution concerned should be clear as to how the intervention affects their position; and

(c) in line with market practices—intervention should not violate clearing, settlement, payment finality, netting, set-off, or collateral systems and procedures.

Intervention may take the form either of rescue or, if rescue is impossible, of some **2.55** form of insolvency procedure.[7] However, these are not alternatives—a rescue may well involve the liquidation of some part of the rescued group, and a good bank/ bad bank rescue will inevitably result in the eventual liquidation of the bad bank. There are therefore in broad terms three possible policy responses to bank failure:

Policy	Techniques
Rescue not involving insolvency proceedings	Government guarantees, capital injections, liquidity arrangements
Rescue involving insolvency proceedings	Good bank/bad bank approaches
Insolvency	Administration, liquidation

There are a variety of reasons why government should seek to rescue an individual **2.56** bank. However, the most commonly encountered in recent practice has been the

---

[6] IMF, 17 April 2009.

[7] There are a wide range of available procedures in the major jurisdictions, ranging from administration regimes whose object is to rescue the underlying business to liquidation regimes whose object is to realize assets and distribute them amongst creditors. For the purposes of this book we refer to all of these collectively as 'insolvency proceedings'. These proceedings almost invariably involve the appointment of one or more persons to conduct the proceeding under the supervision of the court. We refer to such persons as 'office holders'.

public function of the banking system as a conduit for payments, and the ambiguity which that creates as regards deposits. The difficulty is that it is not possible to draw a bright line between deposits maintained for the purpose of payment services and deposits maintained as savings. Thus governments which seek to protect the payment services elements of an institution will necessarily be required to protect the deposits maintained with that institution. It should also be noted that the determination of which institutions should be supported because they are significant providers of payment services is an entirely different determination from that as to whether an institution is systemically significant. This can be seen in the UK in the case of institutions such as Northern Rock, where the basis of the government decision to support depositors was based on the extreme dislocation that the suspension of bank accounts would create, and despite the fact that the institution concerned was not systemically significant. What this demonstrates is that governments may frequently find themselves in a position where they feel forced to intervene in the failure of an institution which is neither systemically significant nor 'too big to fail'. Thus the current paradigm—that banks should ordinarily go into 'normal' insolvency, and that special regimes are the exception—may in practice be the mirror image of the true position.

Bank insolvency regimes

2.57 There are certain attributes of normal insolvency law which should be capable of being varied in the context of a bank insolvency. The most important of these is that it is desirable for jurisdictions to have legislation or other provisions in place setting out the powers and authorities of government, the courts, and other actors in the event of a bank rescue which is undertaken for systemic reasons. These provisions should reinforce that where an intervention is undertaken for reasons other than those for which a 'normal' insolvency is undertaken, all those involved should be empowered to and required to act so as to promote that objective. Governments should not have to grant themselves ad hoc powers in such cases, as was the case in the UK during the Northern Rock collapse. In addition to promoting the efficiency of resolutions, the idea that government will act on an ad hoc basis from case to case creates deep uncertainty in the markets and damages the legal certainty which is the underpinning of those markets.

2.58 The second is that there should be a 'regulatory' as well as a 'solvency' ground for the making of an application to the court for an order commencing insolvency proceedings against the bank. This is because regulators should be able to ensure that proceedings are commenced at an appropriate time as regards the business of the bank concerned, and that time could be well before the onset of formal insolvency as normally measured.

2.59 The third can be summarized as that the office holder should be placed under a positive obligation to pursue the objective of the rescue, even where this results in discrimination between creditors. Although the principle of equal treatment of creditors is one of the fundamental principles of insolvency law, in the case of bank rescues it should, in appropriate cases, give way before the overriding objective of reducing systemic damage. Thus, for example, an office holder should have the power to deliver securities and make payments to close out transactions, even before the full list of creditors and assets has been drawn up. Although most jurisdictions have implemented regimes which focus on business rescue rather than simple recovery maximization, even within such regimes there is often limited scope for the office holder to take account of the interests of wider systemic considerations. One of the consequences of this is that when public authorities seek to engage in rescues, they may find themselves working against rather than with the insolvency regime.

The fourth is that such provisions should operate with rather than against existing   **2.60** financial markets law. The creation of broad discretionary powers to vary existing contracts would clearly make restructuring existing institutions easier. However, the market uncertainty which this would create would have a substantial detrimental effect on every market contract, and would do significant damage to the markets as a whole. This is because the basis of financial markets is legal certainty, and in particular the confidence of counterparties that settlement finality, set-off and collateral rights will be broadly respected in the insolvency of any particular system participant. Thus, for example, in the failure of Lehman Brothers, the reason that the credit derivative markets remained robust was because market participants had confidence that the set-off provisions contained in open contracts would survive, and be effective in, the insolvency. If there had been doubt as to this point it is likely that the impact of the failure on the system as a whole would have been substantially greater than it in fact turned out to be.

The fifth is that it should be possible for financial regulators and treasuries to play   **2.61** a greater role in bank insolvencies. The public sector has a number of relevant roles to play in the context of bank failure. The most important is as the operator (and ultimate guarantor) of the relevant deposit or investor protection system—it should be possible either for one authority or for a number of authorities acting together to determine the optimal balance of assets and liabilities to ensure that protected deposits are repaid with minimal loss to the taxpayer and to other contributories. To this end it should be possible to reverse or amend the terms of inter-group transactions entered into prior to the insolvency, although not transactions with external counterparties. Another potential role is as guarantor and creditor—where a bank which has received public support becomes insolvent, it is important for the public authorities to be confident that the terms on which they have guaranteed liabilities or assumed obligations cannot be undercut by subsequent intra-group transfers, and, if they are, that such transfers can be reversed. In one respect this is simply a particular instance of the general principle that agreements with external entities should be respected; however, in the context of international banks it may be necessary for governments to provide reassurance to each other.

2.62 Finally, it should be noted that there are some other specific areas where the intervention of a regulator could be economically optimal for the markets. One example is the use of central clearing systems. The use of central clearing systems can be perceived as increasing competition within a market, since it enables clients to deal with a larger number of intermediaries without having to take credit risk on those intermediaries. Whether or not this is correct, it highlights the fact that the reduction of risk for the users of any particular market is not always an unalloyed benefit for the participants in that market. Regulators may at times determine that customers will benefit from changes to market structures even where those changes are not in the interest of every individual participant in those markets.

2.63 The role of the regulator in requiring firms to be appropriately managed should be considered. In theory firms have a strong interest in managing their own risk exposures and their own decision taking systems, and regulators should need to have no involvement in this. In particular, firms have no business turning to regulators for assistance in their own internal management. However, there is nonetheless a valid ground for intervention here, in that the cost/benefit analysis of particular risk control measures at individual banks may be positive for the system as a whole by sub-optimal for any individual relevant bank. Since such requirements will only be effective if they are promulgated across the entire industry, we can get to a position where each individual bank is prepared to 'sign up' to a level of risk control which is higher than it would have adopted for its own account in order to have the reassurance that other industry participants subscribe to the same standards. This argument will apply equally to other requirements (for example liquidity requirements).

3

INTERNATIONAL BANK REGULATION

A. The Basel[1] Committee and the Basel Accord

A historic approach to bank regulation is of little use or relevance, but it may be **3.01**
helpful to say a few words about the Basel committee, and how it has come about
that an organization with no powers, constitution, or even legal existence has
come to be the dominant power in bank regulation.

As the financial markets internationalized in the 1970s, it became increasingly **3.02**
clear to supervisors that some form of co-operation would be needed between
them in order to supervise the larger banks. The failure of Bankhaus Herstatt in
1974—a failure of a German bank which had significant repercussions in the
London market—was the event which triggered the establishment of an entity for
this purpose. Thus towards the end of 1974 the governors of the central banks of
the G10 countries established a committee to discuss international supervision.
The Basle (later Basel) Committee on Banking Supervision (BCBS) was afforded
a secretariat by the Bank for International Settlements (BIS) (which existed to
manage payments between central banks) based in Basel. The key point here is
that since the committee was founded by central bank governors (who at the time
were responsible for bank supervision) it could not be given any formal role or
status, and remained an entirely informal body. In 1975 the committee produced

---

[1] A note on spelling. The 1988 accord was referred to as the 'Basle accord', using the French
spelling, since this was at the time the working language of the Bank for International Settlements,
which provides the secretariat for the committee. However, the city itself is in the German-speaking
part of Switzerland, and the German spelling is Basel. At some point between the first and second
Accords the BIS was prevailed upon to adopt the local variant—hence Basle I but Basel II.

its first major document, the Basle Concordat, which laid down a division of responsibilities between the national supervisors of international banks with the aim of ensuring that there were no gaps in the regulatory coverage of such banks.

3.03   Another consequence of the increasing internationalization of the financial markets was that banks established in different countries were beginning to compete head to head in the London syndicated loan markets, and this competition was beginning to highlight the fact that banks from different countries were subject to very different regulatory constraints in terms of the level of capital which they were required to hold. It is generally suggested that the Bank of England's paper of 1980 entitled 'The Measurement of Capital' constituted the first formal imposition by a central bank regulator of a formal capital adequacy regime based on risk-weighted assets, but the US followed almost immediately afterwards, imposing a leverage ratio (a capital requirement not based on the riskiness of assets) by 1985, as did the Japanese regulator. Each jurisdiction had different rules for what counted as capital and what requirement should apply to what type of asset, and many countries (particularly European countries) operated a system whereby the capital requirement imposed on each individual bank was simply a matter for the judgement of the relevant regulator. At the same time banks were increasingly trying to improve their return on equity by financing themselves with a wider range of instruments and by reducing the equity proportion of their balance sheets. Thus there was considerable concern amongst regulators that a 'race to the bottom' could only be averted if the regulatory community established and promulgated a common standard.

3.04   The result of this initiative was the Basle Capital Accord of 1988. This set out a simple weighting system for different types of assets, standardized the rules as to what should count as capital, and set out the basic requirement that banks must maintain an amount of tier one (broadly equity) capital equal to at least 4 per cent of their risk-weighted asset value, and an amount of tier one and tier two equal to 8 per cent of their risk-weighted assets. The BCBS designed the 1988 Accord as a simple standard so that it could be applied to many banks in many jurisdictions. It required banks to divide their exposures up into a few broad 'classes' reflecting similar types of borrowers. Exposures to the same kind of borrower—such as all exposures to corporate borrowers—were subject to the same capital requirement, regardless of potential differences in the creditworthiness and risk that each individual borrower might pose.

3.05   While the 1988 Accord was applied initially only to internationally active banks in the G10 countries, it quickly became acknowledged as a benchmark measure of a bank's solvency and is believed to have been adopted in some form by more than 100 countries. The Committee supplemented the 1988 Accord's original focus on credit risk with requirements for exposures to market risk in 1996.

In theory no-one was (or is) obliged to take any notice of the Basel Committee. **3.06**
However, the Basel Accord was rapidly adopted as the standard bank regulatory
approach, both by the G10 banks which composed the Committee but also by
almost every other bank supervisor worldwide which supervises international
banks. Thus by the time the proposal for an updated Accord was introduced in
1999, the original Accord could justifiably be said to form the basis for global
bank supervision. That updated Accord, published in June 2004, is the document
commonly referred to as Basel II and whose provisions form the subject of the
bulk of this work.

One oddity which requires comment here is the interaction between the Basel **3.07**
Accords and the EU. The broad provisions of the Basel Accord were enacted in the
EU in 1989 in the form of the Solvency Ratio Directive,[2] and the EU has subsequently sought to embed the various updates to the Accord into EU law reasonably rapidly. Since the major EU banking supervisors are themselves direct members
of the BCBS, and all EU supervisors adhere to the Accord in practice, this may
appear to be pure supererogation. There is, however, a logic for this embedding in
EU law of the provisions of the Accord. That logic is that the basis of the EU
system is the concept of the passport—the idea that a bank established in one
member state has an absolute right to do business in any other state subject to
compliance with certain notification formalities. EU member states take the
view—not unreasonably—that they will only agree to other banks having a right
to operate in their jurisdictions if they can be sure that the national supervisor of
any such bank is under a strong legal obligation to regulate that bank to at least the
minimum acceptable international standard. EU member states are, of course,
free to impose on their national banks requirements which are more onerous than
those proposed in Basel—what the directives prevent them from doing is imposing obligations which are less onerous. The current directives implementing Basel
II in the EU are the Bank Capital Directive,[3] which sets out the rules which apply
to banks, and the Capital Adequacy Directive,[4] which sets out the rules which
apply to investment firms and to the trading books of banks.

EU implementation of Basel is not a simple copying out of the Accord. There are **3.08**
some uniquely European provisions in the directives which have no counterpart
in Basel—for example the directives contain a regime which applies to covered
bonds, a specifically European security with which many of the Basel members
would have been unfamiliar. More importantly, the EU passporting regime applies
to investment firms as well as banks, so the EU has applied the Basel rules to
almost all investment firms across the EU. This tends to mean that EU investment

---

[2] 89/647/EEC, now repealed.
[3] 2006/48/EC.
[4] 2006/49/EC.

firms are subject to significantly more sophisticated regulation than those in many other jurisdictions (including, for many years, the United States).

B. Addressing Failures of Multinational Banks

3.09 There is, as yet, no international agreement which would address the required co-ordination of governmental and regulatory action on the failure of a multinational bank with significant activities in more than one jurisdiction. It is frequently said that banks are 'global in life but national in death', but this is an unhelpful oversimplification. It is in fact more than likely that an international bank will operate through more than one significant subsidiary, as well as through a number of less significant subsidiaries. This means that there are likely to be several different courts seized of different parts of the group restructuring, all struggling with each other to establish title to assets. More importantly, the question of which assets are held by which legal entity when the bank finally does become insolvent may be determined by the accident of the last few transactions entered into by the group management, which may be untypical or part of an attempted rescue.

3.10 The issue for governments is therefore as to how the failure of such groups should be best managed. The first point is that the legal distinctions within the institution should be respected—creditors of the group will have performed credit analysis and based decisions on the legal separateness of group members, and the threat of abolition of these distinctions would make the making of such determinations much harder. Any legal provision which has the effect of reducing legal certainty on insolvency would have a detrimental effect on the markets as a whole which would be more severe than the benefit which might accrue in the face of an actual failure. However, that having been said, governments do need to create a situation where office holders of individual parts of the failed institution should be required to have regard to the situation of the group as a whole, and should be expressly permitted to work with office holders of other parts of the group and the management of any group entities which are not insolvent or the subject of proceedings in order to maximize returns to creditors and to minimize disruption to the financial markets as a whole. This should not be at the expense of existing rights such as collateral, set-off, or clearing and settlement systems, but it should be permissible for a court to approve a scheme which may result in creditors in its own jurisdiction being potentially worse off if creditors of the group as a whole are better off in aggregate.

3.11 Another issue which arises in the context of cross-border resolution of bank crises is the issue of domestic depositor preference. Governments derive their tax revenue from their domestic taxpayers, and may feel that the first call on such revenues is the compensation of domestic customers of a bank. This principle would be unobjectionable if applied consistently, since it would result in a position where each government compensated customers in its jurisdiction regardless of the place of establishment of the bank. However, in the absence of a global intergovernmental agreement it is unlikely that each government will adopt identical policies and that customers in different jurisdictions will all be equally protected. As a result, the resolution of such crises may be slowed by (and in extreme cases prevented by) a suspicion of free-riding or unequal benefit. It should be noted that this issue is in fact different from that which arises under deposit protection schemes, since it may also arise as regards guarantees or other sureties which governments may offer on crises to depositors with troubled institutions.

In terms of the appropriate policy response to this congeries of issues, it is impor- **3.12** tant to be realistic about what can be achieved. It may well be true that the optimal way of dealing with the failure of an international banking group would be the establishment of an international insolvency regime, but this is not a short-term deliverable. In the same way and for the same reason it is not helpful to suggest the establishment of global funded compensation schemes.

The most important short-term practical steps to be taken should be that govern- **3.13** ments should engage in intense dialogue with each other about the way in which they would deal with creditors, depositors, and other claimants in respect of the failure of a cross-border institution. It would clearly be optimal if such negotiations could take place within the scope of an international framework, and the conclusions reached embedded in a treaty, convention or similar instrument. However, even if this is not practicable, the substantive discussions should nonetheless be undertaken and progressed to a reasonably advanced stage. It is accepted that government cannot commit itself firmly to pursuing a particular course of action in every imaginable circumstance, since governments cannot commit their own fiscal position in the future; however, this should not inhibit the establishment and development of agreement on broad principles. It would also significantly aid the market as a whole if such agreement, having been achieved, could be formalized—perhaps as a treaty or concordat amongst states.

The foundation of any such treaty or concordat would be that signatory states **3.14** would agree to put in place mechanisms within their national legislation which would enable their national regulators to act as part of a single, concerted, co-ordinated rescue, restructuring, or failure management effort. This would in practice be tantamount to the formation of an ad hoc global supervisor in the event of a significant failure, composed of the relevant national regulators but capable of acting on a global basis.

It is important to make the distinction between inter-government co-operation **3.15** and inter-regulator co-operation for this purpose. It is probably not possible to formalize intergovernmental co-operation at this time, since the approach of government to specific crises is a matter for public policy at the relevant time in the context of the relevant circumstances. Such policy may or may not involve international co-operation. However, inter-regulatory co-operation generally does envisage international co-operation, since regulators generally work with the grain of institutional management and that management is generally cross-border in nature. Put another way, governments can rationally commit their regulators to international co-operation almost regardless of the nature of the crisis to be addressed, whereas the same is not necessarily the case for governmental crisis response—in particular where such response involves the commitment of public funds.

C. International Institutional Co-Operation in Bank Regulation

3.16 The primary obstacle to international co-operation between regulators of banks is the lack of any legal architecture to support such co-ordination. The following are the areas where this lack is most keenly felt, and which therefore form the skeleton of the international agreement which is generally acknowledged to be required in this area.

Provide a legal basis for colleges of supervisors

3.17 Colleges of supervisors work reasonably well in a benign environment, but come under significant stress where the institution which they supervise faces a real risk of failure. This is because the national regulators who constitute the college of supervisors are generally constrained in their ability to act collectively by national legislation which requires them to act in the interest of their national markets, consumers and creditors.

To create a principle of optimal recovery for all clients in cross-border insolvencies of financial sector companies

3.18 This is potentially controversial. However, the principle that would be established would be that regulators and governments should seek the solution to the crisis in respect of the relevant institution which would optimize the position of the clients as a whole of the relevant firm. The aim would be to prevent a 'scramble for assets' between national regulators, and to remove the basis for policies which may be non-optimal for clients as a whole but which might confer a particular advantage on clients established in one particular jurisdiction. It is almost certainly impractical to prescribe equal treatment for all clients, since many jurisdictions have different policies in place as to the treatment of different types of clients of financial sector companies. Optimal recovery for clients as a whole is therefore the best practical solution.

*Provide a basis for mutual development of client protection measures
and for mutual recognition of those measures*

It would not be possible for the international agreement to establish these meas- **3.19**
ures directly, since there is insufficient common ground between putative members for useful conclusions to be reached. However, regulators and governments
are expected to develop their thinking on the mechanisms for dealing with financial institution failure significantly in the near future, and if a common international approach to cross-border failure can be worked out, it is likely that a degree
of commonality will emerge in the thinking of national governments as to the
correct approach to the development of client protections in the event of such
failure. It would clearly benefit the emerging international system considerably if
a mechanism existed for encouraging this harmonization.

*Mandate information-sharing and co-operation amongst supervisors and economic
stability regulators, and enable them to co-operate in multinational work-outs*

The key principle is that any regulator in any jurisdiction should be able to have **3.20**
information and some degree of control—direct or indirect—over a branch of a
foreign bank operating in its jurisdiction where the branch is sufficiently large to
cause that supervisor concern.

Whilst a bank remains solvent informal co-operation between supervisors is gen- **3.21**
erally sufficient to allow the college to function effectively. However, it is at the
point which the stability of the institution is brought into question that the college
most needs to operate effectively. Sadly, it is likely to be at this point that national
laws and regulations may act to inhibit or prevent regulatory co-operation.

It is generally accepted as a matter of policy that where a cross-border institution **3.22**
becomes unstable, the optimum result for creditors and customers in aggregate is
likely to be achieved by managing the problem at the level of the institution as a whole.
Conversely, if national priorities conflict, or if individual regulators seek to secure
windfalls for creditors in their jurisdictions at the expense of others, the problem is
likely to become worse, confidence in the institution will weaken, and significant
resources will be absorbed in inter-governmental and cross-border legal disputes.

The minimum aim should therefore be to require states to legislate to designate **3.23**
any institution which is not incorporated in their territory but whose operations
in their territory give rise to systemic concern. The group of all of the supervisors
who have such concerns as regards any particular entity should constitute the college of supervisors of that entity. Some jurisdictions may have more than one
member of the college.[5]

---

[5] For example where a firm is both a bank and a securities firm in a particular jurisdiction, both the
central bank and the securities supervisor may have concerns about its activities in their jurisdiction.

3.24 Such supervisors should thereupon become party to multilateral exchange of information as to the activities of the relevant institution. Such a supervisor should, at a minimum, be required to agree that in exercising any power conferred upon it by its national legislation, it will have regard to the implication of its decisions on the financial stability of any other state which is a party to the treaty.

3.25 In general, every international entity will have a head office from which its business is managed. The supervisor in this jurisdiction will necessarily have the best overview of the position of the institution globally. This supervisor should assume primary responsibility for passing information to other supervisors, and other supervisors should agree that the supervisor of the head office jurisdiction should be the leading supervisor for the institution. The lead supervisor should co-ordinate the activities of other relevant supervisors, and should seek to arrive at a common agreement between them as to crisis management measures when they are required.

3.26 States agreeing to these principles would in practice have to amend their domestic law in order to permit national supervisors to act in accordance with the treaty. The issue here is that national supervisors are frequently required by national legislation to act exclusively in the interests of customers and/or creditors who are situated within their jurisdictions. Governments would have to permit their regulators to act in the interests of the rescue of an international financial entity, even where there was a chance that consumers or creditors in their jurisdiction might end up worse off than they would have been had the international action not been undertaken.

Provide for multilateral co-operation in the supervision of markets which do not have a single identifiable seat (such as derivatives, syndicated loans, and foreign exchange markets)

3.27 Although there are regulatory and legislative initiatives currently on foot which aim to concentrate these markets through exchanges and clearing houses, it is unlikely that financial markets will ever operate exclusively through such mechanisms. A machinery therefore needs to exist whereby regulators can gather information on these markets, and obtain information about the exposures which individual institutions have through them. Obtaining this information is likely to involve sharing by national regulators of information, some of which will be covered by confidentiality obligations. This is in fact a different issue from that discussed above. It is relatively clear that where an institution is subject to extraordinary stresses that the ordinary confidentiality obligations which may bind its supervisors should be relaxed. What is under discussion here, however, is a situation where there is no extraordinary stress, but where a comprehensive picture of the relevant market can only be constructed by pooling information from a large number of market participants. This obligation would therefore be at once more general—in that it would be independent of any specific crisis—and more constrained—in that it would permit the exchange of a more limited amount of information—than that which would pertain in the event of a significant market crisis.

4

THE BANK CAPITAL CALCULATION

A. The Basic Bank Capital Calculation

The basis of the calculation of a bank's capital requirements is very straightforward **4.01** under the Basel II regime. Basel adopts a three-pillar approach, set out below.

Pillar One	Pillar Two	Pillar Three
Minimum Capital Requirements	*Supervisory Review Process*	*Market Discipline*
Pillar one is classical 'arithmetical' prudential supervision, involving the allocation of percentage capital requirements for individual asset items. There are three approaches within Pillar One: Standardized, Foundation IRB, and Full IRB.	Pillar two is the 'discretionary' element of regulation, and is based on an assessment of the supervision functions within the institution concerned. Pillar two looks at the bank's internal risk control procedures.	Pillar three is based on a compulsory disclosure regime, and operates on the principal that if the financial markets are given sufficient information on the position of an institution then the market price of the risk of that institution will be a useful tool of supervision. It is therefore based on compulsory disclosure and careful monitoring by the regulator of the market price of the risk of the institutions which they regulate.

4.02 The calculation of the amount of capital required by a bank is relatively straightforward:

Credit Risk requirement + Market Risk requirement + Operational Risk requirement = Pillar one requirement

Pillar one requirement + Pillar two requirement = total capital requirement

The calculation of the individual requirements is calibrated such that the capital requirement should be 8 per cent of risk-weighted assets.

The Credit Risk requirement is the sum of:

(1) the credit risk capital requirement;
(2) the counterparty risk capital requirement; and
(3) the concentration risk capital requirement.

The Market Risk requirement is the sum of:

(1) the interest rate position risk requirement (including the basic interest rate position risk requirement for equity derivatives);
(2) the equity position risk requirement;
(3) the commodity position risk requirement;
(4) the foreign currency position risk requirement;
(5) the option position risk requirement; and
(6) the collective investment undertaking position risk requirement.

Exposures which do not fit into any of these categories must, for this purpose, be allocated to one or other of them—thus every exposure which is recognized on the bank's balance sheet must be allocated a capital requirement calculated in some way or other.

4.03 This simple calculation is the basis of the regulatory capital system. The bulk of this book addresses the issues involved in calculating the Pillar one and Pillar two requirements. However, before turning to this topic we must first establish what we mean when we speak of 'capital'.

B. What is Capital?

The topic of regulatory capital really ought to be entirely straightforward. The **4.04** essence of regulatory capital requirements as originally conceived was to procure that banks had sufficient capital to absorb both expected and unexpected losses. Thus, went the theory, any losses actually suffered would affect only the contributors of the capital of the institution; leaving depositors, bondholders and other senior creditors to be paid in full. This would ensure the smooth operation of the market, remove most of the credit risk exposure inherent in dealing with banks, and ensure that the function of operating the payment system would proceed unaffected by credit losses by individual institutions. Capital in this context therefore could mean anything which absorbed losses which would otherwise fall on senior creditors.

This unsophisticated analysis is broadly accurate. However, recent market devel- **4.05** opments have made clear that it conflates two different but important functions of capital. The distinction is best set out in the FSA's Discussion paper 'Definition of Capital',[1] which distinguishes between the functions of capital:

> first, the role of capital while a firm is solvent, including in times of stress, and second, the role of capital if a firm is wound up. We can summarize this distinction between the two main purposes of capital as follows:
> * to absorb losses while the firm is a going concern, both when the firm is in a state of financial health and during periods of financial stress, thus maintaining market confidence in the financial system and avoiding disruption to depositors; and
> * to absorb losses in a gone concern scenario, protecting depositors in a winding up.

The events of the credit crisis of the mid-2000's provided a salutary reminder to **4.06** regulators that subordinated capital might be effective to protect senior creditors, in a 'gone concern' scenario, but was of little or no value to a bank struggling to remain afloat. The key point here is that capital is useless to a firm if any loss impacting on that capital item immediately results in the failure of the firm. Mere subordination is insufficient—capital must be capable of absorbing losses in such a way as to permit the firm concerned to continue in business without adverse consequences, and in particular without inhibiting the ability of that firm to raise further capital. This means that the regulatory criteria for what constitutes acceptable capital must be significantly more complex than a mere requirement that capital instruments be subordinated to ordinary creditors.

---

[1] FSA Discussion paper 07/6.

4.07 As a result the focus of regulators, credit analysts and rating agencies switched almost completely to core tier one capital, and in some cases the primary focus became the sub-division of core tier one known as tangible common equity (ordinary shares less intangible assets). The other forms of subordinated capital (tier three, tier two and non-core tier one) became widely perceived as almost irrelevant, as both regulators and industry analysis concentrated on core equity rations.

4.08 It is probably an error to deduce from this development that tier two is of no use. Tier two provides comfort to those assessing those credit risk exposures which will arise on the insolvency of an institution, and this may well be relevant where an institution fails for idiosyncratic reasons. However, where all institutions face a systemic threat, then contagion risk rapidly places government in a position where it must maintain institutions on a going concern basis rather than dealing with their assets on a gone concern basis, and in a crisis of this kind then ordinary share capital becomes the primary—if not the only—indicator of soundness.

C. The Bank Capital Hierarchy

4.09 There are currently no fewer than seven possible types of bank capital.

Core tier one	Permanent share capital
	Profit and loss account and other reserves (taking into account interim net losses)
	Eligible LLP members' capital
	Share premium account
	Externally verified interim net profits
Non-core, non-innovative tier one	Perpetual non-cumulative preference shares
Innovative tier one	Innovative tier one instruments
Upper tier two capital	Perpetual cumulative preference shares
	Perpetual subordinated debt
	Perpetual subordinated securities
	Revaluation reserves
	General/collective provisions[2]
	Surplus provisions
Lower tier two capital	Fixed term preference shares
	Long term subordinated debt
	Fixed term subordinated securities
Upper tier three	Short term subordinated debt
Lower tier three	Net interim trading book profit

---

[2] Specific provisions are not available to be included in capital since they are, by definition, already committed to absorb specific losses and are not generally available: see para 4.68.

At each stage of the calculation of capital certain deductions are made. These **4.10** deductions constitute a sort of regulatory provisioning, and are generally calculated by specifying certain assets whose value is to be deducted from capital. It should be clear that the effect of requiring a particular asset to be deducted from capital is equivalent to assuming that its value has been wholly lost.

There are a complex set of rules which specify which capital can be used in what **4.11** proportions in respect of which exposures. The principal is that firms are encouraged to hold as much 'core' tier one as possible. Quantitative limits are applied to other forms of capital—thus, a firm may only hold a certain percentage of its capital in the form of any of the other tiers.

D. Capital Monitoring

Firms are required to monitor their capital requirements on an ongoing basis. It **4.12** has never been entirely clear what this requirement actually entails—at the extreme, it could be said to require real-time monitoring. Most large institutions confine themselves to formal assessment on an end-of-day basis (although they will have risk systems which monitor exposures—particularly in trading areas— more frequently). The FSA provides that:

> This [requirement] does not necessarily mean that a firm needs to measure the precise amount of its capital resources and its CRR on a daily basis. A firm should, however, be able to demonstrate the adequacy of its capital resources at any particular time if asked to do so by the FSA.

Firms are required to report not only any actual breach of the requirement, but also any expected breach of the requirement—thus a firm which discovers that its capital will be inadequate at some point in the future is required to notify the FSA.

In this context it is worth noting that in addition to capital adequacy as normally **4.13** defined, most regulators impose a threshold capital requirement in respect of authorization to engage in specific business—thus, for example a bank is required under the EU capital requirements directives ('CRD') to maintain minimum capital of EUR 5m, a non-bank investment firm EUR 730,000, and so on. These requirements are generally only relevant in two circumstances. One is where the institution is starting out—the minimum amount of capital must be subscribed regardless of whether the firm has any exposures at all (and it generally will not). The second is where a firm is being wound up—even after all assets and exposures have been eliminated, there is still a requirement for the firm to maintain this minimum amount of capital until its licence is formally withdrawn. In general, whilst a firm is engaged in investment or banking business, these requirements are not substantial, since the threshold requirement is imposed in parallel with the risk requirement. A firm's capital requirement is therefore the higher of the threshold requirement or the risk requirement.

E. 'Gearing' Rules

4.14 There are rules which regulate the maximum amounts of the different forms of capital which can be used to meet regulatory capital requirements. In broad terms, the effect of these rules is to limit the amount of lower quality capital which can be used to a specified percentage of the total requirement. The rules do not restrict the amount of lower quality capital which can be raised by banks, but have the effect that amounts of capital in excess of the permitted limit are disregarded for the purpose of determining whether the bank has sufficient regulatory capital.

4.15 The gearing rules can be summarized as follows:

(1) There is no limit on the amount of core tier one that can be used to make up capital requirements. There are, however, limits on every other tier.

(2) Where a firm has more of a certain type of capital than it is permitted, that capital may be used to make up any other level which is further down the scale up to the limit applied to that lower amount. Thus surplus upper tier two, for example, may be used as lower tier two or tier three if there is unused capacity in any of these tiers. However, capital which is surplus to all of the applicable gearing rules is simply disregarded.

(3) At least 50 per cent of total tier one capital (after deductions) must be accounted for by core tier one capital.

(4) No more than 15 per cent of total tier one capital (after deductions) may be accounted for by innovative tier one capital.

(5) Innovative tier one capital may not be used to meet Pillar one requirements

(6) Tier one capital and tier two capital are the only type of capital resources that may be used to meet:
  (a) the credit risk capital component;
  (b) the operational risk capital requirement;
  (c) the counterparty risk capital component; and
  (d) the base capital resources requirement.

(7) Total tier two (before deductions) may not exceed total tier one after deductions.

(8) Lower tier two capital resources must not exceed 50 per cent of total tier one after deductions.

(9) The total of unused tier two and tier three may not exceed 250 per cent of total amount of tier one capital (after deductions) which is left after meeting the credit risk and operational risk requirements for the institution as a whole. The easiest way to think of this is to imagine that tier one is applied first in

meeting these two requirements, and anything which is left is used as the base of a trading book which can then be supplemented by 2.5 that amount of tier three. Non bank investment firms which are subject to a Basel regime have a slightly different and more favourable treatment as regards tier three—this is explained below.

F. The Components of Capital

Traditionally capital meant share capital, and some regulators have apparently **4.16** reverted back to that simple definition in assessing the robustness of bank balance sheets. However, over the last decade a flourishing industry has developed in creating instruments which perform the function of capital without having its legal form. In general, the commercial drivers for the creation of these instruments are either to gain tax advantages for the issuers (interest paid to noteholders is deductible from the bank's taxable profit, whereas dividends paid to shareholders are not) or to improve earnings per share (by reducing the number of shares in issue whilst retaining the level of earnings). It is debatable how much lasting value the instruments themselves have brought to the market. However, the construction of these instruments has led to a flourishing debate as to what the characteristics of capital should be, and it is useful to encapsulate here the conclusions of that thought process.

G. Tier one

The core characteristics of tier one are that it: **4.17**

(1) is able to absorb losses;
(2) is permanent;
(3) ranks for repayment upon winding up, administration or similar procedure after all other debts and liabilities; and
(4) has no fixed costs, that is, payments to holders of these instruments are entirely within the control of the management of the institution in broadly the same way as dividends on ordinary shares.

There are a number of different types of 'permanent equity' capital depending on **4.18** the legal nature of the institution. These include:

(1) permanent share capital;
(2) eligible partnership capital;
(3) eligible LLP members' capital;
(4) a perpetual non-cumulative preference share; and
(5) (in the case of a building society) permanent interest-bearing shares (PIBS).

Issuance

4.19 Core tier one must be issued directly by the institution concerned, and must be fully paid, with the proceeds of issue immediately and fully available to the firm. Partially paid up share capital counts as capital only to the extent of the amount paid.

Redeemability

4.20 Redemption, for this purpose, includes repayment. Tier one should be, according to its own terms, either irredeemable or redeemable only on the winding up of the issuer. This does not mean quite what it says. The UK Companies Act, for example, gives all issuers the right to redeem their shares in certain circumstances, and most instruments are drafted with certain redemption rights vested in the issuer—for example an issuer may give itself the right to redeem innovative tier one instruments in the event that changes in tax law render the structure of them not disadvantageous for holders or for the issuer. In general such provisions are permitted, provided that they are at the discretion of the issuer, cannot be exercised without the consent of the relevant regulator, and it is unlikely that the events will arise over the life of the instrument. In the UK, any redemption within five years under such a term requires a formal request to the FSA for a waiver, whereas redemption after five years requires the FSA's consent.

4.21 A common arrangement is for instruments to be convertible or exchangeable for new securities, or for arrangements to be made whereby the redemption price of the existing securities will be paid through the issue of new securities. These sorts of arrangements include convertible preference shares. There is an issue with arrangements of this kind as to how the conversion process should be regarded for capital purposes. Where the new securities to be issued would qualify in the same tier of capital as the existing security, the existing security is treated as continuously existing, and the redemption and issue of new securities is disregarded.

Permanence

4.22 The issuer of the instrument must be under no obligation to redeem the instrument or to make any distribution or other payment in respect of it. This means that a tier one instrument should not count as a liability of the issuer, in the way that (for example) a bond would count as a liability, in that the issuer should never be obliged to make a payment to any holder of a tier one instrument.

4.23 The requirement that capital be permanent means that the terms on which it is issued should not provide for any repayment date. However, there is a small difference between a provision which requires that an instrument be repaid on a particular date, and a provision which, although not mandating repayment, provides that something unpleasant will happen if the instrument is not repaid by a particular date. These are known as 'step-ups'.

A step-up is a provision in a security whereby the coupon payable on that security **4.24** increases after a certain date. The aim of a step-up is to create an incentive for the issuer of the security concerned to redeem it. Thus, for example, if the terms of a security provided that the interest rate payable on it would double after 10 years, investors could reasonably assume that it was virtually certain that the issuer would in fact redeem that security after 10 years and replace it with new securities rather than pay the higher rate.

It may be asked why, if the issuer wished to achieve the aim, it would not simply **4.25** issue 10-year securities. The reason in this context is that for capital to count as tier one, it must be perpetual (that is, undated). For investors, however, the longer the term of a security the higher the risk to them of not getting their money back. Thus the longer the term of a security, the higher the return investors will demand for investing in it. The step-up is an attempt to bridge the gap between investors, who would like to see shorter-term redemption, and the issuer, which requires longer-term capital certainty.

Finally, it should be noted that the unpleasant consequence which attends non- **4.26** redemption is by no means limited to step-ups. To take an extreme example, a provision that, if an instrument were not redeemed by a particular date, the CEO of the issuing institution would be publicly executed would be highly effective in ensuring redemption but would not qualify as a step-up per se.[3] More practically, an instrument which automatically converts into equity on a particular date may also have adverse consequences for the issuer if the conversion goes ahead, since the coupon will cease to be deductible for the issuer for tax purposes and the earnings per share figure for the institution as a whole may be diluted. However, such provisions are not generally recognized by regulators, whose rules in this regard tend to focus exclusively on coupon step-ups.

Unlike core tier one (which must be ordinary equity), the terms of non-core tier **4.27** one (including innovative tier one) may permit a 'moderate' step-up in the coupon due to be paid on the instrument. There is no formal definition of what constitutes a 'moderate' step-up in this context, but it is generally interpreted to mean a cumulative step-up of less than 100 basis points[4] (less the swap spread between the two rates). However, even a 'moderate' step-up is only permitted after the tenth

---

[3] Such an arrangement would also fail the legal certainty test due to doubts about enforceability.

[4] A basis point or 'bp' (plural 'bps') is one-hundredth of a percentage point. Thus 100 bps is one per cent.

anniversary of the issue of the instrument—thus, for a proposed tier one instrument, any step-up at all in the first 10 years of its life makes it ineligible.

4.28 An issuer should be under no obligation to make any payment in respect of a tier one instrument if it is to form part of its permanent share capital unless and until the firm is wound up. A tier one instrument that forms part of permanent share capital should not therefore count as a liability before the firm is wound up. The fact that relevant company law permits the firm to make earlier repayment does not mean that the tier one instruments are not eligible. However, the firm should not be required by any contractual or other obligation arising out of the terms of that capital to repay permanent share capital. Similarly a tier one instrument may still qualify if company law allows dividends to be paid on this capital, provided the firm is not contractually or otherwise obliged to pay them. There should therefore be no fixed costs.

Power to defer payments

4.29 The firm must be under no obligation to pay a coupon; unless the obligation can be satisfied by issuing further securities of the same or better quality. In this case any coupon must be either non-cumulative or must, if deferred, be paid by the firm in the form of tier one capital. An arrangement under which coupons must be paid if they have been paid on other securities (known as 'dividend pushers') is generally regarded as breaching this requirement for unfettered discretion, and as a result dividend pushers may not be included in the terms of tier one capital, unless the firm has the option to fund the 'pushed' payment in stock.

Loss absorption

4.30 The capital must be able to absorb losses to allow the firm to continue trading and, if it is an innovative tier one instrument should not constitute a liability.

Subordination

4.31 To count as innovative tier one an instrument may rank for repayment upon winding up, administration or any other similar process no higher than a share of a company. A company may, by its own articles, provide for the securities which it issues to rank in any order which it likes, and although there are doubts as to whether a company could provide that an instrument should be subordinated below the level of ordinary shares,[5] it can certainly provide that an instrument may rank pari passu with ordinary shares.

---

[5] The doubt is logical rather than legal—an ordinary shareholder is entitled to what is left after all other creditors have been paid out, and it is hard to see how it would be possible for any instrument to rank after such a claim.

Moral hazard

This requirement has come into sharp focus as a result of the credit crisis. The key **4.32** issue here arises where an instrument whose legal form is a deeply subordinated perpetual note is marketed on the basis of promises—explicit or implicit—that the issuer will redeem it at a specified time and will maintain coupon payments regardless of economic performance. Marketing in this way has the effect of creating 'moral' obligations on the issuer which it will in practice be obliged to honour unless it is prepared to suffer lasting damage to its reputation. In many respects this issue is not dissimilar to the step-up issue, in that where an issuer has deliberately created an expectation that it will act in a particular way, it should be treated as if it were in fact legally bound to act in that way.

Associate transactions

An item of capital should not be able to qualify for inclusion as tier one capital if **4.33** the issue of that item of capital by the firm is connected with one or more other transactions which, when taken together with the issue of that item, could result in that item of capital no longer displaying all of the characteristics required. A simple example might be a security issued as part of a deal whereby the issuer promises to repurchase it from the investor on demand.

Reserves

Accumulated profits, in the form of various reserves, constitute core tier one. It is **4.34** sometimes possible to increase these directly—for example a capital contribution should be treated as an increase in reserves. Negative amounts, including any interim net losses must be deducted from reserves. Where trading book valuation adjustments give rise to losses in the current financial year, a firm must also deduct them from reserves. A dividend is foreseeable at the latest when it is proposed by the directors. This creates an asymmetry, in that valuation losses reduce tier one, but valuation gains do not always increase it. Dividends must be deducted from reserves as soon as they are foreseeable—not when they are declared. Revaluation reserves do not count as tier one, but form part of tier two, since they relate to gains which have not yet been realized.

Some movements on reserves are reversed out by the system. An example is the **4.35** capitalization of future interest which arises where an interest-bearing asset is sold to a securitization vehicle. The increase in reserves resulting from such capitalization does not count as tier one.

A revaluation reserve is not included as part of a bank's profit and loss account **4.36** and other reserves. It is dealt with separately and forms part of upper tier two capital.

Share premium account

4.37 Share premium accounts arising on the issue of capital instruments are treated as constituting capital of the same form as the instrument to which they relate. Thus the share premium account arising on the issue of cumulative tier two preference shares would qualify as tier two capital, whereas the share premium account arising on the issue of ordinary shares will count as tier one capital. This is, however, subject to the exception that if the terms of the tier two instrument provide that the instrument can only be repaid out of new revenue, and that the share premium arising on issue may not be used for the repayment, then the share premium will be treated as tier one. This creates the unusual situation in which tier one capital can be created by issuing a tier two instrument.

Externally verified profits

4.38 Externally verified interim net profits count as tier one, but only once they have been verified by a firm's external auditors. The amount credited to tier one is the amount after deduction of tax, forseeable dividends and other appropriations.

Innovative tier one

4.39 The boundary between innovative and non-innovative non-core tier one is not a clear one. The investment banking industry has spent many happy years structuring perpetual non-cumulative preference shares and other instruments with features designed to indicate to investors that they will be regularly paid and rapidly redeemed without actually specifying this in the instrument terms. Such features will generally result in the instrument being classified as an innovative instrument, but since the list of possible structural features for instruments of this kind is almost infinite, it is sometimes surprisingly difficult to classify them. The FSA's rule,[6] for example, provides that:

> If a tier one instrument
> (1) is redeemable; and
> (2) a reasonable person would think that:
>   (a) the firm is likely to redeem it; or
>   (b) the firm is likely to have an economic incentive to redeem it;
> that tier one instrument is an innovative tier one instrument.

> Any feature that in conjunction with a call would make a firm more likely to redeem a tier one instrument . . . would normally result in classification as innovative.

4.40 In order to constitute an instrument an innovative tier one instrument, it is necessary that the obligations of the issuer under it do not constitute a financial obligation.

---

[6] BIPRU 2.2.114.

There are a number of branches of this test. First, the terms of the instrument should not constitute a liability which a person could rely on in seeking to wind up the issuer in court on the basis that it was unable to meet its liabilities. The point here is that in the same way that a company does not treat itself as indebted to shareholders in reckoning its solvency, it should be able to disregard the claims of innovative tier one holders in the same way. Second, the institution should not be required to take any obligation to innovative tier one holders into account in deciding for itself whether it is able to continue trading; and this assessment must be valid in respect of eg the insolvency law assessment of whether a firm is wrongfully trading.

Any tier one instrument—including ordinary shares—with a cumulative or man-   **4.41**
datory coupon should be regarded as an innovative tier one instrument.

Any tier one instrument—including ordinary shares—which has or may have a   **4.42**
step-up; and which is redeemable at any time (whether before, at or after the time of the step-up) is an innovative tier one instrument.

Indirectly issued tier one arises where instruments are issued by a special-purpose   **4.43**
vehicle (SPV). These structures can operate in two broad ways—one is where the SPV is a subsidiary of an institution and contributes the capital so raised to the institution concerned; the other is where the SPV raises financing and applies that financing to subscribe for new capital in the institution. In the first case, the capital so raised is only permitted to be recognized if the SPV is controlled by the institution, (ie may not operate independently of it—the rights of external investors in the SPV do not affect this control) and all or virtually all of the SPV's exposures are to the institution or its group. If the SPV is a partnership, this means that the institution must be or control the general partner. In the second case, the capital issued by the SPV must themselves comply with the conditions for qualification as tier one as if the SPV was itself an institution seeking to include that capital in its tier one, and must be exchangeable into tier one non-innovative instruments issued by the institution at a fixed conversion ratio in the event that the institution enters a period of distress. The capital issued by the institution itself must have a first call date not sooner than the instrument issued by the SPV, and must match—in terms of its repayment terms—the terms of the instrument issued by the SPV. Where there is more than one SPV, the intermediate SPVs are ignored for this purpose. In some European jurisdictions transactions of this kind have been done through operating subsidiaries or asset owning companies—in the UK the FSA requires any such proposal to be pre-approved, and would be unlikely to give such approval.

Convertible and exchangeable instruments

Where a tier one instrument is redeemable into another tier one instrument, there is   **4.44**
in theory no reason to limit the terms on which the new instrument is to be created.

However, in some old tier one structures the terms of the conversion were set by the price of the new instrument at the date of conversion—for example, each £1 preference share converts into as many ordinary shares as may be worth £1 at the market price in the conversion date. The aim of such a structure is of course to give the investor the coupon entitlement of the preference share whilst enabling it to count as nearly as possible as ordinary equity. In accounting terms such a structure is entirely permissible. However, in practice such a structure would create a serious problem for an institution suffering severe credit losses and seeking to raise more capital. This is because in this case the value of the shares in the institution would probably have fallen substantially, the number of shares which would need to be created to satisfy claims under such a note would be very large, and the obligation to issue a large number of new shares would act as a substantial deterrent to any new equity investment being raised by the institution. The FSA has addressed this by providing that any such instrument must be limited in its conversion terms, and in particular the conversion terms must not permit a conversion rate which is more than double the rate prevalent at the time of the issue. The firm is also prohibited under the terms of any such note from issuing on conversion shares with a greater value than the instrument being converted.

4.45 There is also an issue as to whether the firm would be permitted to issue such new instruments. Many company law provisions in many jurisdictions restrict the right of a company to issue new ordinary shares or preference shares, and it is not always possible for either an institution or an investor to be able to say with certainty whether it will be able, on conversion, to issue the securities into which the note is to be converted. Again, the FSA addresses this issue by requiring that an institution may only include such convertible capital as capital if it has obtained authority to issue sufficient securities to satisfy the requirements of the holders on conversion. Thus for a UK entity subject to pre-emption rights, such capital may only be included in regulatory capital if such rights have been disapplied.

Deductions from tier one

4.46 It will be recalled that the gearing rules limit the different types of capital which a bank may recognize as a percentage of tier one capital, and the amount of tier one capital which may be recognized for this purpose is the amount of qualifying tier one capital less certain deductions. The most important of these is intangible assets—an institution must deduct intangible assets from tier one capital. This is one of the most significant divergences between regulatory capital and accounting treatment. Intangible assets include capitalized expenditure, licence rights, and numerous other types of property, some of which are clearly valuable—however, for regulatory purposes all are treated as valueless. There is a particular issue here arising from the treatment of goodwill, in that for accounting purposes goodwill may be capitalized and amortized over time. 'Goodwill' in this context almost always arises as the result of acquisition—where a firm acquires another, if there is a difference between the price paid and the value of the balance sheet assets, the difference is 'goodwill'. Thus if a bank with 100 of capital pays 20 to acquire another with capital of 10, for accounting purposes it will continue to have a value of 100 (made up of 80 of old capital, 10 of newly-acquired capital, and 10 of goodwill), but for regulatory purposes it will have assets of 90. This makes it exceptionally difficult for banks to make cash acquisitions.

Deferred acquisition cost assets should not be deducted as intangible assets. **4.47**

Revaluations of investment properties and equities held in the 'available for sale' **4.48** category may also give rise to tier one deductions. Negative revaluations (ie losses on the initial holding value) are deducted from tier one, but positive revaluations (ie established but unrealized profits) are included in tier two capital.

H. Tier two

Tier two capital includes forms of capital that are subordinated, but do not meet **4.49** the requirements for permanency and absence of fixed servicing costs that apply to tier one capital.

Upper tier two

Upper tier two capital includes capital which is perpetual (that is, has no fixed **4.50** term) but cumulative (that is, servicing costs cannot be waived at the issuer's option, although they may be deferred—for example, cumulative preference shares).

Lower tier two

Lower tier two comprises subordinated capital which is not perpetual (that is, it **4.51** will be repaid after a fixed term) or which has fixed servicing costs that cannot be either waived or deferred (for example, most subordinated debt). To be fully valued lower tier two must have a residual maturity of at least five years—debt with a shorter maturity than this will be discounted on a sliding scale as its residual maturity decreases. If a tier two instrument is or may be subject to a step-up that does not meet the definition of 'moderate' (broadly, the step-up is not more than 100 bps),[7] then the instrument will be treated as maturing on the date when the step-up takes effect (or, if there are multiple smaller steps up, on the first date that the cumulative step-up exceeds the 'moderate' limit). However, a lower limit is imposed on tier two instruments between the fifth and the tenth years of

---

[7] See para 4.27.

their lives. During this period any step-up which would exceed 50 bps (less the swap spread) has the same effect, in that the instrument would be treated as maturing on the date when the spread first exceed the 50 bps limit. Any step-up at all arising in the first five years of an instrument's life makes it ineligible as tier two.

4.52 Tier two also includes certain revaluation reserves such as reserves arising from the revaluation of land and buildings, including any net unrealized gains for the fair valuation of equities held in the available-for-sale financial assets category; and general or collective (ie not specific) provisions.

Upper tier two requirements

4.53 Tier two must be subordinated to ordinary creditors—however, there is no requirement that tiers must rank in order of regulatory seniority—it is permissible (although unusual) for upper tier two to rank in priority to lower tier two. The difference is primarily in the dating.

4.54 Upper tier two will, in the UK, constitute instruments such as perpetual cumulative preference shares and perpetual subordinated debt. The base requirements are that it:

(1) has no fixed maturity date;
(2) provides for the firm to have the option to defer any coupon on the debt, except payments to be made in kind through the issue of new capital of equivalent seniority;
(3) provides for the loss-absorption capacity of the capital instrument and unpaid coupons, whilst enabling the firm to continue its business;
(4) either the instrument or debt is not redeemable or repayable or it is repayable or redeemable only at the option of the firm. If a firm gives notice of the redemption or repayment of an upper tier two instrument, the firm must no longer include it in its upper tier two capital resources;
(5) as with tier one, a firm may not include a dividend pusher in upper tier two unless the 'pushed' dividend is payable in stock.

4.55 Tier two may be created by issuing securities or by borrowing on subordinated terms—unlike tier one, there is no requirement that tier two be composed of securities. However since loan capital is relatively rare amongst banks, the remainder of this discussion refers to instruments. Tier two must be unsecured and fully paid up, and any variation of the terms of existing tier two requires consent.

4.56 Although tier two securities are debt instruments and have the effect of rendering the holders creditors of the issuer, there are very substantial limitations on the rights which holders of tier two securities may acquire as a result of their creditor status. The instrument constituting a tier two security may not contain any of the events of default found in a normal security, and the only permitted events of default are non-payment of any amount falling due under the terms of the capital instrument or the winding-up of the firm, and the event of default must not affect the subordination (in other words, even if an event of default occurs the claim must still be subordinated). This means that in the event of a non-payment the holder cannot sue the issuer for the debts due, but is restricted to petitioning for the user to be wound up and/or proving for the debt in a liquidation—in which event he will be paid in subordination to other senior creditors. This is achieved through the terms of the note. The company and other laws of the issuer may prescribe that creditors may not renounce all of their rights in this way—where this is the case the notes will still be qualifying tier two provided that the rights are renounced to the greatest degree possible under the applicable legal system. Investors must also agree to forego any right of set-off, since if the holder of sub-ordinated debt could set off the debt due to him against amounts due by him to the institution, this would have the effect of promoting the debt due to him to the status of a senior debt.

Investors need not be deprived of other remedies—it is immaterial whether or not   **4.57**
an investor has a non-financial remedy against an issue provided that the non-financial remedy does not in substance amount to a mechanism for obtaining payment. Where such other remedies may result in an award of damages, the claim for damages arising out of such a remedy must, to the greatest extent possible, be subordinated under the subordination provisions of the agreement.

As with tier one, an instrument will only qualify as eligible tier two if the way in   **4.58**
which it is marketed corresponds with its formal structure—thus an instrument sold on the basis of an indication by the issuer that it would buy back the instrument within a few years would not qualify as tier two. In the same way, an instrument will not be accepted as eligible tier two if it is issued as part of a larger transaction the overall effect of which is that the holder of the tier two instrument is effectively preferred.

It is a requirement of the FSA that an issuer must obtain an external legal opinion   **4.59**
that an instrument complies with the requirements for tier two in order for it to be recognized. There is no obvious reason why this should be required for tier two but not tier one issuance.

The debt agreement or terms of the instrument creating tier two capital should   **4.60**
not contain any clause which might require early repayment of the debt—cross default clauses, negative pledges, and restrictive covenants. A cross default clause is a clause which says that the loan goes into default if any of the borrower's other loans go into default. It is intended to prevent one creditor being repaid before other creditors, eg obtaining full repayment through the courts. A negative pledge is a clause which puts the loan into default if the borrower gives any further charge over its assets. A restrictive covenant is a term of contract that prevents the issuer

from doing something whilst the security remains in force, and, if breached, results in early repayment of the debt. Some covenants, eg relating to the provision of management information or ownership restrictions, are likely to be permissible as long as monetary redress is ruled out, or any payments are covered by the subordination clauses.

Lower tier two requirements

4.61 Lower tier two must comply with all of the requirements for upper tier two save for those concerning repayment. Because lower tier two has a fixed repayment date, the issuers capital will, on that date, fall by the amount to be repaid. For this reason issuers of tier two are generally required to notify their regulator before the fixed repayment date and to satisfy that regulator that they will have sufficient new capital in place on the repayment date that they will not breach any regulatory requirement by reason of the repayment.

4.62 Lower tier two capital means capital which complies with the requirements for upper tier two except that it is dated. Where an instrument fails to qualify as upper tier two because of a step-up, it is likely that it will qualify as lower tier two provided that the step-up does not occur less than five years after the date of issue of the instrument.

4.63 When a lower tier two instrument gets within five years of its maturity date, its value as regulatory capital is amortized on a straight line basis over that period—thus when it has four years of life remaining it will count for 80 per cent of its value, when it has three years left it will count for 60 per cent and so on.

4.64 Tier two capital includes positive revaluations of equities held in the available for sale category, other investment property, and land and buildings. The amount to be included in capital is the revaluation amount less any probable taxes which would fall to be paid if the property were actually disposed of.

4.65 Firms using the standardized approach may include general/collective provisions in tier two. However, the value of the general/collective provisions which a firm may include in its tier two capital resources may not exceed 1.25 per cent of the sum of: (1) the market risk capital requirement and the operational risk capital requirement, multiplied by a factor of 12.5; and (2) the sum of risk-weighted assets under the standardized approach for credit risk.

4.66 Where capital is issued in a currency other than the accounting currency of the institution, a problem arises in that the value of the capital to the institution will fluctuate in line with the exchange rate between its reporting currency and the currency in which it has issued. This is a particular problem for issuers based in countries with minor currencies who wish to issue in $US or EUR. In general, firms are likely to wish to hedge such exposures, and if they do so then the regulatory system will recognize such hedges. However, in order to obtain regulatory recognition of such hedges, their terms must be broadly those of the capital which they hedge—that is, the hedge counterparty must be subordinated in the same way and to the same extent as the claims of the holders of the instrument being hedged. This makes such swaps very rare in practice.

Provisioning and expected loss

Where total provisions exceed total expected loss, the balance can be treated as tier two capital. This apparently simple outcome requires a certain amount of explanation to justify.   **4.67**

In broad terms the position under both IFRS and US GAAP is that banks may make specific provisions and collective provisions but not general provisions in their accounts. For this purpose a specific provision is a provision which reflects an actual impairment in the value of a specific asset (classically an event of default such as a breach of a covenant), a collective provision is a provision made as a result of an analysis of a portfolio of exposures on the basis of historical loss experience, and a general provision is a provision in respect of a loss on a portfolio as a whole based on anything other than historical loss data.   **4.68**

For banks which apply the IRB approaches, provisions can be charged against expected loss. This somewhat uncontroversial-sounding development is in fact the culmination of more than a decade's discussion on the appropriate treatment of provisions within the regulatory framework.   **4.69**

A general principle of bank risk management is that capital should only need to be held against the risk of unexpected losses (UL). Expected losses (EL) should be covered either by specific provisions, or by pricing them into the cost of the transaction (known as future margin income).   **4.70**

Specific provisions are taken through the bank's profit and loss account, where they are a charge on profits and therefore reduce retained profit (or increase retained loss). However, where an entity takes a provision, the amount provided is taken to a separate provision maintained on the balance sheet. When the loss is actually incurred, the value of the asset is reduced and the value of the provision is equally reduced, thereby ensuring that the loss has no impact on retained profits. Thus provisioning is simply a form of capital creation in respect of future losses— current profits are capitalized to absorb future losses. A provision therefore performs functionally the same purpose as capital.   **4.71**

The reason that regulators are not happy to regard provisions as capital is that provision balances can be rapidly changed if the bank increases them or runs them down, and they therefore do not meet the ordinary criteria of permanence which regulators require from capital items. Nonetheless, in their capacity as elements of capital whose effect is to absorb losses they require some form of recognition.   **4.72**

4.73 The original approach proposed was that specific provisions should be applied to reduce the risk-weighted assets ('RWAs') of the items in respect of which they were taken, whilst collective provisions would count as tier two capital (up to 1.25 per cent of RWA). This is the approach which remains in place for banks on the standardized approach. However, this has the result that the treatment of specific provisions is far more favourable than the treatment of collective provisions because, mathematically, the impact of using provisions to offset RWAs in the denominator is greater than adding provisions to the numerator. Because it reduces risk-weighted assets, the latter approach also boosts the ratio of tier one.

4.74 This would not be a problem if all banks followed broadly the same policies as regards provisioning. However, banks' collective provisioning policies vary widely (sometimes in order to take account of local tax and other factors), and as a result, banks in different jurisdictions may maintain very different levels of provisions against similar portfolios.

4.75 The solution adopted in Basel to this problem was to pool specific and collective provisions. The regulator then compares the total of all provisions (except for any provisions made against equity or securitization exposures, which are disregarded) with the bank's total expected loss ('EL') figure.[8] Where eligible provisions are higher than EL, the surplus may be included in tier two up to a maximum of 0.6 per cent of RWA. Where provisions are lower than EL, the difference must be deducted from capital, 50 per cent from tier one and 50 per cent from tier two.

4.76 It may be easiest to explain this by way of an example. For a typical fully drawn corporate receivable with 1 per cent PD, and 45 per cent LGD, the risk weight produced by the IRB function is £97.44 per £100 nominal. The capital requirement in respect of this exposure (ie £97.44 × 8%) is £7.79. The EL for this exposure would be 1% × 45% × £100 (ie £0.45). If the bank has provisions of £0.40 to apply to the exposure, it will be treated as underprovisioned, and the balancing £0.05 will be deducted from capital. If it has provisions of £0.50, the remaining £0.05 will be added to tier two capital.

4.77 The effect of these rules is that the pool of provisions is directly matched against the pool of expected losses. Both pools can be removed from the risk capital ratio, leaving only unexpected losses in the denominator, covered by capital in tier one and tier two.

4.78 The upshot of all of this in practice is that an IRB bank may include in its upper tier two capital resources positive amounts resulting from the calculation of

---

[8] EL for any defaulted asset is the bank's best estimate of expected loss. EL for each non-defaulted asset is PD × LGD × EAD. See para 5.08 for details.

expected loss amounts up to 0.6 per cent of the risk weighted exposure amounts calculated under that approach.

I. Deductions

Qualifying holdings (holdings in non-financial undertakings)

A qualifying holding is a direct or indirect holding in a non-financial undertaking **4.79** which represents 10 per cent or more of the capital or of the voting rights of that undertaking, or which makes it possible to exercise a significant influence over the management of that undertaking.

For this purpose a non-financial undertaking is an undertaking other than: **4.80**

(1) a credit institution or financial institution;
(2) an undertaking whose exclusive or main activities are a direct extension of banking or concern services ancillary to banking, such as leasing, factoring, the management of unit trusts, the management of data processing services or any other similar activity; or
(3) an insurer.

Shares do not constitute material holdings if they are not held as investments, are held temporarily during the ordinary course of underwriting, or are held on behalf of others.

The amount of qualifying holdings that an institution must deduct is: **4.81**

(1) (if the firm has one or more qualifying holdings that exceeds 15 per cent of its adjusted capital resources) the sum of such excesses; and
(2) to the extent not already deducted in (1), the amount by which the sum of each of that firm's qualifying holdings exceeds 60 per cent of its adjusted relevant capital resources.

Material holdings (holdings in financial undertakings)

Material holdings only arise in respect of holdings in banks, credit institutions or **4.82** other financial institutions. The area of material holdings is one in which there is a strong difference of opinion between different regulators around the world. Although there is broad agreement that investments in unconsolidated subsidiaries engaged in banking and financial activities should be deducted, some regulators strongly believe that cross-holdings of bank capital by other banks should not be deducted, since such holdings are necessary to promote 'significant and desirable changes taking place in the structure of domestic banking systems'.[9]

---

[9] Basel, para 49(xvii).

The Basel compromise has been to permit national regulators to require deduction of such cross-holdings where they exceed a materiality threshold in relation to the holding bank's capital.

4.83 The FSA's implementation of this policy is that a holding must be deducted as a material holding if it exceeds 10 per cent of the share capital of the issuer.[10] When an institution has a holding of this kind, any other subordinated exposure which it has to such an institution will be counted as part of the material holding for the purposes of establishing the total value to be deducted. When such deductions have been made, each individual remaining holding must be assessed, and where the totality of the holding of share capital and subordinated debt in that institution exceeds 10 per cent of the capital of the institution, the excess must be deducted. Finally, the value of all undeducted holdings of share capital or other capital of such institutions must be aggregated, and if the total of all such holdings is greater than 10 per cent of the institutions tier one plus tier two less deductions, the excess must also be deducted.

4.84 The position of holdings in insurance companies is anomalous in this respect, in that where an institution has a material holding in an insurance company, the amount to be deducted will be the higher of the value of the holding or the proportionate capital resources requirement of the institution attributable to that part of its capital.

4.85 Finally, all holdings in subsidiaries and participations in any other entities must be deducted. This in effect requires the deduction of all holdings which constitute more than 20 per cent of the capital of any entity. It may be noted that whereas subsidiary status arises automatically when share ownership in an entity goes above 50 per cent, for a holding to qualify as a participation (between 20 per cent and 50 per cent) there must be some right of control. This means, amongst other things, that if a bank has no say at all in the affairs of an entity in which it has a substantial equity interest (of less than 50 per cent), the equity interest is not deducted, since the holding will not constitute a participation.

4.86 An important and sometimes misunderstood aspect of material position calculation is that the position to be deducted is the gross position. Where a firm has a material position in another but has hedged that position, the hedge is not taken into account in the material position deduction calculation. This is true whether the position is held in the banking book or the trading book.

---

[10] GENPRU 2.2.20 et seq.

Connected lending of a capital nature

Because of the rules requiring investments in subsidiaries to be deducted, institu- **4.87**
tions sometimes seek to characterize the provision of finance to corporations as
lending where the true nature of the transaction is the provision of capital. The
'connected lending of a capital nature' rule is an anti-avoidance rule intended to
tackle such structures.[11] It applies only to loans provided by an institution to a
body which is connected with it—ie it is an associate of or closely connected with
the institution, or it and the institution are under common control (but not an
entity which is solo-consolidated). The essence of this status is that the loan is
made on terms which, whether through contractual, structural, reputational, or
other factors, have the economic characteristics of share capital or subordinated
debt. This includes situations where the position of the lender from the point of
view of maturity and repayment is inferior to that of the senior unsecured and
unsubordinated creditors of the borrower. A loan may also be treated as connected
lending of a capital nature if it is made to an unconnected party but is made for
the purpose of funding directly or indirectly a loan to a connected party of the
institution, and conversely will not be treated as connected lending of a capital
nature if it is provided to a connected party for the purpose of providing funding
to an unconnected party.

A loan will generally not be treated as connected lending of a capital nature if it is **4.88**
appropriately secured or is repayable on demand. A guarantee may be treated as
connected lending of a capital nature.

Expected losses and other negative amounts

As noted elsewhere,[12] an IRB firm must calculate its total expected loss amount **4.89**
and deduct it from total provisions and value adjustments. As we saw above, where
this amount is positive it may be added to capital up to the 0.6 per cent limit.
Where the result is negative, however, it must deduct that negative amount.

Securitization positions

An IRB firm must deduct the exposure amount of securitization positions which **4.90**
receive a risk weight of 1250 per cent if it does not include such positions in its
calculation of risk-weighted exposure amounts.

In order to complicate matters, the last-named deductions (material holdings, **4.91**
expected losses, and securitization positions) are made for some purposes but not
others. Specifically, they are deducted wholly from tier two only for the purposes

[11] BIPRU 2.2.221.
[12] See para 4.75.

of establishing the levels of tier one, tier two and tier three which are permissible for the institution. For the purposes of publicly reporting the levels of capital which the institution has (ie for tier three purposes) they are deducted 50 per cent from tier one and 50 per cent from tier two. This explains why a reporting institution may have slightly more tier two than its level of reported tier one may seem to permit.

J. Tier three

4.92 Tier three is uncommon amongst banks. In broad terms it is tier two capital with a two-year maturity, and can only be used to support trading book exposures. The only real reasons for firms to issue it are flexibility, and the price advantage derived from its shorter maturity. This latter does not always overcome the costs of repeat issuance. It is most commonly encountered in Europe, where the Basel regime has been applied to pure investment firms, and such firms frequently do issue substantial amounts of tier three.

Upper tier three

4.93 Tier three capital (ie upper tier three) must have an original maturity of at least two years, and payment of interest or principal is permitted only if, after that payment, the firm's capital resources would be not less than its capital resources requirement. In broad terms the requirements which apply to tier two also apply to tier three, save that an institution which includes subordinated debt in its tier three capital resources must notify the FSA one month in advance of all payments of either interest or principal made when the firm's capital resources are less than 120 per cent of its capital resources requirement.

Lower tier three

4.94 Lower tier three means unaudited interim trading book profits. These profits should be adjusted for this purpose so that they are net of any foreseeable charges, dividends or losses on other business; and must not already have been taken into account in the calculation of capital.

Deductions from tier three

4.95 The excess trading book position is the excess of an institution's aggregate net long (including notional) trading book positions in shares, subordinated debt or any other interest in the capital of credit institutions or financial institutions over 25 per cent of that institution's capital resources. This must be deducted from total capital (where an institution has tier three, this is equivalent to deduction from tier three).

K. Capital Arising from Revaluation of Assets

Marking to market (or to model) raises the difficult issue of how regulators should **4.96** treat the impact of changes in the value of such assets on regulatory capital. The reason that this is a problem is that if the value of an available for sale asset goes up, a corresponding adjustment must be made to the other side of the balance sheet, and this is conventionally done in accounting terms by increasing reserves—in regulatory terms, increasing core tier one. However, the new capital thus created does not meet the regulator's requirement that in order to be recognized for supervisory purposes capital must be 'permanent'—indeed, this capital is of the most ephemeral kind, since it may disappear again overnight in the event of a downwards revaluation.

The solution which regulators have adopted is to disallow some elements of the **4.97** accounting gain as capital. A bank must therefore not recognize as capital either the fair value reserves related to gains or losses on cash flow hedges of financial instruments measured at amortized cost; or any unrealized gains or losses on debt instruments held in the available-for-sale category. However, this rule applies only to financial instruments. For equities held in the available-for-sale financial assets category, a bank should deduct any net losses from tier one capital, and include any net gains (after deduction of deferred tax) in upper tier two capital.

The IAS standard, in its entirety, permits firms to designate liabilities at fair value. **4.98** The EU has adopted the IAS standards in a modified form, and EU IAS 39 does not permit the recognition of liabilities at fair value. For non-EU institutions, however, the issue still exists. This has a magnificent consequence for regulated entities, since if a bank becomes insolvent the value of its liabilities will shrink. This would result in the reduction of the balance sheet value of its liabilities, with the difference being taken to reserves as an unrealized profit. This would mean that as the bank approached insolvency its nominal capital would increase substantially. The supervisors of the world have therefore created a 'prudential filter' to be applied in this case, which in summary operates as a rule that where a company designates its liabilities as held at fair value and takes changes in value through profit and loss, it must add back unrealized losses or subtract unrealized gains in determining the asset value.

L. Deductions for Investment Firms

It should be mentioned at this point that within the EU (but not generally else- **4.99** where) non-bank investment firms are subject to the requirements of the Basel II regime. At one level this makes good sense, since the Basel market risks regime is a good match for the exposures of such firms (although certain investment firms, such as commodities traders, do not fit easily within the Basel framework). However, the difficulty which this creates is that whereas the Basel rules on exposure quantification may be a good fit, the rules on capital composition are not. There are two primary issues arising from this fit:

(1) An investment firm is primarily a market-oriented entity which takes positions in liquid instruments, and which therefore needs more short-term capital and—in theory—less long-term capital.

(2) As a result of this, an investment firm which takes long-term illiquid positions (such as making loans) and which seeks to rely on investment firm capital should suffer a much heavier regulatory capital charge for such illiquid assets than would a bank.

4.100   This policy is implemented for investment firms through the 'liquidity deduction' regime. The essence of this is that in response to item 1 above, an investment firm is permitted to hold considerably more of its total capital requirement in the form of short-term tier three capital than a bank would be permitted to hold. The limit which applies to the two organizations is the same—250 per cent of the tier one left after credit, counterparty and operational risk charges are deducted from tiers one and two. However, for an investment firm the value of these deductions should be considerably lower, and as a result a considerably larger percentage of the total capital of an investment firm may constitute tier three.

4.101   The working assumption for investment firms, and the approach outlined above, is that they hold only trading book assets, and if they report on this basis they deduct illiquid assets. A firm which deducts illiquid assets is allowed to use 250 per cent of tier one less deductions as its qualifying tier three limit. However, where an investment firm wishes to hold and weight illiquid assets, it may do so, opting instead to deduct material holdings. A firm which deducts material holdings is subject to a lower tier three limit—200 per cent rather than 250 per cent—will be limited in its trading activities (in that it will not be able to hold more than 10 per cent of any individual entity), and will be obliged to maintain more higher-quality capital relative to its trading book. In some respects the deduction of material holdings approach is a half-way house between the illiquid asset deduction approach and ordinary banking book treatment.

M. Bank Capital Resources—Summary Table

4.102

Core tier one	Permanent share capital Profit and loss account and other reserves (taking into account interim net losses) Eligible LLP members' capital Share premium account Externally verified interim net profits
Non-core, non-innovative tier one	Perpetual non-cumulative preference shares
Innovative tier one capital	Innovative tier one instruments
Deductions from tier one capital	Investments in own shares Intangible assets Excess of drawings over profits Net losses on equities held in the available-for-sale financial asset category Other deductions
Upper tier two capital	Perpetual cumulative preference shares Perpetual subordinated debt Perpetual subordinated securities Revaluation reserves General/collective provisions Surplus provisions
Lower tier two capital	Fixed term preference shares Long-term subordinated debt Fixed term subordinated securities
Deductions from the total tier one and two	Qualifying holdings Material holdings Expected loss amounts and other negative amounts Securitization positions Reciprocal cross-holdings Investments in subsidiary undertakings and participations* Connected lending of a capital nature
Upper tier three	Short-term subordinated debt
Lower tier three	Net interim trading book profit and loss
Deductions from total capital	Excess trading book position Free deliveries

* Excluding any amount which is already deducted as material holdings or qualifying holdings.

Part II

COMMERCIAL BANKING

5

CREDIT RISK

A. Background

Of all the risks that banks are exposed to, credit risk is the most important and the most intuitively obvious. A one-sentence definition of a banker might be a man who judges credit; a decision which can be characterized as a decision on how much to lend to whom on what terms. It is, however, important to remember that credit means more than simply loans. If I lend money, I have a credit exposure to the borrower. However, if I buy debt securities I have a credit claim on the issuer; if I enter into a derivative I have a credit claim on the counterparty; if I enter into an agreement to lend money at a future time (a commitment) I still have a contractual exposure to the credit of the borrower. Credit exposures are at the heart of financial transactions. For an economist, the function of a bank is maturity transformation and intertemporal transfers of resources, but in a world where debts were always repaid these functions would be as mechanical as the transmission of water or electricity. It is the unpredictability of credit that differentiates banking from sewerage as a business. **5.01**

Finance is, however, about more than credit. The old banker's maxim 'lend on the credit, not the security', is frequently broken in modern banking, and transactions are frequently encountered which are financial transactions but not credit transactions. To take a simple example: a loan to a special purpose vehicle whose only asset is an office block is not, in any meaningful sense, an exposure to the credit of the borrowing entity; it is an exposure to the value of the underlying asset (or, to be precise, to the cashflows which that asset may generate). Thus, although most **5.02** bank assets are credit exposures, some are not, and there is more to bank capital adequacy than simply weighting credit. However, credit does remain the single most important component of the system.

5.03   Although we are accustomed to think of credit as arising from loan exposures, credit risk goes well beyond loans. In broad terms almost any financial transaction will involve a credit risk, and sometimes more than one credit risk may arise out of the same transaction. The regulatory system distinguishes between simple credit exposures and complex credit exposures—a simple credit exposure is an exposure which arises out of future payment obligations, where the amount due is certain and it is only the likelihood of repayment which varies, and a complex credit exposure is an exposure which arises out of a transaction (such as a derivative) where both the amount due and the likelihood of repayment may vary over the life of the transaction. This section deals (broadly) with simple credit exposures, where the amount of the exposure can be either known or easily estimated. Complex exposures, which typically arise under derivatives, securities lending or long settlement transactions, are dealt with in the chapter on investment banking.

B. Risk Weighting of Assets

5.04   The basis of bank capital regulation is that banks should be required to maintain sufficient capital to make it unlikely that they will become insolvent in the event of a number of credit defaults. The issue for regulators is to determine the extent of the defaults which a bank should hold capital against. Clearly this is in some respect an arbitrary determination—any institution faces the risk that all of its exposures may simultaneously default. This eventuality is treated as sufficiently unlikely to be disregarded. Nonetheless, although the chances of everything defaulting simultaneously can be disregarded, the chances of a number of different exposures defaulting the same time cannot be—indeed, this is the most common explanation for bank failures. Consequently, the challenge for the regulator is to decide the level of unlikelihood which he is seeking to protect against. The fundamental mechanism by which this is done is to 'weight' the asset concerned. Since the basic Basel requirement is that the amount of capital held in relation to each individual exposure should be 8 per cent of the risk weighted value of that exposure, then by varying the 'weighting' which is applied to each asset we can reflect the relative riskiness of each asset.

5.05   Under the original Basel framework, there was a single calculation methodology applied to all exposures. This had the important consequence that all banks calculated their exposures in the same way; and the same asset would have the same regulatory capital weighting for all banks. Neither of these are true under the Basel II system.

C. The Basel Approaches

Basel II gives banks three ways to calculate the credit weightings to be applied to **5.06** assets.[1] The first—the *'standardized'* approach—employs a prescribed set of weightings based on asset type and external credit ratings. The second—the *'internal ratings based approach'*, known as IRB—permits banks to use their own statistical models to generate weightings. The IRB approach is then subdivided into two further approaches, *'foundation'* and *'advanced'*, depending on the sophistication of the models operated by the relevant bank.

Each bank must decide whether it is a standardized bank, a foundation IRB bank **5.07** or an advanced IRB bank. Broadly, once a bank has classified itself it may elect to use a lower approach for some exposures, but may not elect a higher one. Thus, an advanced IRB bank can elect to use a standardized approach for certain exposures, but a standardized bank cannot elect to use the advanced IRB approach for any exposures. The general policy of regulators is to encourage all banks to progress towards advanced IRB status, but it is accepted that the advanced modelling capabilities required for advanced IRB status may not be cost-effective for some classes of institutions to develop.

In order to explain the basic distinction between the three approaches it is neces- **5.08** sary to explain a little about the basics of weighting. In theory, it is possible for any given exposure to estimate Probability of Default (PD), Loss Given Default (LGD) and the Exposure At Default (EAD). PD and LGD are reasonably self-explanatory—PD is the probability of a default occurring on a particular facility, LGD is the estimate of the loss which will be suffered if there is a default (ie the amount by which any recoveries eventually made will fall short of the amount of the exposure). EAD is a little more complex. For a facility such as a term loan, EAD is simply the amount of the loan—on a loan of £100, the expected exposure at default is £100. However, for a revolving credit facility of £100, the amount drawn at any given time may fluctuate, and for such exposures it is also necessary to make an estimate of the amount which is likely to have been drawn when a default occurs, and this is the EAD. EAD also has to be estimated in the context of undrawn commitments, derivative exposures and a variety of other exposures.

If these three are simply multiplied together, the result is the expected loss amount, **5.09** or EL—thus:

$$\text{Expected Loss (EL)} = \text{PD} \times \text{LGD} \times \text{EAD}$$

---

[1] Technically four, since there is a simplified standardized approach available for institutions of such simplicity that even the standardized approach is unreasonably demanding. However, this is a relative rarity in practice, and is not discussed further in this work.

Bank capital requirements must clearly be sufficient to meet expected losses. However, in order to protect depositors, it is also necessary for banks to have sufficient capital to be able to withstand unexpected losses. It is clear that there is no limit to the scale of potential unexpected losses. However, by setting appropriate parameters it is possible to quantify what can perhaps best be described as 'probable unexpected loss'. The ultimate aim of the bank regulatory capital system is to ensure that a bank has sufficient capital to cover both expected loss and probable unexpected loss. In the IRB world this 'probable unexpected loss' amount is derived by using the PD as one of the inputs into a formula, the full glory of which is set out in para 7.08. However, for our purposes we can represent it as f(PD).

Probable Expected and Unexpected Loss $(UL) = f(PD) \times LGD \times EAD$

f(PD) is always larger than PD, and UL is therefore always larger than EL.

5.10 The basis of weighting is to express UL as a percentage. In the Basel I world, the starting assumption was that the UL for all assets was 8 per cent, but this 8 per cent was varied by a factor (the 'weighting') which represented the level of riskiness of the relevant asset—thus government securities were weighted at 0 per cent, mortgage loans were weighted at 50 per cent (equivalent to a UL of 4 per cent) and so on. The weightings used in the Basle I approach (10 per cent, 20 per cent, 50 per cent and 100 per cent) were therefore a composite estimate of PD and LGD in respect of each asset—EAD was dealt with through the credit conversion factor (CCF) regime.

5.11 The Basel two regimes are distinguished by the fact that they arrive at the weighing figure in different ways. In the standardized approach PD and LGD are not visible, since the prescribed weightings embed them. EAD remains visible in the form of the prescribed CCF figures. Within the IRB approach, in contrast, PD, LGD and EAD must be identified and used. The difference between the IRB approaches is that under the foundation approach the bank uses its own models to calculate PD, whilst under the advanced IRB approach it calculates all three. This can be expressed diagrammatically as follows:

	PD	LGD	EAD
Standardized	Weighting		CCF
Foundation IRB	Bank	Regulator	CCF
Advanced IRB	Bank	Bank	Bank

Shaded = prescribed within the Basel framework
Unshaded = calculated by the bank itself using its own risk models

5.12 It may appear from this table that advanced IRB banks will be free to set their own capital requirements in respect of unexpected loss, but this is not quite the case. Although advanced IRB banks will be permitted to determine all of the inputs to the formula to be used for calculating capital requirements, they will still be required to use the formula and the methodology prescribed by the regulator. The Accord also prescribes considerable operational requirements in respect of the systems used by banks to make calculations for the purposes of the IRB approaches. There will therefore continue to be substantial differences between the capital requirement of an advanced IRB bank and its own assessment of its own risk position.

D. Valuation of Exposures

The calculation of the capital requirement for any exposure is a matter of ascribing **5.13** a weighting to that exposure—in other words, multiplying the value of the exposure by a percentage figure to arrive at a weighted valuation. The bulk of this chapter concerns the calculation of the weighting percentage, but before considering this we should first think about the number to be weighted—the value of the exposure.

Even the valuation of simple exposures is by no means always straightforward. It **5.14** is a fundamental principle of the Accord that an exposure must be valued at the value given to it in its financial accounts. However, this is not as simple a rule as it may appear. UK firms, for example, may account using either International Accounting Standards or UK Financial Reporting Standards and Statements of Standard Accounting Practice, and some may account in accordance with insurance accounts rules, friendly societies accounts rules, building societies accounts rules, or various approved statements of recommended practice. However, the key issue is that the fundamental valuation for any asset is what the auditors say it is. This imports the applicable accounting rules to determine issues such as:

- netting of amounts due to and from the firm;
- the effect of securitization of assets and liabilities;
- leasing of assets;
- assets transferred to or received under a sale and repurchase or stock lending transaction; or
- assets transferred and received by way of initial or variation margin under a derivative or similar transaction.

However, it is important not to confuse the rule that an exposure has its account- **5.15** ing valuation with the proposition that the capital system follows accounting rules. Once exposures have been identified and valued using the applicable accounting principles, they must be dealt with according to the relevant regulatory capital rules. Thus, for example, the question of whether an asset is part of the trading book or not is a regulatory issue which is determined using regulatory rules, and this determination may well come to a different conclusion than the accounting analysis as to whether the relevant asset is held on an available for sale basis. It is therefore possible that there may be assets which are valued for accounting purposes as available for sale which are held in the banking book.

E. Mark to Market

5.16 The issue of marking exposures to market is one which has recently attracted considerable controversy, and the discussion here is confined to the mechanics of the requirements of the current rules. A short summary of the position as it is in the UK is that for institutions reporting under International Accounting Standards, assets are divided into four classes.

Financial assets at fair value through profit or loss

5.17 Where an asset is held at fair value through profit and loss, it is accounted for at 'fair value', and fair value is defined for this purpose as 'the amount for which an asset could be exchanged, or a liability settled, between knowledgeable, willing parties in an arm's length transaction'.[2]

5.18 What this means in practice is that if the value of the asset has increased, the holder books an unrealized profit on the asset, and if it has gone down, the holder books an unrealized loss. This profit or loss is recognized in the profit and loss account and is ultimately reflected in an increase or decrease in the accounting capital of the entity.

5.19 An asset can fall into this category in one of two ways. One is if it is a derivative (except designated hedging instruments) or a financial asset acquired or held for the purpose of selling in the short term or for which there is a recent pattern of short-term profit taking held for trading.[3] The second is by designation. The original principle enshrined in the accounting standard was that when a firm acquired any asset, it was required to make a once-for-all determination as to whether the asset was to be held in this category or not. Thereafter the asset could not be reclassified. This rule was intended to prevent firms from avoiding recognizing unrealized losses by reclassifying assets out of the fair value through profit and loss category. However, under the stress of the credit crunch this rule was changed to provide that firms were permitted to reclassify assets out of this category provided that the reclassification was the result of a genuine determination

---

[2] International Accounting Standard 39, para 9.
[3] In general any asset of which this is true will fall into the trading book and outside the scope of this chapter.

that the asset would now be held to maturity, and that such redesignation occurred only in 'rare circumstances'.[4]

Available-for-sale financial assets

These are non-derivative financial assets designated on initial recognition as available for sale, and are measured at fair value in the same way as financial assets at fair value through profit and loss. The difference between the two classes is that changes in the value of available for sale assets are not taken to the profit and loss account, but are recognized directly in equity, through the statement of changes in equity. Thus if a bank makes a gain or loss on an asset which is held as available for sale, its total accounting capital is raised or lowered accordingly, but its profit or loss will remain unchanged.   **5.20**

Loans and receivables

Loans and receivables may not be marked to market, and must be accounted for 'at amortized cost using the effective interest method'. What this means in broad terms is that if you lend £100 the asset value of the loan is likely to be £100 for as long as the loan remains fully performing, and this will be true regardless of fluctuations in interest rates. The full calculation rule is as follows: amortized cost of a financial asset or financial liability is the amount at which the asset or liability is measured at initial recognition (usually 'cost') minus any repayments of principal, minus any specific provision or write-off, and plus or minus the cumulative amortization of the difference between that initial amount and the maturity amount calculated using the effective interest method. This is done by looking at the cash flows involved in the transaction and treating any variation as an amortization or overdrawing. Thus if a five-year facility of £100 with an effective interest rate of 10 per cent provided for no repayment of interest at all in the first year (but a double payment in the final year), at the end of the first year the facility would be treated as having increased in value to £110. Conversely if it provided for a double payment in the first year and no payment in the final year, it would be regarded as having dropped in value to £90.   **5.21**

Held-to-maturity investments other than loans and receivables

This class comprises all assets held by a bank other than those designated as financial assets at fair value through profit and loss and loans and receivables. They are valued in the same way as loans and receivables.   **5.22**

---

[4] IAS 39, new para 50B, inserted 1 July 2008. The standard also required that the transfer be at the then prevailing market valuation—in other words, accrued mark to market losses prior to the transfer would be made permanent by the transfer, regardless of any subsequent upward movement in the price of the instrument.

5.23 Wherever possible, a firm must use a 'mark to market' approach in order to arrive at fair value. 'Mark to market' means, for this purpose, valuing positions at readily available close out prices from independent sources. Where securities are traded on an exchange then exchange closing prices should be used, but where this is not the case screen prices or quotes from independent brokers satisfy the requirement. Marking to market should be done at the price at which a firm could deal—thus positions should normally be marked at buy or sell price of the dealing spread (as appropriate) unless the firm is a significant market maker in a particular position type or is otherwise satisfied that it could close out at the mid-market.

5.24 Where marking to market is not possible, a firm must use mark to model. 'Marking to model' means any valuation which has to be benchmarked, extrapolated or otherwise calculated from a market input. Where a bank wishes to mark its positions to model, it should be able to demonstrate to its regulator that the model concerned is suitably robust. There is no formal threshold within the regulatory system as to when mark to model valuations may be used; and in practice accounting conventions are followed.

5.25 Finally, in valuing any individual asset banks are required to deduct any asset recognized in respect of deferred acquisition costs and add back in any liability in respect of deferred income (but exclude from the deduction or addition any asset or liability which will give rise to future cash flows), together with any associated deferred tax.

6

THE STANDARDIZED APPROACH

The standardized approach remains the bedrock of the Basel system. Although **6.01** many of the largest banks are IRB banks, there is probably no bank currently existing which does not use some elements of the standardized approach as part of its overall capital calculation. For such banks the standardized approach provides the fallback in respect of exposures arising out of areas of business where the bank may not have the resource nor the data to model exposures.

The standardized approach is similar to the Basle I regime in a number of respects. **6.02** The principal similarity is that a simple pre-determined risk weighting percentage is applied (and, in respect of off-balance sheet exposures, a credit conversion factor) to each exposure of the bank. Credit risk mitigation may then be recognized and serve to reduce the amount of the exposure.

A. Classification of Exposures, Credit Conversion Factors, and Credit Risk Mitigation

6.03 In the standardized approach assets are divided into various different classes. The FSA's articulation of this classification is as follows:

- claims or contingent claims on central governments or central banks;
- claims or contingent claims on non-central government regional governments or local authorities;
- claims or contingent claims on administrative bodies and non-commercial undertakings (public sector entities or PSEs);
- claims or contingent claims on multilateral development banks (MDBs);
- claims or contingent claims on international organizations;
- claims or contingent claims on banks and regulated investment firms;
- claims or contingent claims on corporates;
- retail claims or contingent retail claims;
- claims or contingent claims secured on real estate property;
- past due items;
- items belonging to high-risk categories;
- covered bonds;
- securitization positions;
- short-term claims on institutions and corporates;
- claims in the form of funds (collective investment undertakings, or CIUs);
- other items.

B. Ratings and Rating Agencies

6.04 The standardized approach is based on standardized credit risk exposure classes. The Basel Accord links these to S&P ratings, but the EU implementation of Basel (the Banking Co-ordination Directive) identifies these classes merely as 'credit quality steps' 1 through to 6, a piece of nomenclature deliberately designed to avoid referring to any particular rating provider. However, standardized firms are permitted to determine the credit quality step to which to ascribe any particular exposure by reference to the ratings published by External Credit Assessment Institutions (ECAIs). In the UK the Capital Requirements Regulations 2006 prescribe a mechanism by which the FSA may recognize certain ECAI's—at the time of writing only Moody's, Standard and Poor's, and Fitch-IBCA had been recognized for this purpose.[1] An institution may nominate more than one ECAI to use

---

[1] The criteria which are to be applied in making this determination are set out in reg 22 of, and Sch 1 to, the Capital Requirements Regulations, are made up of the following: objectivity;

across its product range, but may not 'cherry-pick' different ratings for different purposes—the use of different ECAI ratings must be consistent. It is a condition for the use of an ECAI rating that it takes into account both principal and accrued interest (in other words, that it looks at the risk of default on interest as opposed to mere recovery of principal).

The relevant mappings are as follows: **6.05**

Standardized—Long term

Credit Quality Step	Fitch	Moody's	S&P	DBRS
1	AAA to AA-	Aaa to Aa3	AAA to AA-	AAA to AAL
2	A+ to A-	A1 to A3	A+ to A-	AH to AL
3	BBB+ to BBB-	Baa1 to Baa3	BBB+ to BBB-	BBBH to BBBL
4	BB+ to BB-	Ba1 to Ba3	BB+ to BB-	BBH to BBL
5	B+ to B-	B1 to B3	B+ to B-	BH to BL
6	CCC+ and below	Caa1 and below	CCC+ and below	CCCH and below

Standardized—Short term

Credit Quality Step	Fitch	Moody's	S&P	DBRS
1	F1+, F1	P-1	A-1+, A-1	R-1 (high), R-1 (middle), R-1 (low)
2	F2	P-2	A-2	R-2 (high), R-2 (middle), R-2 (low).
3	F3	P-3	A-3	R-3
All other Credit assessments	Below F3	NP	All short-term ratings below A3	All short-term ratings below R- 3

Securitization—Standardized approach

Credit Quality Step	Fitch	Moody's	S&P	DBRS
1	AAA to AA-	Aaa to Aa3	AAA to AA-	AAA to AAL
2	A+ to A-	A1 to A3	A+ to A-	AH to AL
3	BBB to BBB-	Baa1 to Baa3	BBB+ to BBB-	BBBH to BBBL
4	BB+ to BB-	Ba1 to Ba3	BB+ to BB-	BBH to BBL
5	B+ and below	B1 and below	B+ and below	BH and below

independence; international access/transparency; disclosure; resources; and credibility. An ECAI which has been recognized as eligible in another member state may be recognized by the FSA without carrying out another evaluation process.

Securitization—IRB approach

Credit Quality Step		Credit Assessments		
	Fitch	Moody's	S&P	DBRS
1	AAA	Aaa	AAA	AAA
2	AA	Aa	AA	AA*
3	A+	A1	A+	AH
4	A	A2	A	A
5	A-	A3	A-	AL
6	BBB+	Baa1	BBB+	BBBH
7	BBB	Baa2	BBB	BBB
8	BBB-	Baa3	BBB-	BBBL
9	BB+	Ba1	BB+	BBH
10	BB	Ba2	BB	BB
11	BB-	Ba3	BB-	BBL
Below 11	Below BB-	Below Ba3	Below BB-	Below BBL

* Note: AA includes the assessments AAH to AAL.

Once an ECAI has been recognized by a regulator, the relevant regulator is obliged to carry out a mapping process under which the ratings of that ECAI will be attributed to these credit quality steps.[2]

6.06 Where there is only one relevant ECAI rating for a particular issuer, that rating will determine the treatment of all claims on that issuer which are not otherwise rated. Where there are two ratings, the higher of the two should be used. Where there are three or more, the higher of the two lowest should be used.

6.07 Where a rating relates only to a specific claim on an issuer, and the bank has an unrated claim on that issuer, the unrated claim will take the weighting applicable to the rated claim if the unrated claim ranks pari passu with or senior to the rated claim. Similarly, where an issue-specific rating is a low quality assessment (ie maps into a risk weight equal to or higher than that applying to unrated claims) the low quality assessment will apply to claims pari passu with or subordinate to the rated claim. An exception to this is the position as regards covered bonds, which may have a rating higher than the general rating of their issuer because of overcollateralization within the asset pool.

6.08 Where credit risk mitigation is taken into account in arriving at an issue specific rating, that credit risk mitigation will not be recognized for regulatory purposes, since that would constitute double-recognition.

---

[2] Annex 2 of the Basel Accord sets out a description of the approach to be taken in performing this mapping.

Short-term ratings may only be used for short-term claims, and may not be used **6.09** to support long-term ratings. Short-term ratings are taken to be issue-specific—in other words, where an issuer has two short term exposures ranking pari passu, one rated and one unrated, the rating of the rated issue cannot be applied to the unrated issue.

Ratings used should ordinarily be solicited ratings. Regulators have the power to **6.10** recognize only solicited ratings, but may in special circumstances recognize unsolicited ratings.

Institutions may also in certain circumstances use the assessments made by **6.11** export credit agencies so long as the agency complies with the OECD agreed methodology and publishes its risk scores—in the alternative the risk scores used pursuant to the Arrangement on Officially Supported Export Credits may be used.

The essence of the risk weighting system is that an exposure is treated as having a **6.12** value equal to its weighted value rather than its actual value. Thus an exposure to a 20 per cent weighted counterparty is treated as five times less risky than an equivalent exposure to a 100 per cent weighted counterparty. In capital terms, this means that the amount of capital required within Pillar one in respect of each exposure is 8 per cent of the weighted amount—thus the capital required for a £100 exposure to a 100 per cent counterparty is £8, whereas the capital required for a £100 exposure to a 20 per cent weighted counterparty is £1.60.

C. Exposures to Sovereigns

Credit Quality Step	1	2	3	4	5	6
Risk Weight	0%	20%	50%	100%	100%	150%

All claims on sovereigns and their central banks will be weighted as set out above, **6.13** and the differential treatment for non-OECD sovereigns contained in the Basle I Accord is now abolished. National regulators will have an important discretion in this area allowing them to give a zero weighting in respect of exposures to their own government or central bank where those exposures are both denominated and funded in the domestic currency, regardless of the credit rating of that government. Where a regulator has zero weighted its own sovereign in this way, other regulators may zero weight that sovereign in respect of their own bank's exposures to it if they see fit. It is highly likely that most national supervisors will exercise this power where necessary, so the result of this will be that most sovereign exposures to significant countries will be 0 per cent weighted where the exposure is in the domestic currency of the sovereign.

6.14 Exposures to sovereigns may also be weighted using the risk scores produced by export credit agencies, using the following weightings:

Export Credit Agency Minimum Export Insurance Premium (MEIP) ranking

Risk Score	0–1	2	3	4	5	6	7
	0%	20%	50%	100%	100%	100%	150%

The risk scores published by any ECA may be used so long as that agency complies with the OECD agreed methodology and publishes its risk scores. As an alternative, the risk scores used pursuant to the OECD 'Arrangement on Officially Supported Export Credits' may be used.

6.15 For any sovereign where there is no available eligible rating or ECA score, the weighting will be 100 per cent.

Regional governments or local authorities

6.16 This class includes a wide variety of government and quasi-government entities— for example, churches or religious communities with taxation powers[3] fall within it. For this purpose regional authorities and local governments may be divided into two classes—those with revenue raising power and those without. Exposures to local authorities which have their own revenue raising powers may be treated as exposures to central government, and other such exposures are treated as below. It is the responsibility of the relevant regulator in each EU member state to compile a list of the entities within its jurisdiction which have revenue raising powers—the FSA's list is to be found in BIPRU 3 Ann 2R. Where an EEA local authority is included on the list prepared by the relevant authority in that jurisdiction, institutions in other member states may treat that classification as determinative.

Sovereign weighting	1	2	3	4	5	6
Risk weight for regional government	20%	50%	100%	100%	100%	150%

6.17 Regional governments must be assigned a weighting according to the credit quality step which applies to the government of the territory in which they operate. There is an important difference between regional governments and central governments in that a central government in an EU territory or in a territory which has fully implemented Basel II gets an automatic 0 per cent weighting for borrowings in its domestic currency. A local authority, by contrast, does not— thus in a jurisdiction where the rating of the central government is below Level 2, borrowing by the central government in local currency would be 0 per cent

---

[3] More of these exist in the EU than might be supposed.

weighted whereas borrowing by a local authority would be 50 per cent weighted. Where the national government is unrated, the weighting must be not more than 100 per cent.

Exposures to local authorities with a duration of less than three months attract a **6.18** 20 per cent weighting in all cases.

Public sector entities

Public sector entities (PSEs—ie non-commercial bodies which carry out public **6.19** functions) will in principle be treated as local authorities. National authorities have the option to recognize their own PSEs as sovereign weighted where there is no difference in the risk exposure because of the existence of appropriate guarantees. Foreign authorities may then elect to treat the relevant PSEs in the same way.

Multilateral Development Banks (MDBs)

MDBs will be treated as banks and not as sovereigns. However, claims on 'strong' **6.20** MDBs will attract a 0 per cent weighting. A 'strong' MDB will be one whose debt is largely rated AAA, whose shareholder structure is composed of 'high quality' sovereigns with a demonstrated commitment to the institution, which has an adequate level of capital and liquidity and which has conservative financial and lending policies. Claims on the Bank for International Settlements, the International Monetary Fund, the European Central Bank and the European Community automatically receive a 0 per cent weight.

D. Exposures to Banks and Financial Institutions

Basle I provided that all claims on banks incorporated in OECD countries and **6.21** claims of less than one year's maturity on banks incorporated in non-OECD countries were weighted at 20 per cent, with all other claims on banks weighted at 100 per cent. However, as noted above the OECD/Non-OECD distinction has been eliminated within the Basel II framework.

Basel II offers two options to weighting claims on banks, indicating that supervi- **6.22** sors should choose between them. One of these approaches simply reflected the rating of the institution itself, the other reflected the rating of the sovereign in whose territory the bank was incorporated. The latter has been discarded in the EU, but lingers in the EU rule that a bank may never be given a lower risk weighting than that applicable to the government of the territory in which it is established. Since this rule reflects normal rating agency practice, this situation is unlikely to arise in practice.

Credit quality step	1	2	3	4	5	6
Risk weight for long term exposures	20%	50%	50%	100%	100%	150%
Risk weight for exposures below three months	20%	20%	20%	50%	50%	150%

It should be noted that the concessionary three-month treatment should only be used to weight a claim on a bank where either the bank has no separate short-term rating, or there being a short-term rating which is better than the long-term rating. Where a short-term rating exists, a bank would ordinarily be expected to use the short-term rating regime set out below (see para 6.59). In a situation where an institution has a short-term rating in existence but that short-term rating gives a less favourable result than the normal rating, the concessionary treatment may not be used. Also, by concession, an institution may opt to treat three-month paper issued by an institution in its domestic currency using a risk weight one category less favourably than that which would apply had the instrument been issued by the relevant national government.

6.23 These weights apply to exposures to securities firms as well as banks, provided that the securities firm in question is subject to equivalent regulation. Securities firms not subject to equivalent regulation will be treated as corporates.

6.24 Claims on recognized third country investment firms, clearing houses and exchanges are treated as exposures to banks.

E. Exposures to Corporates

6.25 This class forms the vast majority of the claims owed to any bank. The basis of the standardized weighting system is:

Credit quality step	1	2	3	4	5	6
Risk weight	20%	50%	100%	100%	150%	150%

6.26 The usual weighting of all claims on corporates under Basle I was 100 per cent. One way of looking at the Basel II regime is that this remains the default position, with a concessionary rating of 20 per cent given to claims on corporates with a rating of at least AA-, a concessionary rating of 50 per cent to those with a rating between A+ and A-, and a penal weighting of 150 per cent given to claims on corporates of a rating of below BB- An unrated corporate continues to receive a 100 per cent rating (or the rate applicable to its government, if higher). This is curious, primarily because it means a corporate which would have a credit rating below BB- can substantially improve the marketability of its debt securities by not obtaining a rating.

The EU has provided a concession for exposures to lowly rated corporates,[4] in that **6.27** any exposure with a weighting of 150 per cent may have its weighting reduced to 100 per cent if the lending bank applies a value adjustment of at least 20 per cent of the face value of the asset, or may have its weighting reduced to 50 per cent if the institution applies a value adjustment of at least 50 per cent. On paper this looks like a good deal, since:

- Applying no value adjustment, regulatory capital required would be 100 × 150% × 8% = £12

- Applying a £20 value adjustment, regulatory capital required would be (100 − 20) × 100% × 8% = £6.40

- Applying a £50 value adjustment, regulatory capital required would be (100 − 50) × 50% × 8% = £2

However, the key to this is that the value adjustment may not be included in capital, so that in the examples given above the £20 and £50 value adjustments will effectively be deducted from capital.

F. Exposures to Retail Customers

A portfolio of retail exposures is treated as a single asset and weighted at 75 per **6.28** cent. A portfolio is a retail portfolio if:

- all of the exposures are to an individual or small business;

- the exposure is acquired as part of a diversified portfolio of retail exposures where the effect of the diversification is to reduce the risks on the portfolio as a whole;

- no individual exposure exceeds Eur 1m. For these purposes exposures to connected entities must be aggregated—thus if a bank has a portfolio which contains two EUR 0.6m exposures to two companies with a common parent, the portfolio would not qualify as a retail portfolio. There is a positive obligation on an institution operating under this rule to inform itself as to the degree of connection between persons. For this purpose connected persons includes a company and its owner, as well as two companies in common control.

Retail mortgage lending

Retail mortgage lending will attract a weighting of 35 per cent where the supervi- **6.29** sory authorities are satisfied that the lending is secured by residential property to

---

[4] By BCD, Annex VI, Part 1, point 67.

be occupied or let by the owner. Mortgages granted by personal investment companies also fall within this classification provided that the beneficial owner of the property is a natural person. The 35 per cent weighting is also ascribed to any exposure which constitutes an exposure to a tenant under a property leasing transaction concerning residential property under which the firm is the lessor and the tenant has an option to purchase.

6.30 The primary restriction on this treatment is that the mortgage should not exceed 80 per cent of the value of the property. If the mortgage does exceed 80 per cent, the excess will not be 35 per cent weighted, but will be treated as a retail exposure and weighted at 75 per cent. Thus, where a borrower has a mortgage of £100,000 on a property valued at £100, 000, the bank will have two assets—an £80,000 asset weighted at 35 per cent and a £20,000 asset weighted at 75 per cent. It should be noted in passing that this gives an aggregate weighting for the £100,000 asset as 43 per cent.

6.31 For the purpose of applying this test the property must be valued by the firm at least once every three years, or more frequently if market conditions are subject to significant change. Statistical methods may be used for this monitoring unless the loan is in excess of Eur 3m (or if it exceeds 5 per cent of the capital resources of the firm), in which case an independent valuation every three years is required. The lending firm must also have written policies governing the type of collateral which it is prepared to accept, and the requirement for such collateral to be properly insured.

6.32 It is also a condition of this treatment that the criteria for legal certainty should have been fulfilled. Thus:

- the mortgage must be legally enforceable and filed on a timely basis;
- the mortgage must have been registered or perfected according to all relevant requirements; and
- the firm must be able to realize the value of the mortgaged property under the mortgage within a reasonable timeframe.

6.33 This rule applies to residential property throughout the EU provided that the lending is in accordance with the requirements of the local regulator, and may also be applied to property outside the EU. However, bafflingly, this treatment is only accorded to property in jurisdictions where the relevant government has implement Basel II—in other jurisdictions, the relevant weighting to be applied is 50 per cent rather than 35 per cent. The idea that there is a necessary link between local implementation of Basel II and the robustness of security interest in residential property is one for which there is no clear logical basis.

G. Commercial Mortgage Exposures

Commercial mortgage lending is weighted at 100 per cent. National regulators **6.34** are permitted[5] to ascribe a 50 per cent weighting for the tranche of a commercial mortgage loan where the loan-to-value ratio is the lower of 50 per cent of market value or 60 per cent of mortgage lending value. The FSA has not chosen to exercise this discretion, so that all lending by UK banks on the basis of commercial property mortgages will be weighted at 100 per cent in the standardized approach. However, other countries have implemented this discretion, and UK banks lending to borrowers in such countries may apply a 50 per cent weighting to those loans.

Broadly speaking this concessionary treatment should only be agreed by regula- **6.35** tors where the risk of the borrower is not connected to the risk of the property—a condition which would ordinarily exclude from this treatment 'merchant developer' arrangements whereby a loan is made to a single-purpose company whose business is to buy and develop a particular building or buildings. However, this restriction may be disapplied by a bank which can demonstrate that its total losses on loans of this type does not exceed 0.3 per cent over a year and that its total losses on commercial mortgage lending of all types has not exceeded 0.5 per cent over a year. If the bank ceases to satisfy that criteria in any year, its ability to disapply the requirement ceases.

H. Overdue Undefaulted Exposures

Not every overdue asset is defaulted, and an asset need not be written off in full until **6.36** some time after it has become overdue. There is therefore an issue of how to deal with overdue assets which do not yet satisfy the criteria for default. The treatment is:

- Loans secured on commercial property are to be risk-weighted at 100 per cent as soon as past due.

- Amounts due under residential mortgage loans, net of specific provisions, are to be weighted at 100 per cent once 90 days past due, provided that a 50 per cent weighting may be applied at national discretion where specific provisions have reached 20 per cent of the outstanding amount of the loan.

- All unsecured portions of other loans are to be risk weighted once 90 days past due as follows:

  - 150 per cent risk weighting when the regulatory haircut which has been taken ('value adjustments' in the language of the directive) are less than 20 per cent of the unsecured part of the outstanding amount of the loan;

---

[5] Footnote 29 of the Accord and BCD, Annex VI, Part 1, para 51.

- 100 per cent risk weight when value adjustments are no less than 20 per cent of the outstanding amount of the loan;
- 100 per cent risk weight for residential mortgages where value adjustments are less than 20 per cent of the gross debt, falling to 50 per cent if specific provisions exceed 20 per cent;
- 100 per cent for all commercial mortgages.

I. High-Risk Exposures

6.37 This is in some respects the residual class. The Accord makes provision for regulators to have a discretion to designate specific asset classes which they consider to be 'high-risk' and to impose upon them a 150 per cent risk weighting. There is no requirement for such designation to be co-ordinated between regulators, and each national regulator may make up its own mind as to what is high risk and what is not. This provision has been carried through into the EU regime, where it also remains unharmonized. By way of illustration, the FSA has exercised this discretion as regards two specific asset classes:

(1) Exposures arising out of venture capital business (whether or not the institution itself actually carries out that business).
(2) Any exposure to a collective investment undertaking that is illiquid and held with a view to long-term sale or realization.

J. Covered Bonds

6.38 The covered bonds regime is unique to the EU—it is not derived from the Accord (which does not specifically mention covered bonds) but is a response by EU lawmakers to local conditions. In broad terms, a covered bond means a bond issued by a bank secured by assets (usually real estate mortgages) owned by that bank. The essence of the product is therefore that the holder benefits from both the credit of the issuing bank and rights over the security pool in the event of the institution's failure, and these instruments are therefore recognized in the securities markets as having exceptionally low risk. The German Pfandbrief is the most commonly encountered type of covered bond, but most EU member states have a mechanism by which covered bonds may be created.

6.39 Covered bonds must be assigned a risk weight on the basis of the risk weight assigned to senior unsecured exposures to the credit institution which issues them. The following correspondence between risk weights applies:

(1) if the exposures to the institution are assigned a risk weight of 20 per cent, the covered bond must be assigned a risk weight of 10 per cent;

(2) if the exposures to the institution are assigned a risk weight of 50 per cent, the covered bond must be assigned a risk weight of 20 per cent;

(3) if the exposures to the institution are assigned a risk weight of 100 per cent, the covered bond must be assigned a risk weight of 50 per cent; and

(4) if the exposures to the institution are assigned a risk weight of 150 per cent, the covered bond must be assigned a risk weight of 100 per cent.

A covered bond is defined as a bond that is issued by a credit institution which has **6.40** its registered office in an EEA State and is subject by law to special public supervision designed to protect bondholders and in particular protection under which sums deriving from the issue of the bond must be invested in conformity with the law in assets which, during the whole period of validity of the bond, are capable of covering claims attaching to the bond and which, in the event of failure of the issuer, would be used on a priority basis for the reimbursement of the principal and payment of the accrued interest. However, a bond which satisfies this definition will only be afforded concessionary weighting if its underlying assets fall within the list specified in the directive.

The listed permitted underlyings are: **6.41**

(1) (a) exposures to or guaranteed by central governments, central bank, public sector entities, regional governments and local authorities in the EEA;

   (b) (i) exposures to or guaranteed by non-EEA central governments, non-EEA central banks, multilateral development banks, international organizations that qualify for the credit quality step 1;

      (ii) exposures to or guaranteed by non-EEA public sector entities, non-EEA regional governments and non-EEA local authorities that are risk weighted as exposures to institutions or central governments and central banks and that qualify for the credit quality step 1;

      (iii) exposures in the sense of this point (b) that qualify as a minimum for the credit quality step 2, provided that they do not exceed 20 per cent of the nominal amount of outstanding covered bonds of issuing institutions;

   (c) exposures to institutions that qualify for the credit quality step 1 but so that:

      (i) the total exposure of this kind must not exceed 15 per cent of the nominal amount of the outstanding covered bonds of the issuing credit institution;

      (ii) exposures caused by transmission and management of payments of the obligors of, or liquidation proceeds in respect of, loans secured by real estate to the holders of covered bonds must not be comprised by the 15 per cent limit; and

      (iii) exposures to institutions in the EEA with a maturity not exceeding 100 days are not comprised by the step 1 requirement but those institutions must as a minimum qualify for credit quality step 2;

(d) loans secured:

    (i) by residential real estate or shares in Finnish residential housing companies up to the lesser of the principal amount of the liens that are combined with any prior liens and 80 per cent of the value of the pledged properties; or

    (ii) by senior units issued by French Fonds Communs de Créances or by equivalent securitization entities governed by the laws of an EEA State securitizing residential real estate exposures provided that at least 90 per cent of the assets of such Fonds Communs de Créances or of equivalent securitization entities governed by the laws of an EEA State are composed of mortgages that are combined with any prior liens up to the lesser of the principal amounts due under the units, the principal amounts of the liens, and 80 per cent of the value of the pledged properties and the units qualify for credit quality step 1 where such units do not exceed 20 per cent of the nominal amount of the outstanding issue;

(e) (i) loans secured by commercial real estate or shares in Finnish housing companies up to the lesser of the principal amount of the liens that are combined with any prior liens and 60 per cent of the value of the pledged properties; or

    (ii) loans secured by senior units issued by French Fonds Communs de Créances or by equivalent securitization entities governed by the laws of an EEA State securitized commercial real estate exposures provided that, at least, 90 per cent of the assets of such Fonds Communs de Créances or of equivalent securitization entities governed by the laws of an EEA State are composed of mortgages that are combined with any prior liens up to the lesser of the principal amounts due under the units, the principal amounts of the liens, and 60 per cent of the value of the pledged properties and the units qualify for credit quality step 1 where such units do not exceed 20 per cent of the nominal amount of the outstanding issue; or

    (iii) a firm may recognize loans secured by commercial real estate as eligible where the loan to value ratio of 60 per cent is exceeded up to a maximum level of 70 per cent if the value of the total assets pledged as collateral for the covered bonds exceed the nominal amount outstanding on the covered bond by at least 10 per cent, and the bondholders' claim meets the legal certainty requirements; the bondholders' claim must take priority over all other claims on the collateral; or

(f) loans secured by ships where only liens that are combined with any prior liens within 60 per cent of the value of the pledged ship.

(2) For the purposes of (1)(d)(ii) and (1)(e)(ii) exposures caused by transmission and management of payments of the obligors of, or liquidation proceeds in

respect of, loans secured by pledged properties of the senior units or debt securities must not be comprised in calculating the 90 per cent limit.

(3) 'Collateralized' includes situations where the assets described in subpoints (1) (a) to (1)(f) are exclusively dedicated in law to the protection of the bond-holders against losses.

(4) Until 31 December 2010 the 20 per cent limit for senior units issued by French Fonds Communs de Créances or by equivalent securitization entities specified in subpoints (d) and (e) does not apply, provided that those senior units have a credit assessment by a nominated ECAI which is the most favourable category of credit assessment made by the ECAI in respect of covered bonds.

(5) Until 31 December 2010 the figure of 60 per cent in (1)(f) can be replaced with a figure of 70 per cent.

Covered bonds whose pool of underlying assets do not meet these requirements but which meet the definition of Article 22(4) of the UCITS Directive and were issued before 31 December 2007 are also eligible for the preferential treatment until their maturity.

K. Securitization Exposures

There is no standardized approach for securitization paper per se—exposures to **6.42** securitizations are to be weighted in accordance with the securitization regime. However, the securitization regime itself contains a 'standardized' approach, which is compulsory for any standardized bank holding securitization paper.

The securitization regime is deliberately structured so as to give securitization **6.43** exposures a higher weighting relative to their credit assessment than equivalent exposures to non-securitization vehicles: this is intended to eliminate correlation effects which would otherwise be recognized here but not elsewhere in the system. However, it is not always obvious when a particular security should be treated as being securitization paper for this purpose, and since the consequences of classification as a securitization can be very adverse, it is important to examine the tests which will be applied in order to determine whether a structure is a securitization. This topic is treated in more detail in paras 16.07 onwards.

What is a securitization?

It is generally relatively straightforward to identify a securitization, and therefore to **6.44** identify securitization paper. However, the definition which is used in the Accord is effects-based, and captures any transaction or scheme whereby the credit risk associated with an exposure or pool of exposures is tranched in such a way that:

(a) payments in the transaction or scheme are dependent upon the performance of the exposure or pool of exposures; and

(b) the subordination of tranches determines the distribution of losses during the ongoing life of the transaction or scheme.

Thus the securitization exposure class is characterized by three key elements; tranching, performance dependent payments, and subordination.

Tranching

6.45 This means a structure in which the underlying credit risk of the exposures is repackaged into at least two tranches at the inception of the transaction, and those tranches reflect different degrees of credit risk. Any position which constitutes a first loss position—that is, the expected loss on the portfolio—must be counted as tranches even if they are written off and therefore not carried on the books as assets. For example, residual payment claims resulting from a refundable purchase discount that may or may not be accounted for initially as 'loss on sale' have to be counted as tranches.

Performance dependent payment

6.46 This means that the entitlements of the investors are dependent upon the performance of the underlying assets. This must be distinguished from the position as regards a tranched repackaging, where the investor's entitlements are determined without reference to the performance of the underlying assets, but where investors take the risk of default due to an insufficiency of assets.

Subordination

6.47 Subordination differentiates securitization from ordinary senior/subordinated debt instruments, for which the priority of rights is set only in the liquidation process—that is, senior and subordinated debt both default at the same time, and only the liquidation proceeds are distributed unevenly. With a securitization, individual tranches may default at different times, and some tranches may not default at all even if they recover nothing.

6.48 The easiest way to understand the securitization definition is to consider some specific examples.

'Pass through' transactions

In a pass through structure, assets are transferred to a vehicle which issues securities, but all of the securities holders rank pari passu with each other. Such a transaction is not a securitization since there is no tranching. However, some pass through structures have the benefit of a guarantee or other form of credit enhancement provided by the originator or by a wrap provider. These structures will be regarded as securitizations, since the credit enhancement will constitute a first loss position.

Covered bonds

Covered bonds generally do not qualify as securitizations for regulatory purposes, because they do not include at least two different levels of risk, and because they are recourse obligations issued by an institution and not by a bankruptcy remote SPE. However, the funding purpose served by covered bonds is similar to that of traditional securitization, and covered bonds benefit in practice from first loss protection in that the level of collateral in the pool is generally larger than the nominal value of the bonds.

Tranched cover

Where an institution buys funded or unfunded protection to cover part of the risk of an asset, and the protection applies only to a first- or second- loss exposure, such transactions should in principle be treated as synthetic securitizations since they create two different tranches of risk.

Whole loan transactions

These are transactions where a single loan asset is transferred in tranches. Whether or not these transactions constitute securitizations will depend on the terms of the tranching.

Securitization and the specialized lending regime

As noted above, the fact that a transaction is being entered into in respect of a **6.49** single asset does not of itself prevent the transaction constituting a securitization if it falls within the definition set out above. Project and asset finance transactions are therefore vulnerable to recharacterization as securitizations. Senior/subordinate financing structures are common in project and asset finance, with the senior/subordinate structure not necessarily limited to the priority of claims on liquidation proceeds upon default of the borrowing entity, but also encompassing contractual clauses on the deferral of payments to the creditor of the subordinated loan. Furthermore, it is quite common to vest the subordinate creditor with the right to initiate and control liquidation procedures or to require the senior loan creditor to assign the senior loan to the subordinated loan creditor.

Such transactions may be addressed using either the specialized lending regime or **6.50** the PD/LGD approach where practicable for the institution concerned. It seems clear that there is no supervisory rationale for classing project or asset finance transactions as securitizations—the elimination of correlation benefits which the securitization regime seeks to effect is redundant in this context, since the correlation issue does not generally arise in transactions of this type. The Committee of European Banking Supervisors (CEBS) has therefore recommended that such transactions not be treated as securitizations for regulatory purposes on policy grounds, but has not provided any analysis in support of its view. One possibility would be to argue that the specialized lending and securitization definitions are intended to be mutually exclusive, and that a structure which clearly falls within one therefore necessarily falls outside the other. One of the tests proposed for specialized lending is that 'the contractual arrangements give the lender a substantial degree of control over the assets and the income that they generate', and this is in fact a common characteristic of project finance as opposed to securitization structures. The better view is any arrangements which involve the financing of a single asset (or a small number of large assets), under which the lenders have substantial control over the asset financed, constitutes specialized lending and therefore does not constitute securitization.

Weighting of securitization positions—standardized approach

6.51 To calculate the risk-weighted exposure amount of a securitization position under the standardized approach a risk weight must be assigned to the position based on its credit quality. This may be determined by reference to an ECAI credit assessment. Each separate tranche must be considered to be a separate position, as must any credit protection provided to the securitization or any position arising under any derivative, including currency or interest rate contracts—however, overlapping positions may be eliminated, with the position to be weighted being the higher risk position). The exposure value of an on-balance sheet securitization position must be its balance sheet value without regard to valuation adjustments. The exposure value of an off-balance sheet securitization position is its nominal value multiplied by the relevant conversion factor (100 per cent unless otherwise specified).

6.52 The risk-weighted exposure amount of a rated securitization position must be calculated by applying the following table. The outcome varies according to whether the paper held has a long-term or a short-term rating. It will be recalled for this purpose the 'credit quality steps' used are not the ordinary scale but the securitization scale (see above, para 6.05).

Credit quality step	1	2	3	4	5 and above
Risk weight for long term rating	20%	50%	100%	350%	1250%
Risk weight for short term rating	20%	50%	100%	1250%	1250%

A risk weighting of 1250 per cent is, of course, equal to a full deduction of the amount of the securitization position from capital.

6.53 The risk weighting of any unrated securitization position is 1250 per cent unless the composition of the pool of underlying assets is known at all times. For these purposes, 'known at all times' means known sufficiently for the firm to be able accurately to calculate the risk-weighted exposure amounts of the pool under the standardized approach. The firm must know this at the outset of the transaction. During the life of the transaction, it may rely on a contractual prohibition on changes in the composition of the pool that would have the effect of changing the composite weighting to be applied to the pool. In the view of the FSA it would be sufficient for the composition of the pool to be reported to the firm at least daily, via information service providers, secure web-sites or other appropriate sources.

In such a case the firm may apply the weighted-average risk weight that would be **6.54** applied to the securitized exposures under the standardized approach multiplied by a concentration ratio. This concentration ratio is equal to the sum of the nominal amounts of all the tranches divided by the sum of the nominal amounts of the tranches junior to, or pari passu with, the tranche in which the position is held including that tranche itself. Thus if a securitization has a total value of £100, tranched as £85, £10 and £5, and the firm holds the £10 tranche, the concentration ratio will be 6.7 (100/(10+5)). The resulting figure is capped at the equivalent of a 1250 per cent weighting and floored in that it must not be less than the risk weight applied to a rated tranche senior to that held by the firm.

For an originator or sponsor, the risk-weighted exposure amounts in respect of **6.55** their retained positions are capped at the level of the capital requirement to which they would have been subject had they not securitized the assets. Thus, no firm can make its regulatory capital position worse by doing a securitization.

Asset backed commercial paper

An asset backed commercial paper (ABCP) programme is a form of securitization, **6.56** but some special rules are applied to ABCP exposures. The most important of these is that where a firm holds a senior position (only) in an ABCP programme in circumstances where the first loss tranche is significant and the position held is investment grade, it may attribute to that position a risk weight that is the greater of:

(1) 100 per cent, or
(2) the highest of the risk weights that would be applied to any of the securitized exposures under the standardized approach by a firm holding the exposures.

Where a firm provides a liquidity facility to an ABCP conduit, the conversion **6.57** factor to be applied to that facility will be 20 per cent if the facility has an original maturity of one year or less, and 50 per cent if more than one year. The risk weight to be applied is the highest risk weight that would be applied to any of the securitized exposures under the standardized approach by a firm holding the exposures. In order to benefit from these requirements the liquidity facility must satisfy some fairly rigorous conditions; these being:

(1) the facility documentation must identify and limit the circumstances under which the facility may be drawn;

(2) it must not be possible for the facility to be drawn so as to provide credit support by covering losses already incurred at the time of draw—for example, by providing liquidity in respect of exposures in default at the time of draw or by acquiring assets at more than fair value;

(3) the facility must not be used to provide permanent or regular funding for the securitization;

(4) repayment of draws on the facility must not be subordinated to the claims of investors other than to claims arising in respect of interest rate or currency derivative contracts, fees or other such payments, nor be subject to waiver or deferral;

(5) it must not be possible for the facility to be drawn after all applicable credit enhancements from which the liquidity facility would benefit are exhausted; and

(6) the facility must include a provision that results in an automatic reduction in the amount that can be drawn by the amount of exposures that are in default, where default has the meaning given to it for the purposes of the IRB approach, or where the pool of securitized exposures consists of rated instruments, that terminates the facility if the average quality of the pool falls below investment grade.

However, a 0 per cent conversion figure may be applied to a liquidity facility which may be drawn only in the event of general market disruption or that is unconditionally cancellable.

6.58 Credit protection may be recognized in respect of securitization positions in the same way that it is recognized for other positions.

L. Short-Term Claims on Financial Institutions and Corporates

6.59 Where claims on financial institutions and corporates (for example commercial paper) have short-term ratings from External Credit Assessment Institutions (ECAIs), short-term claims on them may be weighted in accordance with those short-term ratings.

Credit quality step	1	2	3	4	5	6
Risk weight	20%	50%	100%	150%	150%	150%

M. Fund Exposures

6.60 'Collective investment undertaking' is the blanket term which catches regulated and unregulated investment vehicles, including hedge funds, private equity funds and regulated funds. The regime for holdings of fund units is another part of the capital requirements jigsaw which is unique to the EU—the topic is not mentioned in the Accord. However, the scope of the regime is unclear, since there is, surprisingly, no definition of a collective investment undertaking in the EU regulatory system. The nearest available definition is the definition provided in the EU Prospectus Directive of 'collective investment undertaking other than of the closed-ended type'. This catches:

a unit trust or investment company –
(a) the object of which is the collective investment of capital provided by the public, and which operate on the principle of risk-spreading; and
(b) the units of which are, at the holder's request, repurchased or redeemed, directly or indirectly, out of the assets of these undertakings.

The second limb of this definition is a description of open-endedness. Thus, if we reason by extension that if it is deleted we can also delete the qualification 'other than of the closed-ended type', we would arrive at a working definition as 'a unit trust or investment company the object of which is the collective investment of capital provided by the public, and which operates on the principle of risk-spreading'. The reference to 'the public' here cannot be interpreted consonantly with other directive references (eg offers to the public), since a hedge fund (for example) raises money exclusively through private placement but is nonetheless a collective investment undertaking. Consequently, we should interpret the reference to the public here as being intended to catch any vehicle which exists to provide an investment service to others.

6.61 The basic treatment for any CIU exposure will be a 100 per cent risk weighting, although a firm must ascribe a 150 per cent weighting to a CIU where it perceives that the CIU is abnormally risky—the FSA suggests that this treatment should be applied where the fund is highly leveraged, lacks transparency or invests substantially in very high risk assets which would ordinarily attract a weighting of over 100 per cent. In the rare circumstances where the CIU has a credit assessment by a nominated ECAI, the weighting to be used should be:

Credit quality step	1	2	3	4	5	6
Risk weight	20%	50%	100%	100%	150%	150%

6.62 An institution may in certain circumstances look through a CIU and report its exposures as being to the underlying assets. This may be done where the CIU is managed by a regulated investment management company (regulated in the EEA or in a recognized third jurisdiction), where the fund's prospectus imposes investment limits which confine its investments to specific asset categories, and where the fund reports in full at least annually. Where the holder is not aware of the fund's actual investments, it may still weight on a 'worst of' basis, assuming that the fund has invested to the greatest extent permissible in the highest weighted assets permissible and so on.

N. Other Assets

6.63 The standard weight for all assets other than those listed above will be 100 per cent. This catches physical assets, and also prepayments and accrued income for which the institution is unable to determine the counterparty. Cash items in the process of collection are 20 per cent weighted; cash in hand is 0 per cent weighted. Gold bullion held in own vaults or on an allocated basis is 0 per cent weighted. Equity and regulatory capital instruments issued by banks and investment firms will be weighted at 100 per cent if they are not deducted from capital.

6.64 For asset sale and repurchase agreements and outright forward purchases, the risk weight ascribed must be that assigned to the asset itself and not that to the transaction counterparty. Thus if I sell a building on a sale and repurchase terms, for the duration of the transaction I will be treated as owning the building.

6.65 It should also be noted here that where a bank is reporting on a solo basis, it is permitted to treat as 0 per cent weighted any exposure to any counterparty which is a parent or subsidiary within its group, provided that the counterparty is included within the same consolidated supervized group as the reporting institution, that both the reporting institution and the counterparty are part of a group risk control policy which is applied in an integrated fashion across the group, and that it is established in a member state (or a state where it is subject to appropriate prudential requirements). This exclusion does not apply, however, to any exposure whose terms are such that it would constitute tier one or two capital if it were invested in an institution.

O. Off-Balance Sheet Items

6.66 An off-balance sheet item means, for this purpose, a potential exposure of the institution concerned which does not appear on its balance sheet. These are (broadly) contractual obligations of the bank which, if performed, would give rise to an asset, such as a commitment to lend at a future date.

6.67 As was the case under Basle I, the mechanism which is used to bring off-balance sheet assets onto the balance sheet is to include them as assets subject to a 'credit conversion factor' or CCF which is intended to reflect the risk of the commitment concerned actually being called upon. The risk-weighted value of off-balance sheet items is multiplied by the credit conversion factor in calculating their capital requirement.

Thus, the risk-weighted exposure value for any off-balance sheet exposure is calculated as:

[Value of exposure] × [credit conversion factor] × [risk weighting]

The credit conversion factor must not be confused with the risk weighting—both must be applied to derive the actual risk-weighted exposure for the commitment. Thus, a £100 exposure to a bank under a one-year facility will, under Basel II, have a risk weighting of:

£100 × 20% (bank risk rating) × 20% (credit conversion factor) = £4

6.68 The starting point for CCFs is that off-balance sheet commitments should receive a 100 per cent credit conversion factor—ie should be treated as if they were present, drawn commitments. This treatment is applied to guarantees, credit derivatives, acceptances, endorsements of bills not bearing the name of another credit institution, transactions with recourse, irrevocable standby letters of credit, assets purchased under outright forward purchase agreements, forward deposits, the unpaid portion of partly paid securities, and asset sale and repurchase agreements. The real issue is therefore as to which commitments may attract a lower weighting.

6.69 A 50 per cent CCF can broadly be applied to exposures which do not constitute direct credit substitutes. There are a number of commitment types—notably standby letters of credit, performance bonds and guarantees which sometimes may and sometimes may not constitute direct credit substitutes, depending upon the circumstances.

6.70 A 0 per cent credit conversion factor is applied to exposures (agreements to lend, purchase securities, provide guarantees or acceptance facilities) which are immediately cancellable by the lender or which provide for automatic cancellation on deterioration in the borrower's creditworthiness. Retail credit lines are treated as being unconditionally cancellable if they can be cancelled to the full extent possible without contravening local consumer protection and related legislation.

6.71 A 20 per cent credit conversion factor is applied to other commitments with an original maturity under one year (other than repo exposures—see below) that do not fall within the 0 per cent band. Commitments with an original maturity over one year that do not fall within the 0 per cent band (other than repo exposures covered below) will default to the 50 per cent CCF category. The 20 per cent CCDF is also applied to documentary credits in relation to exports and other self-liquidating letters of credit—letters of credit which are used for purposes other than trade credit generally carry a 50 per cent weighting depending on their purpose.

6.72 Repos and exposures arising out of securities lending and posting of securities as collateral always attract a 100 per cent CCF regardless of maturity or cancellability.

7

MODEL BASED APPROACHES
TO RISK WEIGHTING

A. Introduction to the Basel Risk Model

7.01 Any and every financial institution expects to suffer some level of default— although no bank advances a facility expecting it not to be repaid, every bank knows from experience that some of the facilities which it advances will in fact not be repaid. Consequently, all properly-run banks make some provision for some level of default on their existing assets. This is known as expected loss.

7.02 Most banks will be sufficiently familiar with their own business to be able to estimate reasonably accurately the expected loss on their portfolio of assets as a whole. Consequently it may be asked why it should be necessary to provide a capital requirement any higher than this level. The answer is that this loss experience will not be experienced evenly across time, but is very likely to occur with significant peaks and troughs. Figure 7.1 illustrates the loss experience of a typical bank:

The point here is that at some points losses will be lower than those expected, and at some points they will be higher. Although the trend is a low, continuing loss

105

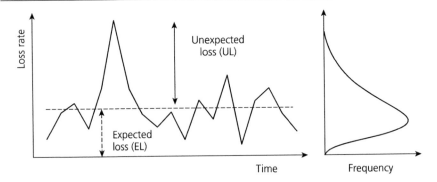

Fig. 7.1 Loss experience of a typical bank

Source: Basel Committee on Banking Supervision *An explanatory note on the Basel II IRB Risk weight Functions* (July 2005).

experience, this experience will be punctuated by incidents of high losses, as well as incidents of very low losses.

7.03 It should be clear from this diagram that the task of the regulator is to set a capital requirement which just skims the top of the actual loss experience curve. If the capital requirement is set significantly higher than this, then banks will be penalized by being required to hold excessive capital, if it is set lower, then the risk of bank failure increases.

7.04 The question therefore becomes one of how to set the capital requirement at a level such that the probability of catastrophic default is sufficiently low to be acceptable. Considering the graph on the left in Figure 7.1, we see that although possible default is unlimited, the probability of that default is reflected by the graph on the right. If this is turned on its side, it becomes recognizable as a probability distribution function (that is, a graph where the total area under the curve is equal to 100 per cent probability) (see Figure 7.2). This is a graph of the probability that losses will exceed the sum of expected losses and unexpected losses. Thus the remaining task for the regulator is to determine what point on this graph constitutes an acceptable risk level. If expected losses are covered by provisions (or revenues), and if the capital requirement set is equal to the unexpected loss element of this distribution, then the probability of the institution defaulting will be equal to the area under the graph to the right of the EL + UL figure (together the Value at Risk, or VaR).

7.05 There are two points to note about this graph. The first is that the area under the graph to the left of the EL element is larger than that to the right—in other words, the majority of losses which are expected to occur fall within the existing provisions for expected loss. The second is that the VaR figure can be set anywhere

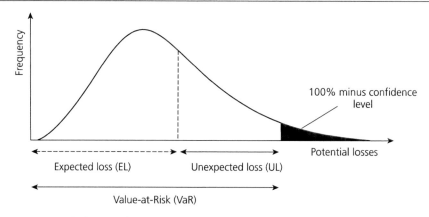

Fig. 7.2. Probability of losses exceeding EL and UL

Source: Basel Committee on Banking Supervision *An explanatory note on the Basel II IRB Risk weight Functions* (July 2005).

along the curve according to taste—the decision as to where to put it is a purely arbitrary one.

In Basel II, this level is set at 99.9 per cent. It used to be frequently pointed out (by **7.06** banks) that this is in theory a standard which guards against events which happen one year in a thousand, and that this was an over-conservative level. However, since the events of the recent past have demonstrated that once in a millennium event may in certain circumstances occur once a week for extended periods, this argument is now less commonly heard.

B. VaR and the Basel Framework

Thus far we have been considering the entirety of the regulated institution, and **7.07** assuming that it is possible to calculate the probability of any given default across the total portfolio of assets of the institution. This approach, known as 'whole bank modelling', would be the perfect approach to bank capital. Unfortunately, it is impossible—at least with current data. Because of this, the Basel Accord is structured so that the VaR calculation is performed in respect of each individual asset, and the result of each of these individual calculations is added together in order to assess the VaR of the total portfolio of credit exposures held by the bank. The effect of this approach is that each asset is examined in isolation without regard to any other asset—in other words, exposures which compose the bank's credit portfolio are treated as granular. It is sometimes argued that this necessarily overstates the capital requirements on the portfolio as a whole—the argument being that no more than a certain number of credits are likely to default at any given time—and more recently it has been argued that it may understate the capital requirements for the portfolio as a whole, since the default of one credit may make the default of another more likely. The statistical tools to resolve this are as yet insufficiently developed to encourage regulators to permit them to be used in the regulatory system any time soon, and as a result we are likely to be left with the Basel system for the foreseeable future.

C. The Basic Basel Formula

7.08 The basis of the Basel II approach, it will be remembered, is the capital requirement per exposure, or K, expressed as a percentage of actual exposure. Thus the actual capital requirement for any position is:

$$\text{Capital Requirement} = K \times EAD$$

There is no pleasant way to deal with what comes next, and those of a sensitive disposition may wish to look away now. The actual expression for K is as follows:

$$K = [LGD * N[(1-R)\char`\^-0.5 * G(PD) + (R/(1-R))\char`\^0.5 * G(0.999)] - PD * \\ LGD * (1-1.5 \times b(PD))\char`\^-1 \times (1+(M-2.5) * b(PD))$$

N{ } represents the expected normal distribution, G{ } represents the inverse of that distribution, and other letters will be defined in the course of the discussion below.

7.09 In order to decode this, it is necessary to go back to what it is trying to do. It should be clear from the graphs above that the effect of the formula should be to arrive at an estimate of the area under the graph to the right of the EL amount and to the left of the confidence level. We will call this the 'default tail'. The percentage capital requirement (K) should therefore be equal to:

$$K = \text{Default tail} \times LGD$$

However, the Basel II model includes one further variable, in that the probability of loss is also a function of the maturity of the exposure, and a further adjustment is made to reflect this. Thus, in the full model:

$$K = \text{Default tail} \times \text{Maturity adjustment} \times LGD$$

We need to look at these piece by piece.

Maturity adjustment

7.10 The maturity factor is expressed as:

$$\frac{1 + (M - 2.5) \times b}{1 - 1.5 \times b}$$

108

where b= $(0.11852 - 0.05478 \times \ln(PD))^2$

b is an adjustment factor based on historic observations, and therefore contains some apparently arbitrary numbers.

The answer to the question 'what on earth does all that mean?' is not important— **7.11** what really matters is how it functions in practice. Where maturity is less than one year, the maturity adjustment ceases to have any function—it is one. Where maturity is between one and five years, it increases in a straight line until five years is reached. All exposures with a maturity of over five years are, in the Basel II world, treated as if they had a maturity of five years, and so at five years the maturity factor reaches a limit.

The maturity factor increases faster for high quality credits than for low quality **7.12** ones. This is because for a low quality credit, the high risk of default is not materially increased by a longer term, whereas for a high quality credit, the longer the maturity the higher the chance that the quality of the credit may deteriorate during the life of the exposure. By way of example, for a AAA credit the effect of the application of the maturity factor is to increase K by a factor of 3.4 times between one year and five years. For a B- credit, by contrast, the increase is only 1.2 times over the same period. For a representative sample of good quality corporate exposures with a 0.25 per cent PD, the weighting at five years would be almost exactly double the weighting at one year.

Default tail

The default tail is, if anything, even less pretty. It is: **7.13**

$$\text{Default Tail} = N \left\{ \frac{\{G\{PD\} + G0.999\}\sqrt{R}}{\sqrt{1-R}} \right\} - PD$$

What is going on here? On the top line, G{PD} is the foundation stone, and is the inverse function of the PD. 0.999 is the 99.9 per cent level of probability which is set for the acceptable level of unexpected loss, and G{0.999} is the inverse function of this level.[1]

---

[1] When it comes to explaining why this inversion and reversion is necessary, the explanation given in the BCBS Explanatory note is that: 'the appropriate default threshold for 'average' conditions is determined by applying a reverse of the Merton model to the average PDs. Since in Merton's model the default threshold and the borrower's PD are connected through the normal distribution function, the default threshold can be inferred from the PD by applying the inverse normal distribution function to the average PD in order to derive the model input from the already known model output. Likewise, the required 'appropriately conservative value' of the systematic risk factor can be derived by applying the inverse of the normal distribution function to the predetermined supervisory confidence level. A correlation-weighted sum of the default threshold and the conservative value of the systematic factor yields a 'conditional (or downturn) default threshold'. In a second step,

7.14 R is the correlation factor which is built in to the model to reflect the risk that loans will default at the same time. R itself is also a function of PD, in that the lower PD for an exposure the more likely the model assumes it to be that it will default at the same time as other defaults.[2] R is arrived at by a formula. The formula for R was derived by looking at historic data for actual correlations, and therefore contains some arbitrary-looking elements. It is:

$$R + 0.12\left[\frac{1-e^{-50PD}}{1-e^{-50}}\right] + 0.24\left[1 - \frac{1-e^{-50PD}}{1-e^{-50}}\right] - 0.04\left[1 - \frac{S-5}{45}\right]$$

You can loosely approximate this as $R = 0.12 + 0.12e^{-50PD}$. Because of the way this formula works, outputs vary between 24 per cent (for a PD of 0.03, the lowest permitted PD for a non-sovereign) and 12 per cent (for a PD above 10 per cent). The 50 (known as the K factor) serves only to regulate the rate of increase between the bottom and the top—since 50 is (in these terms) relatively large, correlation increases rapidly as credit quality improves. The last bit is the size adjustment, which permits firms with a turnover of less than Eur 50m to reduce their R proportionately according to their turnover—a firm with a turnover of less than Eur 5m gets the full 4 per cent reduction. Thus, whereas for large corporates R varies between 12 per cent and 24 per cent, for a very small corporate R varies between 8 per cent and 20 per cent.

7.15 Because the calculation thus far has relied on the inverse normal distribution, it is necessary to turn it right way up again before it can be used under an ordinary normal distribution curve:

- hence the entirety is put within the N{ } function;
- finally, PD is subtracted, since the model is intended to give the probability of total loss, and expected loss must be subtracted in order to yield a figure for unexpected loss.

Consequences

7.16 The formula gives a very roughly 'square root' shaped graph when drawn. Across the curve as a whole the trend line is that an increase in PD of 4 times results in an increase in requirements of around 1.5 times. However, small changes in PD at the top end of the credit curve have a very significant impact. Thus, according to

---

the conditional default threshold is used as an input into the original Merton model and is put forward in order to derive a PD again—but this time a conditional PD. The transformation is performed by the application of the normal distribution function of the original Merton model.'

[2] Events which cause low quality credits to default may vary widely, and may have limited impact on the wider world. An event which causes high quality credits to default, however, is likely to be of more global significance and therefore to affect a wider range of other credits.

Annex V of the Accord, for a representative corporate exposure a PD of 0.10 per cent gives a capital requirement of 30 per cent, whereas a PD of 0.40 per cent gives a requirement of 63 per cent—more than double. More typically, a PD of 1 per cent gives a requirement of 92 per cent whereas a PD of 4 per cent gives a requirement of 140 per cent—almost exactly 1.5 times.

D. Putting It All Together

This is a good moment to revisit the core unexpected loss formula, which it will **7.17** be recalled was either:

£Capital Requirement = EAD × default tail × maturity adjustment × LGD

%Capital Requirement (K) = Default tail × maturity adjustment × LGD

Without doing any arithmetic at all, what can we know about the output of this formula? Well, we know that things which are multiplied together scale linearly—that is, if you double any one element, you double the total. It seems intuitive that if you double the size of the exposure you double the capital charge. However, it is equally true that if you halve loss given default (LGD), you halve the capital requirement; if you double the maturity adjustment, you double the capital requirement. We also know that the default tail changes relatively slowly at the worse end of the credit spectrum but rapidly at the better end—thus a relatively small change in the credit quality of a good exposure will result in a significant change to the capital requirement, whereas an equivalent change in a worse exposure results in relatively little change. Applying this normatively; assuming that you can do nothing about the credit quality of your borrower, you can reduce your credit exposure to that borrower by reducing the size of the outstanding facility, or by reducing its maturity, or by reducing the expected loss on default by taking collateral. All of this seems so intuitively obvious that it is necessary to pause for a moment to realize that this relative coherence between credit risk management and the regulatory capital system is in fact brand new, and is the finest flower of the new dispensation.

E. The Retail Exposures Formula

Because nothing is ever simple, the Accord looks as if it has a number of different **7.18** formulae for different types of exposures—in particular, retail exposures. However, pleasingly this is not quite the case. Residential Mortgages, Qualifying Revolving Retail Exposures and Other Retail Exposures in fact use the same calculation to determine K, but with one fluctuation. This is that instead of the formula for R given above, they use a different mechanism. For the first two of these this is relatively easy to understand; since for residential mortgages R is fixed at

15 per cent and for QRRE at 4 per cent. However, for other retail exposures the correlation is:

$$R = 0.03\left[\frac{1-e^{-35PD}}{1-e^{-35}}\right] + 0.16\left[1-\frac{1-e^{-35PD}}{1-e^{-35}}\right]$$

It should be clear that this is the same formula as used above save with the upper and lower limits changed from 12 per cent and 24 per cent to 3 per cent and 16 per cent. Also since the k-factor is set at 35 rather than 50, the rate of increase between the bottom and the top is flattened. The absence of the size factor should be no surprise, since retail portfolios do not have turnovers.

F. Translating between Capital Requirements and Risk Weightings

7.19 The Basle I approach employed an idea of risk-weighted assets. A weighting factor was applied to an asset value and the result was the risk-weighted asset figure to which the 8 per cent requirement was to be applied. Thus, for an exposure of £100 to a bank, the risk weighting was 20 per cent so the RWA figure was £20 and the capital requirement 8 per cent of £20—that is, £1.60. The Basel II approach calculates a capital requirement (K) for each individual exposure. It is sometimes necessary to translate these into RWAs. This is a reasonably straight-forward process, and is done by grossing up the figure for K by 8 per cent—thus, where an asset has, under Basel II, a capital requirement of £2, the RWA figure is £2/8 per cent, that is, £25 (since, dividing by 8 per cent is equivalent to multiplying by 12.5).

G. Model Types

7.20 The Basel II framework is based on the Asymptotic Single Risk Factor (ASRF) model. Translated, this means a model which has only one variable—in this case PD. The reason that the Basel Committee on Banking Supervision (BCBS) uses this model is not because it is convinced of its essential rightness, but rather because the model which it was required to develop had to apply equally across a wide variety of different portfolios of assets owned by the different types of banks which would be subject to the accord. Thus, the function which the Accord had to perform drove the selection of the ASRF approach. This leads to the slightly counter-intuitive fact that although the ASRF approach is the approach which the BCBS itself uses, it does not take the view that ASRF is necessarily the approach which banks should take—and indeed banks are encouraged to use other models which better reflect their actual risks.

H. Illustrative Risk Weights

For those who did not wish to face the foregoing, some relief is now provided in **7.21** the form of an illustrative table provided as Annex 5 to the Accord itself. These figures were calculated using a representative data series, and are provided only as illustrations of the sorts of output which the Basel model might produce when applied to a relatively typical set of loss data. They are, however, informative.

Illustrative IRB risk weights for UL

Asset Class	Corporate Exposures		Residential Mortgages		Other Retail Exposures		Qualifying Revolving Retail Exposures	
*LGD:	45%	45%	45%	25%	45%	85%	45%	85%
Turnover (millions of €)	50	5						
PD:								
0.03%	14.44%	11.30%	4.15%	2.30%	4.45%	8.41%	0.98%	1.85%
0.05%	19.65%	15.39%	6.23%	3.46%	6.63%	12.52%	1.51%	2.86%
0.10%	29.65%	23.30%	10.69%	5.94%	11.16%	21.08%	2.71%	5.12%
0.25%	49.47%	39.01%	21.30%	11.83%	21.15%	39.98%	5.76%	10.88%
0.40%	62.72%	49.49%	29.94%	16.64%	28.42%	53.69%	8.41%	15.88%
0.50%	69.61%	54.91%	35.08%	19.49%	32.36%	61.13%	10.04%	18.97%
0.75%	82.78%	65.14%	46.46%	25.81%	40.10%	75.74%	13.80%	26.06%
1.00%	92.32%	72.40%	56.40%	31.33%	45.77%	86.46%	17.22%	32.53%
1.30%	100.95%	78.77%	67.00%	37.22%	50.80%	95.95%	21.02%	39.70%
1.50%	105.59%	82.11%	73.45%	40.80%	53.37%	100.81%	23.40%	44.19%
2.00%	114.86%	88.55%	87.94%	48.85%	57.99%	109.53%	28.92%	54.63%
2.50%	122.16%	93.43%	100.64%	55.91%	60.90%	115.03%	33.98%	64.18%
3.00%	128.44%	97.58%	111.99%	62.22%	62.79%	118.61%	38.66%	73.03%
4.00%	139.58%	105.04%	131.63%	73.13%	65.01%	122.80%	47.16%	89.08%
5.00%	149.86%	112.27%	148.22%	82.35%	66.42%	125.45%	54.75%	103.41%
6.00%	159.61%	119.48%	162.52%	90.29%	67.73%	127.94%	61.61%	116.37%
10.00%	193.09%	146.51%	204.41%	113.56%	75.54%	142.69%	83.89%	158.47%
15.00%	221.54%	171.91%	235.72%	130.96%	88.60%	167.38%	103.89%	196.23%
20.00%	238.23%	188.42%	253.12%	140.62%	100.28%	189.41%	117.99%	222.86%

Source: Basel II: International Convergence of Capital Measurement and Capital Standards: A Revised Framework—Comprehensive Version, June 2006, Annex 5.

*where necessary, a maturity of 2.5 years has been assumed.

The way that this works in practice is as follows. As noted above: **7.22**

$$EL = PD \times LGD \times EAD$$

$$\text{Capital requirement} = f(PD) \times LGD \times EAD$$

By way of illustration, take a fully drawn senior £1m facility where the client is a large corporate with a PD of 1 per cent.

$$EL = 1\% \times 45\% \times £1m = £4,500$$

When the 1% PD and the other factors are put into the formula, $f(1\%) = 16.41\%$.

$$\text{Capital requirement} = 16.41\% \times 45\% \times £1m = £73,856$$

The relationship between EL and capital requirement varies as the riskiness of the asset increases. For a more risky asset the formula yields a greater unexpected loss risk relative to the expected loss, and vice versa.

I. Modelling in Practice

7.23 For those who have considered the idea of mathematical modelling in all its purity, there are a number of surprises which are encountered when we turn to consider the way in which models are actually deployed within banks.

7.24 It will appear from the foregoing that a specific calculation can be made for each individual exposure by an IRB bank. However, this would clearly be impossible for a number of reasons, not least that if a bank has actual default data in respect of an individual borrower it is unlikely (except for some very specialized lenders) to lend to that borrower again. Thus, the essence of the use of a model is that it must be used to assess a borrower against a pool of expected loss data, and to grade him within that pool. The most important decision with respect to any exposure is therefore to decide which type of borrower he is.

7.25 It is also clearly possible—in theory—to calculate the risk of every individual borrower to as many decimal places as may be required. However, once a borrower has been allocated to a specific type, it should be clear that this calculation will produce the same result as for any other borrower allocated to that type. The precision generated by the trail of decimal points is in fact spurious.

7.26 The practical consequence of this is that credit risk models are in fact used to allocate quantitative factors to qualitative judgements made by bankers. The way in which this is most commonly encountered is that a bank will operate an internal 'rating' system, with each potential borrower allocated a risk grade which loosely mimics the function of an external rating. Since this is broadly how most large banks have operated for some time, the most interesting aspect of the IRB approach is the extent to which it can be rolled out within a bank without impacting the way in which the bank makes its ordinary commercial decisions. The aim of the exercise is not to affect banks' credit judgements or credit pricing, but to enable their existing judgements to be more accurately translated into credit risk capital requirements.

J. Variations in Credit Risk Weightings between Firms

The single most important aspect of the introduction of the Basel II approach to **7.27** capital requirements is that the capital required in respect of any particular asset will vary over the life of that asset. Each asset must be reassessed at least annually, and certain high risk credits must be reassessed more frequently than this. In addition, any credit must be reassessed when new information comes to light. Under the existing regime, by contrast, the weighting of a drawn asset does not vary, and when a loan is made or an asset purchased the capital required in respect of that asset can be known. Under Basel II, by contrast, a weakening in the credit quality of a borrower will cause the capital requirements in respect of exposures to that borrower to increase. Predicting a bank's capital requirements in the future will therefore become harder.

K. Inputs and Outputs

The 'use' test

Under the Basel regime banks are prohibited from operating two separate risk **7.28** calculation models, one for the regulator and one for themselves. The systems and processes which the bank uses to generate these risks must be consistent with their internal use by the bank (see below). This is known as the 'use' test. The test is set out at para 444 of the Accord as follows:

> 444.   Internal ratings and default and loss estimates must play an essential role in the credit approval, risk management, internal capital allocations, and corporate governance functions of banks using the IRB approach. Ratings systems and estimates designed and implemented exclusively for the purpose of qualifying for the IRB approach and used only to provide IRB inputs are not acceptable. It is recognized that banks will not necessarily be using exactly the same estimates for both IRB and all internal purposes. For example, pricing models are likely to use PDs and LGDs relevant to the life of the asset. Where there are such differences, a bank must document them and demonstrate their reasonableness to the supervisor.

The practical effect of this is that regulators are in effect prescribing both the **7.29** mechanism by which the bank assesses risk and the design parameters by which a bank's risk model should be constructed and maintained. Supervision in this area is backed up by the requirements that all material aspects of the rating and estimation process must be approved by the bank's board of directors and senior management. Further, although a bank is permitted to estimate its PDs, LGDs, and EADs using any mechanism that it desires, the output of its models will be benchmarked against other models and backtested using similar default data. Thus, although the regulators have been careful not to prescribe a specific model for PD estimation, the effect of the regulatory system will be to harmonize these models across institutions.

The meaning of default

7.30 Since the core of the IRB approach is the calculation of PD, and the core of the concept of PD is the definition of 'default', it is reasonable to begin with this. Institutions vary widely in their definitions of what constitutes 'default' and one of the greater problems for banks seeking to adopt the IRB approach has been verifying their historic loan performance information to tally their internal classification of an asset as 'defaulted' with that prescribed by the regulators.

7.31 For the regulators, a default has occurred when:

- The bank considers that the obligor is unlikely to pay its credit obligations to the banking group in full, without recourse by the bank to actions such as realizing security (if held).
- The obligor is past due more than 90 days (for commercial counterparties)or up to 180 days (for retail and public sector entity ('PSE') exposures) on any material credit obligation to the banking group. Overdrafts will be considered as being past due once the customer has breached an advised limit or been advised of a limit lower than current outstandings.

The matters which the regulators suggest be taken into account in determining unlikeliness to pay include:

- The bank puts the credit obligation on non-accrued status.
- The bank makes a charge-off or account-specific provision resulting from a significant perceived decline in credit quality subsequent to the bank taking on the exposure.
- The bank sells the credit obligation at a material credit-related economic loss.
- The bank consents to a distressed restructuring of the credit obligation where this is likely to result in a diminished financial obligation caused by the material forgiveness, or postponement, of principal, interest or (where relevant) fees.
- The bank has filed for the obligor's bankruptcy or a similar order in respect of the obligor's credit obligation to the banking group.
- The obligor has sought or has been placed in bankruptcy or similar protection where this would avoid or delay repayment of the credit obligation to the banking group.[3]

---

[3] BIPRU 4.3.63, BCD Annex VII, part 4 point 45.

For commercial obligors default is a unitary concept, and once an obligor is cate- **7.32**
gorized as being in default then all exposures to that obligor are treated as defaulted.
It should be noted that in this system default is not forever—an obligor may move
from defaulted to non-defaulted status and back again.

There are a number of special provisions relating to default in the context of retail **7.33**
exposures. Most importantly, a good deal of discretion is provided in respect of the
definition of default for retail exposures, with regulators permitted to allow banks
up to 180 days without classifying an exposure as defaulted. Also, for retail obligors default is assessed on a per exposure basis, so that a retail obligor can be in
default on one exposure but in good standing on another. Unauthorized overdrafts count as exposures from the day the credit is granted.

Validation of PD estimates

For retail exposures, a bank is expected to estimate PD primarily by using its own **7.34**
internal data. Other data may be used if the bank can prove that the other data is
strongly linked to the bank's own lending procedures and its internal risk provides. With respect to commercial exposures, a bank may validate its PD estimation techniques in one of three ways:

(a) it may use its internal default data, either on a stand-alone basis or by pooling
    its data with the data of other institutions (provided that that data is compa-
    rable with its own).
(b) it may map its internal grades to the scale used by an external credit assess-
    ment institution, and then attribute the default rate used by the institution to
    its own grades. If this process is relied on, a detailed description of the default
    definitions used and the mapping process must be created.
(c) it may use estimates drawn from statistical default prediction models.

In each of these cases, the approach must be validated by comparison with an
appropriate pool of data. Whether the data is internal, external or pooled, and for
both commercial and retail exposures, there must be at least five years available
data from one of these sources before any PD approach can be considered
validated.

Loss given default

In estimating loss given default ('LGD'), the loss which is to be estimated is eco- **7.35**
nomic loss and not accounting loss. Thus, where a particular exposure has an
economic value higher than that of the mere accounting value (perhaps because it
is a loan at above-market rates), the loss measured must be the full economic
value. Conversely, in considering recoveries from defaulted borrowers, the loss
recorded must take account of the costs incurred by the bank in making recoveries.

For this reason, loss estimates must be grounded in long-run recovery figures, and must not be based on simple valuation of collateral assets.

7.36 A bank is also required to assess LGD by using 'downturn' figures. This means in practice that the bank must estimate an LGD for each facility that aims to reflect economic downturn conditions where necessary to capture the relevant risks. This figure cannot be less than the long-run average loss for the type of facility. Establishing figures for this is remarkably difficult. If a bank has data on losses observed during periods of high credit losses it should of course use them, but such information was until recently unlikely to be readily available. Banks are encouraged to generate appropriate estimates using either internal or external data, but this process is proving to be difficult in practice. However, the regulators view that the less data a bank has, the higher the level of conservatism it should build into its estimates has driven considerable co-operation between banks in developing such databases.

7.37 The rules for calculating LGD vary between exposure classes. For corporate, sovereign and bank exposures, estimates must be based on data that covers 'one complete economic cycle', and in any event at least seven years. It is compulsory to use all available data—in other words, a bank cannot deliberately restrict itself to using only figures from the last cycle. For retail data, by contrast, a bank may deliberately disregard historic data if it can demonstrate that recent data are a better predictor of loss—presumably because of the rapid development of retail credit means that historic data might present an unduly favourable picture. However, even for retail exposures the minimum required data observation period is five years.

Exposure at default

7.38 Exposure at default ('EAD') is the estimated gross exposure at the date of default. For on-balance sheet exposures EAD should never be less than the current drawn amount (after recognizing netting), but otherwise may be estimated in the usual fashion as the long-run average for similar facilities and borrowers in an economic downturn. Given that in many cases there is a positive correlation between EAD and PD (the harder you are pressed for money the more you are likely to want to borrow) the EAD figure should be adjusted to reflect a level of conservatism. In the same way that LGD is to some extent a function of the banks' recoveries expertise, EAD exposure is to some extent a function of the banks' expertise in monitoring such exposures, and this should be taken into account in assessing the level of conservatism to be included in these estimates. Estimates of EAD must be established over historic data covering no less than seven years (for commercial exposure) or five years (for retail exposures). As for LGD, corporate, sovereign and bank exposures must be assessed across the whole of the available data set, whereas retail may be measured on a shorter term with more weight given to recent loss experience.

L. Becoming an IRB Firm

The minimum requirements for eligibility for adoption of IRB include the following: there must be a meaningful differentiation of credit risks; there must be completeness and integrity of rating assignment; there must be oversight of the rating system and processes; the criteria of the rating system; estimation of probability of default (PD); data collections and IT system; the use of internal ratings; internal validation; and disclosure requirements (which are described and required under Pillar 3). **7.39**

In order to adopt the IRB approach, a bank must be able to demonstrate that it is already using IRB methodology to run its business, and has been for the last three years. A bank seeking to use the foundation IRB approach must demonstrate that it has been generating PDs, and a bank seeking to use the advanced IRB basis must demonstrate that it has been generating PDs, LGDs, and EADs, with in each case the output of that system driving both the taking on of credit risk within the bank and the management of the bank's overall credit position by senior management. **7.40**

Once a bank adopts IRB in respect of part of its asset book, regulators will expect it to extend the use of the approach across the entire institution. However, it is accepted that this is unlikely to be possible on day one; consequently, most institutions will find themselves operating a mix of IRB and non-IRB approaches. Regulators accept that there may be issues rolling out the IRB approach both across asset classes and across business units—thus an institution may be permitted to adopt an IRB approach for a particular asset class in one business unit whilst continuing to adopt the standardized approach for that asset class in a different business unit. However, an institution will not be permitted to adopt an IRB for only some of the sub-classes of exposures within a business unit. Put simply, this means that the smallest unit of IRB migration is a business class within a business unit. **7.41**

An exception from this general flexibility is that any bank which adopts an IRB approach for any corporate bank, sovereign or retail asset class must immediately adopt the IRB approach in relation to equity exposures. This is because the treatment of equity exposures under the IRB approach is significantly less favourable than that used under any other approach. **7.42**

Once an institution has adopted an IRB approach, it will not generally be permitted to move back to the standardized approach. In addition, when an institution adopts an IRB approach, the regulators will expect it to have put in place a plan **7.43** covering roll-out to all other significant asset classes and business units over time. However, regulators have expressed their willingness to permit immaterial business units and asset class exposures to remain on the standardized approach.

Eligibility for the IRB approach

7.44 In principle all banks will be forced to adopt the standardized approach unless they can demonstrate that they should be permitted to use one of the IRB approaches. Regulators will only permit a bank to use an IRB approach when it can demonstrate that it has an economic model which is appropriate, effective and can be validated by back testing against live data. The three core requirements are that the rating system must give:

(a) a meaningful assessment of borrower and transaction characteristics;
(b) a meaningful differentiation of risk; and
(c) reasonably accurate and consistent quantitative estimates of risk.

These are continuing tests, and there are some interesting consequences to this. To take a simple example, assume that a bank which has previously conducted a broad range of activities begins to narrow its product range. If it does not refine its model, the level of risk differentiation which the model provides may be insufficient to satisfy the requirements with respect to the asset portfolio. If this happened, the bank would cease to qualify to use the IRB approach, and would be required to revert to the standardized approach until it had developed its model sufficiently to reflect the composition of its new portfolio.

7.45 The model must reflect two distinct factors; the risk of default and transaction-specific factors. The first of these is reasonably straightforward, and in broad terms there will only ever be one PD per borrower, regardless of the form which the exposure to that borrower takes (there are a very few exceptions to this; eg a sovereign borrowing in its own currency may have a different PD from that applied to borrowing in its own currency). The second reflects a wide variety of transaction-specific factors— seniority, security, etc. In both cases, the bank must appropriately differentiate between exposures to different members of the same legal group, and ensure that connected entities with similar credit positions are appropriately classified.

7.46 The output of a bank internal model is conventionally expressed as an internal borrower grading. These systems must contain at least seven non-defaulted grades and at least one defaulted grade. The output of the system must result in exposures being reasonably distributed across the grades, with no concentration. A system which allocated a majority of exposures to any one grade would probably fail this test.

7.47 Where retail exposures are being modelled, borrowers are allocated to pools and modelling is done at the pool level. The key here is that there should be a sufficiently large number of pools, and the exposures within each pool must be broadly homogeneous. Thus, pool allocation becomes paramount. Risk drivers to be considered when assigning exposures to a pool include:

- borrower risk characteristics (such as borrower type, age, and occupation);
- transaction risk characteristics, including product and/or collateral type;
- delinquency of exposure.

The most difficult part of the retail rating requirements is the requirement that **7.48** 'the grade descriptions and criteria must be sufficiently detailed to allow those charged with assigning ratings to consistently assign the same grade to borrowers or facilities posing similar risk.' Banks are permitted to rely on external gradings (such as credit scoring by independent agencies) but may not do this to the exclusion of other information which they have.

It should also be noted that banks' gradings are expected to embody a prudent **7.49** level of conservatism by taking into account adverse economic conditions and/or the occurrence of unexpected events. The scope of this requirement is limited to those conditions 'which are likely to occur over a business cycle within the respective industry/geographic region.' This requirement (known as 'through the cycle rating') poses great difficulty for banks in practice, since small variations in the 'worst case' economic downturn envisaged can have significant repercussions for calculated credit exposures.

Where regulators assess the appropriateness of a bank's use of a model, they will **7.50** require the model to be demonstrated against the bank's own loss database. They will also require the model to be appropriately documented, and for there to be a full description of the structure of the model and the theories on which it is based. This may pose problems for banks which use models bought in from third party suppliers. In principle, the regulators take the view that the fact that the bank is relying on a bought in model is no excuse for the bank not to know the details of its operation. However, where those details are commercially confidential to the model supplier, the regulator will be prepared to deal directly with the supplier to obtain the information which it requires. Where banks are dealing directly with model suppliers, it is therefore important to ensure that suppliers are prepared to furnish this information to regulators upon request.

Because models are tested against historic loss data, the requirements that banks **7.51** must maintain this data in a usable form are particularly important. In particular, banks are required to retain internal data relating to their own internal gradings and the performance of their models as well as loss data relating to exposures in order to track the predictive capabilities of their models.

Models must also be stress tested. Although the bank may broadly determine its **7.52** own requirements as regards stress testing, regulators may prescribe specific scenarios or fact patterns against which the model should be tested.

Corporate governance

7.53 The core of the regulator's requirements as regards the governance of the bank's risk assessment process are set out in paras 438 to 440 of the Accord. These are worth quoting in full:

> 438. All material aspects of the rating and estimation processes must be approved by the bank's board of directors or a designated committee thereof and senior management. These parties must possess a general understanding of the bank's risk rating system and detailed comprehension of its associated management reports. Senior management must provide notice to the board of directors or a designated committee thereof of material changes or exceptions from established policies that will materially impact the operations of the bank's rating system.

> 439. Senior management also must have a good understanding of the rating system's design and operation, and must approve material differences between established procedure and actual practice. Management must also ensure, on an ongoing basis, that the rating system is operating properly. Management and staff in the credit control function must meet regularly to discuss the performance of the rating process, areas needing improvement, and the status of efforts to improve previously identified deficiencies.

> 440. Internal ratings must be an essential part of the reporting to these parties. Reporting must include risk profile by grade, migration across grades, estimation of the relevant parameters per grade, and comparison of realized default rates (and LGDs and EADs for banks on advanced approaches) against expectations. Reporting frequencies may vary with the significance and type of information and the level of the recipient.

7.54 In addition to involvement in the design, management and operation of the bank's risk systems, the regulators require that the internal risk ratings generated by these systems must be an essential part of the reporting to these parties. These reports must include risk profile by grade, migration across grades, estimation of the relevant parameters per grade, and comparison of realized default rates (and LGDs and EADs for banks on advanced approaches) against expectations.

7.55 Part of the responsibilities of the board of the bank under the Accord is to ensure that the bank has appropriate credit risk exposure management procedures in place. These will include establishment of independent credit risk control units which are responsible for the design and implementation of internal rating systems. The unit must be functionally independent of the business units, and its areas of responsibility must include:

- testing and monitoring internal grades;
- production and analysis of summary reports from the bank's rating system, to include historical default data sorted by rating at the time of default and one year prior to default, grade migration analyses, and monitoring of trends in key rating criteria;

- implementing procedures to verify that rating definitions are consistently applied across departments and geographic areas;

- reviewing and documenting any changes to the rating process, including the reasons for the changes; and

- reviewing the rating criteria to evaluate if they remain predictive of risk. Changes to the rating process, criteria or individual rating parameters must be documented and retained for supervisors to review.

It is a sensible rule—and one which has been formalized by many regulators— **7.56** that the person responsible for initial assignment and periodic review of ratings should not stand directly to benefit from the extension of credit. In simple terms, this means that the salesman whose bonus depends on the deal being executed should not be the man making the credit decision. The more mechanized the rating process is the easier this will be to achieve, and conversely the greater the degree of human judgement involved, the harder it will be. The requirements here are for both written policies of independence as regards the rating process, and a more nebulous requirement that 'credit policies and underwriting procedures must reinforce and foster the independence of the rating process.'

At a practical level, procedures to be followed at the point of deciding upon a **7.57** credit exposure must be carefully documented. The first, and most difficult, flashpoint is the situation where the decision of those charged with assessing the exposure differs from the output of the risk model. Where the bank's systems permit the internal rating to be overridden by expert human judgement, the mechanisms by which this can be achieved must be particularly carefully documented.

It is also important to ensure that procedures are in place to ensure that: **7.58**

- all exposures are reassessed at least annually;

- high risk exposures are assessed more frequently;

- the bank has a process in place to obtain and update relevant material on the borrowers financial condition, and on other relevant information (such as the quality of collateral);

- receipt of new information by the bank automatically triggers reassessment.

In the context of retail pools, the periodic review requirement may be satisfied by a representative sample of the pool.

8

THE INTERNAL RATINGS BASED APPROACH

The building blocks of the IRB are the asset categories. Each asset category uses a **8.01** different methodology to ascribe risk weightings to exposures, and in many cases the attribution of a particular asset to one class rather than another will have an impact on the amount of regulatory capital it requires. The asset classes are as follows:

Classification	Sub-classifications
Corporate exposures	Specialized lending (SL); comprising Project Finance (PF) Object Finance (OF) Commodities Finance (CF) Income-producing Real Estate (IPRE) High-volatility Commercial Real Estate (HVCRE)
Sovereign exposures	
Bank exposures	
Retail exposures	exposures secured by residential properties qualifying revolving exposures
Equity exposures	
Eligible purchased receivables	Retail receivables Corporate receivables

A. Corporate, Sovereign, and Bank Exposures

8.02 All of these exposures are weighted using the same approach. This approach will therefore apply to the large majority of exposures of an IRB bank.

8.03 The definitions of 'corporate', 'sovereign' and 'bank' ('institution' in the EU, to include investment firms) correspond with those used for the standardized approach. Thus sovereigns includes entities designated as sovereigns and public sector entities under the standardized approach, along with those multilateral institutions which attract a 0 per cent weighting under that approach. A corporate exposure for this purpose includes any exposure to a firm apart from 'specialized lending' (see below).

8.04 A key step in estimating any IRB parameter is preparing the Reference Data Set (RDS) for that parameter. This involves a variety of challenges, including choosing the sample size, the length of time series, reliance on external data, the treatment of defaulted positions that have generated no loss, and the length of recovery processes (incomplete workout).

PD

8.05 The probability of default for all three types of exposure is calculated in the same way. However, for bank and corporate exposures a 0.03 per cent floor is imposed, so that only sovereign exposures may be treated as absolutely risk-free in this respect. The PD of an obligor in default must be 100 per cent—that is, the PD may not reflect the possibility of the default being cured.

LGD

8.06 The primary difference between foundation and advanced IRB banks is that foundation IRB banks must use the prescribed figures for LGD, whereas an Advanced IRB bank may model it. LGD is an important component of risk weighting. Given the fundamental equation that:

$$f(PD) \times LGD \times EAD = RWA$$

it will be seen that any change in LGD changes RWA proportionately—halve LGD and you halve RWA, double LGD and you double RWA. Thus the calculation and attribution of LGD figures are sensitive and important.

LGD—Foundation IRB Banks

8.07 Under the foundation IRB approach, LGDs are prescribed by the regulator according to asset type. The table of applicable LGDs is:

Covered Bonds	12.5% (11.25% until 2010)
Senior exposures	45%
Subordinated exposures	75%
Equity exposures	90%

The key issue here is the distinction between ordinary, senior, and subordinated exposures. In some circumstances (where there is express subordination in the constitutive documents) the point will be free from doubt, but issues such as economic subordination (senior unsecured debt owed by a borrower whose assets are pledged as security to other creditors) and structural subordination (senior unsecured debt owed by a company whose assets are held in a subsidiary will create difficulties in implementation.

LGD—Advanced IRB Banks

Where LGD is modelled by the bank, the LGD calculation should be based on the definitions of default and economic loss used by the institution, which should be consistent with the provisions contained in the CRD. LGD estimates should reflect the experience and practices of the individual institution. This means in practice that institutions cannot rely on industry-wide estimates without adjusting them to reflect their own position where necessary. **8.08**

An advanced IRB bank's LGD model should generally take collateral into account. Advanced IRB banks reflect collateral through their LGD modelling rather than through the collateral framework set out in Chapter 9. **8.09**

Estimated LGDs are assigned to current facilities (both defaulted and non-defaulted) and used to calculate capital requirements for its exposures. Estimated LGDs are based on the realized LGDs for the applicable Reference Data Set (RDS). However, estimated LGDs are likely to differ from the historic average realized LGDs in the RDS because the former needs to incorporate expectations of future recovery rates. This involves calculating a long-run forward looking recovery rate for the facility grade or pool, taking both current and future economic circumstances into account. The institution should produce an LGD estimate appropriate for an economic downturn ('downturn LGD') if this is more conservative than the long-run average. **8.10**

In addition to expected LGD, an institution must also produce a best estimate of expected loss for defaulted exposures given current economic circumstances and exposure status. The difference between this amount and the estimated LGD derived from the RDS stems from the possibility of additional losses during the recovery period, and represents the unexpected loss capital requirement for the defaulted exposure. **8.11**

Downturn LGDs

Conditional expected loss is calculated by applying a function to the PD figure and by using a 'downturn' LGD figure. The key to the idea of the 'downturn' LGD is that the regulator was either unwilling or unable to apply a meaningful function **8.12** to LGD—thus whereas UL PD is the result of a complex formula, banks are able to use their own unfettered discretion to estimate 'downturn' LGD. Thus the full formula is:

$$\text{Conditional EL} = f(PD) \times \text{Downturn LGD} \times \text{EAD}$$

One of the more difficult discussions around LGD is the issue relating to 'downturn LGDs'. An institution is required to use LGD estimates that are 'appropriate for an economic downturn' if those are more conservative than the long-run average. The basis for this requirement is the idea that LGD for a portfolio of loans fluctuates according to the economic conditions, such that in a downturn LGDs would be larger overall—a principle which could be articulated as 'a falling tide sinks all boats'. Possibly more importantly, it is likely that an economic downturn may both increase probability of default and increase loss given default. Accordingly, LGD parameters need to be calculated assuming that conditions where credit losses are substantially higher than the long-run average. Under such conditions default rates are expected to be high, so that if recovery rates are negatively related to default rates, LGD parameters must embed forecasts of future recovery rates that are lower than those expected during more neutral conditions. It is, however, open to an institution do demonstrate to its regulator on the basis of its data and models that in particular sectors recovery rates are expected to be independent of future default rates. If this can be done then there is no requirement to use higher LGD figures.

LGD—Loss Data

8.13 The risk data set ('RDS') for LGD should include only exposures to defaulted obligors, since it is only after a formal default that loss given default can be calculated (note that in this respect the RDS for LGD is different from that for PD, which must also contain undefaulted experience). It should also include factors that can be used to group the defaulted facilities in meaningful ways.

Ideally, the RDS should:

- cover at least one full business cycle;
- contain all defaults that have occurred within the considered time frame;
- contain data for calculating realized LGDs;
- include all relevant information needed to estimate the risk parameters;
- include data on the relevant drivers of loss.

8.14 In some cases realized LGD may be zero. This will happen if, for example, a breach is cured with no material direct or indirect cost associated with collecting on the instrument, and no loss caused by material discount effects (for example, if the default was caused solely by the 90 day past due criterion, and payment obligations were subsequently completely fulfilled). It is also possible for realized LGD to be positive—for example, where a default is cured without loss but the effect of the default is to increase the rate payable by the borrower on the facility over the default period. However, estimated LGDs may never be less than zero. Where the RDS contains a large number of zero-loss LGDs, regulators are likely to be concerned that the institution is, for example, using an inappropriately early definition of default or that the RDS contains some facilities which are not true defaults (for example, technical defaults such as small outstanding charges on repaid loans).

LGD—Risk drivers

Expected LGDs should be allocated to facilities in accordance with risk drivers, **8.15** and the RDS should, where possible, capture for each default the part played by relevant risk factors in the default. Consequently the analysis of risk drivers is important. CEBS[1] has suggested that the risk drivers for assessing LGD exposures can be grouped according to the following five categories:

(1) Transaction related, including facility type, collateral, guarantees from third parties, seniority, time in default, seasoning, loan to value (LTV), and recovery procedures.
(2) Borrower related, including borrower size (as it relates to transaction characteristics), exposure size, firm specific capital structure (as it relates to the firm's ability to satisfy the claims of its creditors in the event that it defaults), geographic region, industrial sector, and line of business.
(3) Institution related, including internal organization and internal governance, relevant events such as mergers, and specific entities within the group dedicated to recoveries such as 'bad credit institutions'.
(4) External, including interest rates and legal framework (and, as a consequence, the length of the recovery process).
(5) Other risk factors.

Each institution is responsible for identifying and investigating additional risk drivers that are relevant to its specific circumstances. Institutions should collect data on what they consider to be the main drivers of loss for a given group of facilities, and should include the most material drivers in their LGD estimation process. The institution's judgements as to which risk drivers are most material should be appropriately documented and should be discussed with supervisors.

LGD—Estimation methodologies

Supervisors do not prescribe any specific technique for LGD estimation (or for that **8.16** matter any other IRB parameters). However, institutions will have to demonstrate

---

[1] Committee of European Bank Supervisors, Consultation Paper 10, Final version 11 July 2005.

that the methods they choose are appropriate to the institution's activities and the portfolios to which they apply. The theoretical assumptions underlying the models should also be justified, and the approach must be based on quantitative information—the CRD does not permit the use of estimates based purely on judgemental considerations.

8.17 The four main approaches to LGD estimation are Workout LGD, Market LGD, Implied Market LGD, and Implied Historical LGD.

(1) **Workout LGD.** This is created by analysing the cash flows resulting from the workout and/or collections process, properly discounted, are calculated. Calculations for the exposures that are currently held by the institution have to be based on actual recovery data in order to produce a forward looking estimate. The calculation should not be based solely on the market value of collateral; appropriate adjustments should be applied. The calculation of default weighted average of realized LGDs requires the use of all observed defaults in the data sources. Observed defaults include incomplete workout cases, although they will not have values for the final realization of LGD because the recovery process has not ended. The Workout LGD technique can be applied using either direct estimates or a two-step approach. Under a direct estimate approach, the specific characteristics of the proposed facility are compared with the factors present in existing defaults, and a quantitative LGD estimate is derived for the specific exposure. Under a two-step approach, an average LGD is estimated for all exposures covered by the same facility grade or pool, and the facility is allocated to that pool.

(2) **Market LGD.** As an alternative to Workout LGD, the RDS may instead be derived from the observation of market prices on defaulted bonds or marketable loans soon after default or upon their emergence from bankruptcy. This approach may be used where data is scarce.

(3) **Implied Market LGD.** It is also possible to derive estimated LGDs from the market prices of nondefaulted loans or bonds or credit default instruments. These are referred to as Implied Market LGDs. Implied Market LGDs may be used where no other data are available to produce reliable estimates, and if validation results show that these estimates are reliable. The market and implied market LGD techniques are unlikely to be acceptable to regulators unless the market from which the price is derived is deep and liquid and there are good reasons for the scarcity of data. According to the Committee of European Banking Supervisors (CEBS) it is unlikely that any use of market LGD can be made for the bulk of the loan portfolio.

(4) **Implied historical LGD.** The implied historical LGD technique is allowed only for the retail exposure class. It is derived by creating a realized loss figure for a retail portfolio by dividing the total loss divided by the total number of exposures

in the pool, while the 'average realized LGD' is the same total loss divided by the number of defaulted exposures in the pool. This is accepted where institutions can estimate the expected loss for every facility rating grade or pool of exposures.

LGD for expected loss

Institutions that calculate their own estimates of LGD should use downturn **8.18** LGDs both in calculating risk-weighted exposure amounts and in calculating expected loss for exposures that are not in default (if this is more conservative than the long-run average). However, for defaulted exposures, the CRD requires the use of an estimate of expected loss (ELBE) that should be the best estimate of expected loss, given current economic circumstances. In such cases, LGD is defined as the sum of ELBE and a measure reflecting possible additional unexpected losses during the recovery period. If downturn conditions are relevant to a certain type of exposures, then this should be taken into account in measuring the possibility of additional unexpected losses during the workout period. This treatment does not apply to exposures under the double default treatment, since, by definition, EL for these exposures is set at zero.

Recognizing double default

This is a special regime available for certain types of credit protection in respect of **8.19** certain assets in certain circumstances. This approach—'the double-default approach'—applies where the protected asset is a corporate, insurance, government, or retail portfolio (ie not an exposure to a bank, securities firm, equity, securitization, or non-credit asset) and the protection provider is an institution, non-guaranteed export credit agency, or insurance undertaking which has 'sufficient' expertise in providing unfunded credit protection and either: (a) is a regulated bank or equivalent and had at the time the protection was provided an external credit rating equal to step 3; or (b) had at the time the protection was provided an external credit weighting equal to step 2; or (c) has at the time of assessment an internal credit weighting equal to step 3.

The rationale for the double-default regime requires a word of explanation. Where **8.20** an exposure has the benefit of a guarantee or credit protection, the normal treatment is to substitute the credit of the guarantor for the credit of the underlying exposure. Where the guarantor is a better credit than the underlying, this results in an improvement in the risk weighting of the exposure. However, where the guarantor is a worse credit than the underlying, this means that the guarantee will have no consequences at all for the regulatory capital treatment of the exposure. This is clearly not an entirely accurate reflection of reality, since in practice the existence of a second credit claim reduces the risk somewhat. However, it is in accordance with the additive structure of the Basel Accord. It was felt, however, that in some cases (notably those where products were 'wrapped' by specialist credit providers) this policy should be relaxed slightly, since in such cases the combination of two very high quality credits could be shown to have a significant impact on overall risk.

8.21 In such cases, the risk-weighted exposure amount calculated using the formula set out above is adjusted. This operates as a two-stage process. In the first stage the exposure value for the underlying obligation is calculated using the PD of the obligor but the LGD of the protection provider. This yields a risk weighting for the exposure (RW). This figure is then reduced by reference to the following formula:

$$\text{New risk weighted exposure amount} = RW \times \text{exposure value} \times (0.15 + 160 \times PDpp)$$

PDpp is the PD of the protection provider.

8.22 It should be clear from this that the application of the formula will only produce a benefit to the bank where the PDpp is less than (roughly) 0.53%, since at any level above this the multiplier will be greater than one. This means that only protection providers of very high quality will confer any benefit under this regime.

B. Exposure at Default

8.23 Crudely put, EAD is an estimate of how much higher an institution's exposure will be to a borrower on default than it is at the time of the calculation. There are two ways in which EAD typically comes into play. One is where the exposure is in the form of a revolving or undrawn commitment, where the amount currently drawn by the borrower is less than that which could be drawn if the facility were fully utilized. The second is where the exposure arises in the form of a guarantee or similar arrangement, where the current obligation is zero but where the bank may at some point in the future incur an obligation to pay. More generally, banking book exposures will change over time for a number of reasons—additional drawings under existing facilities; or under new facilities to existing or even new borrowers; repayments (whether scheduled, voluntary or lender-induced) under facilities; or accrual/payment of interest and charges.

8.24 It is a view widely held by regulators that bank risk systems potentially understate capital requirements on facilities where balances are not fully drawn. Hence the direct focus has been on increased drawings under existing facilities. Some simple rules were incorporated into the Basle I framework to address these, but those rules were primitive and (particularly as regards the nil weighting for exposures of under one year) had spawned structures created specifically to arbitrage those rules.

8.25 It is probably fair to say that for most banks operating under Basle I, the Basle I rules were used internally as a proxy for EAD. As a result, the development of

EAD modelling within institutions seems to have generally lagged well behind that of PD and LGD, and there is considerably less consensus amongst banks or regulators as to the way in which EAD should be calculated.

It is a core principle of EAD estimation that the EAD figure for an exposure may **8.26** never be lower than the amount currently drawn—in other words, the institution may not estimate that there will be a net reduction of exposures prior to default. This is true even if there is good reason to believe that such a reduction will in fact take place. Partially as a consequence of this, EAD is not explicitly affected by the maturity of facilities.

The core requirement for EAD has been stated as that the EAD required for IRB **8.27** purposes is the exposure(s) expected to be outstanding under a borrower's current facilities should it go into default in the next year, assuming that economic downturn conditions occur in the next year; and assuming that, other than any changes resulting from the economic downturn conditions, a firm's policies and practices for controlling exposures remain unchanged from what they are at present. As with other aspects of the IRB framework, the EAD estimates to be used for capital purposes are based on the realized EADs in the reference data set of exposures that have gone into default in the past. This basic historic data needs to be adjusted to take account of, inter alia, changes in policies and practices and to produce an orientation towards an economic downturn. Estimated EAD cannot be less than current drawings.

The exposure value for leases must be the discounted minimum lease payments. **8.28** Minimum lease payments are the payments over the lease term that the lessee is or can be required to make and any bargain option (ie option the exercise of which is reasonably certain). Any guaranteed residual value fulfilling the criteria for unfunded credit protection should also be included in the minimum lease payments.

Where an exposure takes the form of securities or commodities sold, posted **8.29** or lent under repurchase transactions or securities or commodities lending or borrowing transactions, long settlement transactions and margin lending transactions, the exposure value must be the value of the securities or commodities. Where a volatility adjustment is required to be applied by the collateral method used, that volatility adjustment must be added to the exposure. Exposures under derivative instruments are to be calculated in accordance with the rules applicable to derivatives.

For IRB purposes exposures must be measured gross of value adjustments. Where **8.30** on-balance sheet exposures are calculated after taking account of netting, or where netting is used under a repo or lending or borrowing arrangement, the institution must calculate exposure in accordance with the credit risk mitigation netting rules.

Netting and EAD

8.31 In the own estimates approaches, netting is relevant to the calculation of current exposures, but is also relevant to the calculation of future exposures. The circumstance in which this is most clear is where a bank operates a cash pooling arrangement for a group of companies and manages its exposures to that group on a net basis. For such an arrangement some borrowers can be significantly in debt provided that others have countervailing positive balances. In general, such exposures should be treated as net balances, and EAD calculated on a net basis, provided that the firm meets the general conditions for on-balance sheet netting.

8.32 The issue also arises in the case of securities underwritings. Clearly where a firm agrees to buy securities it has an exposure to the securities issuers. The question is as to what recognition should be given within the system to the fact that by the time it receives the securities it will have made arrangements to sell them on to other investors. It is clearly objectionable to regulators to take the view that a firm should reduce its EAD on the basis of an intention to sell off its exposure. However, given the strong and enduring market practice in this area, regulators clearly take some comfort from the fact that underwriters invariably do sell off such holdings, and as a result regulators are prepared to permit IRB banks to alleviate their positions by recognizing this intention.

Commitments—when should a CF/EAD be applied?

8.33 This question can be restated as when does an arrangement become a commitment? Under the Basle I regime a facility attracted a non-zero CF only if it was committed and had a drawdown period of one year or more. However, even then there was considerable scope for debate as to when a facility became sufficiently 'committed' to warrant a capital requirement being applied to it. To take a simple example, a bank is approached by an investor who is contemplating entering a contested auction for a particular asset. The bank agrees in principle that it would be prepared to lend to the investor to finance the asset on specific terms subject to credit review. At this stage the bank may be aware that the investor is in discussion with several other banks. The investor enters the auction, and makes the winning bid subject to diligence. It commences diligence, and simultaneously commences negotiations with the bank as to the detailed terms of the facility. At some point these terms are agreed and documented in a facility letter, subject to documentation. When diligence is completed, the loan agreement will be documented and, on completion the loan will be drawn. The question for the regulator is at what stage the bank should begin to recognize that it has a commitment? Banks have sometimes argued that since they are only formally legally committed at the documentation stage, that no charge should be applied prior to that stage. However, both regulators and bank management recognize that industry practice is that reliance is—justifiably—placed on banks at a very early stage in such discussions, and that in practice a bank could not withdraw from an informal commitment of this kind without doing serious and lasting damage to its commercial reputation and standing. Thus, whatever the point at which the commitment is recognized, it must be at some point earlier than final documentation.

The issue for regulators here is getting the balance right between, on the one hand, **8.34** not wanting to apply a capital requirement too early in the facility negotiation approach and where the prospects of its being completed may be quite low; and on the other of allowing too much liberalism such that the existence of conditions precedent has the effect of setting the regulatory capital charge to zero until the time that a drawing is virtually certain.

The FSA's guidance on calculating CFs is to the effect that 'a firm should treat a **8.35** facility as an exposure from the earliest date at which a customer is able to make drawings under it'. However, this is perceived by FSA as a backstop—that is, that it represents the last possible date on which it may be possible not to allocate a CF to a facility—and is not intended to set out the commencement date for the weighting. The broad principles to be applied seem to be as follows:

(1) An EAD/CF is required on a facility from the time that a borrower is advised by the bank that it has agreed the facility is to be made available. Where there is a strong possibility that the facility will not eventually be taken up, that may be reflected through a reduction in the EAD/CF applied.

(2) Internal indications of willingness to provide facilities in the future which have not been advised to the customer do not generally require an EAD/CF. However, where the bank has taken a firm decision to make funds available to the borrower, an EAD/CF is required from the time that that fact is recorded on its systems, although for a facility where this would ordinarily be confirmed to the borrower, this may be suspended until the communication has been made.

(3) An EAD/CF should not be applied where a facility is subject to a full credit assessment by the bank, resulting in a re-rating or a confirmation of the rating of the borrower.

As with LGD, estimation of EAD is intended to be oriented towards what happens **8.36** in a downturn, either by the expected default weighted average over a long run, or the direct use of estimates appropriate for a downturn if the conversion factors are expected to be higher in a downturn. However, this is difficult, since EAD will be heavily influenced by lender behaviour—either through transactional lenders taking action to cut their lines, through borrowers increasing utilizations, and by the impact on the cash flow of the borrower of the actions of other lenders.

Maturity

One of the more interesting underlying assumptions within the Basel II **8.37** framework is the imposition of a five-year deemed maturity for all long-term facilities—that is, any exposure with a term of more than five years is assumed to be a five-year exposure. Where an exposure is subject to a formal repayment schedule the maturity will be a weighted average of the maturities over the repayment periods (with a maximum of five years). In any situation where the position of the parties does not permit the institution to calculate this amount, the value of M to be used must be the maximum remaining time in years that the obligor is permitted to take to fully discharge its contractual obligations.

8.38 Time to default is primarily a factor for PD—the longer the repayment period the greater the chance of a default during it. However, it also has some relevance to EAD—for example, the EAD would be expected to be different if a borrower defaults in two years' time, than if it defaults in one year's time. However, there is no immediately intuitive association between time and quantum—it does not necessarily follow that a borrower going bust in two years' time will owe more or less than one going bust in one year's time. A bank could argue that the maximum exposure at the end of a two-year period should be reduced by the value of the facilities which would expire in that time—this, the maximum EAD over a period should be the value of the currently existing facilities which would still be drawable at that time (thus, for example, if an institution has credit lines of £200m open to a particular borrower of which £100m would have expired by the end of a two-year period, it could validly argue that the maximum commitment over the two-year period should be the lower figure). However, this would be to disregard the fact that banks conventionally grant new lines to replace existing lines, and to assume that existing lines would not be renewed would be unrealistic.

8.39 CEBS[2] has recommended that the time horizon to be used for EAD calculation should be one year unless a firm can demonstrate that another period would be more conservative. However, where one year is the term used, firms need not hold capital against facilities, or proportions of facilities that cannot be drawn down within the next year; and, where facilities can be drawn down within the next year, firms may in principle reduce their estimates to the extent that they can demonstrate that they are able and willing, based on a combination of empirical evidence, current policies, and documentary protection to prevent further drawings.

C. Specialized Lending

8.40 The specialized lending regime addresses a problem which is inherent in the credit risk weighting system; that being that it weights credit exposures. For the vast majority of banking transactions this works appropriately. However, the approach

---

[2] Committee of European Bank Supervisors, Consultation Paper 10, Final version 11 July 2005.

breaks down to some extent where the exposure undertaken is an exposure to an asset—as is the case with asset finance and some project finance transactions. In these cases a PD/LGD approach can be implemented, but the implementation is considerably more difficult than with other asset types. This is partially due to a smaller universe of experiences, but partly also to the fact that the risk indicators approach does not apply in situations where asset valuations may be driven by a wide variety of factors only some of which can be modelled. Of course, institutions with a sufficiently detailed database of default data may be able to calculate PD and LGD for asset based exposures, and in this case they will be permitted to do so. However, for institutions which do not have this capability but wish to engage in project and other asset finance lending, the specialized lending regime provides a mechanism by which they can do so.

The specialized lending regime may only be applied in particular circumstances. **8.41** These are that:

(1) the exposure concerned is to an entity which was created specifically to finance and/or operate physical assets;
(2) the contractual arrangements give the lender a substantial degree of control over the assets and the income that they generate; and
(3) the primary source of repayment of the obligation is the income generated by the assets being financed, rather than the independent capacity of a broader commercial enterprise.

In general, the following transaction types will fit within the specialized lending **8.42** criteria:

Project Finance.   A method of funding where the lender looks primarily to the revenues generated by a single project for his return, and where the lender's exposure is calculated by reference to the receipts of a single-project company and the collateral value of the project's assets.

Object Finance.   A method of funding the acquisition of physical assets, where the primary income of the borrower will be related to lease or rental contracts and where the borrower is an SPV or otherwise has no independent capacity to repay the loan.

Commodities Finance.   Structured short-term lending to finance inventories or receivables of exchange-traded commodities, where the borrower has no independent capacity to repay the loan.

Income-Producing Real Estate.   Financing the construction of specific buildings where repayment of the finance is to be provided through cash flows generated by the asset in the form of rent or sale proceeds.

High-Volatility Commercial Real Estate.   Investment in types of income-producing real estate which the national regulator considers to be high volatility exposures.

8.43 For each class of asset, the project must be judged against the criteria in Table 8.1.

Table 8.1 Supervisory rating grades for project finance exposures

	Strong	Good	Satisfactory	Weak
Financial strength				
Market conditions	Few competing suppliers or substantial and durable advantage in location, cost, or technology. Demand is strong and growing.	Few competing suppliers or better than average location, cost, or technology but this situation may not last. Demand is strong and stable.	Project has no advantage in location, cost, or technology. Demand is adequate and stable.	Project has worse than average location, cost, or technology. Demand is weak and declining.
Financial ratios (eg debt service coverage ratio (DSCR), loan life coverage ratio (LLCR), project life coverage ratio (PLCR), and debt-to equity ratio)	Strong financial ratios considering the level of project risk; very robust economic assumptions.	Strong to acceptable financial ratios considering the level of project risk; robust project economic assumptions.	Standard financial ratios considering the level of project risk.	Aggressive financial ratios considering the level of project risk.
Stress analysis	The project can meet its financial obligations under sustained, severely stressed economic or sectoral conditions.	The project can meet its financial obligations under normal stressed economic or sectoral conditions. The project is only likely to default under severe economic conditions.	The project is vulnerable to stresses that are not uncommon through an economic cycle, and may default in a normal downturn.	The project is likely to default unless conditions improve soon.
Financial structure				
Duration of the credit compared to the duration of the project	Useful life of the project significantly exceeds tenor of the loan.	Useful life of the project exceeds tenor of the loan.	Useful life of the project exceeds tenor of the loan.	Useful life of the project may not exceed tenor of the loan.
Amortization schedule	Amortizing debt.	Amortizing debt.	Amortizing debt repayments with limited bullet payment.	Bullet repayment or amortizing debt repayments with high bullet repayment.

	Strong	Good	Satisfactory	Weak
Political and legal environment				
Political risk, including transfer risk, considering project type and mitigants	Very low exposure; strong mitigation instruments, if needed.	Low exposure; satisfactory mitigation instruments, if needed.	Moderate exposure; fair mitigation instruments.	High exposure; no or weak mitigation instruments.
Force majeure risk (war, civil unrest, etc)	Low exposure.	Acceptable exposure.	Standard protection.	Significant risks, not fully mitigated.
Government support and project's importance for the country over the long term	Project of strategic importance for the country (preferably export-oriented). Strong support from Government.	Project considered important for the country. Good level of support from Government.	Project may not be strategic but brings unquestionable benefits for the country. Support from Government may not be explicit.	Project not key to the country. No or weak support from Government.
Stability of legal and regulatory environment (risk of change in law)	Favourable and stable regulatory environment over the long term.	Favourable and stable regulatory environment over the medium term.	Regulatory changes can be predicted with a fair level of certainty.	Current or future regulatory issues may affect the project.
Acquisition of all necessary supports and approvals for such relief from local content laws	Strong.	Satisfactory.	Fair.	Weak.
Enforceability of contracts, collateral and security	Contracts, collateral and security are enforceable.	Contracts, collateral and security are enforceable.	Contracts, collateral and security are considered enforceable even if certain non-key issues may exist.	There are unresolved key issues in respect if actual enforcement of contracts, collateral and security.
Transaction characteristics				
Design and technology risk	Fully proven technology and design.	Fully proven technology and design.	Proven technology and design— start-up issues are mitigated by a strong completion package.	Unproven technology and design; technology issues exist and/or complex design.

Table 8.1 (*cont.*)

	Strong	Good	Satisfactory	Weak
Construction risk				
Permitting and siting	All permits have been obtained.	Some permits are still outstanding but their receipt is considered very likely.	Some permits are still outstanding but the permitting process is well defined and they are considered routine.	Key permits still need to be obtained and are not considered routine. Significant conditions may be attached.
Type of construction contract	Fixed-price date-certain turnkey construction EPC (engineering and procurement contract).	Fixed-price date-certain turnkey construction EPC.	Fixed-price date-certain turnkey construction contract with one or several contractors.	No or partial fixed-price turnkey contract and/or interfacing issues with multiple contractors.
Completion guarantees	Substantial liquidated damages supported by financial substance and/or strong completion guarantee from sponsors with excellent financial standing.	Significant liquidated damages supported by financial substance and/or completion guarantee from sponsors with good financial standing.	Adequate liquidated damages supported by financial substance and/ or completion guarantee from sponsors with good financial standing.	Inadequate liquidated damages or not supported by financial substance or weak completion guarantees.
Track record and financial strength of contractor in constructing similar projects	Strong.	Good.	Satisfactory.	Weak.
Operating risk				
Scope and nature of operations and maintenance (O & M) contracts	Strong long-term O&M contract, preferably with contractual performance incentives, and/or O&M reserve accounts.	Long-term O&M contract, and/or O&M reserve accounts.	Limited O&M contract or O&M reserve account.	No O&M contract: risk of high operational cost overruns beyond mitigants.
Operator's expertise, track record, and financial strength	Very strong, or committed technical assistance of the sponsors.	Strong.	Acceptable.	Limited/weak, or local operator dependent on local authorities.

	Strong	Good	Satisfactory	Weak
Off-take risk				
(a) *If there is a take-or-pay or fixed-price off-take contract*	Excellent creditworthiness of off-taker; strong termination clauses; tenor of contract comfortably exceeds the maturity of the debt.	Good creditworthiness of off-taker; strong termination clauses; tenor of contract exceeds the maturity of the debt.	Acceptable financial standing of off-taker; normal termination clauses; tenor of contract generally matches the maturity of the debt.	Weak off-taker; weak termination clauses; tenor of contract does not exceed the maturity of the debt.
(b) *If there is no take-or-pay or fixed-price off-take contract*	Project produces essential services or a commodity sold widely on a world market; output can readily be absorbed at projected prices even at lower than historic market growth rates.	Project produces essential services or a commodity sold widely on a regional market that will absorb it at projected prices at historical growth rates.	Commodity is sold on a limited market that may absorb it only at lower than projected prices.	Project output is demanded by only one or a few buyers or is not generally sold on an organized market.
Supply risk				
Price, volume and transportation risk of feed-stocks; supplier's track record and financial strength	Long-term supply contract with supplier of excellent financial standing.	Long-term supply contract with supplier of good financial standing.	Long-term supply contract with supplier of good financial standing—a degree of price risk may remain.	Short-term supply contract or long-term supply contract with financially weak supplier—a degree of price risk definitely remains.
Reserve risks (eg natural resource development)	Independently audited, proven and developed reserves well in excess of requirements over lifetime of the project.	Independently audited, proven and developed reserves in excess of requirements over lifetime of the project.	Proven reserves can supply the project adequately through the maturity of the debt.	Project relies to some extent on potential and undeveloped reserves.
Strength of Sponsor				
Sponsor's track record, financial strength, and country/sector experience	Strong sponsor with excellent track record and high financial standing.	Good sponsor with satisfactory track record and good financial standing.	Adequate sponsor with adequate track record and good financial standing.	Weak sponsor with no or questionable track record and/ or financial weaknesses.

Table 8.1 (*cont.*)

	Strong	Good	Satisfactory	Weak
Strength of Sponsor (*cont.*)				
Sponsor support, as evidenced by equity, ownership clause and incentive to inject additional cash if necessary	Strong. Project is highly strategic for the sponsor (core business—long-term strategy).	Good. Project is strategic for the sponsor (core business—long-term strategy).	Acceptable. Project is considered important for the sponsor (core business).	Limited. Project is not key to sponsor's long-term strategy or core business.
Security Package				
Assignment of contracts and accounts	Fully comprehensive.	Comprehensive.	Acceptable.	Weak.
Pledge of assets, taking into account quality, value and liquidity of assets	First perfected security interest in all project assets, contracts, permits and accounts necessary to run the project.	Perfected security interest in all project assets, contracts, permits and accounts necessary to run the project.	Acceptable security interest in all project assets, contracts, permits and accounts necessary to run the project.	Little security or collateral for lenders; weak negative pledge clause.
Lender's control over cash flow (eg cash sweeps, independent escrow accounts)	Strong.	Satisfactory.	Fair.	Weak.
Strength of the covenant package (mandatory prepayments, payment deferrals, payment cascade, dividend restrictions . . .)	Covenant package is strong for this type of project. Project may issue no additional debt.	Covenant package is satisfactory for this type of project. Project may issue extremely limited additional debt.	Covenant package is fair for this type of project. Project may issue limited additional debt.	Covenant package is insufficient for this type of project. Project may issue unlimited additional debt.
Reserve funds (debt service, O&M, renewal and replacement, unforeseen events, etc)	Longer than average coverage period, all reserve funds fully funded in cash or letters of credit from highly rated bank.	Average coverage period, all reserve funds fully funded.	Average coverage period, all reserve funds fully funded.	Shorter than average coverage period, reserve funds funded from operating cash flows.

Table 8.2 Supervisory Rating Grades for Income-Producing Real Estate Exposures and High-Volatility Commercial Real Estate Exposures

	Strong	Good	Satisfactory	Weak
Financial strength				
Market conditions	The supply and demand for the project's type and location are currently in equilibrium. The number of competitive properties coming to market is equal or lower than forecasted demand.	The supply and demand for the project's type and location are currently in equilibrium. The number of competitive properties coming to market is roughly equal to forecasted demand.	Market conditions are roughly in equilibrium. Competitive properties are coming on the market and others are in the planning stages. The project's design and capabilities may not be state of the art compared to new projects.	Market conditions are weak. It is uncertain when conditions will improve and return to equilibrium. The project is losing tenants at lease expiration. New lease terms are less favourable compared to those expiring.
Financial ratios and advance rate	The property's debt service coverage ratio (DSCR) is considered strong (DSCR is not relevant for the construction phase) and its loan to value ratio (LTV) is considered low given its property type. Where a secondary market exists, the transaction is underwritten to market standards.	The DSCR (not relevant for development real estate) and LTV are satisfactory. Where a secondary market exists, the transaction is underwritten to market standards.	The property's DSCR has deteriorated and its value has fallen, increasing its LTV.	The property's DSCR has deteriorated significantly and its LTV is well above underwriting standards for new loans.
Stress analysis	The property's resources, contingencies and liability structure allow it to meet its financial obligations during a period of severe financial stress (eg interest rates, economic growth).	The property can meet its financial obligations under a sustained period of financial stress (eg interest rates, economic growth). The property is likely to default only under severe economic conditions.	During an economic downturn, the property would suffer a decline in revenue that would limit its ability to fund capital expenditures and significantly increase the risk of default.	The property's financial condition is strained and is likely to default unless conditions improve in the near term.

Table 8.2 (*cont.*)

	Strong	Good	Satisfactory	Weak
Cash-flow predictability				
(a) *For complete and stabilized property*	The property's leases are long-term with creditworthy tenants and their maturity dates are scattered. The property has a track record of tenant retention upon lease expiration. Its vacancy rate is low. Expenses (maintenance, insurance, security, and property taxes) are predictable.	Most of the property's leases are long-term, with tenants that range in creditworthiness. The property experiences a normal level of tenant turnover upon lease expiration. Its vacancy rate is low. Expenses are predictable.	Most of the property's leases are medium rather than long-term with tenants that range in creditworthiness. The property experiences a moderate level of tenant turnover upon lease expiration. Its vacancy rate is moderate. Expenses are relatively predictable but vary in relation to revenue.	The property's leases are of various terms with tenants that range in creditworthiness. The property experiences a very high level of tenant turnover upon lease expiration. Its vacancy rate is high. Significant expenses are incurred preparing space for new tenants.
(b) *For complete but not stabilized property*	Leasing activity meets or exceeds projections. The project should achieve stabilization in the near future.	Leasing activity meets or exceeds projections. The project should achieve stabilization in the near future.	Most leasing activity is within projections; however, stabilization will not occur for some time.	Market rents do not meet expectations. Despite achieving target occupancy rate, cash flow coverage is tight due to disappointing revenue.
(c) *For construction phase*	The property is entirely preleased through the tenor of the loan or pre-sold to an investment grade tenant or buyer, or the bank has a binding commitment for take-out financing from an investment grade lender.	The property is entirely pre-leased or pre-sold to a creditworthy tenant or buyer, or the bank has a binding commitment for permanent financing from a creditworthy lender.	Leasing activity is within projections but the building may not be pre-leased and there may not exist a takeout financing. The bank may be the permanent lender.	The property is deteriorating due to cost overruns, market deterioration, tenant cancellations or other factors. There may be a dispute with the party providing the permanent financing.
Asset characteristics				
Location	Property is located in highly desirable location that is convenient to services that tenants desire.	Property is located in desirable location that is convenient to services that tenants desire.	The property location lacks a competitive advantage.	The property's location, configuration, design and maintenance have contributed to the property's difficulties.

	Strong	Good	Satisfactory	Weak
Asset characteristics (*cont.*)				
Design and condition	Property is favoured due to its design, configuration, and maintenance, and is highly competitive with new properties.	Property is appropriate in terms of its design, configuration and maintenance. The property's design and capabilities are competitive with new properties.	Property is adequate in terms of its configuration, design and maintenance.	Weaknesses exist in the property's configuration, design or maintenance.
Property is under construction	Construction budget is conservative and technical hazards are limited. Contractors are highly qualified.	Construction budget is conservative and technical hazards are limited. Contractors are highly qualified.	Construction budget is adequate and contractors are ordinarily qualified.	Project is over budget or unrealistic given its technical hazards. Contractors may be under qualified.
Strength of Sponsor/Developer				
Financial capacity and willingness to support the property	The sponsor/ developer made a substantial cash contribution to the construction or purchase of the property. The sponsor/developer has substantial resources and limited direct and contingent liabilities. The sponsor/developer's properties are diversified geographically and by property type.	The sponsor/ developer made a material cash contribution to the construction or purchase of the property. The sponsor/ developer's financial condition allows it to support the property in the event of a cash flow shortfall. The sponsor/ developer's properties are located in several geographic regions.	The sponsor/ developer's contribution may be immaterial or non-cash. The sponsor/ developer is average to below average in financial resources.	The sponsor/ developer lacks capacity or willingness to support the property.
Reputation and track record with similar properties	Experienced management and high sponsors' quality. Strong reputation and lengthy and successful record with similar properties.	Appropriate management and sponsors' quality. The sponsor or management has a successful record with similar properties.	Moderate management and sponsors' quality. Management or sponsor track record does not raise serious concerns.	Ineffective management and substandard sponsors' quality. Management and sponsor difficulties have contributed to difficulties in managing properties in the past.

Table 8.2 (*cont.*)

	Strong	Good	Satisfactory	Weak
Strength of Sponsor/Developer (*cont.*)				
Relationships with relevant real estate actors	Strong relationships with leading actors such as leasing agents.	Proven relationships with leading actors such as leasing agents.	Adequate relationships with leasing agents and other parties providing important real estate services.	Poor relationships with leasing agents and/or other parties providing important real estate services.
Security Package				
Nature of lien	Perfected first lien.*	Perfected first lien.*	Perfected first lien.*	Ability of lender to foreclose is constrained.
Assignment of rents (for projects leased to long-term tenants)	The lender has obtained an assignment. They maintain current tenant information that would facilitate providing notice to remit rents directly to the lender, such as a current rent roll and copies of the project's leases.	The lender has obtained an assignment. They maintain current tenant information that would facilitate providing notice to the tenants to remit rents directly to the lender, such as current rent roll and copies of the project's leases.	The lender has obtained an assignment. They maintain current tenant information that would facilitate providing notice to the tenants to remit rents directly to the lender, such as current rent roll and copies of the project's leases.	The lender has not obtained an assignment of the leases or has not maintained the information necessary to readily provide notice to the building's tenants.
Quality of the insurance coverage	Appropriate.	Appropriate.	Appropriate.	Substandard.

* Lenders in some markets extensively use loan structures that include junior liens. Junior liens may be indicative of this level of risk if the total LTV inclusive of all senior positions does not exceed a typical first loan LTV.

Table 8.3 Supervisory Rating Grades for Asset Finance Exposures

	Strong	Good	Satisfactory	Weak
Financial strength				
Market conditions	Demand is strong and growing, strong entry barriers, low sensitivity to changes in technology and economic outlook.	Demand is strong and stable. Some entry barriers, some sensitivity to changes in technology and economic outlook.	Demand is adequate and stable, limited entry barriers, significant sensitivity to changes in technology and economic outlook.	Demand is weak and declining, vulnerable to changes in technology and economic outlook, highly uncertain environment.

	Strong	Good	Satisfactory	Weak
Financial strength (*cont.*)				
Financial ratios (debt service coverage ratio and loan-to-value ratio)	Strong financial ratios considering the type of asset. Very robust economic assumptions.	Strong/acceptable financial ratios considering the type of asset. Robust project economic assumptions.	Standard financial ratios for the asset type.	Aggressive financial ratios considering the type of asset.
Stress analysis	Stable long-term revenues, capable of withstanding severely stressed conditions through an economic cycle.	Satisfactory short-term revenues. Loan can withstand some financial adversity. Default is only likely under severe economic conditions.	Uncertain short-term revenues. Cash flows are vulnerable to stresses that are not uncommon through an economic cycle. The loan may default in a normal downturn.	Revenues subject to strong uncertainties; even in normal economic conditions the asset may default, unless conditions improve.
Market liquidity	Market is structured on a worldwide basis; assets are highly liquid.	Market is worldwide or regional; assets are relatively liquid.	Market is regional with limited prospects in the short term, implying lower liquidity.	Local market and/or poor visibility. Low or no liquidity, particularly on niche markets.
Political and legal environment				
Political risk, including transfer risk	Very low; strong mitigation instruments, if needed.	Low; satisfactory mitigation instruments, if needed.	Moderate; fair mitigation instruments.	High; no or weak mitigation instruments.
Legal and regulatory risks	Jurisdiction is favourable to repossession and enforcement of contracts.	Jurisdiction is favourable to repossession and enforcement of contracts.	Jurisdiction is generally favourable to repossession and enforcement of contracts, even if repossession might be long and/or difficult.	Poor or unstable legal and regulatory environment. Jurisdiction may make repossession and enforcement of contracts lengthy or impossible.
Transaction characteristics				
Financing term compared to the economic life of the asset	Full payout profile/ minimum balloon. No grace period.	Balloon more significant, but still at satisfactory levels.	Important balloon with potentially grace periods.	Repayment in fine or high balloon.

Table 8.3 (*cont.*)

	Strong	Good	Satisfactory	Weak
Operating risk				
Permits/ licensing	All permits have been obtained; asset meets current and foreseeable safety regulations.	All permits obtained or in the process of being obtained; asset meets current and foreseeable safety regulations.	Most permits obtained or in process of being obtained, outstanding ones considered routine, asset meets current safety regulations.	Problems in obtaining all required permits, part of the planned configuration and/ or planned operations might need to be revised.
Scope and nature of operation and management (O&M) contracts	Strong long-term O&M contract, preferably with contractual performance incentives, and/or O&M reserve accounts (if needed).	Long-term O&M contract, and/or O&M reserve accounts (if needed).	Limited O&M contract or O&M reserve account (if needed).	No O&M contract: risk of high operational cost overruns beyond mitigants.
Operator's financial strength, track record in managing the asset type and capability to re-market asset when it comes off-lease	Excellent track record and strong re-marketing capability.	Satisfactory track record and re-marketing capability.	Weak or short track record and uncertain re-marketing capability.	No or unknown track record and inability to re-market the asset.
Asset characteristics				
Configuration, size, design and maintenance (ie age, size for a plane) compared to other assets on the same market	Strong advantage in design and maintenance. Configuration is standard such that the object meets a liquid market.	Above average design and maintenance. Standard configuration, maybe with very limited exceptions—such that the object meets a liquid market.	Average design and maintenance. Configuration is somewhat specific, and thus might cause a narrower market for the object.	Below average design and maintenance. Asset is near the end of its economic life. Configuration is very specific; the market for the object is very narrow.
Resale value	Current resale value is well above debt value.	Resale value is moderately above debt value.	Resale value is slightly above debt value.	Resale value is below debt value.
Sensitivity of the asset value and liquidity to economic cycles	Asset value and liquidity are relatively insensitive to economic cycles.	Asset value and liquidity are sensitive to economic cycles.	Asset value and liquidity are quite sensitive to economic cycles.	Asset value and liquidity are highly sensitive to economic cycles.

	Strong	Good	Satisfactory	Weak
Strength of sponsor				
Operator's financial strength, track record in managing the asset type and capability to re-market asset when it comes off-lease	Excellent track record and strong re-marketing capability.	Satisfactory track record and re-marketing capability.	Weak or short track record and uncertain re-marketing capability.	No or unknown track record and inability to remarket the asset.
Sponsors' track record and financial strength	Sponsors with excellent track record and high financial standing.	Sponsors with good track record and good financial standing.	Sponsors with adequate track record and good financial standing.	Sponsors with no or questionable track record and/or financial weaknesses.
Security package				
Asset control	Legal documentation provides the lender effective control (eg a first perfected security interest, or a leasing structure including such security) on the asset, or on the company owning it.	Legal documentation provides the lender effective control (eg a perfected security interest, or a leasing structure including such security) on the asset, or on the company owning it.	Legal documentation provides the lender effective control (eg a perfected security interest, or a leasing structure including such security) on the asset, or on the company owning it.	The contract provides little security to the lender and leaves room to some risk of losing control on the asset.
Rights and means at the lender's disposal to monitor the location and condition of the asset	The lender is able to monitor the location and condition of the asset, at any time and place (regular reports, possibility to lead inspections).	The lender is able to monitor the location and condition of the asset, almost at any time and place.	The lender is able to monitor the location and condition of the asset, almost at any time and place.	The lender's abilities to monitor the location and condition of the asset are limited.
Insurance against damages	Strong insurance coverage including collateral damages with top quality insurance companies.	Satisfactory insurance coverage (not including collateral damages) with good quality insurance companies.	Fair insurance coverage (not including collateral damages) with acceptable quality insurance companies.	Weak insurance coverage (not including collateral damages) or with weak quality insurance companies.

Table 8.4 Supervisory Rating Grades for Commodities Finance Exposure

	Strong	Good	Satisfactory	Weak
Financial strength				
Degree of over-collateralization of trade	Strong.	Good.	Satisfactory.	Weak.
Political and legal environment				
Country risk	No country risk.	Limited exposure to country risk (in particular, offshore location of reserves in an emerging country).	Exposure to country risk (in particular, offshore location of reserves in an emerging country).	Strong exposure to country risk (in particular, inland reserves in an emerging country).
Mitigation of country risks	Very strong mitigation: Strong offshore mechanisms. Strategic commodity. 1st class buyer.	Strong mitigation: Offshore mechanisms. Strategic commodity. Strong buyer.	Acceptable mitigation: Offshore mechanisms. Less strategic commodity. Acceptable buyer.	Only partial mitigation: No offshore mechanisms. Non-strategic commodity. Weak buyer.
Asset characteristics				
Liquidity and susceptibility to damage	Commodity is quoted and can be hedged through futures or OTC instruments. Commodity is not susceptible to damage.	Commodity is quoted and can be hedged through OTC instruments. Commodity is not susceptible to damage.	Commodity is not quoted but is liquid. There is uncertainty about the possibility of hedging. Commodity is not susceptible to damage.	Commodity is not quoted. Liquidity is limited given the size and depth of the market. No appropriate hedging instruments. Commodity is susceptible to damage.
Strength of sponsor				
Financial strength of trader	Very strong, relative to trading philosophy and risks.	Strong.	Adequate.	Weak.
Track record, including ability to manage the logistic process	Extensive experience with the type of transaction in question. Strong record of operating success and cost efficiency.	Sufficient experience with the type of transaction in question. Above average record of operating success and cost efficiency.	Limited experience with the type of transaction in question. Average record of operating success and cost efficiency.	Limited or uncertain track record in general. Volatile costs and profits.

	Strong	Good	Satisfactory	Weak
Strength of sponsor (*cont.*)				
Trading controls and hedging policies	Strong standards for counterparty selection, hedging, and monitoring.	Adequate standards for counterparty selection, hedging, and monitoring.	Past deals have experienced no or minor problems.	Trader has experienced significant losses on past deals.
Quality of financial disclosure	Excellent.	Good.	Satisfactory.	Financial disclosure contains some uncertainties or is insufficient.
Security package				
Asset control	First perfected security interest provides the lender legal control of the assets at any time if needed.	First perfected security interest provides the lender legal control of the assets at any time if needed.	At some point in the process, there is a rupture in the control of the assets by the lender. The rupture is mitigated by knowledge of the trade process or a third party undertaking as the case may be.	Contract leaves room for some risk of losing control over the assets. Recovery could be jeopardized.

The analytical process involved is entirely judgemental, and the allocation of char- **8.44**
acteristics to categories is, in practice, one which relies predominantly on the
expertise of the classifier. Once this analysis has been performed, the exposure is
allocated to one of five risk categories, these being:

Remaining maturity	Strong	Good	Satisfactory	Weak	Default
More than 2.5 years	70% (50%)*	90% (70%)*	115%	250%	0%
Less than 2.5 years	50%	70%	115%	250%	0%

*A firm may use the bracketed figures if it has explicit permission to do so from its supervisor.

Expected loss figures for specialized finance exposures should be as follows: **8.45**

Remaining maturity	Strong	Good	Satisfactory	Weak	Default
More than 2.5 years	0.4% (0%)*	0.8% (0.4%)*	2.8%	8%	50%
Less than 2.5 years	0%	0.4%	2.8%	8%	50%

*A firm may use the bracketed figures if it has explicit permission to do so from its supervisor.

D. Retail and Mortgage Exposures

Retail exposures

8.46 Retail exposures are approached in a different way from corporate, bank and sovereign receivables, in that rather than each individual borrower being given a credit rating, exposures are assessed on a portfolio basis. This permits the institution concerned to recognize correlation effects within the portfolio, and as a result a diversified retail portfolio is likely to be treated as a better credit than an equivalent exposure to a corporate borrower.

8.47 The rationale for the existence of the retail exposures regime is to recognize the superior risk characteristics possessed by a highly diversified pool of non-granular exposures. This enables a separate capital calculation to be applied to that portfolio to take those characteristics into account. This means that the approach is only appropriate where exposures are managed as homogeneous pools rather than as individual exposures.

8.48 The criteria used within the IRB approach for an exposure to qualify as a retail exposure are broadly similar to those used in the standardized approach. However, firms are required by the FSA to maintain detailed policies to discriminate between retail and non-retail exposures, and the FSA has said that it does not regard a simple reliance on the EUR 1m threshold as sufficient.[3] The class of assets eligible with the IRB approach may be slightly wider—for example, the present value of retail minimum lease payments is eligible to be treated as a retail exposure. The IRB approach also requires that the exposures be managed as an aggregate and not as individual exposures.

8.49 Firms may group their retail exposures as they wish, and in particular may segment them by collateral type, by obligor risk characteristics, by transaction risk type, or by delinquency. A firm must assess, test and validate its model and its loss data at least as effectively as it updates its corporate model, and the retail model must meet IRB standards. As noted in the section on models, the IRB model applied to retail exposures gives a lower figure than that for equivalent corporate exposures.

Specialized retail exposures

8.50 There are two specialized classes of retail exposures, both of which have their exposures calculated slightly differently. For exposures secured by real estate, the correlation formula is not used, but correlation is taken to be 0.15 in all cases. For overdrafts and credit card receivables (known for this purpose as qualifying

---

[3] BIPRU 4.64(5).

revolving retail exposures), the same is true but the factor to be used should be 0.04.

The practical effect of these adjustments is that the risk weighting of qualifying **8.51** revolving retail exposures is for most purposes substantially less than the weighting which would be given to ordinary retail exposures. However, it is notable that the effect of using a fixed factor rather than the formula means that at higher PD levels the risk weighted figure is actually higher than it would be if the formula were used. Thus, the examples set out in Annex 5 of the Accord give the following illustrative risk weights for the three different classes.

	Risk weights assuming 45% LGD and 2.5yr Maturity		
PD	Retail Exposures	Residential Mortgages	Qualifying Revolving Retail Exposures
0.05%	7%	6%	2%
1.00%	46%	56%	17%
2.00%	58%	88%	29%
5.00%	66%	148%	55%
10.00%	76%	204%	84%

The figures for mortgage lending look remarkably high in this table. However, **8.52** this is because all of these figures are calculated using a common LGD of 45 per cent. In reality the LGD for a retail mortgage is considerably smaller than that for any other form of retail exposure, and as a result when the mortgage formula is applied to a realistic LGD the actual risk weightings achieved are significantly lower than those set out above for general retail.

For these purposes the technical definition of a qualifying revolving exposure **8.53** means a portfolio of exposures to individuals where outstanding balances are permitted to fluctuate based on the customers own decisions up to a limit. These balances must be unsecured, uncommitted, must revolve in practice as well as in theory and be subject to a maximum limit of €100,000 per individual exposure. The portfolio as a whole must exhibit a sufficiently high margin income that its expected net (after expenses) future margin income over the next 12 months will cover expected loss on the portfolio in that period by at least two standard deviations. Technically there are a number of types of retail facility which could be made to fit within this definition, but the FSA has expressed the view that it is unlikely that any arrangement other than credit card receivables and overdrafts will be accepted as being within it.[4]

---

[4] BIPRU 4.6.46.

Default in the retail portfolio

8.54 The definition of default is slightly different for the retail portfolio. For exposures to enterprises managed within the retail portfolio, an exposure is treated as defaulted when it reaches 90 days past due—as with any other exposure. However, for true retail exposures this can be extended to 180 days past due if the relevant regulator considers it appropriate. It should be noted that the BCD recognizes that a regulator which has implemented the Basel II Accord is entitled to set a definition of default within its jurisdiction and other regulators are entitled to apply that rule in the interests of competitive equality. Thus, if the Austrian regulator (for example) were to determine that the appropriate period for Austrian retail exposures was 100 days, UK banks lending into Austria would be entitled to use the 100 day figure in respect of their portfolio of Austrian retail exposures.

8.55 A firm must maintain a database of retail exposures and use it to generate estimates of PD, LGD and CCF calculated on long run default experience. It is permissible to use third party databases for this purpose, but only where there is a strong link between the firm's assignment process and risk profile and that of the external data used. At least one of the data sources used (external, internal, or pooled) must include data over a period of at least five years, and if it covers a longer period then that period must be used, unless the firm can convince the FSA that the more recent data is a better predictor of loss.

8.56 For retail losses, further drawings may be reflected either in LGD or in CCF.

E. Eligible Purchased Receivables

8.57 Purchased receivables, as with retail exposures, are assessed on a portfolio rather than an individual basis. There is in practice no difference between purchased and home-grown retail receivables. However, corporate receivables may be treated in accordance with this approach if they satisfy certain conditions.

8.58 In principle, if an institution acquires a portfolio of corporate receivables it is required to treat them as individual corporate exposures. However, if the portfolio satisfies certain conditions, it may be treated as a single asset using the top-down methodology employed for retail exposures. As with retail exposures, use of this approach significantly reduces the total risk exposure of the portfolio. The conditions are:

- the receivables must be purchased from an unrelated third party, and may not be originated by the holder;
- the receivables must have been created at arm's length (thus, for example, inter-company debts are ineligible);

- the maturity of the exposures must not be greater than one year (unless the exposures are fully secured by collateral);

- the portfolio must be sufficiently diversified (this limit may be set by national regulators);

- the claim must be on the whole pool. In general, any tranching of claims will have the effect of disallowing the use of this treatment and requiring the investor to use the securitization treatment (see below). However, the existence of a right of recourse to the seller will not have this effect.

The approach to risk weighting corporate receivables involves the purchasing **8.59** bank estimating a one-year expected loss amount. This expected loss figure is then decomposed into its components of PD and LGD. The exposure is then treated as an exposure to a single corporate borrower with those PD and LGD attributes.

F. Equity Exposures

The regulatory capital system takes a broad definition of the notion of equity. **8.60** Lawyers who are accustomed to consider 'equity' as that which is treated as share capital under the applicable company law are therefore required to refocus their attention on subordination as the primary determinant of equity status. For these purposes, equity means:

(1) non-debt exposures conveying a subordinated, residual claim on the assets or income of the issuer, and

(2) debt exposures the economic substance of which is similar to the exposures specified in (1).

This includes debt-like equity instruments (such as preference shares) and equity-like debt instruments (such as the most subordinated notes issued out of a tranched securitization or repackaging. It also clearly includes instruments whose effect is to pass on the economic equivalent of equities whilst remaining legally debt instruments. However, in some circumstances it may be remarkably difficult to identify precisely which instruments fall within this definition and which do not.

Equity exposures include both voting and non-voting interests. An instrument **8.61** which is irredeemable, does not embody an obligation on the part of the issuer, and grants the holder a residual claim on the assets or income of the issuer and is automatically characterized as equity. However, instruments which have the characteristics commonly encountered in innovative bank tier one instruments (such as stock settlement or infinite deferral of payment obligations) may be characterized as equity at the election of the regulator. The substance over form approach is adopted both ways—preference shares and other instruments which, although legally equity, have the economic characteristics of debt are not caught by this definition.

8.62 If a bank holds sufficient equity in a particular entity, that entity will be treated as part of the bank's group. Thus the broad position in respect of any hold in a financial entity is as follows:

	Financial undertaking*	Non-financial undertaking
Holding over 50%	Consolidated as a subsidiary	Consolidated as a subsidiary
Holding between 20% and 50%	Partially consolidated as a participation	Partially consolidated as a participation
Holding below 20% but above 10%	Material holding—deducted	Qualifying holding—deducted if the aggregate of such holdings exceeds specified limits
Holding below 10%	Weighted asset (subject to aggregate limit of 10% of bank's own capital)	Weighted asset

* 'Financial undertaking' for this purpose means a bank, financial firm or insurer.

8.63 The issue of equity held on bank balance sheets was historically of relatively little importance in the UK system, although in continental Europe the 'relationship' model of banking where banks held equity stakes in their customers was for a time more common. However, the major driver behind the increase in the amount of bank equity investment is the rise of private equity investment.

8.64 Within the standardized approach, equity investments are weighted at 100 per cent. The Accord suggests that regulators should have discretion to weight 'higher risk portfolios' at 150 per cent, but within the EU 100 per cent seems to have been adopted as the default weighting. The reason that this is important here is that many IRB banks have not progressed to any of the IRB approaches to weighting equity holdings, and remain on the standardized approach. The reason for this is not hard to discern—this is one of the relatively few areas in which all of the available IRB approaches are likely to produce a significantly higher capital requirement than the standardized approach.

8.65 Within the IRB approach there are three possible treatments for equity exposures. These are:

(1) the simple risk weight approach;
(2) the internal models approach; and
(3) the PD/LGD approach.

The first two of these are described in the Accord as the 'market-based' approach. This is also one of the areas in which EU (and therefore UK) regulation diverges significantly from the Accord.

In all of these cases the valuation of the exposure requires some thought. Broadly, **8.66** the value is the value used in the accounts, whether the fair value or the lower of cost or net realizable value. However, hedging instruments may be recognized in calculating the value of the holdings as long as they have a maturity of at least one year and, unusually for the banking book, long and short positions may be set off against each other to calculate the net exposure. Unfunded protection may also be recognized as reducing this exposure.

The simple risk weight approach for equity

The simple risk weight approach as set out in the Accord provides that institutions **8.67** should apply a 300 per cent weight to equity holdings that are publicly traded and a 400 per cent risk weight to all other equity holdings.

The BCD, by contrast, provides that equities should be weighted at either of **8.68** 190 per cent, for private equity exposures in well-diversified portfolios, 290 per cent for exchange traded equity exposures, and 370 per cent for all other equity exposures.

The expected loss figures to be used in calculating EL for equity are 0.8 per cent **8.69** for private equity exposures in well-diversified portfolios and for exchange traded equity exposures, and 2.4 per cent for all other equity exposures.

The PD/LGD approach for equity

The idea of using a PD/LGD approach for equity seems to lawyers to be absurd— **8.70** equity, by definition, does not 'default', since it does not embed a payment obligation. Consequently it should not be possible to calculate either PD or LGD. The reason that the concept does make sense may be ascertained by referring back to the definition of 'equity' used for this purpose set out in para 8.59 above. For regulatory purposes equity means the most junior capital within a structure, and does not refer to legal form. Thus the most junior piece of any financing will be likely to be considered to be equity for this purpose.

This approach employs the same approach as the foundation IRB approach for **8.71** corporate exposures. The PD to be used must be estimated in the same way as that applied for debt exposures. Slightly higher minimum PD levels are imposed for equities under the BCD:

- 0.09 per cent for exchange traded equity exposures where the investment is part of a long-term customer relationship;
- 0.09 for non-exchange traded equity exposures where the returns on the investment are based on regular cash flows not derived from capital gains;
- 0.4 per cent for exchange traded equity exposures (including short positions); and
- 1.25 per cent for all other equities.

These figures compare with the 0.03 per cent minimum requirement for corporate debt exposures. The calculation of the RWA of the exposure is the same as for corporate and other exposures under the IRB formula.

8.72 The LGD to be used in the PD/LGD model is prescribed even for advanced IRB banks. It is set as 65 per cent for private equity holdings in sufficiently diversified portfolios, and 90 per cent in all other cases. A minimum risk weighting of 100 per cent is required for all public equities held as part of a long-term customer relationship and all private equity holdings not held for the purposes of achieving capital gain.

8.73 There is also an interesting quirk of the system as regards unfunded credit protection. Ordinarily, the purchaser of credit protection under the IRB approach substitutes an exposure to the protection seller—calculated as a function of the protection seller's PD and LGD—for the exposure to the underlying asset. Broadly, the same approach applies where an IRB bank buys unfunded protection on an equity exposure. However, where protection is bought against an equity exposure, the LGD to be used on the protected portion is that which was initially applicable to the underlying equities—65 per cent for private equity in sufficiently diversified portfolios, 90 per cent for others. Thus the RWA calculation for an exposure subject to this form of protection is calculated using the PD of the guarantor and the LGD of the guaranteed exposure

8.74 The maturity assigned to all equity exposures should be five years.

The internal models approach for equity

8.75 The internal models method requires institutions to use their internal risk models to calculate the potential loss on the institutions equity holdings and to multiply that figure by 12.5 (the reciprocal of 8 per cent) to derive a risk-weighted assets figure for the holding. The main requirement for the internal models approach is that the total risk capital charge across the model as a whole must not be less than that which would have applied if the PD/LGD approach had been used. The requirements which apply to the use of this model are broadly similar to those which apply for the use of any other model—the model must be robust, must have been effectively back-tested against data, must be integrated into the institution's management information systems and must be verified at appropriate intervals.

9

NETTING, COLLATERAL,
AND CREDIT RISK MITIGATION

A. Introduction

Credit risk mitigation is the portmanteau term which covers the various different **9.01** ways in which an exposure can be reduced for regulatory reporting purposes. Formally there are three ways of doing this: netting against an existing exposure owed by the bank to the borrower; taking (certain types of) collateral; and obtaining cover from third parties in the form of guarantees or similar contracts. It may be noted that there are a very large number of techniques which are used in the real world by banks to improve their position as lenders which are simply disregarded by the regulatory system, of which the most important are probably loan covenants. No matter how restrictive the undertakings which a borrower gives a bank as to the way in which it manages its business or the way in which it will repay its loan, this protection will not be recognized for regulatory purposes. It is commonly argued that the fact that covenants are disregarded in this way is part of the reason why, during the credit boom of the mid-2000s, covenants on loans (especially to private equity borrowers) became less and less restrictive. However, the reason why such covenants are generally disregarded by the regulatory system is simply that it is almost impossible to quantify the impact of relatively tighter or looser covenants in the calculation of risk capital, and in risk capital, as in so many areas, that which cannot be reliably quantified must be completely disregarded.

9.02   The other situation in which this problem arises is with regard to arrangements (common in structures such as project and export finance, but found in many areas) where a particular loan is committed to be paid out of a particular stream of income arising from a third party. A typical example of an arrangement of this kind is where a bank finances the construction of a power station on terms that the government of the country concerned commits to buy the output of the power station in a minimum quantity for a fixed term. The purchase price is then paid into a designated account (over which the borrower may have no control) on terms that the money paid into the account will be used to repay the debt to the bank. In such an arrangement the bank may regard itself as particularly safe, but it is almost impossible to bring such arrangements within the Basel collateral regime. Even if the purchase price were paid into the account in advance, the bank could only claim to be formally collateralized if it had some sort of perfected security interest over the account. However, since the account is unlikely to be funded, what the bank has is something economically similar to a guarantee by the relevant government. However, even this is uncertain, since the relevant government is only likely to pay money into the account if the electricity is actually produced. Thus the claim on the government is insufficiently certain to constitute a guarantee, and in any event the claim is indirect, and in broad terms only direct guarantees may be recognized for regulatory capital purposes.

9.03   The upshot of all of this is that there are many ways in which a bank can structure an exposure in such a way as to reduce its credit exposure considerably, but without receiving any formal regulatory capital benefit for that reduction. It may be objected that if the Advanced IRB mechanism were sufficiently effective then in the fullness of time such outcomes would be reflected in the AIRB database of actual recoveries, and would from there find their way into the capital return. The difficulty with this analysis is not that it is not true—it is—but that it is true only after a sufficiently large database of loss exposure has been accumulated. For projects of a type where only a few dozen may be undertaken in any given decade, the relevant database will have been accumulated too late to be any practical help.

B. Netting

9.04   The simplest method of reducing an exposure from a borrower to a bank is to set it off against another exposure owed by the bank to the borrower. Although in general borrowers owe banks more than banks owe them, in practice very many borrowers have at least some claims on their bank, if only in the form of positive balances on current accounts. The issue for regulators is therefore the simple one of whether the two should be permitted to be netted off against each other. The core determination here is a legal one; specifically, whether in the insolvency of the borrower the bank would be able to refuse to pay the positive balance to the liquidator of the borrower by setting off against that balance the amount due to it on the relevant loan or other exposure. Consequently regulators have in the past required banks to obtain formal legal opinions from external counsel before permitting them to set off balances for regulatory capital purposes. The Basel II regime is more liberal, in that it requires banks to be confident that they have a 'well-founded legal basis' for netting exposures,[1] but does not prescribe any requirement for formal legal opinions.

In principal anything which can be netted or set off as a matter of law can be netted or set off for regulatory capital purposes. However there is one very important exception to this principle; that being the rule that on balance sheet exposures and off balance sheet exposures may not be netted off against each other. **9.05**

On balance sheet netting

An on balance sheet exposure means for this purpose a loan or a deposit. This rule is restrictively construed in the EU—even if an exposure is recorded in the accounts of the bank as an asset or a liability, it may not be subject to formal on balance sheet netting unless it is either a loan or a deposit.[2] Thus not every claim which may be netted as a matter of law may be netted for regulatory capital purposes, and claims which are on balance sheet for accounting purposes but which do not fall within the definition of loan or deposit may not be netted for capital purposes. **9.06**

The core rule for on balance sheet netting is that it is only permitted where the exposures are mutual, arise in the same right between the same persons, and would be effective in the insolvency of the counterparty.[3] The effect of recognizing an on balance sheet netting arrangement is not—paradoxically—simply to reduce the relevant exposure to the net balance, but to treat the balance due to the bank as collateralized by cash equal to the value of the deposit held by the bank for the borrower. The rules on cash collateralization will therefore apply. **9.07**

Off balance sheet netting and master netting agreements

Off balance sheet netting is a concept which requires a moment's thought. Where two banks have, for example, entered into a series of contracts between themselves, there will at any given time be a net amount owing between them by one side to the other. This is an on balance sheet exposure, in that in accounting terms it is an amount due or payable. The netting which goes into the calculation **9.08**

---

[1] Basel, para 188.
[2] BCD Annex VIII part 1 point 4, BIPRU 5.3.2.
[3] The UK for many years required legal opinions to cover the insolvency of the bank as well as the insolvency of the borrower as a result of its experience with the BCCI failure. However, this has not been carried through into the Basel approach.

of this amount is not a 'netting' in the regulatory sense of the word, but an accounting process, and the rules which govern the way in which the netting should be performed are the accounting rules. Separately, the regulatory system imposes a risk charge in respect of the notional liability which could arise from changes in the value of the derivative positions. This is a pure regulatory capital charge, and its calculation is discussed in the section on derivatives in Chapter 15.

9.09 The issue which arises as regards master netting arrangements is different from both of these, and is in effect an anti-avoidance rule. The essence of this point is that if a client owes a bank money and delivers securities to it as collateral, the value of those securities will be adjusted (a 'risk haircut') to reflect the risk of future downward fluctuation in their price. However, it is possible to document such transactions on terms that the obligations concerned would ordinarily qualify for netting (for example in a derivative or a repo) it should not be possible for the bank to simply net the two exposures off against each other, since this would provide a mechanism whereby the haircuts applied to collateral could be evaded. This it is necessary to extend the collateral haircuts regime to off balance sheet transactions which have the effect of collateralized transactions—repurchase transactions, securities or commodities lending or borrowing transactions, or other capital market-driven transactions. The effect of this rule is to impose a risk capital charge on the net position which would otherwise be arrived at under derivatives relating to repo transactions, securities or commodities lending or borrowing transactions, or other capital markets transactions.

9.10 The essence of this approach is that it is based on the following formula:

$$\text{Exposure} = (\text{net position}) + (\text{haircut for each security}) + (\text{net FX volatility adjustment})$$

This can be formally stated as:

$$E^* = \max \{0, [(\Sigma(E) - \Sigma(C)) + \Sigma (|\text{net position in each } security| \times H_{sec}) + (\Sigma |E_{fx}| \times H_{fx})]\}$$

where:

(1) E is the exposure value for each separate exposure under the agreement that would apply in the absence of the credit protection;

(2) C is the value of the securities or commodities borrowed, purchased or received or the cash borrowed or received in respect of each such exposure;

(3) $\Sigma(E)$ is the sum of all Es under the agreement;

(4) $\Sigma(C)$ is the sum of all Cs under the agreement;

(5) Efx is the net position (positive or negative) in a given currency other than the settlement currency of the agreement;

(6) Hsec is the volatility adjustment appropriate to a particular type of security;

(7) Hfx is the foreign exchange volatility adjustment; and

(8) E* is the fully adjusted exposure value.

The volatility figures to be used in this formula may be derived using either the 'supervisory volatility adjustments approach' or the 'own estimates of volatility adjustments approach'. The distinction between the two is clear from the names—in the first case the calculation is performed using supervisory figures; whilst in the latter the calculation is performed using the bank's own estimates. **9.11**

There is an 'advanced' approach permitted for firms who have permission to use their internal models to estimate the potential change in value of the unsecured exposure amount (ΣE–ΣC). This model must take into account correlation effects between security positions subject to a master netting agreement as well as the liquidity of the instruments concerned. The formula is: **9.12**

$$E^* = \max \{0, [(\Sigma E - \Sigma C) + (\textit{VaR} \text{ output of the internal models})]\}$$

where:

(1) E is the exposure value for each separate exposure under the agreement that would apply in the absence of the credit protection;

(2) C is the value of the securities borrowed, purchased or received or the cash borrowed or received in respect of each such exposure;

(3) Σ (E) is the sum of all Es under the agreement; and

(4) Σ (C) is the sum of all Cs under the agreement.

C. Collateral

Basel II contains three approaches to collateral. The simplest is that which is applied by Advanced IRB banks, who are permitted to reflect the loss mitigating effects of collateral through their modelling of LGD. Other banks must use one of the 'comprehensive' approach or the 'simple' approach. The simple approach is broadly a replication of the existing Basel approach, where the credit weighting of the underlying asset is replaced by the credit weighting of the collateral, subject to a floor. The comprehensive approach permits a slightly wider range of collateral to be recognized—notably shares traded on a recognized exchange—and operates by reducing the absolute value of the exposure. Firms must operate under either the simple or the comprehensive approach in the banking book—not both. Only the comprehensive approach may be used in the trading book. **9.13**

The simple approach

The simple approach differs from the Basle I approach in two major ways. First, it significantly expands the range of collateral which is available for use. Second, it **9.14** imposes a series of haircuts as to the value of the collateral. The logic of Basle I was that the only assets recognized as collateral (cash and government securities) were treated as risk free, and therefore reduced the exposure pound for pound. However, given the wider range of assets eligible to be used as collateral in the Basel II approach, mandatory regulatory haircuts are applied to the value of both the exposure collateralized and the collateral assets.

9.15 In the simple approach, eligible collateral includes:

- cash on deposit with the bank;
- gold;
- debt securities rated BB- (Sovereigns), BBB- (other issuers) or A3/P3 or above;
- bank issued senior debt securities which are listed on a recognized exchange and are not subordinated, whether rated or not (as long as the bank holding the collateral has no reason to believe that the issue justifies a rating below BBB- or A-3/P-3);
- equities included in a main index;
- units in funds where there is a daily price and the fund invests only in instruments which would themselves be eligible collateral.

9.16 The following conditions apply to both the simple and comprehensive approaches:

- documentation must be legally binding and enforceable in all jurisdictions;
- the firm must take all necessary steps to maintain collateral;
- there must be no material positive correlation between the credit quality of the counterparty and the value of the collateral;
- the firm must have the right to liquidate or take legal possession of collateral;
- the firm must have clear and robust procedures for the timely liquidation of collateral.

Under the simple approach, collateral must be pledged for the life of the exposure and revalued at least every six months. The risk weight of the collateralized asset will be the risk weight of the collateral. This will be subject to a floor of 20 per cent unless:

(a) the transaction is covered by the core repo market participant concession (see para 9.26) (0 per cent);

(b) the transaction is a repo market transaction which is not entered into by a core market participant but complies with the requirements and has no currency mismatch (10 per cent);

(c) the transaction is an OTC derivative transaction which is subject to daily mark to market and cash collateralized without a currency mismatch (0 per cent);

(d) the transaction is an OTC derivative transaction which is subject to daily mark to market and collateralized by PSE or sovereign securities qualifying for a 0 per cent weighting under the standardized approach above (10 per cent);

(e) the collateral is cash on deposit and there is no currency mismatch (0 per cent); or

(f) the collateral is in the form of sovereign/PSE securities and is discounted by 20 per cent of its market value (0 per cent).

It should also be noted that where the exposure collateralized is an OTC transaction, a different calculation is applied.

The comprehensive approach

The comprehensive approach adds two further classes of eligible assets as collateral: **9.17**

- equities which are listed on a recognized exchange but are not included in a main index;
- regulated investment funds which invest in such securities.

The major distinction between the simple and the comprehensive approach is that in the simple approach the weighting ascribed to the collateralized portion of the exposure is the weighting of the relevant collateral. In the comprehensive approach, by contrast, the absolute value of the collateralized exposure is reduced to reflect the collateral, with the balance (if any) being weighted in accordance with the underlying credit. This calculation is performed by comparing the current value of the exposure (subject to a value adjustment) with the current value of the collateral received (also subject to a value adjustment). The value adjustments are intended to reflect the risk of adverse change in value, and are generally referred to as 'haircuts'.

The size of the haircut will vary according to the nature of the asset. The value of   **9.18** the underlying exposure will be increased by a factor and the value of the collateral will be reduced by a factor. The reduced value of the collateral will then be subtracted from the increased value of the original exposure. If the reduced value of the collateral exceeds the increased value of the original exposure, the exposure will be treated as completely collateralized and there will be no capital charge. If the reduced value of the collateral is less than the increased value of the original exposure, the difference will be treated as uncollateralized and weighted according to the appropriate weighting for the original exposure. This can be expressed as:

$$(\text{Original exposure} \times (1 + \text{haircut})) - (\text{collateral value} \times (1 - \text{haircut}))$$
$$= \text{exposure}$$

9.19 Thus, for example, assume that a bank has an exposure of £100 to a counterparty and takes collateral in respect of that exposure, and that the haircut for both original exposure and collateral is 15 per cent.

- For the bank to treat the exposure as completely risk free he would have to obtain £135 or more of collateral: $(100 \times 115\%) - (135 \times 85\%) = 0$
- If the bank receives £100 of collateral, it will be left with an exposure to the client of £30: $(100 \times 115\%) - (100 \times 85\%) = 30$.

An exposure cannot be negative, so if the collateral amount exceeds the amount required to zero weight the exposure, the remaining collateral is disregarded for this purpose.

9.20 If the collateral is denominated in a different currency to the original exposure then its value will be further reduced by an additional 8 per cent haircut to reflect this. Thus in the example above, £149 worth of $US denominated collateral would be needed to achieve a 0 per cent exposure: $(100 \times 115\%) - (149 \times 77\%) = 0$.

Haircuts

9.21 The value of the haircut (H) is based on the price volatility of the asset concerned. It is applied to the exposure collateralized to reflect the risk that this exposure will increase, and is applied to the collateral received to reflect the risk that that the value of the collateral will decrease. The Accord specifies two varieties of haircut: standard supervisory haircuts and own estimates.

Standard supervisory haircuts

9.22 These figures are based on daily marking to market, daily remargining and a 10 business day holding period for the collateralized asset. The haircuts are as follows:

Debt securities

Issue rating	Residual maturity	Sovereigns/strong PSEs/MDBs[*]	Banks/Corporates[†]/other sovereigns and PSEs
AAA/AA	1 year or less	0.5	1
	1 to 5 years	2	4
	5 years or more	4	8
A/BBB	1 year or less	1	2
	1 to 5 years	3	6
	5 years or more	6	12
BB+/BB-		15	N/A

* Credit quality step 4 or above.

† Credit quality step 3 and above.

Other collateral

Main index equities and gold	15
Other equities (including convertibles) listed on a recognized exchange	25
Cash in same currency	0
Mutual funds	Highest haircut applicable to any asset which the fund can invest in

Currency haircut

Additional currency risk	8

Own estimates for haircuts

Own estimates may be used to calculate market price and currency volatility **9.23** haircuts.

Secured lending transactions

Collateralized transactions can be loosely divided into three different types; repo- **9.24** style transactions, capital markets (ie collateralized OTC derivative) transactions and secured lending. In general repo-style and capital-market style transactions will satisfy the requirement for daily valuation and remargining and will be calculated as set out above, whereas secured lending transactions will be revalued less frequently and are unlikely to provide for remargining. The haircuts used for secured lending transactions are calculated by applying to the above haircuts a formula which increases the haircut according to the intervals between revaluations. The formula works on a 'square root of time' basis, and gives the following multipliers:

Revaluation	Monthly	Quarterly	Semiannually	Annually
Haircut increased by	2.2×	3.3×	4.5×	6.1×

These multipliers mean that in some cases collateral will be completely ineffective to reduce exposure, since the haircut to be applied will exceed 100 per cent. However, note that taking collateral can never increase an exposure.

Banks who have received approval to operate a market risk model may be permit- **9.25** ted to use their own H figures instead of those stated above. However, in operating such an approach banks will be required to approach exposures individually, and will not be permitted to take correlation into account.

Government repo market concession

There is a concessionary regime available for government repo market trading. **9.26** A national supervisor may permit firms in its jurisdiction which are 'Core Market

Participants' in its government repo market to apply a 0 per cent H in respect of their exposures in that market, and if a national supervisor has exercised this right then other supervisors may give the same benefit to firms which they regulate which participate in that market.[4] However, firms which use VaR modelling to establish H may not take advantage of this concession.

9.27 Core market participants may include, at the discretion of the national supervisor, sovereigns, central banks and PSEs, banks and securities firms, financial firms, regulated mutual funds, regulated pension funds, and recognized clearing organizations.

9.28 The conditions for using 0 per cent H are that the firm should be a core market participant and the transactions must have the following characteristics:

- the repoed asset is a sovereign or PSE security;
- the exposure and the collateral are denominated in the same currency;
- the transaction is either overnight or subject to daily mark to market and revaluation;
- the transaction is documented using standard market documentation and is settled through a robust settlement system which is usually used for transactions of this type, and that documentation must provide that:
  - Close-out on failure to remargin takes place within four days of the failure;
  - The transaction is immediately terminable on any default or other failure to deliver; and
  - Upon any default the counterparty may seize and liquidate the collateral.

D. Unfunded Credit Protection

9.29 Where an entity receives unfunded credit protection (in the form of a guarantee or credit derivative), the guarantee or credit derivative must satisfy certain requirements. These are that:

(1) the guarantee must represent a direct claim on the protection provider;
(2) the guarantee must be explicitly referenced to specific exposures or a specific pool of exposures, so that the extent of the cover is clearly defined and incontrovertible;

---

[4] In other words, if the supervisor in country A permits its banks to use a 0 per cent H in their repo transactions in A's repo market, the supervisor in country B may permit its banks to do the same in respect of trades on A's repo market, regardless of whether the regulator in country B permits its banks to use 0 per cent H in its own repo market.

(3) unless the protection purchaser (ie the bank) does not pay its consideration, the contract must be irrevocable;

(4) there must be no clause in the contract that would allow the protection provider to unilaterally cancel the contract or that would increase the effective cost of cover as a result of the deteriorating credit quality of the hedged exposure;

(5) the contract must be unconditional; there should be no clause outside the direct control of the bank which could prevent the protection provider from being obliged to pay out in a timely manner in the event that the original counterparty fails to make the payment(s) due;

(6) on the qualifying default/non-payment of the counterparty, the bank must be able to call on the guarantee without the need to commence legal action against the counterparty for payment; and

(7) for a bank to take advantage of the full risk mitigation offered by the guarantee, the guarantee must cover all unpaid obligations of the counterparty. If only certain payments are covered then the guarantee can only be used to mitigate part of the risk.

In addition to the operational requirements, Basel II also requires that eligible guarantors must be rated A- or better and have a lower risk weighting than the original counterparty (Basel II, paragraph 195). Further, under Basel II, paragraph 118, there is a minimum standard of legal certainty that applies to all credit risk mitigation techniques. The requirements for legal certainty, in so far as they apply to the Policy, are as follows:

- the credit risk mitigation instrument must be binding on all parties; and
- the credit risk mitigation instrument must be legally enforceable in all relevant jurisdictions.

A similar set of criteria are in place with respect to credit derivatives. These are **9.30** that:

(a) The credit events specified by the contracting parties must at a minimum cover:

   (i) failure to pay the amounts due under terms of the underlying obligation that are in effect at the time of such failure (with a grace period that is closely in line with the grace period in the underlying obligation);

   (ii) bankruptcy, insolvency or inability of the obligor to pay its debts, or its failure or admission in writing of its inability generally to pay its debts as they become due, and analogous events; and

   (iii) restructuring of the underlying obligation involving forgiveness or postponement of principal, interest or fees that results in a credit loss event (ie charge-off, specific provision or other similar debit to the profit and loss account).

(b) If the credit derivative covers obligations that do not include the underlying obligation, section (g) below governs whether the asset mismatch is permissible.

(c) The credit derivative shall not terminate prior to expiration of any grace period required for a default on the underlying obligation to occur as a result of a failure to pay.

(d) Credit derivatives allowing for cash settlement are recognized for capital purposes insofar as a robust valuation process is in place in order to estimate loss reliably. There must be a clearly specified period for obtaining post-credit event valuations of the underlying obligation. If the reference obligation specified in the credit derivative for purposes of cash settlement is different than the underlying obligation, section (g) below governs whether the asset mismatch is permissible.

(e) If the protection purchaser's right/ability to transfer the underlying obligation to the protection provider is required for settlement, the terms of the underlying obligation must provide that any required consent to such transfer may not be unreasonably withheld.

(f) The identity of the parties responsible for determining whether a credit event has occurred must be clearly defined. This determination must not be the sole responsibility of the protection seller. The protection buyer must have the right/ability to inform the protection provider of the occurrence of a credit event.

(g) A mismatch between the underlying obligation and the reference obligation under the credit derivative (ie the obligation used for purposes of determining cash settlement value or the deliverable obligation) is permissible if (1) the reference obligation ranks pari passu with or is junior to the underlying obligation, and (2) the underlying obligation and reference obligation share the same obligor (ie the same legal entity) and legally enforceable cross-default or cross-acceleration clauses are in place.

(h) A mismatch between the underlying obligation and the obligation used for purposes of determining whether a credit event has occurred is permissible if (1) the latter obligation ranks pari passu with or is junior to the underlying obligation, and (2) the underlying obligation and reference obligation share the same obligor (ie the same legal entity) and legally enforceable cross-default or cross-acceleration clauses are in place.

9.31 When the restructuring of the underlying obligation is not covered by the credit derivative, but the other requirements are met, partial recognition of the credit derivative will be allowed. If the amount of the credit derivative is less than or equal to the amount of the underlying obligation, 60 per cent of the amount of the hedge can be recognized as covered. If the amount of the credit derivative is larger than that of the underlying obligation, then the amount of eligible hedge is capped at 60 per cent of the amount of the underlying obligation.

Effect of unfunded credit protection

Where these requirements are satisfied, the treatment which is applied is that the **9.32** protected portion of the exposure is assigned the risk weighting of the protection provider. The uncovered portion remains attributable to the underlying counterparty, and is weighted accordingly. Thus, no haircuts are applied unless there is a currency mismatch between the underlying obligation and the protection. Where there is a currency mismatch, the amount of the exposure deemed to be protected will be reduced by the appropriate haircut—for a bank using the standard supervisory haircuts this will be 8 per cent, but a bank which uses its own models to generate haircuts will be permitted to use the output of those models for this purpose. The haircuts are scaled up using the square root of time formula depending on the frequency of revaluation.

Where there is a maturity mismatch between the asset protected and the protec- **9.33** tion contract (ie where the protection has a shorter duration than the asset protected), the following hierarchy applies:

(a) If the original maturity of the exposure was less than one year, a mismatching hedge will not be recognized.
(b) If the residual maturity of the hedged exposure is less than three months, a mismatched hedge will not be recognized.
(c) If the residual maturity of the protection is between one and five years, the value of the hedge will be reduced by a formula. Thus the value protected will be taken to be:
$$P \times (t - 0.25)/(T - 0.25)$$
   Where:
   t is the residual maturity of the protection in years (or T, if lower) and
   T is the residual maturity of the exposure in years (or five years, if lower).
(d) If the residual maturity of the protection is more than five years, the mismatch will be disregarded.

Where any protection contract includes a materiality threshold below which no **9.34** payment is due under the protection, that materiality threshold will be treated as a first loss piece and is required to be deducted from capital by the bank purchasing the protection.

Multiple default credit derivatives

A first to default credit derivative is a credit derivative written on a basket of assets **9.35** under which the protection buyer receives a payment on the default of any asset in the basket. Conventionally such derivatives pay out only once—if there is a second or a third default in the basket, no further payment will be made. For these arrangements, the bank may recognize the derivative by assuming that the derivative covers the asset in the basket with the highest regulatory capital charge, provided that the notional amount payable under the derivative is greater than or equal to the value of the asset. For the bank providing the protection, if the product has an external credit assessment from an eligible credit assessment institution, the risk weight applied to securitization tranches will be applied. If the product is not rated by an eligible external credit assessment institution, the risk weights of the assets included in the basket will be aggregated up to a maximum of 1250 per cent and multiplied by the nominal amount of the protection provided by the credit derivative to obtain the risk-weighted asset amount.

9.36 A similar treatment is applied to second-to-default derivatives—that is, derivatives where the second default among the assets within the basket triggers the credit protection. In this case the bank obtaining credit protection through such a product will not be able to recognize any capital relief (unless first-default-protection has also been obtained or when one of the assets within the basket has already defaulted). For banks providing credit protection through such a product, the capital treatment is the same as for a first to default product, except that the asset with the lowest risk-weighted amount can be excluded from the calculation.

Part III

INVESTMENT BANKING

10

THE TRADING BOOK

A. Introduction

Market risk was a relative latecomer to the Basel framework—although the original **10.01** Accord was signed in 1988, it was only in 1996 that the amendment to incorporate market risks was implemented. The original Accord dealt only with credit risk: the working assumption being that bank assets would typically be loans. In strict theory, of course, all financial assets are credit assets; the point being that a person who has lent £100 to company X is, in credit terms, in the same position as a person who owns a £100 security issued by company X. However—again in strict theory—the difference is that whereas the owner of the loan is obliged to wait until it is repaid, the owner of the security will be able to sell it. This means that whereas the owner of the loan is exposed to the whole risk of the creditor for the whole period of the loan, the owner of the security is exposed primarily to the market for the securities for the period that it would take him to find a buyer in the market for the security. The holder of the security is still, of course, exposed to the credit risk of the issuer, since if the issuer suddenly defaults the amount recovered by the security holder will be the same as the amount recovered by the lender. However, whereas the lender may have a multi-year risk exposure, the security holder is treated as having an exposure measured in days.

10.02 In the simplified terms of Basle I (which tended to regard all exposures of less than one year as credit risk free) this meant that the credit risk inherent in securities could be disregarded. This did not, of course, mean that securities were risk free. What it did mean was that the risk inherent in a security was not the credit risk of the issuer but the risk of the market moving against the holder of the security before he could sell it. For market securities, therefore, the measure of risk was an approximation to the risk of the market in which the security was traded. This meant that this risk could be subdivided in two—*specific risk*, or the risk that the price of the specific security would move, and *general market risk*, or the risk that the whole market would move, taking the security with it. More importantly, it meant that the risk on market securities was substantially less than the risk on credit exposures, since the likelihood of the market for a particular security dropping to zero over a short period was clearly much less than the likelihood of a creditor failing to repay over a long exposure period. The trading book therefore became the preferred place to hold any asset which could be held in eligible (ie tradable security) form.

10.03 The inclusion of assets in the trading book has a further advantage for banks. In general netting in the banking book may only be recognized within broad limits, and hedging is not recognized other than within the collateral framework. Thus, in the banking book a firm which held securities issued by an issuer but had a matching short position in those securities would be required to take a full capital charge on the securities without taking the short position into account. In the trading book, however, the risk charge is applied to net trading positions—that is, positions which have been calculated taking into account any relevant long and short positions in the same underlying security or exposure. Thus, a large long and an equally large short in the same securities may result in almost no risk capital charge being applied to either position. It is worth noting that trading book offset is an entirely different thing from netting. In the trading book, a long position arising under a derivative with A can be set off against a short position with B, despite the fact that the two positions could not be legally netted. Conversely, a long position in security X with A cannot be netted against a short position in security Y with A, even if the two arise under a single netting arrangement. Credit risk exposure to A is calculated on the basis of the net value, but the two positions both attract a separate market risk charge.

10.04 One of the biggest single issues in regulatory capital regulation has therefore been for some years the question of which exposures could be held in the trading book. This is a question to which the answer was (and is) surprisingly unclear. The core test is straightforward—as Basel II says:

> A trading book consists of positions in financial instruments and commodities held either with trading intent or in order to hedge other elements of the trading book. To be eligible for trading book capital treatment, financial instruments must either be

free of any restrictive covenants on their tradability or able to be hedged completely. In addition, positions should be frequently and accurately valued, and the portfolio should be actively managed.[1]

For this purpose a 'financial instrument' is any contract that gives rise to both a financial asset of one entity and a financial liability or equity instrument of another entity, whether cash or derivative. The definition of 'trading intent' includes positions:

> 'held intentionally for short-term resale and/or with the intent of benefiting from actual or expected short-term price movements or to lock in arbitrage profits, and may include for example proprietary positions, positions arising from client servicing (eg matched principal broking) and market making.'[2]

These rules, although useful at a high level of generality, do not help much with **10.05** specific cases. Can a listed bond issued by a minor corporate and known to be completely illiquid be held within a trading book? How about hedge fund units; structured notes, tailored derivatives or other structures? Although some of these issues were considered at the Basel level, it was felt that there was little to be gained by becoming more prescriptive on the issue. The position therefore remained (and remains) that responsibility for writing detailed rules on eligibility for trading book has been passed back to the regulated firms. Banks are required to have a clearly defined trading book policy for determining which exposures to include in, and to exclude from, the trading book.

The development in this area which was new to Basel II was an attempt to indicate **10.06** the sorts of criteria which such policies should include. For reasons given above, at the time when Basel II was finalized the pressure on regulated firms to hold assets in their trading books was substantial, and was by no means always effectively resisted. Consequently a list of criteria were identified which banks should have regard to in drafting and implementing their trading book admission policies. These are:

- The activities the bank considers to be trading and as constituting part of the trading book for regulatory capital purposes.
- The extent to which an exposure can be marked to market daily by reference to an active, liquid two-way market.
- For exposures that are marked to model, the extent to which the bank can:
  - identify the material risks of the exposure;

---

[1] Paragraph 686 of the Accord.
[2] Paragraph 687 of the Accord.

- hedge the material risks of the exposure and the extent to which hedging instruments would have an active, liquid two-way market;
- derive reliable estimates for the key assumptions and parameters used in the model.

- The extent to which the bank can and is required to generate valuations for the exposure that can be validated externally in a consistent manner.
- The extent to which legal restrictions or other operational requirements would impede the bank's ability to effect an immediate liquidation of the exposure.
- The extent to which the bank is required to, and can, actively risk manage the exposure within its trading operations.
- The extent to which the bank may transfer risk or exposures between the banking and the trading books and criteria for such transfers.[3]

These points were supplemented by a series of criteria to be applied in deciding whether any individual position should receive trading book treatment:

- Clearly documented trading strategy for the position/instrument or portfolios, approved by senior management (which would include expected holding horizon).
- Clearly defined policies and procedures for the active management of the position, which must include:
  - positions are managed on a trading desk;
  - position limits are set and monitored for appropriateness;
  - dealers have the autonomy to enter into/manage the position within agreed limits and according to the agreed strategy;
  - positions are marked to market at least daily and when marking to model the parameters must be assessed on a daily basis;
  - positions are reported to senior management as an integral part of the institution's risk management process; and
  - positions are actively monitored with reference to market information sources (assessment should be made of the market liquidity or the ability to hedge positions or the portfolio risk profiles). This would include assessing the quality and availability of market inputs to the valuation process, level of market turnover, sizes of positions traded in the market, etc.
- Clearly defined policy and procedures to monitor the positions against the bank's trading strategy including the monitoring of turnover and stale positions in the bank's trading book.[4]

---

[3] Paragraph 687 of the Accord.
[4] Paragraph 688 of the Accord.

A final quirk in relation to the trading book is that banks frequently hedge through **10.07** their trading book positions held in their banking book. This works well for foreign exchange hedges, where exposure is calculated across the entire bank position. However, for exposures which are calculated differently in the banking and trading books (notably credit), it is necessary to create an 'imaginary' derivative between the banking and trading book in order to reflect the effect of such hedging (in effect, the trading book leg of the derivative cancels out the external positions taken on, and the positions are treated as hedged in the banking book. The existence of this 'imaginary' derivative caused some banks to wonder whether such derivatives could be put on without an external leg, so that the hedge between the banking and trading book could be given effect as if it were a real transaction. Not surprisingly, this idea is scotched in the Accord—the existence of the imaginary derivative is affirmed, but it can only qualify as credit protection in the banking book if it is backed up with identical protection purchased from third party protection sellers in the trading book.

B. Trading and Market Exposures

Position risk requirement

The key to market risk is the calculation of position risk requirement (PRR). **10.08** A firm must calculate a PRR in respect of:

- all its trading book positions;
- all foreign exchange positions, including those arising out of banking commitments (such as guarantees in foreign currencies) which may give rise to currency exposures. This must be calculated regardless of whether the exposure is a banking book or a trading book exposure; and
- all positions in commodities (including physical commodities) whether or not in the trading book.

A firm must be able to monitor its total PRR on an intra-day basis. This does not require a real-time information system—PRR is in practice generally controlled on an intra-day basis by setting position limits for individual books.

There are no fewer than six different PRR calculations: **10.09**

(1) Interest rate PRR (includes debt securities).
(2) Equity PRR.
(3) Commodity PRR.
(4) Foreign currency PRR.
(5) Option PRR.
(6) Collective investment undertaking PRR.

Where an instrument does not fall neatly within any of these approaches, the approach to be used is the existing approach which is most closely analogous to it. A firm is not required to use these, and it may use a different system, provided that it can demonstrate that the output of that system is in all circumstances higher than the PRR which would be applied. If the firm is unable to perform this calculation, the ultimate fallback is to a percentage of exposure approach—the percentage being 100 per cent unless a lower value can be agreed with the supervisor.

Interest rate PRR

10.10   The interest rate PRR is likely to constitute the largest component of any bank's PRR, as the greatest market exposure that such banks are likely to have will be in the debt securities market. However, interest rate PRR goes well beyond fixed income securities, and includes:

- futures, forwards or synthetic futures on debt securities;
- futures, forwards or synthetic futures on debt indices or baskets;
- interest rate futures or forward rate agreements (FRAs);
- interest rate swaps or foreign currency swaps;
- deferred start interest rate swaps or foreign currency swaps;
- the interest rate leg of an equity swap (unless the firm uses the basic interest rate PRR calculation for equity derivatives);
- the cash leg of a repurchase agreement or a reverse repurchase agreement;
- cash borrowings or deposits;
- options on a debt security, a basket of debt securities, a debt security index, an interest rate or an interest rate future or swap (including an option on a future on a debt security) (unless the firm calculates a PRR on the option using the option PRR method);
- dual currency bonds;
- foreign currency futures or forwards;
- gold futures or forwards;
- forwards, futures or options (except cliquets) on an equity, basket of equities or equity index unless the firm uses the basic method);
- credit derivatives.

10.11   A firm calculates its interest rate PRR by taking each position that it has in the trading book—whether long or short—and calculating a net position. Derivative and other positions which give rise to interest rate exposure are converted into notional positions in a hypothetical debt security, and positions in such hypothetical securities may be netted off against actual securities. Thus, if a firm has a physical long position in a security and a hypothetical short position of the same size arising out of a derivative, its net position for this purpose will be treated as being zero.

The interest rate PRR calculation divides interest rate risk into the risk of loss from a general move in market interest rates, and the risk of loss from an individual debt security's price changing for reasons other than a general move in market interest rates. These are called general market risk and specific risk respectively. Once the notional positions have been established, two calculations are made for each individual position; the interest rate PRR calculation for general market risk and the interest rate PRR calculation for specific risk. Once these calculations have been made, the totals are added together to establish the total interest rate risk PRR. **10.12**

All net positions, whether long or short, must be converted on a daily basis into the firm's base currency at the prevailing spot exchange rate before their aggregation, and the firm must calculate the capital requirement for general market risk and specific risk in each individual currency separately. **10.13**

A firm's interest rate PRR calculation must include all trading book positions in debt securities, preference shares and convertibles, except for positions in convertibles which have been included in the firm's equity PRR calculation; positions which have already been deducted from capital, or positions which hedge options. It must also include securities which belong to the firm but which have been lent or repo'd (although not securities which have been borrowed and then relent, or reverse repo'd and then repo'd, since these are not regarded as belonging to the firm for this purpose). **10.14**

An alternative (and simplified) method of calculating interest rate PRR is provided within the equity rules. This is the basic interest rate PRR calculation, and is generally used by firms whose trading business is confined mainly or exclusively to equity business, and who find themselves exposed to interest rate risk in their trading books because of the interest rate leg of equity swaps. Equity derivatives are excluded from the interest rate PRR calculation if they have been included in the basic interest rate PRR calculation.[5] **10.15**

The approach to calculation is the same for all instruments—they are converted into notional positions in: **10.16**

(1) the underlying debt security, where the instrument depends on the price (or yield) of a specific debt security; or

(2) notional debt securities to capture the pure interest rate risk arising from future payments and receipts of cash (including notional payments and

---

[5] See para 10.39 below.

receipts) which, because they are designed to represent pure general market risk (and not specific risk), are called zero-specific-risk securities; or

(3) both (1) and (2).

10.17 Notional positions in actual debt securities must be valued as the nominal amount underlying the contract at the current market price of the debt security; and positions in zero-specific-risk securities must be valued using either a present value approach (under which the zero-specific-risk security is assigned a value equal to the present value of all the future cash flows that it represents); or, if this cannot be calculated, the notional principal amount.

Position netting

10.18 As noted above, PRRs are charged on net positions in the trading book. A firm must not net positions (including notional positions) unless those positions are in the same debt security. This requirement is strictly construed—securities are only treated as being capable of being netted against each other if they enjoy the same rights in all respects; and are fungible with each other. Thus identical securities which are not fungible cannot be netted for this purpose. There is a wrinkle here, as where securities are issued as part of a 'tap' of an existing issue, it may take some time before the new securities become fungible with the existing securities. Positions may therefore be netted where securities are not immediately fungible but will become fungible within 180 days and thereafter the debt security of one tranche can be delivered in settlement of the other tranche.

10.19 The reason for this strictness may not be immediately apparent—after all, if securities are functionally identical why should opposite positions not be offsettable? The reason is that although such an economic match may eliminate credit risk, it does not eliminate market risk. If I am entitled to receive securities A and obliged to deliver securities B, then I am exposed to market risk on B since when my obligation to deliver falls due I will not be able to deliver unless I can buy B in the market. The fact that I will own securities A is, for this purpose, irrelevant.

10.20 This analysis becomes more complex for credit derivatives. Where a firm's position in a security arises out of a credit derivative, it does not know precisely which security will be delivered under the derivative. This is because the protection seller under a credit derivative is entitled to deliver whatever security is, at the time of settlement, the cheapest security to obtain and deliver. The position of the two parties is therefore asymmetrical. A protection seller has a notional short position in the cheapest to deliver security. However, he is not required to deliver that security, but may elect to deliver any security which is deliverable under the CDS. Thus, a long position in any security which is deliverable under the CDS may be set off against the short position created by the CDS. A protection buyer, however, cannot set off the long position which he has in the cheapest to deliver security against any other position, since he can never say that the two positions are 'the same' as he does not know what the cheapest to deliver security will be.

Where a firm enters into a derivative or other contract which creates a pure expo- **10.21** sure to interest rates (such as a rate derivative), the position is taken into the trading book by being deemed to be a position in a 'zero-specific-risk security'—in other words, an imaginary security issued by a risk-free issuer with a term and a yield equal to that which has been bought or sold under the derivative. Firms which deal heavily in the interest rate markets amass very large positions in these imaginary securities. Such positions can be netted like any other position, but zero specific risk security positions may only be netted if:

(1) they are denominated in the same currency;
(2) their coupons do not differ by more than 15 basis points; and
(3) they mature:
    (a) on the same day, if they have residual maturities of less than one month;
    (b) within seven days of each other, if they have residual maturities of between one month and one year; and
    (c) within 30 days of each other, if they have residual maturities in excess of one year.

Notional legs

Futures, forwards and similar contracts on debt securities involve the creation of **10.22** a notional leg. This 'leg' is similar to that of Miss Kilmansegg in that it is entirely imaginary. It therefore requires a word of explanation.

When a firm buys a future on a debt security, it agrees to pay money in the future **10.23** in exchange for the delivery of a debt security. This gives it a notional long position in the relevant debt security which, as we have seen, can be netted off against short positions in arriving at the total interest rate PRR. However, a method must be found for reflecting the price which it will pay for that security. This is done by pretending that the firm has a short position in a zero-coupon zero-specific risk security with a maturity equal to the expiry date of the future. The point here is that a zero-coupon security is simply a right to receive a sum of money at a future time, and a short position in a zero-coupon security is simply an obligation to pay money at a future time. For a seller of a future the position is simply reversed—the seller is treated as having a short position in the security to be delivered, and a long position in a zero-coupon zero-specific risk instrument reflecting that amount which will be received on the exercise of the future.

The reason for introducing the notional security concept is that the security so **10.24** introduced enables the payment obligation to be valued—it is simply the amount discounted by the risk-free return rate over the period to maturity. Thus, all derivatives can be reduced to positions in securities. Basket derivatives may be either reduced to a series of derivatives on individual underlying securities, or treated as exposures to a single notional security having the repayment characteristics of the basket and a specific risk PRA and a general market risk PRA equal to the highest that would apply to the debt securities in the basket or index.

10.25 This simple but powerful technique can be used to disassemble complex trades including forward rate agreements, interest rate swaps, options, and swaptions. For trades where one leg is an interest rate swap (ie equity swaps and the forward cash legs of repo and reverse repo agreements), that leg must be converted into a notional position in a zero-specific risk security. A cash borrowing or deposit must be treated as a notional position in a zero coupon zero-specific-risk security which has a value, coupon and maturity equal to the market value of the borrowing or deposit.

Specific risk

10.26 The specific risk portion of the interest rate PRR for each debt security is calculated by multiplying the market value of the individual net position (long or short) by the appropriate PRA from Table 10.1.

Table 10.1 Position Risk Adjustments

Debt securities issued or guaranteed by central governments, issued by central banks, international organizations, multilateral development banks or EEA States' regional governments or local authorities which would qualify for credit quality step 1 or which would receive a 0% risk weight under the standardized approach to credit risk.		0%
(A) Debt securities issued or guaranteed by central governments, issued by central banks, international organizations, multilateral development banks or EEA States' regional governments or local authorities which would qualify for credit quality step 2 or 3 under the standardized approach to credit risk.	Zero to six months	0.25%
(B) Debt securities issued or guaranteed by institutions which would qualify for credit quality step 1 or 2 under the standardized approach to credit risk.	Over 6 and up to and including 24 months	1%
(C) Debt securities issued or guaranteed by an institution which would qualify for credit quality step 3 or which would do so if it had an original effective maturity of three months or less.		
(D) Debt securities issued or guaranteed by corporates which would qualify for credit quality step 1 or 2 under the standardized approach to credit risk.	Over 24 months	1.6%
(E) Other qualifying debt securities.		

(A) Debt securities issued or guaranteed by central governments, issued by central banks, international organizations, multilateral development banks or EEA States' regional governments or local authorities or institutions which would qualify for credit quality step 4 or 5 under the standardized approach to credit risk. (B) Debt securities issued or guaranteed by corporates which would qualify for credit quality step 3 or 4 under the standardized approach to credit risk. (C) Exposures for which a credit assessment by a nominated ECAI is not available.	8%
(A) Debt securities issued or guaranteed by central governments issued by central banks, international organizations, multilateral development banks or EEA States' regional governments or local authorities or institution which would qualify for credit quality step 6 under the standardized approach to credit risk. (B) Debt securities issued or guaranteed by corporate which would qualify for credit quality step 5 or 6 under the standardized approach to credit risk. (C) An instrument that shows a particular risk because of the insufficient solvency of the issuer of liquidity. This paragraph applies even if the instrument would otherwise qualify for a lower PRA under this table.	12%

10.27 There are two important points to note about Table 10.1. One is that for the purposes of this analysis, the classification of debt securities must be performed using the criteria set out in the standardized approach, even by IRB banks (it will be recalled that the classification of exposures differs slightly between the standardized and the IRB approaches). The second is that there is something of a chasm between the treatments afforded for 'qualifying debt securities' and other debt securities. In practice the issue of whether a security can be classified as a qualifying debt security or not is of very great significance as regards the position of investors in that security. A debt security is a qualifying debt security if:

(1) it is rated as investment grade[6]; or
(2) it has a PD which, because of the solvency of the issuer, is at least equivalent to investment grade; or
(3) it is a debt security for which a credit rating by a nominated ECAI is unavailable but which:
    (a) is considered by the bank to be sufficiently liquid;
    (b) is considered by the bank to be investment grade; and
    (c) is listed on at least one regulated market or designated investment exchange; or
(4) is issued by a bank or investment firm subject to Basel-like supervision and is considered by the bank to be at least investment grade.

---

[6] Roughly 'credit quality step 3'—that is, rated Baa or higher by Moody's and BBB by S&P.

General market risk

10.28 The general market risk portion of the interest rate PRR for each currency is calculated using one of three methods:

(1) the interest rate simplified maturity method;
(2) the interest rate maturity method; or
(3) the interest rate duration method.

The interest rate simplified maturity method weights individual net positions to reflect their price sensitivity to changes in interest rates. The weights are related to the coupon and the residual maturity of the instrument (or the next interest rate re-fix date for floating rate items). Under the interest rate simplified maturity method, the portion of the interest rate PRR for general market risk equals the sum of each individual net position (long or short) multiplied by the appropriate PRA, which may vary from 0 per cent to 12.5 per cent according to coupon and duration.

The interest rate maturity method builds on the interest rate simplified maturity method by partially recognizing offsetting positions.

The interest rate duration method produces a more accurate measure of interest rate risk than the maturity methods but it is also more complex to calculate. Details of the calculation mechanism may be found in paras 718(i) to 718(vii) of the Accord.

C. Equity PRR and Basic Interest Rate PRR for Equity Derivatives

10.29 A firm calculates its equity requirement in much the same way as it calculates its interest rate requirement—that is, it calculates a net position in each equity, applying one of two methods: the simplified equity method or the standard equity method. A firm does not have to use the same method for all equities, and may mix the two. The results for each position are then added together to give a total capital requirement. The mechanism used to determine which securities should be treated as being within the trading book calculation for this purpose are the same as those for debt securities.

10.30 Instruments which result in notional positions in equities include:

• depository receipts;
• convertibles where:
  (a) the convertible is trading at a market price of less than 110 per cent of the underlying equity; and the first date at which conversion can take place is

less than three months ahead, or the next such date (where the first has passed) is less than a year ahead; or

(b) the conditions in (a) are not met but the firm includes the convertible in its equity PRR calculation rather than including it in its interest rate PRR calculation;

- futures, forwards, CFDs and synthetic futures on a single equity;

- futures, forwards, CFDs and synthetic futures on a basket of equities or equity index;

- equity legs of an equity swap;

- options or warrants on a single equity, an equity future, a basket of equities or an equity index.

Unless specified otherwise, the value of each notional equity position equals the quantity of that equity underlying the instrument multiplied by the current market value of the equity. Thus, for example, if a share is valued at 250p and a firm goes short of the share by agreeing to sell it in five years' time for 300p, the value of the position is 250p. The risk inherent in the term of the transaction (five years) will be captured by the creation of a notional position in a zero-coupon security which will be captured in the calculation of the interest rate PRR.   **10.31**

A depository receipt is treated as a notional position in the underlying equity. A convertible is also treated as a position in the equity into which it converts. However, since this price may well show a profit or loss on the current value of the convertible, the value of such profits or losses is added to (for losses) or subtracted from (for profits) the firm's equity PRR. As with debt securities, a position in a derivative linked to an index may be treated as a position in a single composite instrument—however, such trades are significantly more common in the equity world.   **10.32**

Where a firm has entered into a swap under whose terms it will either pay or receive the value of an equity, this leg of the swap will be treated as a long or short (as appropriate) position in the underlying equity. The same applies for swaps which reference equity baskets or equity indices.   **10.33**

Standard equity method

The standard equity method divides the risk of loss from a firm's equity positions into the risk of loss from a general move in a country's equity market and the risk of loss from an individual equity's price changing relative to that country's equity market. These are called 'general market risk' and 'specific risk' respectively. Under the standard equity method, a firm must group equity positions into country portfolios and then add the PRRs for specific risk and the PRRs for general market risk for each country portfolio.   **10.34**

Standard equity model—specific risk

10.35 The specific risk calculation is performed by multiplying the net position in each equity, equity index or equity basket, and by multiplying its market value (long or short) by the appropriate PRA from the table.

Qualifying equities	2%
Qualifying equity indices	0%
All other equities, equity indices or equities baskets	4%

10.36 The rule for being a qualifying equity is obscure. In principle, any equity which is a constituent of a main index (in the UK, the FTSE All Share) may be a qualifying equity. However, an equity ceases to be a qualifying equity if either: (a) the issuer has issued debt securities all of which are credit quality step 1, 2 or 3; or (b) it forms too large a component of the country portfolio held by the reporting firm. What this latter test means in practice is that if an equity forms more than 10 per cent of the country portfolio held by that firm it ceases to be a qualifying equity. For these purposes, a qualifying equity index is any index which is composed of equities traded on a main exchange, and is constructed in such a way that:

(a) it contains at least 20 equities;
(b) no single equity represents more than 20 per cent of the total index; and
(c) no five equities combined represent more than 60 per cent of the total index.

Standard equity method—general market risk

10.37 The basic rule for the equity method is that general market risk is the net value (ignoring the sign) of each separate country portfolio multiplied by 8 per cent. This is the 'first method'.

10.38 The FSA permits different country portfolios to be netted off against each other—this approach is known as the 'second method'.[7] It is permissible only in respect of country portfolios which includes at least four OECD member country portfolios, where no individual country portfolio comprises more than 30 per cent of the total gross value of country portfolios included; and the total net value of country portfolios included is zero. At first glance this appears almost irrelevant, since no trading position of this complexity will ever net out to precisely zero except by accident. However, what this rule means in practice is that a reporting firm may select parts of its equity trading portfolio which do net out in this way, treat them as separate country portfolios, and apply this treatment to them.

---

[7] BIPRU 7.3.42.

This will leave the firm with a net zero position treated under this method, and a number of non-zero positions which will each be weighted using the first method. The capital charge which is applied under the second method is calculated using a 'sum of the squares' approach. This results in a significantly smaller weighting for the totality of the positions concerned than would be obtained under the first method.

Simplified equity interest rate PRR

Equity transactions may give rise to interest rate exposure—for example under **10.39** equity forward, future or option calculations. A firm which uses an interest rate risk PRR calculation is permitted to use that calculation in respect of the interest rate component of equity trades. However, there are a number of equity trading firms which do not have the systems in place to calculate interest PRR. Consequently the equity trading rules contain a simplified interest rate PRR calculation which can be used by such firms. This calculation is deliberately calibrated to give a higher capital charge than would be obtained under the interest rate PRR method, largely since it does not permit the offsetting of long and short interest rate positions.

The simplified equity approach may only be applied to a forward, future, option **10.40** or swap on an equity, basket of equities or equity index. It is simply that the market value of the notional equity position underlying the instrument is multiplied by the amount in the table. The results are summed, ignoring the sign, and the balance will be the interest rate risk charge.

0 to 3 months	0.2%
3 to 6 months	0.4%
6 to 12 months	0.7%
1 to 2 years	1.25%
2 to 3 years	1.75%
3 to 4 years	2.25%
4 to 5 years	2.75%
5 to 7 years	3.25%
7 to 10 years	3.75%
10 to 15 years	4.50%
15 to 20 years	5.25%
20 years	6.00%

Finally, a firm is required to take a further risk charge where it nets a position in a **10.41** specific equity against a position held synthetically under equity index future, forward, or contract for differences ('CFD'). This charge is intended to reflect the risk that the index might not move fully in line with the prices of its components. The effect of this is that where a firm holds an equity index future and is short of a basket of equities which exactly replicate that index, the position will not net precisely to zero since this charge will still be incurred. The same applies if a firm holds opposite positions in a future, forward or CFD on an equity index that are not identical in respect of either their maturity or their composition or both.

D. Commodity PRR

10.42 Commodity PRRs are calculated in much the same way as other PRRs. A firm's commodity PRR calculation must be performed over the firm's entire commodity position, regardless of whether the position is a trading book or non-trading book positions. Clearly all physical commodity positions must be included, even if they are lent or repo'd, and conversely such positions need not be included if they are held as part of a repo or stock lending transaction.

10.43 For this purpose gold is regarded as a currency and not a commodity—consequently gold positions are treated under the foreign exchange position risk requirement ('FX PRR').

10.44 An issue which is particularly important for commodities is that there is a separate PRR calculation provided for options. Many commodity trades are in the form of options, and the issue is therefore whether they should be treated under the commodity PRR rules or under the option PRR rules. (A warrant relating to an investment must be treated as an option on that investment.) The broad answer is that where an option or warrant has a substantial in the money value, the reporting institution may choose whether to apply the option PRR or the relevant underlying PRR (in the case of a commodity warrant, the commodity PRR). However, where the option or warrant has negligible in the money value, the option PRR must be applied. Clearly the simplest approach administratively is to apply the option PRR to all option positions, since this avoids the requirement for periodic reclassification. However, the application of the option method generally results in a higher capital charge than the application of the other methods, and as a result performing this exercise may well be justified.

10.45 The synthetic positions which are required to be treated as commodity positions are:

- forwards, futures, CFDs, synthetic futures and options on a single commodity;
- a commitment to buy or sell a single commodity at an average of spot prices prevailing over some future period;
- forwards, futures, CFDs, synthetic futures, and options on a commodity index Commodity swaps.

The approach which is adopted for calculating the commodity PRR is: express **10.46** each relevant commodity position in terms of whatever the standard unit of measurement of the commodity concerned may be; express the spot price in each commodity in the firm's base currency at current spot foreign exchange rates; calculate an individual PRR for each commodity; and sum the resulting individual PRRs.

A forward position in a commodity is treated as having a notional value equal to **10.47** the amount of the commodity due to be delivered under the forward. Commodity index futures and commodity index options are divided into notional positions, one for each of the constituent commodities in the index. A commodity swap is treated as a series of notional positions, one for each payment under the swap.

A firm must calculate a commodity PRR for each commodity separately. There **10.48** are three approaches which can be used—the commodity simplified approach, the commodity maturity ladder approach, or the commodity extended maturity ladder approach. Different approaches may be used for different commodities, although two different approaches may not be used for the same commodity. For this purpose, each different grade or brand of a particular commodity is treated as a different commodity—thus Arabica coffee is treated as a different commodity from Robusta. This can sometimes be a difficult distinction to make—the FSA has provided guidance that different types of a commodity should only be regarded as the same if either: (a) they can be delivered against each other; or (b) they are close substitutes and have price movements which have exhibited a stable correlation coefficient of at least 0.9 over the last 12 months.[8] A firm seeking to rely on the latter must monitor the correlation, and cease to treat the commodities as the same if the relationship relied upon breaks down.

The simplified approach

The simplified approach involves establishing a net position in the commodity **10.49** concerned, and applying a weighting of 15 per cent of the net position multiplied by the spot price for the commodity; plus 3 per cent of the gross position (long plus short, ignoring the sign) multiplied by the spot price for the commodity.

The maturity ladder approach

A firm must use a separate maturity ladder for each commodity. The calculation **10.50** is done in a series of steps:

Step 1: offset long and short positions maturing within 10 business days of each other.

---

[8] BIPRU 7.4.22.

Step 2: allocate the positions remaining after step 1 to the appropriate maturity band in the table below (physical commodity positions are allocated to band 1).

Step 3: match long and short positions within each band. In each instance, calculate a spread charge equal to the matched amount multiplied first by the spot price for the commodity and then by the spread rate of 3 per cent.

Step 4: carry unmatched positions remaining after step 3 to another band where they can be matched, then match them. Do this until all matching possibilities are exhausted. Each time a position is carried, a carry charge is applied of the value of the carried position, multiplied by the 0.6 per cent carry charge, multiplied by the number of 'rungs' on the ladder over which the position is carried. This charge is in addition to the spread charge, which is calculated as in step 3.

Step 5: for any remaining unmatched positions, calculate the outright charge on the remaining positions. The outright charge equals the remaining position (ignoring the sign) multiplied by the spot price for the commodity and the outright rate of 15 per cent.

Band 1	0 to 1 month
Band 2	1 month to 3 months
Band 3	3 months to 6 months
Band 4	6 months to 1 year
Band 5	1 year to 2 years
Band 6	2 years to 3 years
Band 7	3 years

The extended maturity ladder approach

10.51 The extended maturity ladder approach is intended as an accommodation for large commodities firms which have a diversified commodities portfolio but which do not yet have the systems in place to be able to satisfy the FSA's requirements for the use of VAR models. The maturity ladder itself is the same as for the maturity ladder approach, and the difference between the two approaches is simply that instead of applying a fixed outright rate of 15 per cent, carry rate of 0.6 per cent, and spread rate of 3 per cent, the firm may use the figures in the table below.

	Precious metals (ex. gold)	Base metals	Softs (agricultural commodities)	Other (including energy)
Spread rate	2%	2.4%	3%	3%
Carry rate	0.3%	0.5%	0.6%	0.6%
Outright rate	8%	10%	12%	15%

These rates are arrived at on the basis that the reporting firm has positions across a number of different commodities within each of these categories, and are lower than the rates which are applied in the other approaches since they reflect the different risks and volatilities which are likely to apply to different commodities within these categories. As a result, a firm which does not have a number of positions with differing maturities across a number of commodities within each of these categories will not be permitted to use this approach. Where a firm has a position in a multi-commodity index which cuts across these categories, it must use the highest applicable figure to the notional of the entire index.

Finally, firms are required to consider taking a further charge to reflect liquidity. **10.52** This is a particularly important issue in the commodity markets, since a long position deliverable in nine months' time is no safeguard against an obligation to make physical delivery tomorrow. Again, no specific rules are provided in respect of the calculation of such a charge.

E. Foreign Currency PRR

The calculation for foreign currency PRR is structurally similar to other PRR **10.53** calculations. A firm calculates its open currency position in each currency by:

(1) calculating the net position in each foreign currency;
(2) converting each such net position into its base currency equivalent at current spot rates;
(3) summing all short net positions and summing all long net positions calculated under (1) and (2); and
(4) selecting the larger sum (ignoring the sign) from (3).

A separate exercise is performed to establish the firm's net position in gold. Once **10.54** these positions have been established, the absolute value (regardless of whether it is long or short) of the net positions in each currency and in gold are calculated in the bank's reporting currency and added together. This figure is multiplied by 8 per cent to give a capital requirement. The foreign currency PRR calculation is performed over all currency exposures, whether in the trading or the banking book. In this context, a foreign currency exposure is created wherever an asset is held in a currency which is different from the reporting currency of the relevant bank— thus if a UK bank reporting in sterling holds a dollar denominated asset, the result is a foreign currency position which must be included in the currency PRR calculation. Clearly all spot and forward positions on gold and foreign currency must also be included in the calculation, as must foreign-currency denominated irrevocable guarantees (and similar instruments) that are certain to be called and likely to be irrecoverable. The rule on options is the same as for commodities—options with a substantial value may be treated under either method. However, swaps and other transactions which have been entered into in order fully to hedge net future foreign currency income or expenses which are known but not yet accrued are excluded from the foreign currency PRR calculation.

10.55 Where a contract is based on a basket of currencies, the firm can choose either to derive notional positions in each of the constituent currencies or treat it as a single notional position in a separate notional currency.

10.56 Although the calculation applies across the banking and trading books, there is a difference as to how it is applied. Within the banking book, a forward position in a currency is treated as having its nominal value—thus an obligation to pay $100 has a value of $100, whether the obligation falls to be performed today or in a year's time. In the trading book, by contrast, a position is valued at its present value—thus, in the trading book an obligation to pay $100 in a year's time would have a value of (say) $96. This has the effect of reducing the charge applied to the exposure in the trading book. However, this is to some degree offset by the fact that in the trading book the contract which gave rise to the obligation to pay $100 in a year's time would attract an interest rate PRR charge to reflect the implied interest rate exposure on the transaction.

10.57 A foreign currency swap is treated as long notional position in the currency in which the firm has contracted to receive interest and principal; and a short notional position in the currency in which the firm has contracted to pay interest and principal. Currency options, when included in the foreign currency PRR calculation, are treated as foreign currency forwards. A forward, future, synthetic future or CFD on gold must be treated as a notional position in gold with a value equal to the amount of gold underlying multiplied by the current spot price for gold.

10.58 It frequently happens that firms come to own units in funds which are denominated in one currency but where the investments of the fund are made in another currency. An example might be a UK, sterling-reporting fund which invests in US equities. A holding of units in such a fund is treated as a holding in the relevant foreign currency calculated on the basis that the fund has invested to the greatest extent permissible in assets denominated in the relevant foreign currency. Where a firm has an investment in a fund dedicated to more than one market, such that it does not know the exposure of the fund, it must treat the exposure as an exposure in a separate currency which cannot be netted against any other currency position.

F. Option PRR[9]

10.59 All derivatives can be decomposed into puts and calls. This is true both for OTC derivatives and for warrants and other structured securities. Consequently the

---

[9] It may be helpful to consult the Annex provided at the end of the chapter, which gives a guide to the most commonly encountered forms of option.

option PRR methodology gives the basis for the calculation of PRR for all derivatives trading.

An option is necessarily an option over something, and that something is likely to be a financial asset. The first question about any option is therefore likely to be that of whether it is to be treated as an option or as a synthetic holding in whatever the underlying asset is. When does a FTSE option cease to be a synthetic position in FTSE shares and become an option? The answer which the regulatory system applies to this question is that broadly a derivative position is an option position if its value (ie the amount by which it is 'in the money'[10]) is less than the capital charge which would apply to the underlying. If the option is: (a) heavily in the money; and (b) is a relatively simple structure (American, European, Bermudan or Asian), then the reporting institution may choose to treat the position either as an option position or as a synthetic position in the underlying asset. Complex option structures are always treated under the option method.

10.60

Firms are required to use the option PRR calculation for options which do not have a substantial value, but may elect whether to use the option method or a method based on the underlying where the option does have a substantial value. Thus, in principle a firm's option PRR calculation must include:

10.61

(1) each trading book position in an option on an equity, interest rate or debt security;

(2) each trading book position in a warrant on an equity or debt security;

(3) each trading book position in a CIU (Collective Investment Undertaking); and

(4) each trading book and non-trading book position in an option on a commodity, currency or gold, except to the extent that the firm is permitted, and has elected, to use one of the other approaches.

An option has a substantial value for this purpose if its in the money percentage is greater than the appropriate Position Risk Adjustment ('PRA'). Both of these terms require explanation. The 'in the money percentage' is simply the difference between the current market price of the underlying and the strike price of the option expressed as a percentage of the current market price. Thus, where a bank has an option to pay a strike price of 40 to acquire an asset worth 100, the in the money percentage will be 60 per cent, since that is the percentage of the value of the underlying which is embedded in the option. The 'appropriate PRA' for a position is the PRA under this regime for the relevant underlying: this is 8 per cent or 12 per cent for equities, 15 per cent for commodities and so on. For debt securities and interest rate derivatives, the appropriate PRA is the sum, of the specific

10.62

---

[10] See para 10.62 below for an explanation of 'in the money'.

market risk and the general market risk PRA. Notably, CIUs are given a PRA of 32 per cent.

10.63 In broad terms, the option method operates by converting each option into a position in the underlying notional, with positions in interest rate options converted into positions in notional zero specific risk securities with a deemed maturity date of the date of payment under the option. Interestingly, however, before making this calculation a firm may net options themselves off against each other, provided that the options concerned have the same strike price, maturity, and underlying. Firms may also treat as options trades entered into as part of a single strategy for this purpose where the transactions are entered into with the same counterparty as part of the same transaction—thus, for example, where a bank enters into a synthetic long put with a particular counterparty by buying a call option and going short of the underlying, the entire transaction may be treated as a single purchased option. This potentially opens up scope for arbitrage between the option PRR rules and other rules, and as a result the application of this rule is subject to a 'floor' provision that it may not be used to achieve a greater degree of netting than would be possible under other approaches.

The option standard method

10.64 Capital for options is relatively straightforward for purchased options—a purchased option gives rise to a long or short position in the underlying asset, and has a book value. The simplest approach is therefore to say that the capital requirement should be the PRR for the underlying asset. However, there is a problem with this approach; that being that a very large exposure can be taken on an asset through the purchase of a very cheap option. In these circumstances, the maximum exposure of the owner of the option is the value at which he is carrying the option, since the value of an option can never fall below zero, and the maximum loss to which he is exposed is the loss of the value of the option. Consequently the approach which is adopted is that the capital requirement which is applied to the owner of a written option is the lesser of: (a) the market value of the derived position multiplied by the appropriate PRA; and (b) the market value of the option. Equally, there can be circumstances in which an option has a positive net value. If I own an option whose value is positive by more than the PRA attributable to the securities concerned, then I am treated as being in a risk free position. This is because the inherent value in the option is greater than the risk charge which would be attributed to a direct holding in the underlying assets.

10.65 The position for the writer of an option is slightly more complex. In principle the writer of an option is exposed to the whole of the value of the underlying position—the writer of a put is at risk of having the underlying delivered to him, and the writer of a call is at risk of having to deliver the underlying—and so in principle the writer of an option is exposed to the full value of the underlying multiplied by the PRA. However, the chance of his having to do so is not 100 per cent, since the question of whether an option will actually be exercised or not depends on whether it is in the money or not on maturity. It is not possible to know whether any particular option will be out of the money at maturity, but a proxy can be obtained by asking whether the option is out of the money at the time when the capital calculation is made. Thus, if an option is out of the money, the PRR which is applied to its writer is the market value of the derived position multiplied by the appropriate PRA, but this amount is reduced by the amount (if any) by which the amount the option or warrant is out of the money. Thus, if a warrant is out of the money by an amount greater than the PRR of the underlying position the writer of the option does not take any capital charge in respect of the option (subject to a maximum reduction to zero).

Under the option standard method, the PRR for underwriting or sub-underwriting **10.66** an issue of warrants is the net underwriting position (or reduced net underwriting position) multiplied by the current market price of the underlying securities multiplied by the appropriate PRA, but the result can be limited to the value of the net underwriting position (or reduced net underwriting position) calculated using the issue price of the warrant.

Options are sometimes purchased or sold for the purpose of hedging a position. **10.67** Where this is done, the option may be treated as a hedge, and not under the option PRR method. Where this is done, the position is broadly that the option hedging method may only be used for the options which actually hedge another position (in other words, there must be a position in an equity, debt security or a currency which the option actually hedges). Where this is the case, the approach (in broad terms) is that instead of applying one PRR to the hedged position and another to the hedge, a single PRR is applied to both positions equal to the PRR which would apply to the one unhedged position.

Exceptions to this treatment are made for digital options (where the PRR is simply **10.68** the maximum loss of the option), Quantos (where a firm must add 8 per cent to the PRA when applying the option standard method), and cliquets (which have a separate and detailed treatment all their own—a good exposition may be found in para 7.6.30 of the FSA's BIPRU sourcebook).

Where the option methods are applied to commodities, the liquidity provision **10.69** relating to the availability of commodities for delivery must be applied to the option in the same way in which they would be applied to any other option position.

Options on funds

Options on funds (or CIUs—as they are referred to by the regulators) present **10.70** interesting problems in this context. Until relatively recently fund units would have been unlikely to be found in trading books. However, the rise of hedge fund business, and in particular prime brokerage services which offered fund unit placement, trading and liquidity provision have resulted in trading in fund units becoming a significant activity.

10.71 The basic principle is that a firm must in general treat a fund unit as a fund unit. Fund units are subject to a very high PRR of 32 per cent, which is assessed in order to reflect the fact that the holder of a fund unit generally does not know what the underlying assets and liabilities of the fund are at the time when he comes to value that unit. However, this is not of course true of all funds, and where an investor can reasonably claim to know what a fund invests in, he may be permitted to treat the holding in the fund unit as a holding in the underlying assets held by the fund. There are two ways in which this is permitted; the standard CIU method and the modified CIU method.

10.72 The basic condition which the fund must satisfy before an investor is permitted to use either of these methods are that the fund's units must be redeemable in cash out of the fund's assets on a daily basis. This of course excludes almost all hedge and other funds, since in general it is only regulated funds which will comply with this criterion. The other criteria which apply are all mandatory for regulated open-ended funds, and include segregation of assets in the hands of a separate custodian and a requirement that the fund must report at least semi-annually in such a way as to permit investors to assess compliance with these restrictions.

10.73 Needless to say a fund would not attract look-through treatment if its manager had absolute power to invest in any type of asset. Consequently, look-through is only available if the fund's prospectus restricts the categories of assets that it is authorized to invest in, the relative limits and the methodologies to calculate them, and limits on leverage and counterparty exposure.

10.74 Where a firm has full transparency into the assets of a fund into which it invests on a daily the firm may treat itself as having a position in those assets, and may calculate the securities PRR for position risk (general market risk and specific risk) for those positions in accordance with the methods set out in the securities PRR requirements or, if the firm has a VaR model permission, in accordance with the methods set out in the section on VaR models. There are two circumstances in which this may happen. One is where the fund is a private arrangement between a relatively small number of investors. The other is where the fund is established with the express intention of replicating an index or static basket of securities. For the first case, actual information about the specific underlying portfolio, and this is uncommon in fund arrangements. For the second case, where the fund is established to track an index, a unit holder may assume without information that the fund is in fact tracking that index, provided that the fund has an explicit mandate to do so, and it can be demonstrated that a very high minimum correlation between the movement of the unit price in the fund and the movements in the underlying basket can be demonstrated over the most recent six months.

Under this approach, netting is permitted between positions in the underlying **10.75** investments of the fund and other positions held by the firm, as long as the firm holds a sufficient quantity of units to allow for redemption/creation in exchange for the underlying investments.

There is also a 'modified' approach, which can be used where a fund is limited in **10.76** its range of permitted investments. The modified approach applies where a fund is only permitted to invest in certain types of investments. It operates by assuming that the fund is fully invested up to its maximum permitted limit in the most 'expensive' type of asset (for risk capital purposes) that it is permitted to invest in. The purpose of this approach is that funds which are limited to high quality assets—(notably money market funds) obtain some relief from the 32 per cent weighting which they would otherwise attract—thus if a fund is limited to investing in a range of assets of which the worst available PRA would be 8 per cent, the holding of the units may be given a PRA of 8 per cent. It does not matter that the investor knows that some of the fund's investments are in assets which would attract a lower PRA—the calculation is made on the 'worst permissible investments' basis. This approach clearly does not give rise to netting of positions.

G. Annex—A Guide to Option Terminology

10.77

American option	An option that may be exercised at any time over an extended period up to its expiry date.
European option	An option that can only be exercised at expiry.
Bermudan option	A half-way house between an American option and a European option. The Bermudan option can only be exercised at specific dates during its life.
Asian option	The buyer has the right to exercise at the average rate or price of the Asian option underlying over the period (or part of the period) of the option. One variant is where the payout is based on the average of the underlying against a fixed strike price; another variant is where the payout gives at expiry the price of the underlying against the average price over the option period.
Barrier option	An option which is either cancelled or activated if the price of the underlying reaches a pre-set level regardless of the price at which the underlying may be trading at the expiry of the option. The knockout type is cancelled if the underlying price or rate trades through the trigger; while the knock-in becomes activated if the price moves through the trigger.
Corridor option	Provides the holder with a pay-out for each day that the underlying stays within a defined range chosen by the investor.
Ladder option	Provides the holder with guaranteed pay-outs if the underlying trades through a pre-agreed price(s) or rate(s) at a certain point(s) in time, regardless of future performance.
Lock-in option	An option where the pay-out to the holder is locked in at the maximum (or minimum) value of the underlying that occurred during the life of the option.
Look-back option	A European style option where the strike price is fixed in retrospect, that is at the most favourable price (ie the lowest (highest) price of the underlying in the case of a call (put)) during the life of the option.
Forward starting option	An option that starts at a future date.
Compound option	An option where the underlying is itself an option (ie an option on an option).
Interest rate cap	An interest rate option or series of options under which a counterparty contracts to pay any interest costs arising as a result of an increase in rates above an agreed rate: the effect being to provide protection to the holder against a rise above that agreed interest rate.
Interest rate floor	An interest rate option or series of options under which a counterparty contracts to pay any lost income arising as a result of a fall in rates below an agreed rate: the effect being to provide protection to the holder against a fall below that agreed interest rate.
Performance option	An option based on a reference basket comprising any number of assets, where the payout to the holder could be one of the following: — the maximum of the worst performing asset, or — the maximum of the best performing asset, or — the maximum of the spreads between several pairs of the assets.

Quantos	Quanto stands for 'Quantity Adjusted Option'. A quanto is an instrument where two currencies are involved. The payoff is dependent on a variable that is measured in one of the currencies and the payoff is made in the other currency.
Cliquet option	A cliquet option consists of a series of forward starting options where the strike price for the next exercise date is set equal to a positive constant times the underlying price as of the previous exercise date. It initially acts like a vanilla option with a fixed price but as time moves on, the strike is reset and the intrinsic value automatically locked in at pre-set dates. If the underlying price is below the previous level at the reset date no intrinsic value is locked in but the strike price will be reset to the current price attained by the underlying. If the underlying price exceeds the current level at the next reset the intrinsic value will again be locked in.
Digital option	A type of option where the pay-out to the holder is fixed. The most common types are all-or-nothing and one-touch options. All-or-nothing will pay out the fixed amount if the underlying is above (call) or below (put) a set value at expiry. The one-touch will pay the fixed amount if the underlying reaches a fixed point any time before expiry.

11

SECURITIES UNDERWRITING

Underwriting poses special problems for investment firm capital adequacy. **11.01** An underwriting position is in principle a trading position—it is bought in order to be sold—and is generally properly dealt with in the trading book. However, unissued or unallocated securities have a number of anomalous features—for example, they do not give rise to specific market risk, since their price does not change—and the structure of underwriting does not fit easily within either the option or the 'synthetic short' analysis which is used for ordinary trading activities. Consequently, a specialized regime exists to deal with it. It should be noted that the underwriting regime only applies to new securities—meaning either securities which are created for the purpose of the offer being underwritten, or securities which have not previously been offered for sale to the public at large or admitted to trading on a regulated market. A placing of securities already in existence, for example, would not be permitted to take advantage of the underwriting regime. It should also be noted that the regime does not apply to underwritings of syndicated loans, since it is restricted to offerings of securities. The regime also does not catch grey market dealings—that is, dealings entered into on a 'when issued' basis which are effected before the securities concerned become tradable.

The CRD therefore provides a special regime to accommodate the particular risks **11.02** inherent in underwriting.[1] The essence of the underwriting capital regime is that the charge varies through the period of the offering. For this purpose, there are two key periods. The first is the period from the date of 'initial commitment' (the date on which the institution first gave a commitment to underwrite) to the date of firm commitment (generally referred to as 'working day 0'). The second is the period from working day 0 until the end of the fifth day thereafter ('working day 5'). After working day 5 the regime ceases to apply, and firms must deal with any positions arising out of the underwriting in the normal fashion.

---

[1] CRD Annex 1 Part 1 points 41–46.

11.03 The date of initial commitment is the date on which a firm commits to under-write. This may be a commitment given to the issuer, or to a third party, or to a sub-underwriter. The commitment need not be a legal commitment, and the fact that it is conditional or subject to conditions precedent is not relevant for this purpose. The rule here appears to be the same as that which applies to loan com-mitments, and is subject to the same carve-out—that a firm which would other-wise be treated as committed is not treated as committed if it has an absolute and unconditional right to withdraw from the underwriting at any time.

11.04 Working day 0 is the day on which the underwriter becomes unconditionally committed to acquire a known quantity of securities at a specified price. For an equity offer this is generally the day on which the lists are closed and the allocation announced (or, for a rights issue, the date on which the offer becomes closed to acceptances). For a debt offer, it is generally the date of allotment and payment.

11.05 In respect of an underwriting, a firm must calculate its net position in the securi-ties underwritten. The net position is the position which the firm has agreed to assume through underwriting, net of any sub-underwriting arrangements which it has put in place and which are confirmed in writing. For this purpose, forward sales in the grey market which have been confirmed in writing may be treated as equivalent to sub-underwriting. If a firm is required to assess its commitment before allocation, it must assess that commitment at the size of the largest amount of securities which it could be compelled to receive. Informal arrangements, and undocumented grey market sales, are not effective to reduce these positions.

11.06 Firms who are lead managers in an underwriting may overallot the securities being offered. When this is done, it is usual (in the equity but not in the debt market) for the lead manager to have an arrangement with the issuer (known as a 'green-shoe') by which the issuer agrees to make further securities available to the lead manager if the offering goes so well that the overallotted shares are fully taken up. Where a lead manager has overallotted and has the benefit of a greenshoe, he may set off the greenshoe against the overallotment position for the purposes of calcu-lating his net underwriting position.

11.07 The approach to the capital calculation begins with calculating the net underwrit-ing position in the securities which the underwriter has. For equities, this amount is then reduced by a factor. The percentage of the net underwriting position which is included in the capital calculation is as follows:

Initial Commitment to working day 0	0%
Working day 1	10%
Working day 2	25%
Working day 3	25%

Working day 4	50%
Working day 5	75%
After working day 5	100%

Equity positions arising out of underwriting may only be treated under the simplified equity method.

The position for debt securities is slightly more complex, in that these reductions **11.08** are only applied to the specific market risk of the position—the position itself is applied in full in the calculation of the general market risk from the day of initial commitment. By way of counterbalance, however, the reduction in specific risk between the date of initial commitment and working day 0 is to 0 per cent, rather than 10 per cent as for equities.

It should also be noted that there is a concession within the regime for large expo- **11.09** sures. Underwriting can involve firms with relatively small capital accepting large underwriting positions on the basis that they have sub-underwritten them. In this context, even the 10 per cent percentage could be too large for their capital bases. Consequently, for the purposes of calculating the amount of an underwriting position to be included in the large exposures calculation, a discount of 0 per cent is applied from the date of initial commitment until the end of working day 1. Thereafter the position size used for large exposures purposes is the same as above.

12

TRADING BOOK MODELS

Risk models come in a bewildering variety of types. However, for market risk **12.01** purposes there are two types which may be used within the framework. The simplest is the 'CAD 1' model—named after the first Capital Adequacy Directive, which permitted such models to be sued in the calculation of regulatory capital. The VaR model is more complex.

A. 'CAD 1' Models

CAD 1 models come in two forms—interest rate risk pre-processing models, and **12.02** option risk aggregation models. An interest rate pre-processing model may—at its simplest—be applied to collections of interest rate forwards, futures, options and warrants along with bonds giving rise to such positions, and used to resolve all of these into a single notional position which can be plugged into the interest PRR calculation. Their function is, broadly, to avoid the necessity for analysing complex portfolios by resolving those portfolios into simpler positions which are then put through the normal PRR calculation. An option risk aggregation model performs roughly the same function for interest rate, equity, foreign currency, commodity, and fund options.

Use of a model for trading book purposes is much like the use of a model for credit **12.03** modelling purposes in that it is in the discretion of the regulator. Thus in order to permit a bank to use a model the regulator must be satisfied not only with the model itself, but with the way in which it is integrated into the management and operations of the bank. Before granting a waiver, the FSA generally engages in a detailed due diligence process which is likely to involve a programme of visits to the institution concerned, meetings with management, financial control, front office, operations, systems and development, IT, and internal audit. It will generally commission an expert report from a firm of consultants on the model before approving its use. One of the consequences of this is that the making of changes to a model may well require regulatory consent.

B. VaR Models

12.04 We have already examined the broad outline of a VaR model (see above, Chapter 7). In the context of a trading book, the function of the model is to estimate the worst case potential loss on a particular trading position in the event of a market downturn.

12.05 The function of a VaR model is as a risk management model which uses a statistical measure to predict profit and loss movement ranges with a confidence interval. What this means in practice is that the output of a VaR model should be an estimate of the worst expected loss on a portfolio resulting from market movements over a period of time within a specified confidence level. In general, the specified confidence level is 99 per cent, and the specified period is 10 days, so in which case the VaR models should estimate the worst possible outcome for 99 out of 100 periods in which the holder of the portfolio was unable to liquidate any of the portfolio for 10 days and during that time the market responded in accordance with its historic tendencies. In theory, of course, the worst possible loss is a 100 per cent loss, but the unlikelihood of the market going from any level to absolute zero over a 10-day period is more than 99 per cent improbable, so is disregarded. The question, therefore, is what is the greatest drop in values which has a more than 1 per cent chance of happening.

12.06 From these results PRR charges can be calculated. Regulators are careful not to prescribe any particular type of model, but encourage forms to experiment with differing approaches in the interests of maximizing risk analysis capability. VaR models may be applied to interest rate general and/or specific market risk, equity general and specific risk, CIU risk, foreign currency risk, and commodity risk. A VaR model is a complex beast, and in general can only be established once it has been validated through application to historical data and after a period of parallel running, in which its output can be tested against real-time price movements.

12.07 The 'use test' is applied to VaR models in the same way as it is to credit models. That is, a firm may not operate a VaR model solely for the purpose of calculating PRRs—the VaR model must be fully integrated into the daily risk management proves of the firm, and serve as the basis for risk reporting to senior management who, in turn, are required to be actively involved in the risk control process. The firm must also have a Risk Control Unit, which is required to produce and analyse daily reports on the output of the model and to conduct initial and continuing validation of the model itself.

The FSA divides types of securities into four broad classes, and in general each **12.08** application by a bank to extend its VaR model to another of these will require FSA approval. However, the FSA takes the view that once an institution has developed a VaR model and applied it to one of these classes, it should seek to extend the model to all of them. The classes are:

(1) linear products, which comprise securities with linear pay-offs (eg bonds and equities) and derivative products which have linear pay-offs in the underlying risk factor (eg interest rate swaps, FRAs, total return swaps);
(2) European, American and Bermudan put and call options (including caps, floors and swaptions) and investments with these features;
(3) Asian options, digital options, single barrier options, double barrier options lookback options, forward starting options, compound options and investments with these features; and
(4) all other option based products (eg basket options, Quantos, outperformance options, timing options) and investments with these features.

C. The Multiplication Factor

A 'multiplication factor' is generally built into the mechanism by which the output **12.09** of the model is incorporated into the PRR calculation. In general, the multiplication factor is three, although it may be increased if there have been instances where the model has not performed accurately in backtesting, or if the regulator perceives that there are weaknesses in systems and controls around the model. Thus, once the VaR model has been established, the model PRR resulting from it will be the average of the daily VaR over the last 60 days multiplied by the appropriate multiplication factor for the model. By exception, if the model's VaR assessment for the day is higher than this number, then this is taken.

13

CREDIT DERIVATIVES

A. Introduction

Credit derivatives require special treatment in the trading as well as the banking **13.01** book. The structure of a credit default swap ('CDS') is relatively straightforward— one party (the protection buyer) agrees that it will pay a fee to another (the protection seller). The operative part of the agreement is triggered if one of a number of events occurs in relation to an underlying entity (conventionally referred to as 'defaults', although these events include events which would not necessarily constitute defaults under a normal loan agreement). The underlying entity is generally referred to as the 'reference entity'. If a default occurs with respect to the reference entity, the protection buyer may deliver a specified type of asset issued by the reference entity to the protection seller. In return, the protection seller must pay to the protection buyer an amount equal to the non-defaulted value of the asset. Thus, if A owns a bond worth £100 issued by X, it may purchase credit protection on that bond from B. In this example, A is the 'protection buyer', B is the 'protection seller', and X is the 'reference entity'. If X defaults, A is entitled to deliver the bond to B and B is obliged to pay £100 to A. This is a 'physically settled' CDS, referred to as such because of the requirement to actually make physical delivery of the relevant asset to the protection seller. A more commonly encountered variant is the 'cash settled' CDS. In a cash settled CDS there is no physical delivery, and the protection seller is required to pay to the protection buyer an amount equal to the difference between the nominal value of the reference asset and the current market value of the reference asset post default.

It should be clear from this example that the essence of what is going on here is **13.02** that A is entering into an at the money put option with B in respect of the reference asset in exchange for an option premium. The ordinary treatment for this transaction in the trading book would be relatively straightforward—A would be treated as having a long position in a put, and B would be treated as having a short position in that put. However, credit derivatives are generally more complex than this. The reasons for this are twofold.

13.03 First, a credit derivative generally references credit rather than a specific asset. Thus, in the example given above, what A is seeking to do is to buy protection not on a specific asset, but on any credit exposure to X. This is generally done by identifying a fairly wide class of 'reference assets' issued by X—which may include public bonds, private bonds or loans existing from time to time—and provide that a default on any one of these may constitute a 'credit event' giving rise to a claim under the CDS. Thus, the terms of the contract will provide that the right to claim against B will be triggered by the occurrence of an event of default in respect of any asset falling within the class of reference assets.

13.04 Second, the terms of the contract will provide that once a credit event has occurred, A may deliver to B any asset issued by X which falls within the class of 'deliverable obligations'. The class of deliverable obligations may be the same as the class of reference obligations, but it need not be. Thus it could well be the case that loans to X fall within the class of reference obligations (such that a default on a loan by X would constitute a credit event) but the class of deliverable obligations could include only securities issued by X.

13.05 Thus the essence of the CDS is that if a particular event happens with respect to one class of obligations of X, the protection buyer will be entitled to put to the protection seller any asset of its choosing falling within the class of deliverable obligations. This is clearly quite far removed from a traditional option structure, since neither the buyer nor the seller of the option know which security the option relates to.

13.06 It is important, for a variety of reasons, that there is no engagement anywhere that the person buying protection should actually own (or be exposed to) any asset relating to X at the time when he enters into the contract. It is therefore perfectly possible that A might enter into the CDS with B at a time when he had no exposure to X at all. A's motivation for doing this might be that he believed that a default would take place with respect to X, and that, if this happened, he would be able to purchase assets in the market at a discounted value reflecting the default and then deliver them to B in order to receive their full pre-default value. By buying 'bare' protection in this way, A in effect goes short of the credit of X. Conversely, by selling protection B in effect goes long of the credit of X, since if X does not default he will receive the premium payments over the life of the contract for no cost. It should also be clear that the premium received by B should be the difference between the actual market rate charged to X by the market (the credit spread) and the hypothetical risk-free rate which the market would charge to a risk-free borrower, since B is effectively assuming this risk. Thus B would be placed in the economic position of a person who borrows risk-free and lends to X at a normal market spread. There is one final refinement to bear in mind, and that is that the protection buyer should discount the premium paid to B to reflect the cost of the credit exposure which it is assuming to B. Thus, the position in which B should end up should be the net position which it would have if it borrowed at its normal credit risk spread and lent on the basis of X's normal risk spread.

It should be clear from the foregoing that although CDSs can be simplistically **13.07** regarded as options, in practice they are sufficiently unlike normal option transactions as to be a fairly bad fit with the option regime. Consequently a separate regime is created for them.

The starting point is the position as regards a total return swap. Where a person **13.08** has written a total return swap with another—ie has agreed to pay to that other the costs of owning the asset, in exchange for its agreement to pay over the benefit of the asset—he must treat himself as having a long position in the general and specific market risk of the reference obligation, and a short position in the general market risk of a zero-specific-risk security with a maturity equivalent to the period until the next interest fixing and which is assigned a 0 per cent risk weight under the standardized approach to credit risk.

The difference between this position and the position of a protection seller under **13.09** a credit default swap is that the protection seller does not have a position for general market risk. For the purposes of specific risk, the protection seller must treat itself as having a synthetic long position in an obligation of the reference entity. Premium or interest payments due must be represented as notional positions in zero-specific-risk securities.

Credit derivatives are sometimes embedded in structured securities, known as **13.10** 'credit linked notes' ('CLNs'). The easiest way to think of a credit linked note is that it replicates the position where the protection seller writes the CDS but at the same time advances to the protection seller the value of the protected asset as collateral. When wrapped together in note form, this cocktail produces an arrangement under which the note buyer pays to the issuer the value of the note, and receives back an enhanced coupon which is the sum of the interest rate payable by the issuer and the protection premium due in respect of the underlying reference entity. In the event that a credit event occurs in respect of the reference entity, the issuer simply reduces the amount which it is due to pay back under the note— thus if a CLN is issued for £100 in respect of reference entity X, there is a credit even in respect of X and the value of the deliverable assets is 50% of the protected value, the terms of the notes will provide that the repayment of £50 by the issuer will discharge all of its obligations under the notes. Note that with CLNs, the note issuer is the protection buyer, and the note investor is the protection seller.

B. Notional Positions

13.11   A single name credit linked note creates a long position in the general market risk of the note itself, as an interest rate product. For the purpose of specific risk, two notional positions are created; one in an obligation of the reference entity, another in the issuer of the note. However, where the credit linked note has an external rating and meets the conditions for a qualifying debt security, a single long position with the specific risk of the note need only be recorded.

13.12   There is, of course, no reason why CDSs or CLNs should be confined to a single reference entity, and it is not uncommon for protection structures to cover a basket of different reference entities. The terms of such contracts are generally that if any one of a basket of reference entities suffers a credit default, then the asset concerned may be put to the protection provider. These contracts can take a variety of forms, and may provide either that the protection seller is required to cover only the loss suffered by the first default in the basket (a 'first to default structure') or that the protection seller is required to cover all defaults until the principal of the protection amount is exhausted.

13.13   A first to default credit derivative creates a position for the notional amount in an obligation of each reference entity, and the PRRs for each holding are added together. However, if the maximum payment which can be made under the structure is lower than this amount, the maximum payment amount may be taken as the PRR requirement for specific risk.

13.14   Where a protection seller sells a notional amount of protection on a basket of names, it is treated as having a position in each reference entity, with the total notional amount of the contract assigned across the positions according to the proportion of the total notional amount that each exposure to a reference entity represents. Where more than one obligation of a reference entity can be selected, the obligation with the highest risk weighting determines the specific risk.

C. Recognition of Risk Reduction

13.15   In broad terms, the position of the protection buyer is the mirror image of the position of the protection seller. This only really breaks down with credit linked notes, since the issuer of a credit linked note does not have a short position in itself. There is, however, an issue as regards term. A protection seller who sells three-year protection is acquiring a synthetic asset with a three-year maturity, and this is true regardless of the maturity of the underlying assets. For a protection buyer, however, if there is a maturity mismatch between the protection which it has bought and the term of the underlying assets, then it is incompletely hedged. This matters because a firm may take an allowance for protection provided by credit derivatives in respect of cash positions which it holds. The issue here is that if a firm holds an asset, and buys credit protection in respect of that asset under which the asset is both a reference asset and a deliverable asset, then it is in the position that it would be if it held the cash asset and had entered into a forward sale in respect of that asset. Under ordinary trading book principles, this would result in the asset and the future being netted in the calculation of the trading book position. However, as we saw above, CDSs are protean in their structure, and it is frequently the case that the question of whether the two sides of the transaction are matched is not entirely straightforward. CDSs are therefore allocated into three classes for the purposes of determining whether such netting is available.

Full offset. This applies where positions are created by completely identical instruments (ie CDSs with identical terms as to reference and deliverable assets, or total return swaps on identical terms), or where a cash position is hedged by a CDS where the cash asset is the reference obligation (this will generally only arise under a total return swap).

80 per cent offset. This applies where there is an exact match of reference obligation, maturity and currency, and there is no other term in the CDS which would cause its value to deviate materially from the price movements of the cash position.

Partial allowance. A partial allowance is permitted where the reference obligation and the underlying obligation have the same obligor, have legally enforceable cross-default clauses, and the reference obligation is not senior to the underlying obligation. The effect of a partial allowance is that the PRR of both sides of the transaction is calculated but only the higher of the two PRRs applies.

Once these allowances have been made, a specific risk PRR must be taken against the remaining position. Where there is no allowance or set-off, a separate specific risk PRR must be taken for each side of the position. **13.16**

As noted above, a CDS gives rise to a specific risk capital charge, and because the underlying assets are assumed to be credit assets, the charge concerned will be an interest rate PRR. This calculated as the higher of the charge which would be arrived at under the normal interest rate PRR method and the result of the 'ordinary credit default swap PRR method.' The ordinary credit default swap method is broadly six times the loss which would be caused by a change in credit spreads plus four times the PRR of the long position to which it is exposed. A different (and more onerous) calculation is applied to securitization CDSs. **13.17**

13.18 Many CDSs entered into in the trading book are likely to be components of synthetic securitizations. There is a separate treatment provided for such CDSs which is more onerous—and more complex—than that imposed on other types of CDSs. The specific risk portion of interest rate PRR for securitization swaps is the sum of the valuation change capital charge (a calculation based on a prescribed stress test matrix) and the default capital charge (loosely a grossed-up figure based on the risk weight which the position would attract under the normal securitization framework). If the result of this calculation is lower than the charge which would have been arrived at under the normal trading book rules for CDS, that charge is used instead.

14

COUNTERPARTY RISK

A. Introduction

Trading book exposures are generally assessed as giving rise to position risk ('PR') **14.01** rather than counterparty or credit risk ('CR'). However, a number of trading book exposure types may give rise to both. To take a simple example, if a firm purchases a security in the cash market it will have a position risk on that holding. If it enters into a derivative under which it is liable to receive the value of the security it has two risks—a position risk on the security, and a counterparty risk on the derivative counterparty. Such exposure can also arise under free deliveries, unsettled transactions and repo agreements as well as margin lending arrangements and long settlement transactions.

The broad principle is—unsurprisingly—that once a firm has calculated its **14.02** exposure values to any particular counterparty, it must risk weight the resulting exposures in accordance with the approach which it uses to calculate its ordinary credit risk exposures—standardized or IRB, as the case may be.

No CCR is attributed in the trading book to a transaction entered into with a **14.03** central counterparty, to which an exposure of 0 per cent is allocated.

B. Credit Derivatives

No CCR is attributed to a credit derivative entered into in the banking book, **14.04** since these are already dealt with under the existing banking book rules. For credit derivatives in the trading book (including total return swaps), a PFCE (potential future credit exposure) figure must be calculated by multiplying the nominal amount of the instrument by 5 per cent where the reference obligation would be a qualifying debt security, or 10 per cent otherwise. Where the notional exposure arising from the swap represents a long position in the underlying, 0 per cent is used.

14.05 For a first to default transaction, the appropriate percentage for the potential future credit exposure will be determined by the lowest credit quality of the underlying obligations in the basket. If there are non-qualifying items in the basket, the percentage applicable to the non-qualifying reference obligation should be used. For second and subsequent to default transactions, underlying assets should continue to be allocated according to credit quality—ie for a second to default transaction, the applicable percentage figure is the percentage applicable to the second lowest credit quality.

14.06 Where a credit derivative included in the trading book forms part of an internal hedge and the credit protection is recognised for the purposes of the calculation of the credit risk capital component, there is deemed to be no counterparty risk arising from the position in the credit derivative.

C. Collateral in the Trading Book

14.07 Credit exposures can clearly be mitigated by collateral whether they are in the banking or the trading book. The treatment of collateral in the trading book is in principle the same as in the banking book, and firms are required to apply in the trading book the same collateral treatment which they apply to their banking book positions. However, the collateral rules which are applied to trading book exposures are slightly more generous than those which apply in the banking book. In particular, in the context of repo transactions, securities or commodities lending or borrowing transactions, all instruments and commodities eligible to be held in the trading book may be recognised as eligible collateral. For long settlement transactions and financial derivatives in the trading book, commodities eligible to be held in the trading book may be recognised as eligible collateral. The volatility adjustment which is applied in such cases is the adjustment which applies to non-main-index equities.

14.08 A particular problem arises in this context as regards master netting agreements where such agreements cover both trading book and banking book transactions. Where such a master agreement covers repo or securities lending in the trading book, all of the transactions which the agreement covers must comply with the stricter eligibility rules which apply in the banking book. What this means in practice is that the relaxation in collateral eligibility described above is not available for agreements which are subject to a master netting agreement which also covers banking book transactions.

D. Double Default in the Trading Book

The double default calculation provided for in the IRB approach is based on the formula involving an IRB risk weighting multiplied by a function of the protection provider, and this approach applies in the trading book as well as the banking book. There are, however, some ways in which this approach is applied differently in the trading book. First, in the trading book value adjustments made to take account of the credit quality of the counterparty may be included in the calculation of total exposure—this is an exception to the usual rule that valuation adjustments taken in respect of credit quality may not be included in exposure calculations.[1] Second, if the trading book approach recognises the credit risk of the counterparty in full, then the expected loss for the counterparty risk exposure (and therefore the risk weighted amount under the IRB approach) must be zero.

14.09

There is a wrinkle as regards credit exposures to clearing houses. In general, exposures to clearing houses have a weighting of 0 per cent. However, this only applies to exposures 'resulting from' transactions cleared by the clearing house. A clearing house member may make payments to the clearing house for reasons which are not directly related to particular transactions (for example, where a clearing house enters into money market transactions with banks as part of its proprietary treasury operations. These payments are not covered by the 0 per cent weighting, and are therefore treated as exposures to a regulated financial institution.

14.10

For the purposes of counterparty credit risk, a firm may net exposures arising from items in the trading book against exposures arising from items in the non-trading book. Where this is done, the net balance must be allocated to whichever book had the greater gross balance—thus if there is a large positive exposure in the trading book and a smaller negative exposure in the banking book, the resulting net positive balance must be dealt with under the trading book rules. However, this calculation must be performed carefully, since some rules may not tally—for example, if the net balance falls within the banking book, the calculation will have to be reperformed, since some of the collateral recognized in the trading book may not be eligible under the banking book rules.

14.11

---

[1] Note that valuation adjustments used in this way may not also be counted towards upper tier two.

E. Rules Common to Banking and Trading Books

Unsettled transactions

14.12 Unsettled transactions may arise in respect of both the trading and the non-trading book, and this rule applies in respect of both. No transaction is instantaneously settled, and all transactions are unsettled for some period of time, even if that period is measured in minutes. The effect of this rule is therefore to define the point at which a capital charge is required to be taken on the basis that the period for which the transaction has remained unsettled has become excessive.

14.13 The rule applies to securities, currency and commodities transactions but does not apply to repo or securities lending exposures. It begins with the establishment of the due settlement date. This will be determined by reference to practice in the particular market concerned. Once this date has passed, the firm must calculate its potential settlement exposure. This is defined as the amount which the firm could lose if the trade were not to settle, and is calculated as the difference between the agreed settlement price of the transaction and the current market value. Thus, if a firm has agreed to buy 100 securities at £1 each, if the price of the securities rises to £2 after the settlement date then the potential settlement exposure is £100 (£1 × 100 = £100, less £2 × 100 = £200). Note that if the price of the securities were to fall rather than rise, there would be no potential settlement exposure, since the firm would not be exposed to any risk of loss.

14.14 The capital requirement for an unsettled transaction is calculated by multiplying the potential settlement exposure by a factor. The factor is set out in the following table.

Number of working days after due settlement date	Factor
5–15	8%
16–30	50%
31–45	75%
46 or more	100%

Note that this rule may be disapplied in cases of a system-wide failure of a settlement or clearing system until the situation is rectified.

Free deliveries

14.15 In modern securities, currency and commodities markets, the ordinary mechanism for the settlement of transactions is delivery against payment, or DVP, by which delivery of securities and the payment of the price occur simultaneously.

However, there may be circumstances in which, for a variety of reasons, one side is prepared to permit one half of a transaction to be performed before the other half. For the reporting bank, this could happen in one of two ways—it could either pay for assets before receiving them, or deliver assets before receiving payment for them. Both of these circumstances are caught by the free delivery rule. The rule on free deliveries applies in respect of the trading book and the non-trading book. It applies only where at least one day has elapsed between the payment and the non-delivery.

Free delivery treatment varies according to whether the free delivery is in the **14.16** banking or the trading book. In the banking book, the treatment resembles that for unsettled transactions, in that it begins with a determination of the positive exposure of the firm. Thus, if the firm has paid for but not received 100 securities valued at £1, if the value of the securities increases to £2 then the firm's exposure is £100. For a banking book exposure, from the payment date to a day four days thereafter, the firm may treat itself as having a counterparty exposure to the transaction counterparty calculated in accordance with its normal means of calculating banking book counterparty exposures. However, when the transaction becomes more than five days old, the transaction—plus any positive exposure arising on the unsettled transaction—must be deducted from capital.

In the trading book, the position is slightly different, in that up to the first capital **14.17** payment leg there is no capital charge, but thereafter the position is treated as for the banking book. An IRB firm may, however, elect not to perform this calculation, but simply to allocate standardized weighting to all such exposures in the trading book. Finally, a blanket 100 per cent weighting may be applied to all free delivery exposures where the total firm exposure arising from such exposures is not material.

15

COUNTERPARTY CREDIT RISK FOR DERIVATIVES, SECURITIES FINANCING, AND LONG SETTLEMENT EXPOSURES

A. Introduction

The effect of the rules set out in this chapter is that certain exposures whose value **15.01** can fluctuate over time should be treated as having a greater degree of risk than their actual mark to market value. In order to explain why this is, consider a bank which owns 100 of shares in A, but also has a derivative in place with X under which it is entitled to be paid the value of 100 shares in A. Clearly both positions give rise to the same risk as to the future price of A, and both will be valued by reference to the value of the shares in A. There is, however, a difference between the two. For the physical position, fluctuations in the value of the shares will result simply in gains or losses to the holder. Fluctuations in the value of the derivative, however, bring in an extra factor. This is that if the value of the shares in A increases, the bank's credit exposure to X will increase. The rules set out in this chapter seek to capture this extra level of risk by treating the value of the derivative as being slightly higher than its mark to market value; thereby requiring a slightly higher level of capital to be held against it. This is the counterparty credit risk requirement ('CCR').

What is being calculated here is either the valuation amount (for standardized **15.02** banks) or the EAD (for IRB banks)—that is, the value of the credit exposure.

The rules apply to three different types of transaction: derivatives, securities financing, and long settlement transaction.

15.03 'Derivatives' is not a term with a defined meaning, but for this purpose the BCD helpfully essays an inclusive definition. For BCD purposes a derivative means:

(1) an interest-rate contract, being:
  (a) a single-currency interest rate swap;
  (b) a basis-swap;
  (c) a forward rate agreement;
  (d) an interest-rate future;
  (e) a purchased interest-rate option; and
  (f) other contracts of similar nature.
(2) a foreign currency contract or contract concerning gold, being:
  (a) a cross-currency interest-rate swap;
  (b) a forward foreign currency contract;
  (c) a currency future;
  (d) a currency option purchased;
  (e) other contracts of a similar nature; and
  (f) a contract concerning gold of a nature similar to (2)(a) to (e).
(3) a contract of a nature similar to those in 1(a) to (e) and 2(a) to (d) concerning other reference items or indices, including as a minimum all instruments specified in points 4 to 7, 9 and 10 of Section C of Annex I to the MiFID not otherwise included in (1) or (2).[1]

15.04 The term 'securities financing transaction' is a portmanteau term which includes a number of different transaction types. The most significant of these are repo (short for repurchase) transactions, in which one party sells securities to another on the basis that it will buy them back again at a future date at a specified price, and stock lending transactions, in which one party transfers title to securities to another on the basis that it will be able to call for the return of those securities on the specified date. It may be helpful to note at this point that although repo and stock lending transactions look almost identical to lawyers, in economic terms they are very different. A repo is economically equivalent to a borrowing of a specific amount of money secured on the stock transferred, with an interest rate charged on that money in terms of the differential between the purchase price and the repurchase price. This effectively gives the participants a long or short interest rate position on the repo price. A stock loan is economically equivalent to a borrowing of stock against collateral, and the lender is in principle rewarded with a lending fee rather than an interest rate. Amongst other advantages, this makes stock loans easier to administer for lending institutions. The best way to envisage

---

[1] BCD Annex IV.

the difference between the two is that in a repo, the amount of the repayment is fixed and the amount of securities collateral therefore varies. In a stock loan, the value of the repayment varies, so the amount of securities used does not.

Securities financing transactions also include margin lending transactions, where **15.05** an institution lends money to a customer in order for that customer to purchase, sell, hold or otherwise trade in securities. The aim of this provision was to catch 'prime brokerage' and similar arrangements, where banks provided leverage to securities investors by extending credit based exclusively on securities portfolios. A distinction is drawn here between securities financing transactions (that is, loan transactions entered into for the express purpose of financing securities business) and lending transactions which just happen to be collateralized by securities. The distinction is, however, not exactly a bright line.

The rules also apply to long settlement transactions. In some respects this is an **15.06** anti-avoidance measure. If I agree to sell securities on terms that the buyer need only pay for them in 12 months time, what I have created is in fact a securities financing contract, but in legal and regulatory terms it is a contract for sale. The rule which is applied is therefore that any contract for the sale of a security, a com-modity, or a foreign currency amount against cash, other financial instruments, or commodities, or vice versa may be treated as a long settlement transaction. This will be the case where the settlement or delivery date is contractually specified as more than the lower of the market standard for the particular transaction and five business days after the date on which the firm enters into the transaction. Thus any sale of securities which has a settlement period of more than five days will be a long settlement transaction.

Finally, it should be noted that the fertile minds of derivatives lawyers and finan- **15.07** cial structurers have produced—and still produce—a bewildering array of instru-ments and structures. Regulators in general accept that any set of rules developed for generic classes of derivatives will produce anomalous results in certain circum-stances. Consequently the FSA has adopted a 'non-standard transactions' rule[2] which provides simply that: (a) where a transaction is non-standard as regards the market as a whole; and (b) the application of the stated rules would result in a material understatement of the counterparty credit risk to which the firm is exposed, the firm must adjust the credit risk applied to the particular transaction and must consult the FSA as to that treatment. Although there is a slight air of desperation in the drafting of this rule, this does no more than reflect the practical impossibility of developing a credit regime which will apply across all conceivable transaction types.

---

[2] BIPRU 13.2.

B. Calculating Exposures

15.08 Derivative exposures are generally effected under ISDA or other master documents which provide for broad netting. Exposures with any given counterparty are assessed using netting sets (see below). Where there is more than one netting set, there is more than one exposure (see below).

15.09 Exposures to certain central counterparties attract a CCR of zero. This is a concession designed to encourage central counterparty use, and applies only where the central counterparty's credit risk exposure with all participants in its arrangements are fully collateralized on a daily basis. However, this concession is not available for exposures arising from collateral held by the central counterparty for the participant to mitigate losses in the event of the default of other participants in the central counterparty's arrangements—broadly, default fund contributions.

15.10 The basis of the valuation mechanism prescribed for derivative and other variable transactions is first to establish the amount due under the transaction, and then to apply a regulatory 'haircut' to that amount to arrive at the appropriate exposure value or EAD. This calculation is performed using one of three approaches; being:

- mark to market method;
- standardized method;
- internal model method.

One or other of these methods must be applied to derivatives and securities financing transactions within a single entity—they cannot be mixed for different derivative types. There is one exception to this rule which arises from the fact that the rules require a firm to use the mark to market approach for any non-linear exposure for which it cannot calculate a model value.[3] Methods may be mixed across different group members in accordance with the consolidation rules. A firm must calculate the exposure value of a long settlement transaction in accordance with either one of these methods or, if it is permitted to use it, the master netting agreement internal models approach. If a firm enters into a transaction which is structurally a long settlement transaction in order to execute a trade which is structurally a derivative or securities financing trade, it may opt to simply treat that trade as a derivative or securities financing trade and apply to it whatever calculation method it applies to such transactions. The use of the long settlement approach is therefore, in effect, optional for derivatives trading firms with established processes.

15.11 The inclusion of long settlement transactions within this framework focuses attention on the fact that although a firm is most unlikely to engage in derivatives

---

[3] Netting may not be recognized in calculating such an exposure, which must be treated as if it constituted a separate netting set containing only itself.

or financing transactions by mistake or through inadvertence, it may well, for a variety of good reasons, find itself party to long settlement transactions. There is therefore a concessionary rule which has the effect that a firm may, if it wishes, weight long settlement transactions using the mark to market method and the standardized approach to credit weighting regardless of any other factor.

Finally, the collateral rules apply where credit protection is purchased against an **15.12** asset held in the banking book. Where such protection is held, the credit exposure on the relevant credit derivative is, for the purpose of this section set to zero. This is because the counterparty risk concerned is already accounted for in the collateral rules. Equally, where a firm has sold protection out of the banking book and as a result is treated as having the asset protected on its books, the CCR for the sold derivative is also set to zero.

C. The Mark to Market Method

The basis of the mark to market method is that the firm concerned must under- **15.13** take a two-stage calculation. First, it must determine the current replacement cost of all contracts with positive values at market prices. This gives a mark to market value for each contract. Secondly, the firm must determine the 'add-on' to be applied to each contract, known as the potential future exposure ('PFE'). The exposure value for this purpose is then calculated as the sum of the mark to market value and the PFE.

Since the market value of a particular contract will be the value of the net obliga- **15.14** tion arising under the contract, the netting of the different legs of the derivative contract is already embedded in the valuation. Consequently the adjusted value of the mark to market value of these contracts will constitute the capital requirement to be applied to these positions.

PFE calculation

The PFE is calculated my multiplying the nominal principal amount of the under- **15.15** lying contract by the percentage set out in the table below.

Residual maturity	Interest rate contracts	Contracts concerning foreign currency rates and gold	Contracts concerning equities	Contracts concerning precious metals except gold	Contracts concerning commodities other than precious metals
One year or less	0%	1%	6%	7%	10%
Over one year but under five years	0.5%	5%	8%	7%	12%
Over five years	1.5%	7.5%	10%	8%	15%

Any contract not falling within one of the columns is treated as falling within the highest column. Where a contract requires more than one payment of principle, a separate multiplier should be applied to each payment to be made as if it were the only payment, and the PFEs for each payment are then totalled. For resetting contracts, maturity should be treated as the period until the next reset date.[4]

15.16 Once again, we note that this table is onerous for commodity dealings. For firms which apply the commodity extended maturity ladder (a regime created for commodity specialists—see above at para 10.48) there is a concessionary regime which applies the following percentages to commodity derivative exposures.

Residual maturity	Precious metals (except gold)	Base metals	Agricultural products (softs)	Other, including energy products
One year or less	2%	2.5%	3%	10%
Over one year but under five years	5%	4%	5%	6%
Over five years	7.5%	8%	9%	10%

15.17 PFEs should in theory be applied to all contracts, whether or not they have a positive mark to market value. Thus a fixed floating interest rate derivative which currently has a negative value for the reporting bank will nonetheless attract a PFE. However, this only applies where there is some possibility of a positive amount being paid to the institution at some point. For a contract such as a written option—where the bank receives a payment up-front and the only remaining issue is as to how much (if anything) it will have to pay out to the counterparty, no PFE should apply.

15.18 When a PFE is applied to a position where the mark to market exposure of the contract is negative, the exposure value of the contract is not deducted. However, where the exposure relates to collateral provided to cover a contract with a negative mark to market value—for example, where the reporting bank has provided a counterparty with £100 of collateral to cover the bank's obligations under a contract which has a negative mark to market for it of £20—it is permitted to deduct the £20 from the £100 before calculating the PFE.

15.19 The determination of the principal amount of the contract is not always straightforward—some derivatives may provide that the principal will change on the

---

[4] Subject to a restriction that a rate of 0 per cent may not be applied to any exposure arising under a resetting contract with a term of over one year, even if the next reset is within one year and a rate of 0 per cent would otherwise be applicable under the table. In such a case a 0 per cent weighting is used instead.

occurrence of particular events. In the case of such contracts firms must reflect the effect of such provisions in their calculation.

Netting within the mark to market method

Where a number of obligations arise under a contract which provides for netting **15.20** by novation (that is, where the terms of the contract have the effect that no matter how many individual transactions are entered into under the contract, only a single net amount will ever be payable), both the mark to market value and the PFE should be calculated on the net balance payable under the novation. However, it is relatively unusual to encounter full netting by novation arrangements in derivatives, and the vast majority of derivatives transactions are done under close-out netting provisions. Under a close-out netting arrangement, multiple transactions done under the relevant agreement continue to be separately settled unless an event of default occurs, whereupon the netting provisions take effect and the obligations under the contract are reduced to a single net amount. Where a contract contains close-out netting provisions, the mark to market amount is calculated on a net basis in the same way as for novation netting. However, the PFE is increased by a factor which represents the increased level of risk which regulators consider to attach to close-out netting over novation netting. The relevant calculation is:

$$PCEred = 0.4 * PCEgross + 0.6 * NGR * PCEgross$$

where:

(a) PCEred = the reduced figure for potential future credit exposure for all contracts with a given counterparty included in a legally valid bilateral netting agreement;

(b) PCEgross = the sum of the figures for potential future credit exposure for all contracts with a given counterparty which are included in a legally valid bilateral netting agreement and are calculated by multiplying their notional principal amounts by the PFE percentages;[5] and

(c) NGR = 'net-to-gross ratio': the quotient of the net replacement cost for all contracts included in a legally valid bilateral netting agreement with a given counterparty (numerator) and the gross replacement cost for all contracts included in a legally valid bilateral netting agreement with that counterparty (denominator).

---

[5] Perfectly matching contracts included in the netting agreement may be taken into account as a single contract with a notional principal equivalent to the net receipts.

D. The Standardized Method

15.21 The basis of the standardized method is that derivatives are disaggregated into one or more 'payment legs'. A transaction which involves mutual payments—for example, a fixed-floating interest rate swap—has two payment legs. Unless these obligations are denominated in the same currency and are payable on a net basis, they are treated as gross obligations even if the contractual documentation permits netting of payments. This includes the notional principal of the transaction. Where a payment leg gives rise to interest or FX risk, the position must be included in the calculation of the appropriate foreign exchange risk or interest rate risk calculation (however, payments with a remaining maturity of less than one year are disregarded for interest rate risk purposes).

15.22 In general, the risk position for any transaction relating to financial instruments with a linear risk profile is the effective notional value of the position—that is the value of the underlying financial instruments established as current market price multiplied by quantity. Where the obligation is to make payments of a specified calculated amount (such as a fixed-floating swap), the exposure is the notional value of the outstanding gross payments multiplied by modified duration. Modified duration is a measure of the weighted average term to maturity of a security, and for this purpose is calculated as the delta of the value of the position divided by the delta of the interest level. In this calculation risk positions are assigned 'signs' according to whether the position is positive or negative for the reporting institution.

15.23 Collateral must be reflected in the calculation of the position, with collateral posted treated as an obligation immediately due to the counterparty, and collateral received treated as a claim immediately due from the counterparty. The effect of this is to net the collateral against the claim due. Where the collateral is the 'wrong way'—eg where an institution has provided collateral to a counterparty, but at the time of the transaction has money due to that counterparty rather than receivable from it, the collateral simply increases the credit risk exposure of the institution to the counterparty.

15.24 The standardized method may only be used for financial derivative instruments and long settlement transactions—it does not apply to securities financing arrangements. Also, it may only be used for derivatives with a 'linear' risk profile. A linear risk profile is a term which describes a transaction where the amount due under the transaction varies directly with another factor. An example might be an obligation to deliver a specified number of specified securities, where the value of the derivative is the number of securities multiplied by the market price of those securities, as the amount due will vary directly with the market price. A non-linear risk profile would arise under a transaction where the obligation was to pay a variable amount on the occurrence of a specified uncertain event, since for such a transaction the return does not vary directly with any single underlying factor. In general, non-linear risks must be dealt with by applying the mark to market method. This must be applied even where the form has a CAD 1 model or a VaR model if that model is not capable of estimating the delta or modified duration of the position. Each such exposure must be treated as a separate exposure—that is, no two non-linear positions treated under the mark to market method may be netted against each other.

E. Credit Risk Exposure Calculation

Once the reporting firm has established its individual risk positions, it must cal- **15.25** culate its net exposure. In principle, the exposure calculation is done instrument by instrument—thus, long and short notional positions in any identical instrument may be set off against each other. Positions in each instrument constitute a 'hedging set' of positions—thus long and short positions in any particular instrument are treated as hedging each other.

Underlying financial instruments other than debt instruments must be assigned **15.26** by a firm to the same respective hedging sets only if they are identical or 'similar' instruments.

- For equities, similar instruments are those of the same issuer. An equity index is treated as a separate issuer.

- For precious metals, similar instruments are those of the same metal. A precious metal index is treated as a separate precious metal.

- For electric power, similar instruments are those delivery rights and obligations that refer to the same peak or off-peak load time interval within any 24-hour interval.

- Actual and synthetic positions in debt instruments of a certain issuer, or from reference debt instruments of the same issuer that are emulated by payment legs, or that underlie a credit default swap, may be included in the same hedging set.

- For certain low risk instruments, positions in different instruments may be grouped together into a 'hedging set'. Instruments may be included in a hedging set if: (a) they are in the same currency; (b) they satisfy the criteria for an interest rate specific risk PRR of less than 1.6 per cent (see para 10.26 above); and (c) they fall within the same grouping in the table set out below.

	Government referenced interest rates	Non-government referenced interest rates
Maturity	<= 1 year	<= 1 year
Maturity	>1– <= 5 years	>1– <= 5 years
Maturity	5 years	>5 years

- There is one hedging set for each issuer of a reference debt instrument that underlies a credit default swap.

15.27 It is important to remember that the exposure which is being calculated here is the exposure to one particular counterparty. It is therefore a precondition for the inclusion of any exposure in a hedging set that it be covered by a netting agreement which permits the exposure to be set off against other exposures to the same counterparty. Thus if a reporting institution has an exposure to a particular counterparty which arises under a stand-alone agreement which is not covered by the general netting arrangements between it and the counterparty, it may not include that position within any hedging set, and must treat it as giving rise to a separate standalone exposure.

15.28 Once the net positions in the various different notional underlying instruments and exposure classes have been calculated, those positions must be turned into a credit requirement through the use of a CCR multiplier. The weightings to be used are those set out in Table 15.1 below.

Table 15.1 CCR multipliers

Hedging set categories	CCR multiplier
Interest rates	0.2%
Interest rates for risk positions from a reference debt instrument that underlies a credit default swap and to which a capital charge of 1.60% or less applies under the IRR approach	0.3%
Interest rates for risk positions from a debt instrument or reference debt instrument to which a capital charge of more than 1.60% applies under the IRR approach	0.6%
Exchange rates	2.5%
Electric power	4.0%
Gold	5.0%
Equity	7.0%
Precious metals (except gold)	8.5%
Other commodities	10.0%
Underlying instruments of financial derivative instruments that are not in any of the above categories.	10.0%

15.29 Once all this has been done, the firm must finally calculate its actual exposure value net of collateral. This is done by calculating:

(a) the current market value of the total portfolio of transactions included in the netting set, less the current market value of all of the collateral held in respect of those transactions;

(b) the sum of the risk positions (after collateral) of each hedging set within the netting set, weighted using the CCR multiplier above.

The higher of these two figures is the actual exposure value. The effect of this is that each netting set exposure has a floor equal to market value less collateral (ie the exposure can never be less than the net mark to market value of the exposure to the counterparty), but that where the risk adjusted calculation gives a higher figure, it is that higher figure which is used. This would generally be expected to be the case.

Finally, the total exposure calculated in this way is multiplied by a scaling factor if **15.30** 1.4 (β or beta). This scaling factor was introduced at the Basel level in order to ensure a degree of robustness within the system, and its calculation is well beyond the scope of this work. However, its effect is that if the product of the calculation described above is £10m, then the credit exposure which will arise from the CCR standardized method will be taken to be £14m, and this will be the exposure at default of the position.

F. The CCR Internal Model Method

A CCR internal model is, as it sounds, a model which is used by an institution to **15.31** counterparty credit risk. The output of a CCR model is the credit risk requirement (CRR) for the exposures modelled. There are few generally applicable rules which can be specified in respect of such models—they are developed by banks and approved and reviewed independently by regulators. Such models may well not catch all of the types of derivatives which fall within the CRR regime—where this is the case the firm may use one of the other CRR methods for such exposure. However, a firm which has introduced a CRR model for part of its CRR exposures is expected to roll out that model to their exposures (except immaterial exposures) within a reasonable period of time, and in particular is expected to apply that model to new types of derivative transaction which it enters into. However, in general, regulators will try very hard to avoid a firm 'cherry-picking' its exposures, using a CRR model where it gains an advantage from doing so but using the stand-ardized or mark to market methods where this would produce a lower risk charge.

CCR models, like any other CCR calculation, work at the level of the netting set. **15.32** They must compute the exposure value for the netting set at each future date, and should catch movement in collateral values. The output of a model should be an estimate of effective positive exposure (EPE). EPE is defined as the weighted aver-age effective exposure level (EE) at a series of times during the first year of exposure based on a variety of estimates of different market risk factors. The principle for the calculation of effective EE is simply that it can go up but not down—thus if the output of the firm's model suggests that EE over the next 12 months would be:

t0	t1	t2	t3	t4	t5
£10m	£20m	£20m	£30m	£20m	£10m

then effective EE would be:

£10m £20m £20m £30m £30m £30m[6]

15.33 It is a principle that the output of the CCR model—no matter how high it may be—must be multiplied by α (alpha). α, like β, is 1.4, but whereas β is set by regulatory fiat at 1.4, α is in principle either 1.4 or such higher number as the regulator may choose to require. However, if a firm can demonstrate that the output of its model is always at least 1.2 times EPE, then the regulator may give the firm permission to disapply the modifier.

15.34 A CRR model may take into account collateral by reducing the exposure to the relevant counterparty. However, if this is done it is important that the collateral not be reflected in any other calculation, since this would result in double-counting.

15.35 The requirements for the establishment, verification and operation of a CCR model are very similar to those which apply to the development and operation of a credit model. The firm must have a control unit that is responsible for the design and implementation of its CCR management system, including the initial and on-going validation of the model, and this unit must control input data integrity and produce and analyse reports on the output of the firm's risk measurement model, including an evaluation of the relationship between measures of risk exposure and credit and trading limits. The unit must be independent from the parts of the business responsible for originating, renewing or trading exposures and free from undue influence; it must be adequately staffed; and it must report directly to the senior management of the firm.

15.36 CCR models are also subject to the use test, in that a CCR model may not be sued for regulatory reporting if it is not closely integrated into the actual credit risk management process of the firm. It is not permitted to use a model for regulatory reporting unless the results of the same model are also used by the firm itself for that purpose. CCR models must be appropriately stress-tested.

15.37 Firms must be able to demonstrate to their regulator that their models have sufficient flexibility to capture general and specific wrong-way risk. General wrong-way risk is the risk that the probability of default of counterparties is correlated with another factor which is sued in the calculation. An example would be an interest rate derivative with a highly leveraged counterparty—the effect of this could be that increases in interest rates could reduce the exposure to the counterparty on the specific transaction, but increase the likelihood of the counterparty

---

[6] Note that a firm should be capable of establishing EE daily, and should be able to establish sufficient data points in the forthcoming year to adequately reflect the time structure of future cashflows.

actually defaulting. Specific wrong way risk arises where the risk is embedded in a particular transaction—taking a synthetic exposure to the credit of X and accepting collateral in the form of other credit claims on X would be an example. There is no specific rule relating to the way in which this is done, but regulators will require firms to show that they have considered and incorporated into their model the existence of wrong-way risk.

As with all of the model provisions of Basel, the ruse specify that the model must be validated and operated by reference to data which are validated independently of the business line, cover at least three years, and reflect a full business cycle. **15.38**

Contractual netting within the CCR regime

The netting requirements imposed in calculating CCR risk are slightly different from those applied in the calculation of on-balance sheet netting, since they must contemplate close-out and novation netting as well as simple set-off. However, the basic principle remains the same—netting may not be recognized unless it is legally robust and supported by appropriate legal opinions. **15.39**

The CCR netting regime applies to simple bilateral agreements relating to individual products or groups of products (generally referred to as master agreements). There are three groups of products for this purpose: **15.40**

(1) financial derivatives;
(2) repo and securities lending;
(3) margin lending.

Within these groups netting may be recognized across different agreements. However, in order to net across these groups—in other words, to net exposures arising under a repo agreement against exposures arising under a derivative transaction two criteria must be met. First, the firm must have in place with the counterparty 'contractual cross product netting agreements'—that is, written bilateral agreements which create a single legal obligation covering all included bilateral master agreements and transactions belonging to different product categories. Multilateral arrangements do not fall within this classification. Second, the firm must have a recognized CCR internal model. Firms which operate the CCR mark to market or standardized methods may not net across these classes.

The criteria which must be satisfied before netting can be recognized are as follows: **15.41**

(1) the firm must have a contractual netting agreement with its counterparty which creates a single legal obligation, covering all included transactions, such that, in the event of a counterparty's failure to perform owing to default, bankruptcy, liquidation or any other similar circumstance, the firm would

have a claim to receive or an obligation to pay only the net sum of the positive and negative mark-to-market values of included individual transactions;

(2) the firm must be in a position to provide its regulator, if requested, written and reasoned legal opinions to the effect that, in the event of a legal challenge, the relevant courts and administrative authorities would, in the cases described under (1), find that the firm's claims and obligations would be limited to the net sum, as described in (1), under:

   (a) the law of the jurisdiction in which the counterparty is incorporated and, if a foreign branch of an undertaking is involved, also under the law of the jurisdiction in which the branch is located; or

   (b) the law that governs the individual transactions included; or

   (c) the law that governs any contract or agreement necessary to effect the contractual netting;

(3) the firm must have procedures in place to ensure that the legal validity of its contractual netting is kept under review in the light of possible changes in the relevant laws;

(4) the firm must maintain all required documentation in its files;

(5) the effects of netting must be factored into the firm's measurement of each counterparty's aggregate credit risk exposure and the firm must manage its CCR on such a basis; and

(6) the firm must aggregate credit risk to each counterparty to arrive at a single legal exposure across transactions; this aggregation must be factored into credit limit purposes and internal capital purposes.

15.42 There is an interesting quirk in the position of EU national supervisors as regards netting. Ordinarily, the judgement as to whether a particular legal opinion constitutes a 'clean' legal opinion is a matter for the home regulator alone. However, under the BCD, where a regulator in one of the jurisdictions required to be covered by (2) above is not satisfied that the laws of its jurisdiction are sufficiently robust to permit netting, no other regulator may recognize netting which involves that jurisdiction.[7] Thus, regulators cannot designate their jurisdictions as 'good' jurisdictions, but they can designate them as 'bad' jurisdictions, and if they do the latter then their decision is unquestionable by other regulators.

15.43 A firm must not recognize for netting purposes any contract which contains a 'walkaway' clause—that is, a clause which permits a non-defaulting counterparty to make limited payments only, or no payments at all, to the estate of the defaulter, even if the defaulter is a net creditor. This is true whether or not it is possible to obtain a clean netting opinion on the contract in the relevant jurisdictions.

---

[7] BCD Annex III part 7 point (b), BIPRU 13.7.7.

In order for a cross-product netting agreement to be recognized for netting purposes, the netting effected under the agreement and the legal opinions relating to the agreement must include all of the agreements within the cross-product netting agreement. Thus a cross-product netting agreement may only be recognized if: **15.44**

(a) the netting it effects captures all (and not some only) of the master agreements which it covers;
(b) the legal opinions address the validity of the entire agreement across all of the relevant products; and
(c) the bilateral agreements included under the cross-product master continue to comply on a standalone basis with the requirements for recognition.

CCR models and securities financing transactions

Where a firm has a CCR model which covers securities financing transactions, it should use that model to calculate its exposure. If it has a master netting agreement internal model, it may use that model. If it has both, it may choose which approach to apply. If it has neither, it may either use the master netting agreement approach contained in the collateral rules (if it is permitted to do so—a firm which uses the financial collateral simple method will not be permitted to do this). If all of this fails, then it will be obliged to treat the exposure as a collateralized receivable and apply the relevant collateral method (simple or comprehensive, as appropriate) to recognize the securities financed as collateral. However, it should be noted that the financial collateral simple method is not available in respect of securities financing transactions in the trading book. **15.45**

16

SECURITIZATION AND REPACKAGING

A. Introduction

Given that the Basel Accord is intended to reflect credit risk, it might have been **16.01** expected that the rationale for a separate treatment of securitization exposures would have disappeared, and that exposures to securitization vehicles would be evaluated in exactly the same way as exposures to other types of vehicles, based on credit characteristics. In fact, exactly the opposite is the case.

The reason for this lies in the difference between 'top-down' and 'bottom-up' **16.02** portfolio valuations. Top-down valuations take correlation effects into account—therefore, the risk of default on a portfolio valued on a top-down basis is less than the sum of the risks of default of the individual components, since not all of the constituents of the portfolio are likely to default at once. Conversely, bottom-up valuations are simply the sum of the risk of default of the individual components. Thus, for any portfolio, the top-down risk will be less than the bottom-up risk. The principle which the Accord applies is that a top-down approach should only be used for certain classes of assets (retail loans and purchased receivables), and all other classes of receivables should be assessed using a bottom-up approach.

Securitization presents a problem for this approach. The problem is that once a **16.03** pool of assets has been securitized, the capital which is required to be held against such notes must be calculated by assessing the default risk of these notes. This is calculated by assessing the risk arising on the portfolio of assets owned by the securitization vehicle. This calculation is, necessarily, made using a top-down approach, since the risk of default of notes issued by the securitization vehicle is necessarily the risk on the individual assets held by that vehicle adjusted for correlation risk.

16.04 The problem which this creates for the Basel structure is that it creates the theoretical possibility that a firm could take assets which it is required to evaluate using a bottom-up approach, securities them, buy back the securitization notes, and obtain a reduction in its total capital requirement (since the total risk of all of the securitization notes will reflect correlation effects within the securitization vehicle, and will therefore be a top-down evaluation—which, by definition, will be less than the bottom-up figure).

16.05 The draftsmen of the Accord have responded to this problem by creating a series of approaches to securitization exposures which have the effect of imposing a higher capital requirement on those exposures than their rating or PD would require if they were any other class of exposure. Where an interest is defined as a securitization interest, it therefore has a heavier capital requirement than would be the case were it not so defined.

16.06 A further, and potentially more serious, problem is that the standardized approach to unrated assets gives a 100 per cent default weighting—a weighting which would be very advantageous for many securitization tranches. As a result, the securitization framework proceeds from the fundamental principle that securitization exposures should be deducted unless there is a good reason to give them some better treatment. Good reasons can be manufactured, but it is still the case that a bank purchasing an unrated note in a securitization where it does not have full information in respect of the underlying asset pool should expect to have to deduct it.

B. What is a Securitization?

16.07 It should therefore be clear that the potential consequences of a structure being held to be a 'securitization' are significant. It is therefore distressing that the regulatory system almost goes out of its way to avoid delivering precision on this point.

16.08 As with many public decisions this, although uncomfortable, is not unjustifiable. The core principle on which the Accord proceeds is that:

> Since securitisations may be structured in many different ways, the capital treatment of a securitisation exposure must be determined on the basis of its economic substance

rather than its legal form. . . [S]upervisors will look to the economic substance of a transaction to determine whether it should be subject to the securitisation framework for purposes of determining regulatory capital.[1]

The test is therefore one of economic substance rather than legal form.

The Accord provides some more helpful definitions of 'traditional' and 'synthetic' securitizations.   **16.09**

> A traditional securitisation is a structure where the cash flow from an underlying pool of exposures is used to service at least two different stratified risk positions or tranches reflecting different degrees of credit risk. Payments to the investors depend upon the performance of the specified underlying exposures, as opposed to being derived from an obligation of the entity originating those exposures. The stratified/ tranched structures that characterise securitisations differ from ordinary senior/ subordinated debt instruments in that junior securitisation tranches can absorb losses without interrupting contractual payments to more senior tranches, whereas subordination in a senior/subordinated debt structure is a matter of priority of rights to the proceeds of liquidation.[2]
>
> . . .
>
> A synthetic securitisation is a structure with at least two different stratified risk positions or tranches that reflect different degrees of credit risk where credit risk of an underlying pool of exposures is transferred, in whole or in part, through the use of funded (e.g. credit-linked notes) or unfunded (e.g. credit default swaps) credit derivatives or guarantees that serve to hedge the credit risk of the portfolio. Accordingly, the investors' potential risk is dependent upon the performance of the underlying pool.[3]

Given the significance of the drafting of these provisions, it is appropriate to provide the equivalent definition as it has been translated into the CRD. The relevant sections (subsections 37 to 39 of Article 4) read:

> (37) 'traditional securitisation' means a securitisation involving the economic transfer of the exposures being securitised to a securitisation special purpose entity which issues securities. This shall be accomplished by the transfer of ownership of the securitised exposures from the originator credit institution or through sub-participation. The securities issued do not represent payment obligations of the originator credit institution;
>
> (38) 'synthetic securitisation' means a securitisation where the tranching is achieved by the use of credit derivatives or guarantees, and the pool of exposures is not removed from the balance sheet of the originator credit institution;
>
> (39) 'tranche' means a contractually established segment of the credit risk associated with an exposure or number of exposures, where a position in the segment entails a

---

[1] Accord, para 538.
[2] Accord, para 539.
[3] Accord, para 540.

risk of credit loss greater than or less than a position of the same amount in each other such segment, without taking account of credit protection provided by third parties directly to the holders of positions in the segment or in other segments

This latter forms the basis of the rules of the FSA and other EU regulators.

16.10 At first glance this looks alarming. The drafting is clearly effective to catch mainstream securitizations, along with asset-backed securities, mortgage-backed securities, credit enhancements, liquidity facilities, interest rate or currency swaps, credit derivatives and tranched cover. It is also notable that there is nothing in the definition which limits the concept by reference to types of underlyings—on this basis you could securitize racehorses. However, there are many financing structures which involve tranching of some form or other which are not intended to be securitizations, and which would cause great difficulty for banks if they were to fall within the securitization framework.

16.11 The reason that this is not more problematic is that there are three substantial 'safer harbours' for tranched financings. The first is the fact that a securitization, by definition, involves a pool of underlying assets. An arrangement with respect to a single asset cannot constitute a securitization. The second is the exclusion for 'subordination' set out in the Basel definition of a traditional securitization. The logic of this statement may be questionable, but in policy terms the exclusion of subordination arrangements from the class of securitizations saves the majority of leveraged finance and structured lending transactions. The third substantial safe harbour is the 'specialized financing' regime, which covers real estate, project and asset financing arrangements. It seems to be established (although it is nowhere positively stated) that an exposure which falls within both the securitization and the specialized finance definitions will fall within the specialized finance rather than the securitization field. Thus another substantial chunk of tranched financing is preserved from the securitization regime.

16.12 Unfortunately, however, there is still considerable scope for structured finance transactions to fall within the securitization regime inadvertently, and considerable care must be taken in analysing structures for this reason.

16.13 The selection of tranching as the touchstone for securitization has the interesting consequence that any single-tranche repackaging of a pool of assets is not a securitization. This applies to credit derivative exposures as well as formal repackagings. However, it is remarkably difficult in many cases to be satisfied that a repackaging is in fact single tranche—for example, a single tranche repackaging which has the benefit of a liquidity facility may well be classified as tranched if the liquidity facility is repayable in advance of the securities issued. In the same way, including features such as synthetic yield traps in credit derivative structures could give rise to arguments that the CDS had become a synthetic securitization, with potentially adverse consequences for bank protection sellers.

It is not, in general, possible to resolve issues as to the securitization or otherwise **16.14** status by textual analysis of the relevant rules. In practice dialogue with supervisors is likely to be the only way in which a meaningful set of ground rules come to be developed in this regard.

C. True Sale and Derecognition of Assets

The starting point for the securitization regime is that where a bank originates a **16.15** securitization, the assets concerned should appear on its balance sheet unless the criteria for derecognition of those assets can be satisfied. A bank may act as originator in a number of ways. The most common is the situation where a bank accumulates assets on its own balance sheet and then sells them to a securitization vehicle. However, banks may be originators with respect to assets even if they never own the relevant assets directly. A bank which funds an SPV which then acquires assets is an originator, as is a bank which neither sells not funds assets, but merely acts as a sponsor of a vehicle which raises money from third parties and acquires assets from other third parties—this is common with asset backed commercial paper (ABCP) vehicles. Thus wherever a bank is involved in the establishment of a securitization or repackaging vehicle, the management or advising of such a vehicle, the placement of securities for such a vehicle or the provision of liquidity or credit enhancement to it, it is at risk of having the vehicle's assets treated as its own (and therefore of having to hold capital against them) unless it can satisfy the derecognition conditions.

A bank may originate a securitization by putting into the securitization assets which **16.16** it currently owns. Where this happens, the question is as to whether the assets should be treated as no longer owned by the bank. However, a bank may also originate a securitization by arranging for a vehicle to raise money from third parties and then spend that money on acquiring assets from third parties. In this case the starting point is that the assets are brought onto the balance sheet of the bank by reason of the fact that they have been acquired by a securitization vehicle in respect of which the bank is the originator. This produces the apparent paradox that the bank is seeking to remove from its balance sheet assets which, on an accounting analysis, were never on it in the first place. This helps to illustrate the fact that in the context of securitization and its treatment for regulatory purposes, the accounting and regulatory analyses of any given situation may be very different.

There is an interesting issue here about the scope of the securitization regime as **16.17** regards the origin of the assets securitized. The FSA states that the rules on the treatment of assets which are securitized only apply to assets originated in the non-trading book, and do not apply to assets in the trading book.[4] Although not

---

[4] BIPRU 9.1.9.

immediately intuitively obvious, this is in fact correct. Where assets are purchased into the trading book and sold on to a securitization vehicle, the ordinary trading book rules will apply, and those assets will be netted through the ordinary trading book mechanics. For a synthetic securitization of trading book assets the treatment which will apply will be the ordinary trading book treatment of CDSs, which again will result in a net exposure. Thus it is only in the context of assets originated in the banking book that the securitization assets regime really applies.

16.18 Once assets have been identified as securitization assets in a securitization where a bank is an originator, the bank can only remove those assets from its regulatory report if it satisfies the criteria for derecognition. The most important of these is the requirement that the transaction result in some actual transfer of risk, and that that transfer be 'significant'. For this purpose the FSA has suggested that a transfer should be treated as 'significant' where the proportion of risk transferred is at least equal to the proportion by which the capital requirement is reduced[5]—put simply, if the effect of the transaction is to reduce the capital requirement for the originator by 25 per cent, then at least 25 per cent of the risk must have been transferred outside the bank group.

16.19 Where a securitization transfers no meaningful risk, or where the amount of risk transferred does not meet the test for being 'significant' (as would be the case where, for example, the originator retained the risky pieces of the transaction) then it is disregarded. This is important, since as noted above the effect of the securitization regime is to increase the overall capital requirement which is applied to securitization exposures. The guiding principle here is that the originator should never find himself in a worse position than he would have been in had he retained the securitized assets on his own balance sheet.

16.20 Provided that a securitization satisfies the basic test of transferring significant risk, the assets concerned will be derecognized providing that the securitization structure satisfies certain minimum tests. Given that the securitization regime captures both traditional and synthetic securitizations, a separate set of tests are provided in each case.

16.21 For traditional securitizations the tests are as follows:

(1) The transferor does not maintain effective or indirect control over the transferred exposures. A transferor will be presumed to have maintained effective control over the transferred credit risk exposures if it:
   (a) is able to repurchase from the transferee the previously transferred exposures in order to realize their benefits; or
   (b) is obligated to retain the risk of the transferred exposures; but not

---

[5] BIPRU 9.3.2.

    (c) if it is merely appointed as servicer in respect of the assets.

(2) The assets are effectively legally isolated from the transferor and its creditors on insolvency (eg through the sale of assets or through subparticipation). This test is not satisfied unless a legal opinion as to the effectiveness of the transfer has been obtained from appropriate external legal counsel.

(3) The securities issued confer no rights against the originator, but only a claim to the underlying assets.

(4) The transferee is a special purpose entity ('SPE') and beneficial interests in that SPE are freely transferable.

(5) Clean-up calls[6] must satisfy the conditions:

    (a) their exercise must not be mandatory, in substance or in form;

    (b) they must not be structured to provide credit enhancement (ie to avoid allocating losses to be absorbed by credit enhancements or positions held by investors or otherwise structured); and

    (c) they must only be exercisable when 10 per cent or less of the original underlying portfolio or reference portfolio value remains.

(6) Certain prohibited provisions must not appear in the securitization framework:

    (a) the originating bank must not be required to alter systematically the underlying exposures such that the pool's weighted average credit quality is improved unless this is achieved by selling assets to independent and unaffiliated third parties at market prices;

    (b) the framework must not allow for increases in a retained first loss position or credit enhancement provided by the originating bank after the transaction's inception;

    (c) there must be no provision for an increase in the yield payable to parties other than the originating bank, such as investors and third-party providers of credit enhancements, in response to a deterioration in the credit quality of the underlying pool ('step-ups').

(7) The documentation must reflect the economic reality of the transaction.

For synthetic securitizations, the tests are: **16.22**

(1) The contractual arrangements must satisfy the same tests as for a traditional securitization—that is, the documentation must be effective, legally binding and covered by external legal opinions. The obligations of the originator must be limited in the same way—thus if the underlying quality of the pool

---

[6] A clean-up call is an arrangement whereby if the total pool of assets falls below a certain level (conventionally 10% of the initial value), the sponsor may elect to buy back all of the outstanding notes and collapse the structure. They are used to avoid sponsors having to pay for the maintenance of a financing structure after most of the assets held within it have matured.

deteriorates the originator should not be required to improve the pool or increase the amount of premium to be paid.

(2) The protection provided should not:
   (a) be subject to significant materiality thresholds below which credit protection is deemed not to be triggered even if a credit event occurs, or
   (b) allow for the termination of the protection due to deterioration in the credit quality of the underlying exposures.

(3) The protection should not contain clauses that provide for increases in a retained first loss position or credit enhancement provided by the originating bank after the transaction's inception.

(4) Any clause in a synthetic securitization which provides for a feature which is economically equivalent to a clean-up call must comply with the requirements for a clean-up call in a traditional securitization.

'Derecognition' for synthetic securitizations

16.23 Derecognition for traditional securitizations is a relatively straightforward concept—the assets concerned are simply removed from the balance sheet. Derecognition for synthetic securitizations is slightly more complex. We need here to restate the basis of the definition of a synthetic securitization—an arrangement where a bank has transferred a significant portion of the risk of a pool of assets held on its own balance sheet by buying protection from eligible protection providers on a tranched basis. The difficulty here is that many CDS's are 'tranched' in the sense that they provide for a 'threshold' loss amount which, if it occurs, constitutes a loss borne by the protection buyer rather than a protection seller. Such arrangements are economically identical to a first loss/second loss tranching arrangement, and therefore constitute tranching. Thus, in a situation where an issuer has purchased protection directly on a pool of receivables whilst retaining a 'first loss' exposure in the form of a minimum threshold before the protection can be called, the arrangements will constitute a synthetic securitization.

16.24 The regulatory treatment of this position is that the bank must analyse the entire portfolio as a securitization, identifying tranches which it has retained and tranches which it has sold. It must then treat those tranches as it would any other securitization tranche. Thus, in the example given above, the bank would analyse the transaction into a first loss and a senior piece. It would apply to the exposure which it retained (the minimum threshold amount) the treatment accorded to first loss pieces of securitizations—generally deduction from capital. It would then consider the second loss piece. In general there are two possible ways that this can come out. One is where the credit protection purchased is unfunded. In this case the treatment applied to the assets composing the pool is simply the substitution of the risk weight of the protection provider for the risk weight of the underlying asset. The other is where the protection is funded—that is, where the protection provider has put up cash collateral equal to the value of the assets. In this case the ordinary cash collateralization rules will apply, and the risk exposure on the assets will generally be reduced to zero.

There is one wrinkle to this treatment. Where an asset is sold to a securitization **16.25** special purpose vehicle (SPV), the transfer is generally permanent (or, if it is not, off-balance sheet treatment for the assets transferred is unlikely to be achieved). Synthetic securitizations are based on guarantees and credit default swaps, both of which almost invariably exist for a specified period of time and have a termination date. This creates no issues where the termination date of the protection must necessarily fall due after the relevant assets have matured. However, it is clearly the case that sometimes the duration of the protection will be less than the maximum theoretical duration of the assets (this is a particular problem in the mortgage markets, since the legal maturity of a mortgage in the UK is generally 25 years). This problem is particularly acute since the duration of protection for this purpose is taken to be the first date on which it can be cancelled by the protection provider, in the same way as any other item of unfunded credit protection (see para 9.33 above).

The simplest approach to this problem would be to require that protection must **16.26** equal the duration of the assets protected in order to be eligible for recognition. However, this would place insupportable difficulties in the way of many synthetic securitizations. A mechanism is therefore provided for the resolution of this problem, based on two assumptions. The first is that any asset or protection with a maturity of over five years should be treated as if it had a maturity of five years—thus if a bank owns assets with a 20-year maturity and has protected them with synthetic securitization protection with a five-year maturity there is deemed to be no mismatch. The second is that maturity mismatches are deemed to have an impact on a sliding scale over time, with a six-month mismatch between (say) five-year assets and four-year six-month protection having relatively little impact, whereas a six-month mismatch between two-year assets and one-year six-month protection being very significant. The relevant formula is slightly different from that which is normally applied to maturity mismatches (see para 9.33 above), and is:

$$\text{Risk Weighted Exposure Amount} = [RW(SP) \times (t - t^*)/(T - t^*)] + [RW(Ass) \times (T - t)/(T - t^*)]$$

where:

RW(Ass) is risk weighted exposure amounts for exposures if they had not been securitized calculated on a pro-rata basis;

RW(SP) is risk weighted exposure amounts calculated under BIPRU 9.6.3 G as if there was no maturity mismatch;

T is maturity of the underlying exposures expressed in years;

t is maturity of credit protection expressed in years; and

t* is 0.25.

Implicit support, or 'de-derecognition'

16.27 In certain circumstances an originator who has transferred assets via a securitization may be compelled by the regulator to take the assets back again. This will arise where the originator is held to have provided 'implicit support' for the securitization. Implicit support may be defined as any action taken by the sponsor which would have the effect of reducing potential or actual losses to investors. Classical examples of implicit support would include repurchase of securitization notes at a price above the market price or substituting assets into the pool with the aim of improving the quality of the overall pool.

16.28 In order for support to constitute implicit support it must be implicit—that is, it must not be pursuant to a formal obligation on the originator set out in the securitization documentation. Where a sponsor commits itself in securitization documentation to do certain things which have the effect of supporting the pool, it may do those things without being held to have provided implicit support. The converse of this, of course, is that where an originator sets out in a document that it may do certain things, for regulatory capital purpose it will be treated as having done them in full. Thus, if a sponsor agrees that it may if called upon contribute up to a certain percentage of the pool in the form of capital support, that capital support will be treated as having been contributed in full, and the relevant deduction made from its capital.

16.29 The most common forms of implicit support are the buying back of notes from investors and the recomposition of asset pools. As to note buybacks, there is no prohibition on originators purchasing interests in their own securitizations, provided that such purchases are undertaken at fair market value on an arm's length basis and have been subjected to the normal credit and liquidity review processes of the relevant bank.

16.30 There is also an issue as regards sanctions for implicit support. The FSA, for example, treats the provision of implicit support as a free-standing breach of its rules, capable of being sanctioned like any other regulatory breach. However, the draftsmen of the Accord (and, to be fair, the BCD, with less excuse), did not feel that they could provide for disciplinary consequences for breaches of prudential rules, not least because of the wide variety of different consequences. Consequently the Accord provides only that a bank which has provided implicit support to a securitization vehicle must publicly acknowledge the fact that it has done so.

D. Risk Weighting of Securitization Exposures

Any exposure to a securitization must be weighted under the securitization regime **16.31** and not under the ordinary regime. This includes exposures arising from interest rate or currency derivatives, as well as any credit protection provided to a securitization vehicle. Where an exposure to a securitization arises through an off balance sheet arrangement, the arrangement must be converted into an on balance sheet exposure using a credit conversion factor of 100 per cent.

Where an IRB bank calculates the weighting of a securitization position, the size **16.32** of the position used to calculate the exposure is the gross position before value adjustments. However, the risk weighted exposure amount of any securitization position may be reduced by 12.5 times the amount of any value adjustments actually made. However, where the position is carried with a risk weight of 1250 per cent, value adjustments used in this way may not also be taken into account in the expected loss calculation.

It may sometimes happen that a bank which holds a securitization position receives **16.33** credit support in relation to that securitization position, either from the SPV or from a third party. In broad terms the position here is the same as that for any other position subject to credit support—where the credit support is cash collateral the value of the exposure will be reduced in accordance with the rules set out above in Chapter 9.

It may sometimes occur that a firm has overlapping positions in a securitization— **16.34** that is, two or more positions which have the characteristic that only one of them can be actually lost, or (more usually) that the occurrence of a loss on one will reduce *pro tanto* the loss on the other. Where this is the case the exposures should be netted against each other to produce an exposure value equal to the largest loss actually capable of being made, and this exposure should be weighted using the approach which gives the highest weighting.

E. Weighting Holdings of Securitization Positions— the Standardized Approach

The position of a standardized bank which holds securitization positions is set out **16.35** in paras 6.51 to 6.55 above. The basis of the standardized approach is that securitization exposures with a rating of BBB- or above will carry the same capital requirements as notes issued by a corporate with the same rating. Divergence begins in the BB- to BB- range, where notes issued by a corporate would carry a 100 per cent weighting but securitization exposures held by independent investors carry a 350 per cent weighting. Below this level, notes issued by a corporate would carry a 150 per cent weighting whereas notes issued by a securitization vehicle will be deducted from capital.

16.36 In the standardized approach, the risk weighting of the originator or sponsor is capped at the amount which would be applied to the relevant exposures had they not been securitized. Thus an originator or sponsor can never suffer a higher charge as a result of a securitization than they would have done had they held the entirety of the pool on their own balance sheet. However, this rule applies only to the portfolio as a whole—it would be perfectly possible for an originator to sell 50 per cent of the risk on a portfolio and find itself with a capital charge equal to 90 per cent of the charge to which it was originally subject.

16.37 In general, all positions in unrated securitizations must be deducted. However, there are some securitizations where external ratings are not sought. In such circumstances there is a relaxation of the rule that all securitization exposures which are not rated must be deducted. This arises in two circumstances; where the investor holds an exposure to a defined portfolio in which it has full transparency as to the underlying assets, and where the investor holds a second loss or better piece of an asset-backed commercial paper programme. Where the investor has full transparency,[7] it may calculate the capital requirement which would be applied to the underlying asset pool and weight its exposure as a proportion of that exposure multiplied by a concentration ratio. Thus, there are three parts to this process, which can be expressed as:

Capital weighting of pool × % holding in pool × concentration ratio

The concentration ratio here is the sum of all of the nominal amounts of all of the tranches divided by the sum of the nominal amounts of the tranches junior to that held, including the position itself. Thus, imagine an unrated securitization with a value of £100 divided into £60 senior, £30 mezzanine and £10 first loss. Imagine that a bank holds £15 of the mezzanine tranche. The concentration ratio which will be applied will be £100 (the nominal amount of all the tranches) divided by £40 (the sum of the tranches junior to and including the one held), or 2.5. The risk-weighted exposure amount will therefore be 15 per cent of the amount which it would be if the assets were held on balance sheet multiplied by 2.5. The concentration ratio could get very large if such holdings were to extend to very junior tranches, and the total is therefore capped at full deduction of 1250 per cent weighting. This approach may also be used for unrated tranches of securitizations where there are more senior rated pieces, but in this case the charge is floored at

---

[7] The FSA, in BIPRU 9.11.7 (4), suggests that this means access to pool composition at least daily.

the risk-weighted exposure amount which would apply if the holding were a holding in the rated tranche—in other words, this approach cannot be used to give a junior tranche a lower requirement than that which would apply to a more senior tranche.

A different rule applies where the holding is a holding in an unrated ABCP programme. In this case, where the position is in an investment grade tranche other than a first loss position (generally a second loss position) and where the holder of the tranche does not also provide first loss support, the position may be given a weighting equal to the higher of 100 per cent or the weighting which would apply under the standardized approach to the highest rated of the underlying assets in the pool—thus if some of the assets in the pool would carry a 150 per cent weighting then the weighting to be applied to the tranche would be 150 per cent, but if the highest rated asset in the pool were 50 per cent, the weighting to be applied to the tranche would be 100 per cent. **16.38**

Liquidity facilities

Where a standardized bank has advanced a liquidity facility to a securitization, **16.39** it may treat the exposure as carrying a risk weight of the highest weight which would apply to any asset in the pool under the standardized approach without the 100 per cent floor, and in addition may apply a 20 per cent conversion factor if the term of the liquidity facility is under one year, and a 50 per cent conversion factor if the term is over one year. This treatment only applies if the liquidity facility satisfies some fairly rigorous requirements; notably:

- the liquidity facility documentation must clearly identify and limit the circumstances under which the facility may be drawn;

- it must not be possible for the facility to be drawn so as to provide credit support by covering losses already incurred at the time of draw—for example, by providing liquidity in respect of exposures in default at the time of draw or by acquiring assets at more than fair value;

- the facility must not be used to provide permanent or regular funding for the securitization;

- repayment of draws on the facility must not be subordinated to the claims of investors other than to claims arising in respect of interest rate or currency derivative contracts, fees or other such payments, nor be subject to waiver or deferral;

- it must not be possible for the facility to be drawn after all applicable credit enhancements from which the liquidity facility would benefit are exhausted; and

- the facility must include a provision that results in an automatic reduction in the amount that can be drawn by the amount of exposures that are in default, where default has the meaning given to it for the purposes of the IRB approach, or where the pool of securitized exposures consists of rated instruments, that terminates the facility if the average quality of the pool falls below investment grade.

These requirements go to both the terms of the facility document and the way in which it is to be used in practice.

16.40 A further concession—although one rarely encountered in practice—is granted for a liquidity facility which meets all of the conditions set out above and, in addition, either:

(a) may be drawn only in the event of general market disruption, or
(b) is unconditionally cancellable and where repayment of draws on the facility are senior to any other claims on the vehicle.

Such facilities have a 0 per cent conversion factor and are therefore treated as credit risk free.

16.41 For synthetic securitizations under the standardized approach a credit conversion factor must be applied to the exposure. The credit conversion factor prescribed for such exposures is 100 per cent, regardless of tenor (this may be compared with the figure used in the standardized approach of 50 per cent for exposures of more than one year and 20 per cent for exposures of less than one year.

F. The IRB Approach

16.42 There are three methods available to IRB firms for calculating the capital charge to be applied to securitization positions. It is important to understand that the default position for any securitization holding is deduction—thus the default treatment for any exposure which does not fit within one of these approaches is deduction.

16.43 The fundamental approach is the ratings based approach (RBA), which—as it implies—derives securitization capital charges from the external ratings given to the relevant position. The RBA may be applied both to securitization tranches which are actually rated and securitization tranches which have an 'inferred' rating—that is, which are unrated but which are senior to or pari passu with tranches which are rated, and which have maturities which are longer than those of the rated positions.

16.44 Firms which are able to do so may use the supervisory formula approach (SFA)—however, it is relatively rare for any firm other than an originator or sponsor to be able to calculate an SFA requirement, and in general bank investors in securitization paper are not in a position to use the SFA to calculate their requirement for that paper.

The ABCP internal assessment approach (IAA) is, as it sounds, only available for **16.45** ABCPs.

The ratings based approach

The basis of the ratings based approach is, as it sounds, the external rating of the **16.46** paper issued by the securitization vehicle.

Credit quality step	Most senior tranche(1)	Normal treatment	Non-granular pools (3)
1	7% (6%)(2)	12%	20%
2	8%	15%	25%
3	10%	18%	35%
4	12%	20%	35%
5	20%	35%	35%
6	35%	50%	50%
7	60%	75%	75%
8	100%	100%	100%
9 and 10	250%	250%	250%
11	425%	425%	425%
12	650%	650%	650%
13	1250%	1250%	1250%

(1) The most senior tranche for this purpose means the most senior tranche disregarding any super-senior items due in respect of interest or currency derivatives or senior liquidity facilities.

(2) A senior tranche which is senior to a tranche which would qualify for credit quality step 1 may be weighted at 6 per cent rather than 7 per cent.

(3) In principle a non-granular pool is a pool which contains less than six items. However, the calculation of the number of items in a pool is done by using a weighted average rather than by simply counting—thus a pool containing one £1m asset and six £1 assets will not count as granular for this purpose. The formula for calculating the effective number of exposures is:

$$N = (((\Sigma_i)(EAD_i))^2)/((\Sigma i)(EAD_i^2))$$

where EAD_i represents the sum of the exposure values of all exposures to the ith obligor. Where a securitization is a resecuritization this means that the bank must count the number of exposures in the immediate pool rather than the number of underlying assets—thus a resecuritization containing three tranches of bonds issued by a mortgage securitization vehicle would be non-granular for this purpose, even though there may be many thousands of mortgages underlying the bonds.

The supervisory formula approach

The basis of the supervisory formula approach is the calculation of K_{irb} figure. K_{irb} **16.47** is the regulatory capital requirement which would be arrived at under the IRB methodology if the assets held in the securitization were held directly on the balance sheet of the bank concerned. This assessment must be made on an asset-by-asset basis, and it is unlikely that any institution which is not the originating bank will be able to calculate K_{irb}. Thus, again, it is likely that the only use of the SFA which will be encountered in practice will be where it is used by sponsoring banks to weight commitments such as liquidity lines and credit support arrangements.

16.48 In order to use the SFA a bank must have sufficient information about the underlying assets to calculate K_{irb}—the level of capital which would have been required had the assets not been securitized, and must further be able to calculate the level of credit enhancement for a relevant tranche, the tranche thickness, the pool's effective number of loans and the pool's exposure-weighted average loss-given-default.

16.49 The overall effect of the regime is that if assets were securitized and all of the paper issued by the securitization vehicle were held by institutions, the total capital requirement of the system as a whole would increase slightly. This is because prior to the securitization the capital requirement would have been K_{irb}, whereas after the securitization a charge equal to K_{irb} must be taken by the owner of the equity piece and a further charge must be taken by the owners of the senior pieces. As a result, one of the more important features of the proposed regime is that the position of the originating bank is capped at K_{irb}—thus an originating bank can never be worse off than it would have been had it not securitized the assets at all.

16.50 The formula for the SFA is absurdly complicated, and is not reproduced here. It is set out in para 624 of the Accord, and explained in paras 623 to 636.

16.51 The concessions available for liquidity facilities within the IRB approach are as for the standardized regime (see above para 16.39).

The ABCP IAA

16.52 The ABCP IAA does not—again paradoxically—apply to commercial paper. What it does apply to is exposures such as liquidity facilities and credit enhancements which are advanced by a bank to an ABCP of which it is the sponsor. The essence of the IAA is that where the ABCP conduit itself is rated, the bank may treat its unrated exposures to the conduit as having the benefit of an inferred rating derived from the rating of the CP issued by the conduit.

G. Revolving Credit Securitizations

16.53 A revolving credit securitization is a securitization of (usually retail) revolving assets (such as credit card balances, overdrafts and similar assets), and its distinguishing characteristic is that the pool of assets underlying the securitization is continually maturing and being redrawn. It should be emphasized that the starting point for the approach set out in the Accord is that revolving credit securitizations should, in principle, be treated like any other securitization, and investors in notes issued by revolving credit securitization vehicles are in this respect in no different a position than holders of any other type of securitization. The position of the originator, however, is different. This is because of the effect of a feature of a standard revolving credit securitization known as early amortization. The treatment of an originator of a revolving credit securitization is therefore that it should calculate an additional risk charge to reflect this risk.

It must be noted that the concern arises as a specific incident of the securitization **16.54** of revolving assets. Securitizations where the underlying assets do not revolve, but where the life of a vehicle is extended by arrangements whereby the redemption proceeds of assets held within the structure are used to purchase new assets ('replenishment structures') are not affected by these rules, even where the terms of the notes issued provide for early amortization. Equally these issues do not arise where an early amortization provision is triggered only by external factors (change of law and similar events). It is only where the relevant early amortization provision is triggered by a change in the performance of the securitized assets that the provisions of these early amortization rules apply.

The problem with revolving credit assets (such as overdrafts) is that it is never **16.55** possible to be confident what any individual component of the pool will be worth on any specific day in the future. Consequently a revolving credit securitization must be structured so that the pool of receivables is at all times worth at least an amount equal to the amount due to the noteholders. This means that in practice the pool will have to be larger than the value of the notes issued. This means that the originator must contribute into the pool a larger quantity of assets than is required to back the claims of the noteholders, and it will continue to own the excess assets within the pool. The resulting structure is shown in Figure 16.1:

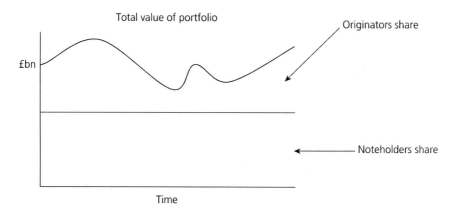

Fig. 16.1 A Revolving Credit Securitization

16.56 An early amortization provision is a provision by which, on the occurrence of a specified event, the revolving structure ceases to revolve. As the assets in the pool are paid down, the amounts received are used to repay noteholders' interests, and further drawings on the facilities become a matter for the originator alone. Thus, the effect of an early amortization is to transfer the assets back to the sponsor. Again in principle this is not problematic. However, the problem in practice is that 'good' assets are likely to repay faster than bad ones, and bad ones—by definition—may not repay at all. Consequently if all of the receipts from the pool on an early amortization were to be used to repay noteholders, the result would be that the noteholders would get cash and the originator would be left with the credit problems—in effect the originator would have first loss exposure. The revolving securitization rules are an attempt to deal with this problem.

16.57 The basis of the approach is to divide early amortization provisions into 'controlled' and 'non-controlled'. In broad terms a 'controlled' early amortization is a structure which seeks to allocate credit risks on the pool as a whole between the originator and the noteholders in a relatively equitable fashion, and an 'uncontrolled' early amortization is one where the noteholders effectively receive priority. A 'controlled' early amortization is defined as an amortization which occurs where: (a) investors remain exposed to losses on the underlying portfolio during the amortization period; (b) investors and originator share pro rata in amounts received; (c) an amortization period is prescribed, and amortization payments are made through that period, at a rate such that investors are not fully paid out until at least 90 per cent of the total underlying assets have either been repaid or become defaulted; and (d) the speed of the repayment is not more rapid than would be achieved by straight line amortization over the amortization period. A 'non-controlled' early amortization is simply any early amortization provision which does not meet these criteria. The position of the originator of a revolving credit securitization is that it must treat itself as being exposed to the originator's share on a normal basis, and to the noteholders' share on a credit conversion basis.

Treatment of the originator's share

16.58 Provided that the originator's share is not subordinate to investor's interests, the originator should treat itself as continuing to own the assets which constitute the originators share—ie it should not treat this exposure as a securitization exposure. The originator's position is capped such that the total charge to the originator of both parts of the securitization should not be greater than the charge which would apply if it had held all of the assets on his own balance sheet.

16.59 For a controlled early amortization structure, the general rule is that the investor is treated as being in a position equal to where he would have been had the assets not been securitized, but may apply a conversion factor equal to 90 per cent to the position he holds. However, for securitizations of retail credit card lines and other retail exposures which are uncommitted and unconditionally cancellable, a lower conversion factor is applied depending on the 'excess spread' (ie the level by which the total income on the portfolio exceeds the interest costs payable to noteholders). Where the three month average level of excess spread is more than 133.33 per cent of the 'trapping point' (ie the early amortization trigger point plus 4.5 percentage points unless the documentation provides a different figure) the conversion factor will be 0 per cent, and the noteholders' portion will be treated as risk free. As the level of excess spread decreases the conversion factor increases, and at a level of excess spread below 25 per cent of the trapping level, the conversion factor will be 40 per cent.

For an uncontrolled early amortization structure, the requirement is 100 per cent **16.60** rather than 90 per cent. Again, for securitizations of retail credit card lines and other retail exposures which are uncommitted and unconditionally cancellable, a lower conversion factor is available, but in this case the limit can vary up to 100 per cent if the three-month average excess spread is below 50 per cent of the trapping level.

PART IV

OTHER RISKS

17

OPERATIONAL RISK REQUIREMENTS

A. Operational Risk

Operational risk is the 'risk of loss resulting from inadequate or failed internal **17.01** processes, people and systems or from external events'.

The key to understanding the operational risk charge is to distinguish between it **17.02** and the Pillar two charge. The Pillar two charge is intended to constitute, inter alia, an assessment by the regulators of the effectiveness of the control systems within the bank. The operational risk charge is intended to be a quantification of the effectiveness of the bank's systems. Put simply, Pillar two assesses the risk that the bank will make the wrong commercial decision, and the operational risk charge assesses the risk that the decision will be incompetently executed in such a way as to lose money for the bank.

The approach which the regulator requires to be taken to operational risk is a **17.03** quantitative one based on historic failures. Risk control systems assessed under Pillar two are assessed on the basis of what they are likely to achieve in the future. Operational risk control systems assessed under Pillar one are measured on their actual historical performance. Changes to operational risk controls may eventually have an impact on loss experience, but should not be reflected in the operational risk charge until this is demonstrable.

At this point, however, it should be noted that it remains a regulatory imperative **17.04** for banks to control their operational risk exposure. The existing requirements on operational risk control (see below) have not been revoked (or even affected) by the Basel II operational risk proposals. The principles require a bank to put in place procedures to control and reduce operational risk;[1] Basel II puts in place a mechanism by which the level of operational risk that a bank is exposed to should be measured. The two are complementary.

17.05 The primary difficulty with operational loss is to capture data and to categorize it. An ideal operational loss database identifies each loss event according to cause and severity. However, although it is not usually difficult to identify an unexpected financial loss to the bank, it is somewhat harder to decide whether it is an operational loss caused by failed systems or a commercial loss caused by a bad business decision. To take a simple example, assume that a bank decided to save money by not employing external counsel to document a transaction, and as a result discovered that the amount advanced was irrecoverable because of a documentation error. Would this be legal operational risk or a loss resulting from unsuccessfully taking a commercial risk? Issues also arise in quantifying operational risks. Assume that a money centre bank which is due to make a $100m payment through the payment system inadvertently makes the payment twice. The second, inadvertent payment is noted by the recipient, who returns it? Is this: (a) not an operational risk, since the process worked and the money was returned; (b) an operational risk with a severity of 0; or (c) an operational risk with a severity of $100m. None of these categorizations seem to fit the facts particularly well.

17.06 Basel II offers three approaches: the basic indicator approach, the standardized approach, and the advanced measurement approach.

17.07 Two of the three mechanisms which Basel provides for calculating operational risk eschew the analysis of operational risks themselves, and operate on a percentage of lead indicator basis. However, the third, known as the 'Advanced Measurement Approach' (AMA), permits banks to assess the actual incidence and severity of operational risk within the institution, and to model a charge based on that information.

B. The Basic Indicator Approach

17.08 The basic indicator approach is exactly that—a bank is required to hold capital equal to 15 per cent of its average annual gross income—interest and non-interest—over the previous three years. Gross income means the sum of the following items:

- interest receivable and similar income;
- interest payable and similar charges;
- income from shares and other variable/fixed-yield securities;
- commissions/fees receivable;

---

[1] See paras 17.23 to 17.24.

- net profit or net loss on financial operations;
- other operating income.

The gross income calculation should exclude: (a) any provisions (eg for unpaid interest); (b) any profit or loss arising from the sale of securities held in the banking book; (c) extraordinary or irregular items; and (d) any income derived from insurance. Technically the sum of these could be negative—where this is the case the three-year average should be calculated taking any negative number as zero.

Clearly gross income means income before the deduction of operating costs. An **17.09** issue does arise, however, where a service is outsourced to another regulated entity, since this would give rise to double counting of operational risk within the system. Thus, by concession, the CRD provides that where a regulated firm outsources an activity to another regulated firm, the outsourcer may deduct the fee paid for the outsourcing from its calculation of gross income.

Profits and losses on securities trades—both unrealized and realized—are excluded **17.10** from the gross income calculation. However, profits and losses arising from the revaluation of trading items (ie items held on an available for sale basis) should be included in the gross income calculation. A justification can be constructed for this—operational risk may arise from a revaluation, but not from an absolute sale, since the completion of the absolute sale will (in theory) reveal any operational risk incurred. However, the consequence in practice is that proprietary trading activities will attract a relatively low operational risk charge compared with other credit operations.

The basic indicator approach is the default approach to operational risk, and as **17.11** such there are no criteria which are to be satisfied before it can be used. However, the Accord notes that operational risk should, at the least, be managed in accordance with the Basel Committee Guidance on Sound practices for the Management and Supervision of Operational Risk, published February 2003, and the FSA requires all firms to meet basic standards of management.

The calculation of operational risk requirements is clearly problematic for firms **17.12** which are start-ups, or which have been through a sufficiently radical restructuring on the last three years to render their gross income data irrelevant. FSA permits such firms to use forecast income instead of historic income in such circumstances.

C. Standard and Advanced Measurement Approaches— Criteria for Use

An institution must comply with certain operational risk management criteria **17.13** before using the Standard or Advanced Measurement Approaches. It is interesting to compare these criteria, as shown in Table 17.1.

Table 17.1 Comparison of Standardized Approach and Advanced Measurement Approach

Standardized Approach (1)	Advanced Measurement Approach (2)
The bank must have an operational risk management system *with clear responsibilities assigned to* an operational risk management function. The operational risk management function is responsible for developing strategies to identify, assess, monitor and control/mitigate operational risk; codifying firm-level policies and procedures concerning operational risk management and controls; for the design and implementation of the firm's operational risk assessment methodology; and for the design and implementation of a risk-reporting system for operational risk.	The bank must have an independent operational risk management function *that is responsible for the design and implementation of the bank's* operational risk management framework. The operational risk management function is responsible for codifying firm-level policies and procedures concerning operational risk management and controls; for the design and implementation of the firm's operational risk measurement methodology; for the design and implementation of a risk-reporting system for operational risk; and for developing strategies to identify, measure, monitor and control/mitigate operational risk.
As part of the bank's internal operational risk assessment system, the bank must systematically track relevant operational risk data including material losses by business line. Its operational risk assessment system must be closely integrated into the risk management processes of the bank. Its output must be an integral part of the process of monitoring and controlling the bank's operational risk profile. For instance, this information must play a prominent role in risk reporting, management reporting, and risk analysis. The bank must have techniques for creating incentives to improve the management of operational risk throughout the firm.	The bank's internal operational risk measurement system must be closely integrated into the day-to-day risk management processes of the bank. Its output must be an integral part of the process of monitoring and controlling the bank's operational risk profile. For instance, this information must play a prominent role in risk reporting, management reporting, *internal capital allocation*, and risk analysis. The bank must have techniques for *allocating operational risk capital to major business lines* and for creating incentives to improve the management of operational risk throughout the firm.
There must be regular reporting of operational risk exposures, including material operational losses, to business unit management, senior management, and to the board of directors. The bank must have procedures for taking appropriate action according to the information within the management reports.	There must be regular reporting of operational risk exposures and *loss experience* to business unit management, senior management, and to the board of directors. The bank must have procedures for taking appropriate action according to the information within the management reports.
The bank's operational risk management system must be well documented. The bank must have a routine in place for ensuring compliance with a documented set of internal policies, controls and procedures concerning the operational risk management system, which must include policies for the treatment of non-compliance issues.	The bank's risk management system must be well documented. The bank must have a routine in place for ensuring compliance with a documented set of internal policies, controls and procedures concerning the operational risk management system, which must include policies for the treatment of non-compliance issues.

The bank's operational risk management processes and assessment system must be subject to validation and regular independent review. These reviews must include both the activities of the business units and of the operational risk management function.

Internal and/or external auditors must perform regular reviews of the operational risk management processes and measurement systems. This review must include both the activities of the business units and of the *independent* operational risk management function.

The bank's operational risk assessment system (including the internal validation processes) must be subject to regular review by external auditors and/or supervisors.

The validation of the operational risk measurement system by external auditors and/or supervisory authorities must include the following:
— verifying that the internal validation processes are operating in a satisfactory manner; and
— making sure that data flows and processes associated with the risk measurement system are transparent and accessible. In particular, it is necessary that auditors and supervisory authorities are in a position to have easy access, whenever they judge it necessary and under appropriate procedures, to the system's specifications and parameters.

---

(1) Accord, para 663.

(2) Accord, para 666.

D. The Standardized Approach—The Charge

Provided that a bank satisfies the eligibility criteria, it is entitled to use the standardized approach to set its operational risk charge. This approach involves segmenting the business of the bank into eight business lines. In each case, the average gross income of that business line for the last three years is established, and that figure is multiplied by the multiplier for that business line. The sum of these calculations is the total operational risk charge for the bank. The business lines and their multipliers are as shown in Table 17.2. **17.14**

Table 17.2 Business lines and their multipliers

Business Line	Detail	Multiplier
Corporate finance	Underwriting of financial instruments and/or placing of financial instruments on a firm commitment basis.	18%
	Services related to underwriting.	
	Investment advice.	
	Advice to undertakings on capital structure, industrial strategy and related matters and advice and services relating to the mergers and the purchase of undertakings.	
	Investment research and financial analysis and other forms of general recommendation relating to transactions in financial instruments.	

Table 17.2 (*cont.*)

Business Line	Detail	Multiplier
Trading and sales	Dealing on own account. Money broking. Reception and transmission of orders in relation to one or more financial instruments. Execution of orders on behalf of clients. Placing of financial instruments on a best efforts basis. Operation of multilateral trading facilities.	18%
Retail banking		12%
Commercial banking		15%
Payment and Settlement		18%
Agency services		15%
Asset management		12%
Retail brokerage (activities with individual physical persons or a retail SME as defined under the standardized approach)	Reception and transmission of orders in relation to one or more financial instruments. Execution of orders of behalf of clients. Placing of financial instruments without a firm commitment basis.	12%

E. Advanced Measurement Approach—The Charge

17.15 A bank may initiate AMA use by applying it to only part of its operations, and it may continue to use the Basic Indicator Approach or Standardized Approach for the balance. As with the IRB, it is intended that once a bank commences using the AMA for part of its undertaking, it will commit itself to rolling out the AMA across all of its business. There are no hard rules as to the segments which the AMA should be applied—a bank can segment its business according to business line, legal structure, geography, or any other internally determined basis, and may apply the AMA within any one or more of those segments.

17.16 The threshold conditions which must be satisfied before a bank is permitted to use the AMA in any part of its business are:

- all operational risks of the bank's global, consolidated operations for the relevant area are captured;

- all of the bank's operations that are covered by the AMA, meet the qualitative criteria for using an AMA, while those parts of its operations that are using one of the simpler approaches meet the qualifying criteria for that approach;

• on the date of implementation of an AMA, a significant part of the bank's operational risks are captured by the AMA;

• the bank must commit to a timetable to roll out the AMA across all material legal entities and business lines.

Once a bank has been approved to use the AMA, it is to some extent on its own— **17.17**
Basel does not specify the structure of the calculation or the factors which should be taken into account. However, it does require that the system must measure at least the risks prescribed by Basel in Annexe 7 of CP3 as being components of operational risk (see Table 17.3).

Table 17.3 Components of operational risk

Event-Type Category (Level 1)	Definition	Categories (Level 2)	Activity Examples (Level 3)
Internal fraud	Losses due to acts of a type intended to defraud, misappropriate property or circumvent regulations, the law or company policy, excluding diversity/ discrimination events, which involve at least one internal party	Unauthorized activity	Transactions not reported (intentional)
			Trans type unauthorized (w/monetary loss)
			Mismarking of position (intentional)
		Theft and fraud	Fraud/credit fraud/worthless deposits
			Theft/extortion/ embezzlement/robbery
			Misappropriation of assets
			Malicious destruction of assets
			Forgery
			Check kiting
			Smuggling
			Account take-over/ impersonation/etc
			Tax non-compliance/evasion (wilful)
			Bribes/kickbacks
			Insider trading (not on firm's account)

Table 17.3 (*cont.*)

Event-Type Category (Level 1)	Definition	Categories (Level 2)	Activity Examples (Level 3)
External fraud	Losses due to acts of a type intended to defraud, misappropriate property or circumvent the law, by a third party	Theft and fraud	Theft/robbery Forgery Check kiting
		Systems security	Hacking damage Theft of information (w/monetary loss)
Employment practices and workplace safety	Losses arising from acts inconsistent with employment, health or safety laws or agreements, from payment of personal injury claims, or from diversity/ discrimination events	Employee relations	Compensation, benefit, termination issues Organized labour activity
		Safe environment	General liability (slip and fall, etc) Employee health and safety rules events Workers compensation
		Race and discrimination	All discrimination types
Clients, products & business practices.	Losses arising from an unintentional or negligent failure to meet a professional obligation to specific clients (including fiduciary and suitability requirements), or from the nature or design of a product	Suitability, disclosure and fiduciary	Fiduciary breaches/guideline violations Suitability/disclosure issues (KYC, etc) Retail customer disclosure violations Breach of privacy Aggressive sales Account churning Misuse of confidential information Lender liability
		Improper business or market practices	Antitrust Improper trade/market practices Market manipulation Insider trading (on firm's account) Unlicensed activity Money laundering

		Product flaws	Product defects (unauthorized, etc)
			Model errors
		Selection, sponsorship & exposure	Failure to investigate client per guidelines
			Exceeding client exposure limits
		Advisory activities	Disputes over performance of advisory activities
Damage to physical assets	Losses arising from loss or damage to physical assets from natural disaster or other events	Disasters and other events	Natural disaster losses
			Human losses from external sources (terrorism, vandalism)
Business disruption and system failures	Losses arising from disruption of business or system failures	Systems	Hardware
			Software
			Telecommunications
			Utility outage/disruptions
Execution, delivery and process management	Losses from failed transaction processing or process management, from relations with trade counterparties and vendors	Transaction capture, execution and maintenance	Miscommunication
			Data entry, maintenance or loading error
			Missed deadline or responsibility
			Model/system misoperation
			Accounting error/entity attribution error
			Other task misperformance
			Delivery failure
			Collateral management failure
			Reference data maintenance
		Monitoring and reporting	Failed mandatory reporting obligation
			Inaccurate external report (loss incurred)
		Customer intake and documentation	Client permissions/disclaimers missing
			Legal documents missing/incomplete
		Customer/client account management	Unapproved access given to accounts
			Incorrect client records (loss incurred)
			Negligent loss or damage of client assets
		Trade counterparties	Non-client counterparty misperformance
			Miscellaneous non-client counterparty disputes
		Vendors & suppliers	Outsourcing
			Vendor disputes

17.18 Having identified these loss categories, each loss category must be analysed in relation to a number of risk factors. There are a number of ways of doing this, but one of the most common is the use of so-called Key Risk Indicators (KRI). These may include:

- Control environment drivers—eg
  - policy;
  - personnel;
  - processes;
  - management information systems.
- Business environment drivers—eg
  - legal complexity;
  - process complexity;
  - regulatory complexity;
  - speed of change.

17.19 There are several hundred KRIs floating around the industry, since each operational risk unit is exposed to different risks. For each KRI, a risk level should be established. Clearly, each business line within the bank will have a different set of KRIs, and frequently different KRIs may apply to business units operating in different jurisdictions. The key is to identify 'operational risk units' within the bank; that is, parts of the bank's business which have the same basic operational risk exposures. A set of KRIs should then be compiled for each operational unit. The result of this process should be a matrix.

Business lines		B1	B2	B3
Internal fraud	Unauthorized activity			
	Theft and fraud			
External fraud	Theft and fraud			
	Unauthorized activity			
&c	&c			

Each cell of the matrix looks like this:

KRI 1 (as percentage) × historic loss ($)	=	$n
KRI 2 (as percentage) × historic loss ($)	=	$n
KRI 3 (as percentage) × historic loss ($)	=	$n
Total		$n

The process of calculating the operational risk charge is therefore, in theory very **17.20** simple. For each risk category one multiplies each KRI by the loss severity in respect of losses to that business from that particular risk source and totals the result. The sum of the value of all of the cells of the matrix is then the operational risk charge of the organization.

The bank must also meet a series of regulatory criteria in relation to its AMA **17.21** model:

- It must be able to demonstrate statistically to its regulator that the output from its model meets the same test of model reliability as the advanced IRB model (ie a one year holding period and a 99.9 per cent confidence interval).

- Its model must operate on an additive rather than a correlation-based approach (ie it must sum the risks arising from the various exposures without taking account of the correlation between them and the unlikelihood of all these risks occurring in the same period).

- The system must use collected internal data. The bank must operate an internal data collection system which maps data to a matrix allocating loss both by business area and by loss category, which is comprehensive in that it captures all losses wherever occurring caused by operational factors (including recovery values) and which is able to map failures in central functions (such as IT) to business areas.

- The model must use relevant external data (such as public or pooled industry data), at least in respect of exposure to infrequent but potentially severe loss.

- The system must refer to factors reflecting the business environment and internal control systems and must be capable of scenario analysis using expert inputs from business managers and others to assess plausible severe losses.

- The system must be based on a credible, transparent, well-documented and verifiable process, which must enable regulators and others to identify the relative importance placed on the relevant inputs.

- The system must not double-count risk mitigants of processes already recognized in other parts of the system. Conversely, it must not include losses due to credit factors already reflected in other part of the Basel framework.

Under the AMA a bank will be given some credit for risk mitigants (such as opera- **17.22** tional loss insurance) limited to 20 per cent of the total operational risk charge. The criteria for operational risk mitigants to be recognized are that:

- the insurance provider has a minimum claims paying ability rating of A (or equivalent);

- the insurance policy must have an initial term of no less than one year. For policies with a residual term of less than one year, the bank must make appropriate haircuts reflecting the declining residual term of the policy, up to a full 100 per cent haircut for policies with a residual term of 90 days or less;

- the insurance policy has a minimum notice period for cancellation and non-renewal of the contract;

- the insurance policy has no exclusions or limitations based upon regulatory action or for the receiver or liquidator of a failed bank;

- the insurance coverage has been explicitly mapped to the actual operational risk loss exposure of the institution;

- the insurance is provided by a third party entity. In the case of insurance through captives and affiliates, the exposure has to be laid off to an independent third party entity, for example through re-insurance, which meets the eligibility criteria;

- the framework for recognizing insurance is well reasoned and documented;

- the bank discloses the reduction of the operational risk capital charge due to insurance.

F. Corporate Governance and Operational Risk

17.23 Regulators have been concerned about operational risk for some time, and in February 2003 the Basel Committee produced a document entitled 'sound practices for the management and supervision of operational risk'. This document took a corporate governance-based approach to operational risk control, and set out 10 principles as follows:

Principle 1: The board of directors should be aware of the major aspects of the bank's operational risks as a distinct risk category that should be managed, and it should approve and periodically review the bank's operational risk management framework. The framework should provide a firm-wide definition of operational risk and lay down the principles of how operational risk is to be identified, assessed, monitored, and controlled/mitigated.

Principle 2: The board of directors should ensure that the bank's operational risk management framework is subject to effective and comprehensive internal audit by operationally independent, appropriately trained and competent staff. The internal audit function should not be directly responsible for operational risk management.

Principle 3: Senior management should have responsibility for implementing the operational risk management framework approved by the board of directors. The framework should be consistently implemented throughout the whole banking organisation, and all levels of staff should understand their responsibilities with respect to operational risk management.

Senior management should also have responsibility for developing policies, processes and procedures for managing operational risk in all of the bank's material products, activities, processes and systems.

Risk Management: Identification, Assessment, Monitoring, and Mitigation/Control

Principle 4: Banks should identify and assess the operational risk inherent in all material products, activities, processes and systems. Banks should also ensure that before new products, activities, processes and systems are introduced or undertaken, the operational risk inherent in them is subject to adequate assessment procedures.

Principle 5: Banks should implement a process to regularly monitor operational risk profiles and material exposures to losses. There should be regular reporting of pertinent information to senior management and the board of directors that supports the proactive management of operational risk.

Principle 6: Banks should have policies, processes and procedures to control and/or mitigate material operational risks. Banks should periodically review their risk limitation and control strategies and should adjust their operational risk profile accordingly using appropriate strategies, in light of their overall risk appetite and profile.

Principle 7: Banks should have in place contingency and business continuity plans to ensure their ability to operate on an ongoing basis and limit losses in the event of severe business disruption.

Role of Supervisors

Principle 8: Banking supervisors should require that all banks, regardless of size, have an effective framework in place to identify, assess, monitor and control/mitigate material operational risks as part of an overall approach to risk management.

Principle 9: Supervisors should conduct, directly or indirectly, regular independent evaluation of a bank's policies, procedures and practices related to operational risks. Supervisors should ensure that there are appropriate mechanisms in place which allow them to remain apprised of developments at banks.

Role of Disclosure

Principle 10: Banks should make sufficient public disclosure to allow market participants to assess their approach to operational risk management.

The most important point to make about these principles is that they have not **17.24** been revoked (or even affected) by the Basel II operational risk proposals. The principles require a bank to put in place procedures to control and reduce operational risk; Basel II puts in place a mechanism by which the level of operational risk that a bank is exposed to should be measured.

18

CONCENTRATION AND LARGE EXPOSURES

A. The Large Exposures Regime

The large exposures regime is one of the two substantial components of the **18.01** prudential capital regulatory system—the other being liquidity—which does not fall within the Basel Capital Accord regime. However, unlike liquidity, large exposures are dealt with within the EU capital directives,[1] and it is that regime which forms the basis for this chapter.

The essence of the large exposures regime is the idea that banks should diversify **18.02** their risk. The defining moment in the UK for large exposures risk was the collapse of Johnson Matthey Bankers in 1984. Johnson Matthey, although apparently a creditworthy bank, had concentrated its exposures to such an extent that two exposures to companies controlled by associated businessmen totalled 76 per cent and 34 per cent of the bank's capital base.[2] Failure of two of its customers was sufficient to nearly wipe out the bank's capital. JMB was under an obligation to report these exposures to the Bank of England, but had not done so in a way which indicated their significance. Partly as a result, the large exposures regime was

---

[1] Articles 66, 106 to 117 and para 7 of Annex V of the Banking Consolidation Directive and Arts 28 to 32 and Annex VI of the Capital Adequacy Directive.
[2] Goodhart, *The Central Bank and the Financial System* (Palgrave Macmillan, 1995), p 405.

tightened at the UK and at the EU level, and in particular formal limits were introduced as to the extent of permitted exposure to any given customer.

18.03   There are three core rules which are relevant for the large exposures regime. One is the rule that any exposure which is sufficiently 'large' should be reported to the regulator; the second is that the totality of large exposures should not exceed 8 times the bank's capital; the third is that no single exposure should be permitted to exceed 25 per cent of capital. The definition of a 'large' exposure for this purpose is an exposure which exceeds 10 per cent of the firm's large exposures capital. Thus, for a bank with £10m of capital, any exposure larger than £1m must be reported, no individual exposure may be larger than £2.5m, and the total of all exposures larger than £1m may not exceed £80m.

18.04   It should be explained at this point that the large exposures capital base is slightly different from ordinary regulatory capital. The differences are not great, and are largely positive—thus large exposures capital base may include surplus provisions above the normal 0.6 per cent limit, and need not deduct expected loss or securitization positions. Banking book limits are assessed using a base figure of tier one plus tier two less deductions and subject to these differences, and tier three is included in the capital base which is used in calculating the trading book limits (but not the banking book limits).

18.05   The large exposures rules are in principle straightforward. However, the question of what constitutes an 'exposure' is an extremely complex one, and much of the difficulty which the large exposures regime poses for banks arises out of this question. The issue is that banks will in general asses their exposures counterparty by counterparty, treating different legal entities as distinct from each other. The large exposures regime, however, requires exposures to individual counterparties to be aggregated together so that exposures to entities which are 'closely connected' with each other are treated as a single exposure. In this context close connection is intended to catch economic connections, and includes not only companies which are members of the same group, but also companies which are in common ownership or are in other ways mutually dependent on each other.

18.06   The context in which large exposures restrictions cause most difficulty in practice is generally within banking groups. Banking and financial groups are generally run as a whole rather than on legal entity lines—indeed the major advantage of being a member of a bank group is the ability to rely on group resources. Thus, in practice cash management and credit exposure analysis will tend to be done primarily on a group basis. The large exposures regime is therefore applied to a bank group on a group basis. However, it is also applied on an individual basis to the legal entity which takes deposits. This is because the bank regulator is concerned that where a group contains both regulated and unregulated entities, cash raised from depositors through the bank entity could be paid out to the non-bank entity and placed at risk. Thus a regulator will tend to wish to impose limitations on the exposure which a group bank has to the other members of its group. The problem which this creates is of course that from the perspective of a bank which is a member of a group, the other members of the group are closely connected with each other in exactly the same way which the members of any group are connected. This means that a bank which lends money to more than one other company within its own group must add those exposures together in order to ascertain whether the total exceed its 25 per cent permitted ceiling. The tension between groups seeking to manage cash centrally and bank regulators seeking to ensure that individual banks remain prudently exposed is what has given much of the existing large exposures regime its complexity.

B. Exposure

An exposure for this purpose means the totality of the economic exposure which **18.07** an institution has to a particular counterparty or group of connected counterparties. It may arise across many transactions involving different types of financial instruments with several counterparties within the same group of companies.

Exposures are aggregated for this purpose regardless of whether they fall within the **18.08** trading book or the banking book. An exposure is simply the accounting value of the money exposure—no account is taken of risk weightings—thus a £100 asset weighted at 20 per cent would give rise to the same £100 exposure as a £100 asset weighted at 100 per cent. However, exposures which have been deducted from capital (or which are fully provided against) do not count as exposures for this purpose.

Technically an exposure is an exposure regardless of its term. However, it is **18.09** accepted that banks may have large short-term exposures to each other arising from normal unsettled transactions, and such balances are excluded from the exposure calculation provided that they are outstanding for a short period of time. The limits are 48 hours for foreign exchange transactions and five working days for securities—if a transaction remains unsettled after this period it should be included in the relevant exposure calculation.

Because the basic test for an exposure is the accounting treatment, there are certain **18.10** types of arrangements which give rise to legal liability but which do not give rise to a large exposure for regulatory purposes. Examples of these include transactions entered into by a bank as trustee or agent in circumstances where it has no personal liability, and potential liability under contractual warranties. Thus, if a bank sells an asset on the basis of warranties as to its condition[3], the exposure which

---

[3] This may happen in lease finance transactions.

arises under those warranties will not count as an exposure for this purpose unless it becomes sufficiently certain as to appear on the balance sheet as a liability.

C. Counterparty

18.11 All exposures to the same counterparty are necessarily part of a single exposure. An individual counterparty may be any sort of person—legal or natural. Where the counterparty is a partnership, it is conventional to treat the partnership as a single counterparty, even though the exposure may be technically to the partners of the partnership. Where a bank gives a guarantee, the exposure is taken as being to the person whose obligation it has guaranteed. For a derivatives contract, the exposure is to the person with whom the contract was made unless the contract was made on exchange. When a derivatives contract is made on exchange, the contract as made between the exchange members will immediately be novated into two new contracts, one each between the parties to the original contract and the clearing house for the exchange. This means in practice that regardless of who the initial contract was made with, all unsettled contracts will be exposures to the clearing house.

18.12 Exposures frequently have more than one obligor—this most commonly arises where the bank deals with A, and the liabilities of A are guaranteed by B. For this purpose 'guarantee' includes any form of unfunded credit protection which would be recognized under the credit regime, and includes credit derivatives and eligible insurance policies. Where an exposure to a counterparty is guaranteed in this way, a firm may elect whether to treat itself as having an exposure to A or to B. Where (as is often the case) A and B are members of the same group this may be an irrelevant issue, since the two exposures will be classed as connected exposures. However, if the Bank has a large existing exposure to A and cannot take any more, the option to treat the exposure as an exposure to B means that the bank will be able to assume the exposure.

18.13 It frequently happens in such cases that the guarantee will have elements of mismatch with the underlying exposure, possibly as to base currency or as to duration. In these cases, the value of the guarantee is haircutted in the same way as it would be under the unfunded credit protection rules which would apply in the collateral rules. Likewise, a guarantee which would not be recognised as eligible protection under the collateral rules is not recognized for large exposures purposes.

Connected counterparties

18.14 As noted above, the term 'connected counterparties' includes companies in the same group as each other, regardless of the degree of economic connection (if any) between them. It also specifically includes companies which are owned by the same individual or group of individuals (since such arrangements do not generally constitute 'groups' as the term is usually defined). The test also catches 'common control' arrangements, where companies have the same common directors. Finally, companies linked by cross-guarantees are regarded as connected. The problem that this definition sometimes raises is the extent of the economic linkage which is required in order to treat counterparties as connected, since it is possible for companies to be very closely related without being connected. To take a simple example, a small bank in an agricultural region specializing in lending to farmers would be justified in concluding that all of its loans were connected, since the ability of the farmers to repay the loans would all depend on agricultural commodity prices. However, in such a case a regulator would not normally regard the exposures as connected.

It is also important for a bank to identify which entities are connected to itself. **18.15** This is because, in the same way that exposures to other groups are aggregated into single exposures, exposures to other members of the bank's own group are also aggregated into a single exposure, and this exposure is (with exceptions) treated like any other exposure—a bank should not be allowed to be exposed to other members of its own group beyond the levels which it would be permitted to be exposed to any other counterparty. The logic of this may not be immediately apparent in a conventional banking group of which the bank is the primary member. However, its rationale may be easily understood in the context of banks which form a small part of a larger non-financial group. The danger in such situations is that the bank is operated as a finance centre for the group, with depositors' assets being used for the commercial purposes of the group rather than being prudently managed. Thus, in such situations the bank is restricted in the exposures which it can maintain to other group members in total. It will also be clear from this example why the test for entities which are connected to the bank is wider than the normal test for connected counterparties. The key aspect of the test for close connection with the bank is the 'closely connected' test. This catches any entity which either describes a relationship between two or more persons under which one or more of the following applies:

(a) the insolvency or default of one of them is likely to be associated with the insolvency or default of the others;
(b) it would be prudent when assessing the financial condition or creditworthiness of one to consider that of the others; or
(c) there is, or there is likely to be, a close relationship between the financial performance of those persons.

These are not absolute tests, but depend upon judgement calls both by the regula- **18.16** tor and by the reporting institution, and assessments can and do differ. In recent times this test has been used to catch securitization SPVs to which the bank has liquidity lines. Another case where an entity may be regarded as 'connected with' the bank for this purpose are where the entity is an 'associate' of the bank (defined as an affiliate, an appointed representative of a group member, or person having a business or domestic relationship with the bank (or an associate of the bank) which might reasonably be expected to give rise to a community of interest between them which may involve a conflict of interest in dealings with third parties. Finally, an entity is connected with the bank if the same persons significantly influence the governing body of that person and of the bank, or where the bank has an exposure to that person which was not incurred for a commercial purpose on an arms length basis. The test of being arms length for this purpose is not determined simply by the economic characteristics of the transaction—it is also important to determine whether the exposure would be subject to the firm's usual monitoring and recovery procedures if repayment difficulties emerged; in particular where the borrower (or the directors of the borrower) have influence over the governance of the bank itself.

Total exposure

18.17 A firm's total exposure to any client or group of connected clients is simply the sum of the exposures to that person, or to the individual persons within that group. This includes all exposures, both trading book and banking book. The only exception to this rule is where a person acts as agent of another. Thus, for example, where a single fund manager acts as manager of a number of different funds, the bank may treat each exposure as being to the relevant fund, and need not aggregate the exposures as exposures to the manager. However, this in turn is subject to the proviso that where the investors in the fund are connected with the bank itself, the bank may in some circumstances have to treat the fund itself as a connected party with other persons, and that list may well include the manager. Again, the judgement which is required here is a risk and economic judgement rather than a purely technical one.

18.18 An exposure can arise in one of two ways; either as an issuer exposure or as a counterparty exposure. A simple example would be where a bank purchases an option on a security. This will give rise to an issuer exposure against the issuer of the security, and a counterparty exposure to the option counterparty. When calculating a bank's total exposure to a counterparty it must sum the counterparty exposures and the issuer exposures to that counterparty—in other words, if it owns debt securities issued by a borrower and also has loans outstanding to that borrower, the two are added together to determine the total exposure to that borrower.

18.19 Issuer exposure is calculated as the net position in securities issued by the issuer. In the trading book no distinction is made between different types of securities for this purpose, and all securities are netted off against each other to produce a single net balance, regardless of their nature. In the banking book the calculation is more complex. Securities are divided into different pools depending on their currency of denomination, and for each currency pool fixed rate and index linked securities are subdivided into sub-pools of securities with a maturity of under one year, and securities with a maturity of over one year (floating rate securities are not divided in this way). If the balance of any sub-pool is negative, it is disregarded in calculating the exposure. Banking book and trading positions may not be set off against each other. Finally, it should be noted that this process is limited to securities issued by the same issuer. If a bank is long of securities issued by one member of a group of connected counterparties, but short of securities issued by another member of that group, it may not net the two positions against each other for the purpose of calculating the exposure to the group of connected counterparties as a whole.

It is possible for a transaction to give rise to both an issuer and a counterparty **18.20** exposure—this is true of most securities financing transactions, for example. Where this is the case, both the issuer and the counterparty exposure must be taken into account in calculating exposure limits.

Where a bank has a derivative position in securities, it must treat that position as **18.21** a position in the underlying for this purpose—thus a commitment to buy a security (under a future, or as an underwriting commitment) creates a long position, and a commitment to sell creates as short position. An option creates a long (if written) or a short (if bought) position respectively; a put creates a position valued at the strike price of the option; and a bought call creates a position in the underlying valued at book value of the option. Note that a written call does not generate an issuer exposure at all.

In general, exposures in the banking book will give rise to counterparty exposures, **18.22** since security transactions are generally held in the trading book—not least because the trading book netting rules are more generous. However, where an issuer exposure is held within the banking book, a firm may elect to treat the exposure as a counterparty rather than an issuer exposure. If the firm does elect to treat the exposure as an issuer exposure, it may elect to treat other banking book assets as issuer exposures in order to create netting. Thus, where a firm has a long position in securities in its banking book but also has a put option in respect of those securities which hedges that position, it may elect to treat that option as a short issuer exposure and net the two issuer exposures. It will still, however, have a counterparty exposure to the writer of the option.

Counterparty exposure is altogether simpler, since counterparty exposures are **18.23** valued using the valuation used for weighting purposes, and the counterparty is the person who would be treated as the counterparty for risk weighting purposes.

Banks are prohibited from taking on exposures to counterparties in circumstances **18.24** where they do not know the identity of the counterparty (this would arise, for example, when dealing with an agent acting on behalf of an undisclosed principal—a situation which used to be common in the foreign exchange markets and may still arise within some electronic trading systems).

D. Exposure Limits

18.25 The essence of the large exposures regime is the exposure limit rules. In the banking book, there are two limits imposed by the large exposures regime. One is that no single large exposure to a counterparty, group of connected clients or connected counterparties should exceed 25 per cent of the large exposures capital base, the other is that the total of all of the large exposures (ie exposures of greater than 10 per cent of assets) should not exceed 800 per cent of the large exposures capital base. Thus, for a bank with a large exposures capital base of £100m, no single exposure should be allowed to exceed £25m, and the total of all exposures of more than £10m should not exceed £800.

18.26 In principle these rules apply equally across both non-trading and trading book positions, and firms are required to monitor their total aggregate exposure to any one credit across both the trading and non-trading books. However, trading book positions may be exempted from the limits set out above, provided that an appropriate capital charge is taken to reflect the degree of concentration risk actually assumed. In addition, an absolute cap is imposed on trading book positions, so that total exposure to any one credit does not exceed 500 per cent of capital resources, and the total of all excesses arising in this way which have existed for more than 10 days does not exceed 600 per cent of capital. This arrangement permits firms to take very large trading positions in the trading book provided that they are confident that these positions can be sold on relatively rapidly. As with positions which exceed the 10 per cent level, forms are required to report these to the relevant regulator.

18.27 The capital charge which must be taken in respect of large exposures is known as the concentration risk capital component (CNCOM). Each large exposure has a specific charge, and the total of these is taken to the the CNCOM which is applied at firm level. The CNCOM is regarded as part of the credit risk capital requirement. It should be noted that the CNCOM arises in the trading book in addition to the other charges applied—thus, a sufficiently large position in a particular bond will attract PRR and IRR as well as a CNCOM.

18.28 The CNCOM is calculated position by position. First each total trading and non-trading-book position is assessed against the 25 per cent permitted exposure level. Where the total position is less than 25 per cent, no CNCOM arises. Where the total position is in excess of the 25 per cent level, the excess constitutes the weighted holding. The CNCOM which is applies is 200 per cent of the capital requirement for that holding if the position has existed for less than 10 days. If the position has been held for more than 10 days, the scaling factor is increased, such that a maximum 900 per cent requirement is applied for holdings which have existed for more than 10 days and which exceed 100 per cent of the firm's capital resources.[4] The FSA provides a useful example of a CNCOM calculation in its rulebook at BIPRU 10.5.24.

There are a number of different types of exposures which are exempt from **18.29** the large exposures regime. In part this is simply the equivalent of 0 per cent weighting—large exposures is conceptually a part of the credit exposure regulatory regime, and where credits are treated as risk free under one part of the credit regime, it is not rational to require a charge to be applied under a different part. The exempt holdings are:

(1) Claims—whether specific assets or otherwise—which would unsecured receive a 0 per cent risk weight under the standardized approach. This includes claims on central governments, central banks, international organizations, and claims guaranteed by any of these. It should be noted that this applies even to IRB banks, which are likely to apply a small but non-zero weighting even to government debt. This produces the interesting position where an exposure is treated as having a small credit requirement for credit purposes but to fall outside the large exposures charge. The reason for this anomaly is almost certainly simple necessity—banks have to hold so much of the paper of their national governments for so many reasons that a rule which restricted the amount of this which they are permitted to hold would potentially increase rather than reduce systemic risk.

(2) Asset items constituting claims on and other exposures to central governments or central banks which would not receive a 0 per cent weighting under the standardized approach, but which are denominated and, where applicable, funded in the national currencies of the borrowers. This reflects the principle embedded in the regulatory regime that a government or central bank cannot go bust in its own currency, since it can always print more of it.

(3) Asset items constituting claims on and other exposures to financial institutions with a maturity of one year or less. This does not include exposures which form part of the capital resources of the institution—thus a tier two instrument with a residual maturity of less than 12 months would not get the benefit of this exemption.

(4) Any exposure to or guaranteed by an EEA state's regional governments and local authorities which claims would receive a 0 per cent risk weight under the standardized approach. It should be noted that no non-EEA regional government can have the benefit of this concession, no matter how it is constituted or funded.

---

[4] The trading book holdings must be applied so that the lowest regulatory capital cost holdings are used to fill the 25% 'free' bucket. This means that the calculation of the CNCOM must be done by applying the scaling factor to the most 'expensive' portions of the position.

(5) Asset items constituting claims and other exposures on recognized[5] non-EEA investment firms, recognized clearing houses, designated clearing houses, recognized investment exchanges, and designated investment exchanges in CRD financial instruments with a maturity of one year or less but not constituting such institutions' capital resources. Since exchange and clearing house transaction and collateral balances are generally held for a considerably shorter period than this, this means that most of these exposures are outside the large exposures regime.

(6) Loans secured by mortgages on residential property.

(7) Covered bonds. This is because in a covered bond the holder has recourse to both the credit of the issuing entity and the pool of collateral which the relevant legislation requires to be held in respect of that bond. The credit exposure of the holder is therefore to both the issuer and the collateral, and on this ground the exposure is not treated as purely an exposure to the issuer.

(8) Exposures secured by mortgages on offices or other commercial premises which would receive a 50 per cent risk weight under the standardized approach. However, for these exposures the treatment is not a complete exemption, but a reduction of 50 per cent in the value of the exposure.

(9) Bill endorsements on bills with a maturity of one year or less where the relevant bill has already been endorsed by another investment firm.

18.30 There are a number of other circumstances in which an exposure can be disregarded for these purposes. However, these are not altered to the nature of the exposure itself, but to the circumstances in which the exposure arises. They are as follows.

Parental guarantees

18.31 A firm may treat as exempt any exposure which is guaranteed to it by its own parent in circumstances where a direct exposure to that parent would be 0 per cent weighted under the standardized regime. The logic of this is that the exposure is, in effect, guaranteed by a 0 per cent weighted guarantor and should therefore be treated accordingly. This exemption is, however, not available where the exposure exceeds 100 per cent of the firm's capital resources—in other words, it is not a completely free ride. Perhaps more importantly, the exemption only applies where the firm's exposure to connected counterparties (including the parent, and including this and any other exposures guaranteed by the parent) does not exceed 200 per cent of the firm's capital resources. It is therefore not the case that a firm can disregard the large exposures regime completely by having all of its exposures

---

[5] Recognized means for this purpose recognized by the relevant regulator as being subject to appropriate supervision. For an EU firm, a firm established and regulated in any other EU jurisdiction is likely to satisfy that criterion.

guaranteed by its own parent. Although this exclusion is similar in structure to those created under other parts of the large exposures regime, it is in fact a separate concession with different conditions.

This is also permitted where the exposure is an exposure to a person other than a   **18.32** connected counterparty where the parent, instead of guaranteeing that exposure, agrees with the firm that it will promptly on demand by the firm increase the firm's capital resources by an amount that is sufficient to reverse completely the effect of any loss the firm may sustain in connection with that exposure, or by the amount required to ensure that the firm complies with its obligations under the system.

Collateralization

Exposures which are collateralized involve different credit considerations from   **18.33** uncollateralized obligations—consequently the existence of certain types of collateral is recognized as reducing or eliminating the exposure for large exposures purposes. Since there is more than one way of treating collateral under the credit regime—the simple method, the comprehensive method, and the AIRB method—there is more than one treatment available in respect of the large exposures regime. The starting point is the financial collateral simple method as used by a standardized bank.[6] Under this, exposures are in principle exempt if they are collateralized by:

(1) Debt securities issued by central governments, central banks, international organizations, multilateral development banks, or EEA States' regional governments or local authorities, which securities constitute claims on their issuer which would receive a 0 per cent risk weight under the standardized approach.

(2) Cash deposits placed with the lending firm or with a credit institution which is the parent undertaking or a subsidiary undertaking of the lending firm. This includes cash received for the issue of a credit linked note and loans and balancers subject to an on balance sheet netting agreement.

(3) Certificates of deposit issued by the lending firm or by a credit institution which is the parent undertaking or a subsidiary undertaking of the lending firm and lodged with either of them.

(4) Exposures secured by collateral in the form of securities other than those referred to in (1) which are traded or regularly quoted on a recognized investment exchange. However, in order for an exposure to be eliminated it must be overcollateralized to a specified level—150 per cent in the case of shares, 100 per cent in the case of listed debt securities, and 50 per cent in the case of

---

[6] It will be recalled that the financial collateral simple method is only available to firms using the standardized approach, and may only be applied to exposures to which they apply that approach.

securities issued by EEA regional governments or by banks (not including subordinated securities which rank as bank capital).

18.34 A firm which uses the financial collateral comprehensive method under the standardized approach or the IRB approach (but not the advanced IRB approach) effectively uses that method to calculate the value of the exposure itself. The value of its exposures to a counterparty or to a group of connected clients or to connected counterparties therefore becomes the fully-adjusted value of the exposures to the counterparty or group of connected clients calculated in accordance with the financial collateral comprehensive method, taking into account the credit risk mitigation, volatility adjustments and any maturity mismatch (E*) in accordance with those rules. Here again, the eligibility criteria are the same as those for the comprehensive approach—securities to collateral which would not be admissible as collateral under that regime are not recognized for the large exposures approach either.

Advanced IRB firms

18.35 Advanced IRB firms may calculate and use their own estimates of LGDs and EAD (conversion factors). This leads to an interesting issue, in that banks using the advanced IRB approach will typically take financial collateral on banking book exposures into account by using their own internal estimates to adjust the exposure's loss given default (LGD). This effectively means that the bank may use its own model to estimate the value of an exposure, and may then use that value to determine the size of the exposure to be treated for large exposure purposes. Not all advanced IRB banks are permitted to do this—the FSA specifies that an AIRB bank should not be permitted to use its own estimates of LGD exposure unless it can demonstrate that it can estimate the effects of financial collateral on exposures separately from other LGD relevant issues. More importantly; the firm may not pick and choose which exposures it applies its LGD models to—if the firm has permission to apply its won LGD figures for the purpose of calculating exposure size then it must do so for all exposures whose nominal size would otherwise make them large exposures. It should not be possible to apply the comprehensive method to some exposures and the AIRB approach to others. It should also be noted that even where a firm is permitted to value its large exposures using its LGD model, it is still required to report exposures to the FSA on a gross basis. Thus, where a firm has an exposure the nominal value of which exceeds 10 per cent of its capital base, it must still report that exposure to FSA as a large exposure, even if the valuation of the exposure applying an AIRB method results in a lower figure.

18.36 Also, where an AIRB firm uses its own estimates of LGD in calculating large exposures, it must conduct periodic stress tests of its credit risk concentrations including in relation to the realizable value of any collateral taken. The results of these stress tests must be applied in assessing large exposures, and if necessary the value of collateral should be reduced. These tests should be carried out at least once a year.

Treasury concession

The treasury concession is in many respects a concession of necessity. It has its **18.37** origin in the arrangement commonly encountered in corporate groups whereby a single legal entity within the group is charged with operating the treasury function of the group as a whole. The reason that this structure is adopted is that it enables counterparties dealing with the group to net their exposures against a single entity, rather than having to operate multiple credit and debit balances with different entities. This reduces the costs of the counterparties and therefore (in theory, at least) improves the terms on which the relevant treasury business operates. However, in a group which operates a treasury company, individual group entities may from time to time have substantial exposures to that treasury company, and this is a particular problem in a group containing multiple banks or regulated entities. Consequently the treasury concession regime has been created for the purpose of ensuring that a financial group may establish a treasury company and may maintain larger intra-group balances with that treasury company than is generally permitted. It should be noted at this juncture that the concession is required both for group users of a treasury company and for the treasury company itself, since treasury companies are, for a variety of reasons, almost always authorized banks or investment firms.[7]

The essence of the treasury concession is that a group member may disregard for **18.38** large exposure (LE) purposes an exposure to any other group company provided that the exposure is either:

(a) incurred in the course of the firm carrying on a treasury role for other members of its group (this only applies where the exposure has an original maturity of less than one year, and therefore cannot be used to exempt long-term intra-group funding arrangements;

(b) a cash loan to a group member which carries on a treasury role made using cash which is surplus to the needs of the firm and fluctuates regularly (note that in this instance the exposure may be for a term of more than one year); or

(c) arises from the firm's operating of a central risk management function for members of the firm's group in respect of derivatives trades.

The treasury exemption is a partial exemption, in that its effect is to exempt exposures equal to 50 per cent of capital. This exemption may be combined with the

---

[7] This is generally true even in non-financial groups.

ordinary LE rules, such that the total amount of any exposure which a firm can have to its group treasury company is equal to 50 per cent of that bank's capital plus the 25 per cent of capital which would be the ordinary maximum.

Intra-group securities financing transactions

18.39 Groups frequently use securities financing transactions to transfer finance and assets amongst themselves, in particular for the purpose of managing group liquidity. This is a useful and an important function, and regulators do not wish to inhibit it unnecessarily. However, because securities financing transactions can give rise to exposures, it is necessary to establish an exemption from the LE rules to reflect these. Thus, intra-group securities finance transactions are exempt provided that the exposure is at least 90 per cent[8] collateralized by collateral which would be eligible under the comprehensive method,[9] that the counterparty is within the concentration risk group, and the exposure is not caught within a counterparty credit risk model.

National integrated groups

18.40 The issue of large exposures within groups is a complex one. The legal basis of a group structure implies that the separate existence and solvency of each group member be accurately reflected in the supervisory regime. The attitude which was historically taken by UK regulators was therefore that group members should be regulated on the basis of their separate legal personality, and that exposures to other group members should be treated on the basis that they are not different from any other exposure. There is some legal theory to support this approach— most notably that where a member of a group becomes insolvent, the office holder who is appointed to supervise the relevant insolvency procedure is not permitted to deal more favourably with other group members than with any other creditor or debtor of the insolvent firm. On this basis, the very high level of recognition of corporate autonomy embedded in English law made it necessary to disregard group connections when monitoring large exposures. The counterargument to this, however, is that in reality corporate groups do not do business on the basis of their separate legal entities, but as a single business subject to common integrated management, systems and controls. In particular, resources are frequently transferred within the group between group members for a variety of reasons, and it is very unlikely that any group would voluntarily allow a group member company to become insolvent whilst other group members proposed to continue in business.

---

[8] Assessed as a gross value, without haircuts or mismatch discounts.
[9] For some reason the comprehensive method eligibility test is applied even if the bank concerned uses only the simple method.

In short, groups operate as such and not as coalitions of ring-fenced entities. As a result, the industry and some regulators have argued that the correct focus of large exposures regulation is at the group level rather than the individual legal entity level.

It was not possible to resolve this divergence of opinion between national regula- **18.41** tors, and as a result the BCD provides (at Art 113(2)) that member states may exempt individual exposures incurred by banks to members of their groups where the exposure was to a group member which was subject to consolidated supervision in accordance with the BCD or with equivalent standards in force in another country.

This does appear to create a duality, where some EU regulators will restrict intra- **18.42** group exposures whilst others will not. However, nothing is ever this simple. When the FSA began to consider this issue,[10] the conclusion which it reached was that although it agreed in principle that exposures arising within groups should be subject to a lesser degree of control, the legal issues which arose in relation to the interoperation of different national legal systems were such as to make a blanket relief for all intra-group exposures imprudent.

The FSA has thus ended up with what can be regarded as a three-stage approach. **18.43** Within the UK, it broadly exempts any exposure. Between the UK and any other region, it is prepared in some circumstances to exempt exposures. Outside these two safe havens, however, it regards intra-group exposures as subject to the same requirements as any other exposure.

The UK Integrated Group

For the FSA the UK integrated group means that part of a bank group within **18.44** which it is prepared to disregard large exposures. A bank must decide which legal entities will fall within the UK Integrated Group (UKIG), and notify the FSA in advance of the existence and composition of the group.

The basis of the UKIG is the idea of the concentration risk group. A concentration **18.45** risk group consists of a parent and subsidiaries (but not participations) which are subject to consolidation on a full basis (ie not subject to proportionate consolidation) by the FSA, an EEA supervisor, or an equivalent third country supervisor. The UKIG consists of those concentration risk group members which are UK firms and which are subject to the same risk control processes as the UK bank, which are not subject to any restriction which could impede the prompt transfer of capital resources or repayment of liabilities from the bank.[11] It should be noted

---

[10] In CP 97, developed in CP 2005/03 and 2006/03.

[11] It will be noted that these are also the conditions which must be satisfied for an intra-group exposure to be 0% weighted under the standardized approach (BIPRU 3.2.28 and 3.2.30). This means that exposures between UKIG members are effectively disregarded within the regulatory

here that the requirement that the firm be a UK firm is not, as might ordinarily be expected, that the firm be incorporated in the UK. The test which is actually applied is that the firm be either incorporated in the UK or have its centre of main interest deemed to be in the UK within the meaning of the EU Insolvency Regulation.[12] This latter test may possibly be satisfied by any non-financial firm,[13] wherever in the world incorporated, which is managed from the UK—the UKIG may therefore include non-UK incorporated firms.

18.46 Once a UKIG has been established, the LE rules are applied to the members of that group as if they were a single legal entity. This means that where a bank is a member of a UKIG, the LE rules no longer apply to it in a solo basis as regards exposures to concentration risk group members. Instead, they are applied at the level of the UKIG as if it were a single entity. This approach is in some ways similar to solo-consolidation (see para 20.21), in that the separate legal existence of the legal entities is effectively disregarded, with the consolidated balance sheet of the UKIG members treated as if they were a single legal entity. The most important difference is that for the purposes of calculating the capital of the UKIG (important for calculating the applicable exposure limits on a group level) the calculation method prescribed is the aggregation and deduction method—method 2 of the Financial Groups Directive's methods[14] set out in Annex 2. The reason for prescribing this is that since there is no reason to assume or require that the UKIG will be a coherent group with a single identifiable parent, it would be impossible to require ordinary consolidation methodology.[15]

18.47 Many UK groups will have UK group members which, for one reason or another, fall within the concentration risk group but outside the UKIG. For LE purposes the group is required to treat all of these as a single entity (the 'residual block')—the group is therefore divided into two entities, the UKIG and the residual block. The UKIG is required to treat the residual block as if it were a single entity—thus in many respects the concentration group is regarded as being split into two entities, each of which deals with the other as if it were a single entity. There may also, of course, be entities which are connected counterparties but which do not fall

---

capital system as a whole, since they are neither risk weighted nor limited by large exposures regulation.

  [12] 1346/2000/EC.

  [13] Banks and other financial firms are explicitly excluded from the scope of the regulation.

  [14] See below, paras 21.28 to 21.29.

  [15] The reason for selecting Method 2 is that the calculation of capital resources under Method 2 is based on the solo capital resources of members of a financial conglomerate. The definition of solo capital resources depends on what type of undertakings the financial conglomerate contains. For instance, if a financial conglomerate contains a bank the solo capital resources calculation for every group member in the banking sector and the investment services sector is based on the capital resources calculation for banks. Consequently this rule has the effect of applying to the UKIG the corresponding procedure that applies under the consolidation rules.

within the concentration group. These will not form part of the residual block, but will continue to be treated as connected counterparties of the UKIG.

Some of the other LE rules are also modified in their application to the UKIG. For **18.48** example, the treasury concession may be applied on a consolidated basis, but only where the counterparty is a concentration risk group company. The 50 per cent limit is, however, calculated on the UKIG consolidated capital amount. The intra-group securities financing exemption is equally amended.

The concomitant of the UKIG is the Wider Integrated Group (WIG). The WIG **18.49** regime is formally concessionary, in that a firm may only claim the benefit of the regime if it has applied for and received a waiver from the FSA to apply this part of the rules. The WIG regime is an alternate to the UKIG regime—if the latter applies, the former does not. A WIG is composed of all of the entities which satisfy the requirements for inclusion in the UKIG plus all of those who would do so but for the fact that they are incorporated outside the UK. Importantly, the require-ment of common risk control and no obstacle to repatriation of funds still apply, and therefore in the course of a waiver application for a WIG approval a firm will have to satisfy the FSA that the corporate laws in all of the jurisdictions in respect of which a WIG election is made do not have the effect of imposing such restric-tions on transfer of funds.

Once the members of the WIG have been identified, they are then disaggregated **18.50** into a UKIG, one or more diverse blocks and a residual block. It is for the appli-cant to negotiate with the FSA as to what exactly constitutes a diverse block, but in principle a diverse block is any group of entities which represents a different grouping of risk, such that there is a low risk correlation between any diverse block and any other diverse block. Blocks may be diverse according to geography, busi-ness, or a combination of both. There will generally be no more than four diverse blocks, and there may well be fewer.

The rule which applies to WIGs is similar to that which applies to UKIGs. In **18.51** essence, each of the UKIG and each diverse block is treated as a different single entity, and exposures between the UKIG and each diverse block are treated as exposures to a different counterparty subject to a limit based on the consolidated capital of the UKIG.

There is a wrinkle which arises where the entity which forms the UKIG has a trad-ing book. The entity will have performed a CNCOM calculation in respect of exposures to other group members. As a first step this is cancelled. A revised CNCOM calculation is made as if the CNCOIM rules were applied to the entire UKIG, and based on the UKIGs total capital. This will result in the CNCOM which would have applied to the totality of all of the exposures of the UKIG. The reporting bank then calculates what percentage of that totality of exposures was its own. It then includes that percentage of the recalculated CNCOM in its own report in place of the originally calculated figure.

18.53 The following tables (Tables 18.1 to 18.3) are reproduced from the FSA's rule-book, and may be helpful in understanding the effect of the interaction of the UKIG and WIG regimes.

Table 18.1 No UKIG or WIG

Situation	Exposure from/to	Summary of the available modifications
1	Intra group exposures but no UKIG or WIG in place	The firm is not subject to an integrated groups treatment of large exposures. The normal large exposure limits (BIPRU 10.5) apply to connected exposures of the firm at the solo level. (This assumes that no other large exposure exemptions are utilised.)
		Although a firm's exposures to connected counterparties may not qualify for an integrated groups treatment, they may still qualify for a treasury and intra-group securities financing transaction concession (BIPRU 10.7).

Table 18.2 UK Integrated Group established but no Wider Integrated Group in place

Situation	Exposure from/to	Summary of the available modifications
2	UKIG firm to another UKIG firm (they are members of the same UKIG)	Exposures between members of a firm's UKIG are exempt from the large exposure limits. This means that the 25%, 800%, 500% and 600% limits are disapplied and that the exposures are not included in the notional CNCOM. (BIPRU 10.8.8 G)
3	UKIG firm to an undertaking within its residual block	In situation 3, there is a UKIG and a residual block. But no WIG has been established.
		The UKIG's exposures to undertakings within its residual block are exempt from the normal large exposures limits at the solo level. Instead, the total of the UKIG's exposures to its residual block is subject to the following limits:
		— 25% non-trading book limit;
		— trading book limits other than CNCOM;
		— 500% limit for excess trading book exposures with the deletion of the 10 day time limit; and
		— Treasury concession and intra-group securities financing transactions.
		The capital resources to which the limits apply are those of the UKIG, rather than those of the solo firm.

Treasury concession and intra-group securities financing transactions) may be applied to exposures of the UKIG to its residual block if the requisite conditions are satisfied.

In respect of the treasury concession, the UKIG's exposures to undertakings within its residual block may be exempt from the 25% limit, subject to a maximum of 50% of the capital resources of the UKIG. These exempt exposures would also be exempt for the purposes of calculating the notional CNCOM. Any exposure that meets the treasury concession conditions but is above the 50% limit would not be exempt from the large exposure limits. They would not be exempt from the notional CNCOM. The UKIG exposures that were eligible for a treasury concession, but which, together with other such exposures, exceeded the 50% limit are not exempt and are treated as other exposures of the UKIG and remain subject to the 25% limit.

4	A firm in the residual block to another undertaking in the residual block	Not within the scope of the preferential large exposure treatments.
5	A firm in the residual block to an undertaking which is a member of the UKIG	Not within the scope of the preferential large exposure treatments.

Table 18.3 UK Integrated Group in place, Wider Integrated Group waiver granted

Situation	Exposure from/to	Summary of the available modifications
6	UKIG firm to another UKIG member (within the same UKIG)	Exposures between members of a firm's UKIG are exempt from the large exposure limits (the modifications available are the same as those noted for Situation 2).
7	UKIG firm to an undertaking in its WIG	In situation 7 there is a UKIG, WIG (comprising diverse blocks agreed under the WIG waiver) and a residual block.

The aggregate exposure of the UKIG to each individual diverse block within the WIG is subject to the following limits:

— 25% non-trading book limit;

— trading book limits other than CNCOM;

— 500% limit for excess trading book exposures with the deletion of the 10-day time limit; and

— Treasury concession and intra-group securities financing transactions.

The capital resources to which these limits apply are those of the UKIG, rather than those of the solo firm.

Table 18.3 (*cont.*)

Situation	Exposure from/to	Summary of the available modifications
		Treasury concession and intra-group securities financing transactions may also be applied to the exposures of the UKIG to each of its diverse blocks within the WIG if the requisite conditions are satisfied.
		In respect of the treasury concession, where there is a WIG, the UKIG's exposures to each individual diverse block may be exempt from the 25% limit up to a maximum amount of 50% of the capital resources of the UKIG. Exempt exposures are also exempt for the purpose of calculating the notional CNCOM for each diverse block. The UKIG exposures to the individual diverse blocks that were eligible for the treasury concession, but which together with other such exposures exceed the 50% limit, are not exempt and are treated as other exposures of the UKIG and remain subject to the 25% limit.
8	UKIG firm to a undertaking within its residual block	In situation 8, there is a UKIG, WIG (comprising diverse blocks agreed under the WIG waiver) and residual block.
		The UKIG's exposures to members of its residual block are exempt from the normal large exposures limits at the solo level. Instead, the total of the UKIG's exposures to the residual block is subject to the following limits:
		— 25 % non-trading book limit;
		— trading book limits other than CNCOM;
		— 500% limit for excess trading book exposures with the deletion of the 10 day time limit; and
		— Treasury concession and intra-group securities financing transactions).
		The capital resources to which these limits apply are those of the UKIG, rather than those of the solo firm.
		Treasury concession and intra-group securities financing transactions may also be applied to exposures of the UKIG to its residual block if the requisite conditions are satisfied.
		In respect of the treasury concession, where, subject to meeting the treasury concession conditions, the UKIG's exposures to undertakings within its residual block may be exempt from the 25% limit, subject to a maximum of 50% of the capital resources of the UKIG. These exempt exposures would also be exempt for the purposes of calculating the notional CNCOM. Any exposure that meets the

		treasury concession conditions but is above the 50% limit would not be exempt from the large exposure limits. They would not be exempt from the notional CNCOM. UKIG exposures that were eligible for a treasury concession, but which, together with other such exposures, exceeded the 50% limit are not exempt and are treated as other exposures of the UKIG and remain subject to the 25% limit.
9	WIG firm to an undertaking in the UKIG	Not within the scope of the preferential large exposure treatments.
10	WIG firm to another undertaking in the same WIG (either within the same diverse block or between diverse blocks)	Not within the scope of the preferential large exposure treatments.
11	WIG firm to an undertaking within the residual block	Not within the scope of the preferential large exposure treatments.
12	A firm within the residual block to an undertaking within the UKIG	Not within the scope of the preferential large exposure treatments.
13	A firm within the residual block to an undertaking within the WIG	Not within the scope of the preferential large exposure treatments.
14	A firm within the residual block to an undertaking in the residual block	Not within the scope of the preferential large exposure treatments.

19

LIQUIDITY

A. Liquidity Supervision

19.01 The purpose of banks is maturity transformation—in effect borrowing money from the future to spend in the present. Banks are consequently structurally illiquid, since they could never repay today all of the obligations that they have. The issue for regulators as regards banking is therefore not whether banks should be permitted to run liquidity risk—they do; that is their function—but as to how much liquidity risk they should be permitted to run.

19.02 Liquidity supervision has historically been applied by national supervisors not only to banks established in their jurisdiction but also to branches in their jurisdiction of banks established elsewhere. This is a breach of the general principle that prudential regulation is generally conducted at a legal entity level by the home state supervisor. However, in the early days of cross-border banking, branch supervisors were all too well aware that in order to protect depositors in their jurisdiction, the most important matter was to ensure that sufficient liquid assets were held locally to enable those depositors to be repaid. When the EU introduced the concept of single authorization accompanied by a right to passport, liquidity remained a matter for host states to the extent that they wished to supervise it. The directives require home and host state supervisors to co-operate in this regard, and a variety of techniques exist by which home state supervisors may, by concession, permit a branch operating in their jurisdiction to deal with its liquidity as part of a whole firm or group liquidity management strategy. Such concessions are common practice both within the EU and across other jurisdictions. However, in principle liquidity is national even in the EU. As mutual confidence has collapsed between regulators in the wake of the credit crisis, the trend is towards resiling from such group arrangements, and we expect to see an increase in the number of national regimes applied to cross-border banks in the future.

19.03 Liquidity is primarily dealt with by regulators as a systems and controls issue—for example the FSA implemented the directive provisions relating to liquidity by inserting provisions in its systems and controls sourcebook (SYSC 11) and by requiring banks to perform scenario analysis (GENPRU 1). The regulation of liquidity is one of the 'hot' areas of modern bank capital regulation, and it is frequently said that it was one of the major failings of the Basel regime that it gave insufficient emphasis to liquidity issues. It is true that the primary Basel recommendations in this area go to systems rather than the imposition of quantitative restrictions. However, there is considerable debate as to whether and to what extent quantitative restrictions on liquidity can be implemented, and the extent to which they may be successful or even useful.

19.04 An important point as regards liquidity supervision is that supervisors start from a very different point as regards liquidity than that from which they start as regards capital. There is a broadly established and generally agreed industry framework for the determination of bank risk calculation, and therefore risk capital requirements. In creating a regulatory bank capital requirement framework, regulators were able to build on this work. This meant that the resulting system, although complex, was broadly acceptable to banks, since it was based on the same general approaches which were used internally within those banks themselves. With liquidity, however, no two banks employ the same control, modelling or risk analysis techniques, and academic writers have not generated a consensus as to the approaches or techniques to be used to model liquidity risk. To complicate matters further, it is frequently noted that liquidity and credit risk are sufficiently intertwined as to be inseparable. The VaR techniques used to model credit risk necessarily take some elements of liquidity risk into account, since market prices for securities—especially in times of liquidity scarcity—will include an element of liquidity exposure risk, and a system which models price changes will necessarily factor in these elements.[1] Thus the regulator seeking to regulate liquidity risk

---

[1] Note that this is an entirely different risk from that which is addressed by the trading book incremental capital risk. Incremental capital risk addresses the risk of credit risk migration—loosely the risk that positions will diminish in value because of deterioration in the credit risk of the issuer. Liquidity risk is the risk that in the event of a disposal there will be no buyer at all (in which case the asset is valueless) or buyers at artificially low levels. This risk is addressed primarily through valuation adjustments, but these in turn only address relative illiquidity. Absolute illiquidity is a harder risk to model.

within banks is faced with a policy choice—either create and impose a quantitative model which the industry does not support, or confine the regulatory process to the non-quantitative aspects of regulation.

B. Qualitative Supervision of Liquidity

The Basel liquidity paper of 2008[2] sets out 17 principles for managing liquidity **19.05** risk, and these still form the best basic summary of the structure of a regulatory liquidity regime.

Fundamental principles for the management and supervision of liquidity risk

Principle 1.   A bank is responsible for the sound management of liquidity risk. A bank should establish a robust liquidity risk management framework that ensures it maintains sufficient liquidity, including a cushion of unencumbered, high quality liquid assets, to withstand a range of stress events, including those involving the loss or impairment of both unsecured and secured funding sources. Supervisors should assess the adequacy of both a bank's liquidity risk management framework and its liquidity position and should take prompt action if a bank is deficient in either area in order to protect depositors and to limit potential damage to the financial system.

Governance of liquidity risk management

Principle 2.   A bank should clearly articulate a liquidity risk tolerance that is appropriate for its business strategy and its role in the financial system.

Principle 3.   Senior management should develop a strategy, policies and practices to manage liquidity risk in accordance with the risk tolerance and to ensure that the bank maintains sufficient liquidity. Senior management should continuously review information on the bank's liquidity developments and report to the board of directors on a regular basis. A bank's board of directors should review and approve the strategy, policies and practices related to the management of liquidity at least annually and ensure that senior management manages liquidity risk effectively.

Principle 4.   A bank should incorporate liquidity costs, benefits and risks in the internal pricing, performance measurement and new product approval process for all significant business activities (both on and off balance sheet), thereby

---

[2] Basel Committee on Banking Supervision, *Principles for Sound Liquidity Risk Management and Supervision*, September 2008.

aligning the risk-taking incentives of individual business lines with the liquidity risk exposures their activities create for the bank as a whole.

Measurement and management of liquidity risk

Principle 5. A bank should have a sound process for identifying, measuring, monitoring and controlling liquidity risk. This process should include a robust framework for comprehensively projecting cash flows arising from assets, liabilities and off-balance sheet items over an appropriate set of time horizons.

Principle 6. A bank should actively monitor and control liquidity risk exposures and funding needs within and across legal entities, business lines and currencies, taking into account legal, regulatory and operational limitations to the transferability of liquidity.

Principle 7. A bank should establish a funding strategy that provides effective diversification in the sources and tenor of funding. It should maintain an ongoing presence in its chosen funding markets and strong relationships with funds providers and Supervision to promote effective diversification of funding sources. A bank should regularly gauge its capacity to raise funds quickly from each source. It should identify the main factors that affect its ability to raise funds and monitor those factors closely to ensure that estimates of fund raising capacity remain valid.

Principle 8. A bank should actively manage its intraday liquidity positions and risks to meet payment and settlement obligations on a timely basis under both normal and stressed conditions and thus contribute to the smooth functioning of payment and settlement systems.

Principle 9. A bank should actively manage its collateral positions, differentiating between encumbered and unencumbered assets. A bank should monitor the legal entity and physical location where collateral is held and how it may be mobilized in a timely manner.

Principle 10. A bank should conduct stress tests on a regular basis for a variety of short-term and protracted institution-specific and market-wide stress scenarios (individually and in combination) to identify sources of potential liquidity strain and to ensure that current exposures remain in accordance with a bank's established liquidity risk tolerance. A bank should use stress test outcomes to adjust its liquidity risk management strategies, policies, and positions and to develop effective contingency plans.

Principle 11. A bank should have a formal contingency funding plan (CFP) that clearly sets out the strategies for addressing liquidity shortfalls in emergency situations. A CFP should outline policies to manage a range of stress environments, establish clear lines of responsibility, include clear invocation and escalation procedures and be regularly tested and updated to ensure that it is operationally robust.

Principle 12. A bank should maintain a cushion of unencumbered, high quality liquid assets to be held as insurance against a range of liquidity stress scenarios, including those that involve the loss or impairment of unsecured and typically available secured funding sources. There should be no legal, regulatory or operational impediment to using these assets to obtain funding.

Public disclosure

Principle 13. A bank should publicly disclose information on a regular basis that enables market participants to make an informed judgement about the soundness of its liquidity risk management framework and liquidity position.

The role of supervisors

Principle 14. Supervisors should regularly perform a comprehensive assessment of a bank's overall liquidity risk management framework and liquidity position to determine whether they deliver an adequate level of resilience to liquidity stress given the bank's role in the financial system.

Principle 15. Supervisors should supplement their regular assessments of a bank's liquidity risk management framework and liquidity position by monitoring a combination of internal reports, prudential reports and market information.

Principle 16. Supervisors should intervene to require effective and timely remedial action by a bank to address deficiencies in its liquidity risk management processes or liquidity position.

Principle 17. Supervisors should communicate with other supervisors and public authorities, such as central banks, both within and across national borders, to facilitate effective cooperation regarding the supervision and oversight of liquidity risk management. Communication should occur regularly during normal times, with the nature and frequency of the information sharing increasing as appropriate during times of stress.

Although not a direct development of these principles, the best summary of **19.06** private sector approach to liquidity management is to be found in the Institute for International Finance's liquidity paper of 2007.[3]

---

[3] *Principles of Liquidity Risk Management*, Institute for International Finance, March 2007.

C. Quantitative Supervision of Liquidity

19.07 Many bank regulators have concluded that systems and control regulations along these lines, although necessary, are not sufficient, and have imposed broad quantitative restrictions on banks. These restrictions vary significantly across jurisdictions, and since they fall outside the scope both of the Accord and of the CRD it is difficult to generalize. We therefore provide a brief summary of the UK regime as one of the more developed regimes of this kind.[4]

19.08 The UK has two liquidity supervision regimes: the maturity mismatch approach; and the sterling stock liquidity approach. The maturity mismatch approach is the approach used for firms generally, with the sterling stock approach used for firms which maintain large sterling retail deposits.

19.09 EEA banks that have a branch in the UK but do not have a UK deposit-taking permission are required to maintain a liquidity policy and monitor their liquidity position at the level of the UK branch (not the bank as a whole), but are not required to comply with the quantitative elements of the UK regime.

'Global concession' policy

19.10 The FSA supervises the liquidity of all banks operating in the United Kingdom. The liquidity of EEA banks and overseas banks is often managed from its head office on an integrated basis. Where this is the case the FSA is prepared in certain circumstances to agree that it will not directly regulate the liquidity position of the branch. The basis on which it is prepared to do this is where:

- the home supervisors liquidity supervision arrangements cover the relevant branch, and the supervisor is prepared to co-operate with the FSA;
- the branch is fully integrated with its head office for liquidity management purposes;
- the branch has little or no autonomy from its head office as regards liquidity exposures; and
- the head office is willing and able to support the branch.

19.11 A branch which lends a considerable proportion of its own balance sheet back to its parent or to other counterparties in its home country risks becoming illiquid if, for any reason, the parent is unable to meet its debt service obligations. Partly for this reason the FSA assesses whether to place limits on home country lending for branches.

---

[4] At the time of writing the UK liquidity regime is reasonably well concealed within the FSA rulebook. The diligent reader is directed to the previous edition of the FSA's bank supervisory rules, designated within its rulebook as IPRU(BANK). IPRU(BANK) has been repealed in its entirety apart from chapters LM and LS, which contain the FSA's quantitative liquidity rules.

Liquidity assessment

The basis of the supervision of bank liquidity is the bank's own statement of its **19.12**
liquidity management policy. This should set out mismatch guidelines and the
procedures for dealing with breaches of the policy, along with the Bank's contingency funding plan.

A bank should be able to quantify precisely the size and date of at least some of its **19.13**
future cash outgoings, such as requirements to repay deposits, provide committed
funds, meet settlement or other obligations and pay other identifiable expenses.
Others—such as drawdowns on committed facilities—may be less predictable.
However, these obligations should still be capable of being estimated. The basis of
quantitative supervision is that a bank should estimate these outgoings and maintain a stock of liquid assets sufficient to meet them. Such outgoings may be met in
a number of ways:

(a) by holding sufficient immediately available cash or marketable assets;
(b) by securing an appropriate matching future profile of cash flows from matur-
    ing assets and liabilities; and
(c) by further borrowing—taking deposits or borrowing on the interbank market.

Banks are generally reluctant to hold a large stock of immediately available cash or **19.14**
marketable assets, as the return on holdings of such assets is generally very low.
There is therefore an inherent tension within the regulatory system between regulators, who wish to see banks holding adequate stocks of existing assets, and banks,
who wish to rely as far as possible on future borrowing capacity. For regulators,
however, the primary concern is precisely that if the bank finds itself in a position
where it needs to raise further funding, the market may be unwilling to provide
that funding to it. Consequently regulators make a significant distinction between
future funding which is proposed to be raised when required, and future funding
which has been pre-agreed under committed borrowing lines. Again, there is a
fundamental tension here between firms—who will not wish to pay for such commitments, but will rely on the assumption that they will be able to borrow in the
future on the same terms on which they can borrow today—and regulators, who
are concerned specifically with circumstances in which lenders may not only not be
prepared to lend new money but may be seeking to withdraw from committed lines
already in place. The one area where there is no obvious tension between regulators
and firms is diversification—regulators require firms to maintain access to a wide
variety of different sources of liquidity, and well-advised firms seek the same end.

D. Mismatch Liquidity

The FSA's mismatch approach measures a bank's liquidity by assessing the mis- **19.15**
match between its inflows (assets) and outflows (liabilities) within different time

bands on a maturity ladder. The difference between the maturities of inflows (assets) and outflows (liabilities) is termed a mismatch. In the maturity ladder, inflows (assets) and outflows (liabilities) are slotted into time bands—in other words, a particular maturity period is identified—say, within the next week or month—and total outflows and inflows during that period are estimated. Maturity is determined on a worst-case view, ie inflows (assets) are put in at their latest maturity and outflows (liabilities) at their earliest maturity. The information provided in the maturity ladder is assessed in these cumulative time bands. The basis of all of these bands is money payable on demand (known as 'sight' money). The bands are sight—8 days, sight—1 month, sight—3 months, etc. A net mismatch figure is obtained by subtracting outflows (liabilities) from inflows (assets) in each time band. Mismatches are then measured on a net cumulative basis. A net overall cumulative mismatch figure is derived by accumulating the net positions in each successive time band. The FSA assesses a bank's liquidity position by means of the net cumulative mismatch position expressed as a percentage of total deposit liabilities. Total deposit liabilities (the total of the deposits held by the bank) are used because they represent a relatively stable approximation of the total external (or withdrawable) funding of the bank. The FSA sets recommended guidelines for the maximum percentage for net cumulative mismatches as a percentage of total deposits. These are known as the mismatch guidelines. These are intended to prevent banks operating with too large a negative mismatch, and therefore running an excessive risk of not being able to raise sufficient funds to cover the mismatch at short notice.

19.16 The FSA normally sets guidelines for maximum mismatches only for the time bands of sight—8 days and sight–1 month. Mismatch guidelines are not usually set for the longer time bands, except in exceptional circumstances, as over a longer time period, in most cases, banks will have a greater opportunity to raise funds, and therefore a larger negative mismatch is not such a concern.

This can be represented schematically as follows:

Band	Inflows	Outflows	Net mismatch	Net overall cumulative mismatch	Net overall cumulative mismatch as percentage of total deposit liabilities
Sight–8 days					
Sight–1 Month					
Sight–3 months					

Inflows and outflows

19.17 The timebands in the maturity ladder are established on a cashflow basis. This means that what is report is actual flows of money (including salaries, fees and interest payments) and not simply principal payments and repayments.

One of the most important aspects of the treatment of cashflows in liquidity **19.18** monitoring is the retail/wholesale divide. A bank must classify its cashflows as being either retail or wholesale, and a bank whose cashflows are heavily dependent on the wholesale markets may be set a tighter mismatch than one with cashflows from the retail sector. This is to reflect the fact that retail cashflows tend to be more 'sticky'—that is, retail customers will be slower to respond to a deteriorating bank than wholesale customers. Retail exposures may also be addressed on a 'behavioural' basis. The point here is that to analyse retail exposures—overdrafts and deposits—on the basis of their legal characteristics would be highly misleading. In theory retail deposits are all withdrawable on demand, but to treat the whole of a bank's deposit base as sight money would result in the bank's liquidity position being unsalvageable. The key point, of course is as to how likely it is that these deposits would actually be withdrawn on mass. This is addressed in practice by behavioural modelling, by which the bank may take into account (with an appropriate degree of conservatism) the probability of substantial withdrawals, taking into account historic experience and any observable trends. Such modelling must also take into account idiosyncratic features of particular asset types—for example, since it is very likely that deposits with the bank of client money by regulated firms would be required to be moved if the bank came under pressure, such deposits should be treated as being immediately withdrawable even though they may be classified as retail exposures. This approach should also be applied in calculating the obligations which will arise from indeterminate commitments such as overdraft and other facilities. Where such an analysis does not produce a robust response, the default treatment is 15 per cent of such liabilities.

A bank is generally required to report to the FSA on a legal maturity basis. A retail **19.19** bank which has received permission to report its retail exposures on a behavioural basis must also report its legal maturity position. Wholesale exposures may never be reported on a behavioural basis—this treatment is unique to retail exposures.

Outflows (liabilities)

These are in principle included in the maturity ladder according to their earliest **19.20** contractual maturity. Retail liabilities may be addressed on a behavioural basis—see above, para 19.18. Contingent liabilities (such as obligations under guarantees) are not included in liabilities for this purpose.

Inflows (assets)

Inflows are generally included in the maturity ladder according to their latest **19.21** contractual maturity. However, this also needs to be flexed to take account of behaviour. An overdraft, for example, is technically repayable on demand, but overdrafts should not for this purpose be treated as capable of being liquidated within days.

Committed facilities available to the bank

19.22   Undrawn committed facilities granted to a bank should not be included as inflows
in the receiving bank's mismatch calculated on a contractual basis. The reason for
this is the sad but observable truth that other banks are liable to withdraw commitments (or to decline to permit drawings under them) to a bank which is clearly
in trouble. However, the FSA may consider that a proportion of undrawn committed facilities granted to a bank should count towards the mismatch calculated
on a behavioural basis, provided that it is satisfied that there is a good chance that
the commitment will not be withdrawn, and that drawing under it will be permitted, by the bank in question. This is, in reality, another behavioural adjustment
(albeit one which is applied to a wholesale exposure), and in assessing the likelihood of a bank permitting another to draw under a committed facility, the issues
to be taken into account will include the following:

(a)   whether the facility is legally binding;

(b)   whether the facility is regularly used to fund a bank's business or whether it is
a standby facility expected to be drawn down in an emergency (the FSA takes
the view that regularly used facilities are less likely to be withdrawn when
most needed than emergency standby facilities, since in the case of the latter
request to draw can suggest to the lender that there is a problem);

(c)   the identity of the provider of the facility;

(d)   the relationship between the provider of the facility and the bank;

(e)   the existence of covenants in the facility documentation. The existence of
covenants means that a facility may be withdrawn under certain circumstances and this, in turn, can threaten a bank's liquidity. The existence of
covenants in a facility is likely to reduce the percentage of the facility allowed
in the mismatch calculation. In assessing any particular covenanted facility,
regard should be given to the amount of headroom a bank has before a covenant is triggered;

(f)   the number of available facilities. Where a bank depends on a single standby (as
opposed to several) which might be judged to be unavailable in a crisis, a supervisor may be inclined to consider appropriate a smaller percentage (if any) of
the standby to count towards the behavioural mismatch calculation. However,
this logic does not apply if there is a cross-default clause that may mean a breach
of one facility that may have a knock-on effect for other facilities.

19.23   Once a bank has drawn down a committed facility, the amount drawn down
should be treated for reporting purposes by the receiver as a potential outflow
according to the final maturity date of the facility.

19.24   Undrawn committed facilities granted by a bank should be included as demand
outflows in the providers' mismatch calculated on a contractual basis. The default
treatment of a committed facility granted by a bank should be 15 per cent of the

total undrawn committed facilities, but this should be varied to reflect the expected performance of the facility, and the varied amount agreed with the supervisor.

Marketable assets

The mismatch liquidity approach does not formally impose a requirement to maintain a stock of liquid assets.[5] However, the best way for a bank to deal with mismatches is to increase stock of short-term assets, and the practical consequence of the approach is that banks subject to this approach generally do hold such stocks. The issue is therefore how such holdings are treated for the purpose of the liquidity analysis. The general rule is that assets should not be considered as liquid except at their maturity date unless they can be offered for discount at a central bank. Some assets which are not eligible for central bank liquidity operations may be accepted as sufficiently liquid to provide immediate liquidity provided that there is a very highly liquid market for such assets. In evaluating such assets, it is necessary to consider the specific attributes of individual securities as well as the nature of the security in the abstract—thus, for example, if a bank holds the majority of an issue it would be unlikely to be able to sell all of its holding without significantly impacting the market price which it would receive on the sale, and that fact should be taken into account in estimating the amount of liquidity which could be raised from sale of the asset within the relevant time band. Where such assets are included as marketable securities, a haircut should be applied to the value of the asset to reflect the likely loss resulting from a forced sale.

19.25

Assets considered to be readily marketable are included in the maturity ladder in the sight—8 days time band, generally at a discount to their recorded value. Some assets which would be subject to an extended settlement period if sold may be included in the 8 days—1 month time band.

19.26

Securities held as a result of reverse repos, or securities which form part of a hedged transaction or synthetic asset (eg bonds attached to an interest rate swap), may be included in a portfolio of discountable assets if such assets are marketable (whether in isolation of their attached swap or as a package). Although banks selling such holdings may face market risk (eg where they sell an asset in isolation of its attached swap), the liquidity framework is not designed to take this into account and, in calculating mismatches, the FSA does not treat such securities in a distinctive way unless there is a restriction on sale.

19.27

Assets which have been pledged as collateral and are therefore no longer available to a bank to meet obligations should be excluded from the maturity ladder as they are no longer available to provide the bank with liquidity.

19.28

---

[5] Although the sterling stock liquidity method does.

19.29 Marketable assets should be reported at a discount in the sight—8 days time band. Banks should note that the marketability of some assets may change both significantly and quickly. It is therefore important that banks review the marketability of assets and the risk to that marketability regularly.

19.30 The discount factors applied to different types of marketable assets in the FSA's mismatch calculations are given in Table 19.1.

Table 19.1 Discount factors applied to different types of marketable assets

Central government debt, local authority paper and eligible* bank bills (and comparable assets from other OECD member countries)	Benchmark discount
Central government and central government guaranteed marketable securities with 12 or fewer months residual maturity, including treasury bills; and eligible* local authority paper and eligible* bank bills.	0%
Other central government, central government guaranteed and local authority marketable debt with five or fewer years residual maturity or at variable rates.	5%
Other central government, central government guaranteed and local authority marketable debt with over five years residual maturity.	10%
Other securities denominated in freely tradable currencies (usually OECD member countries)	
Non-government debt securities falling within the definition of qualifying debt security, and which have six or fewer months to residual maturity.	5%
Non-government debt securities falling within the definition of qualifying debt security, and which have five or fewer years residual maturity.	10%
Non-government debt securities falling within the definition of qualifying debt security, and which have more than five years residual maturity.	15%
Listed equities.	
Other marketable assets (usually OECD countries).	
Holdings in a qualifying money market fund.	5%
Non-OECD central government debt where such debt is actively traded. (However, where such debt is denominated in local currency, it is usually deemed to be available to provide liquidity only in that currency.)	20–40%
Non OECD non-government debt.	No better than that applied to the appropriate government
Non-OECD listed equities.	40%

*Eligible means that the paper is accepted as discountable by the Bank of England in its open market operations.

In setting mismatch guidelines, the following factors are considered in all cases: **19.31**

(a) the volatility, diversity and source of deposits;

(b) the volatility of deposits may be more closely related to a bank's perceived creditworthiness, to its position in the banking system or to current economic or financial conditions, than to the precise term of the deposits;

(c) particular attention is paid to those deposits that are known to be sensitive to a bank's reputation and standing, eg fiduciary deposits;

(d) the presence of concentrations in the deposit base, including single-source introductions or investment firms' client money accounts;

(e) the degree of reliance on marketable assets, the depth of market in such assets and the price volatility of such assets;

(f) the degree of diversification in a bank's portfolio of marketable assets, and the facility with which such assets could be liquidated.

(g) the availability and reliability of undrawn standby lines;

(h) the dependence on drawings of standby lines in order to maintain adequate liquidity, and in particular the possibility of calls for early repayment on lines which have already been drawn (which may result from breaches of material adverse change clauses or other covenants); and

(i) the impact of other business such as off balance sheet obligations, cash flows from FRAs, swaps, forwards etc.

In setting mismatch guidelines consideration should also be given to certain qualitative factors, such as quality of management, market reputation, general ability of management and the particular skills of the treasury area.

Every bank should have systems in place that enable it to calculate its liquidity   **19.32** position on a daily basis, and must report its liquidity profile on a quarterly basis. A bank is required to report all deposits or groups of connected deposits that exceed 2 per cent of total deposit liabilities.

An issue frequently arises where inflows and outflows are denominated in different   **19.33** currencies. In principle, exposures denominated in highly liquid and freely convertible currencies may be aggregated. However, a bank should not rely on the swaps market in less freely convertible currencies as a means of switching liquidity from one currency to another, since difficulties in one deposit market may affect others. An analysis of liquidity by individual currency may be required by the FSA as regards business conducted in a currency which is not quickly and easily convertible.

E. Sterling Stock Liquidity

This regime applies only to retail UK banks, and is intended for banks   **19.34** whose primary business is sterling deposit-taking. UK retail banks which have a substantial non-sterling business may be required to monitor that business using the maturity mismatch approach.

19.35 The reason that the sterling stock liquidity approach exists is that retail banks' wholesale exposures, when measured on a legal maturity basis, may lead to very large maturity mismatches on paper which may not relate to the actual risk exposure of the institution. The sterling stock rules are in this respect a concessionary regime for such banks, allowing them to maintain a smaller liquidity pool than the full mismatch liquidity regime might otherwise require. However, the regulator must also have regard to the importance of preserving retail depositors. One of the objectives of the sterling stock liquidity approach is to ensure that a bank in difficulty can survive short-term crises until an appropriate rescue or restructuring can be put in place. The target for such survival is five working days. This is accomplished by requiring such banks to hold a stock of sterling liquidity in the form of assets which may be immediately converted into sterling.

19.36 It is generally a safe bet that when a bank gets into difficulties wholesale creditors will seek to withdraw funds faster than retail creditors. This is the basis of the sterling stock liquidity approach in a scenario analysis based on the non-renewal of maturing sterling wholesale funding (on a net basis) and the leakage of 5 per cent of gross retail deposits. A bank which operates on the sterling stock basis should be required to maintain an internal limit for its maximum wholesale sterling net outflow over the next five working days.

19.37 A sterling stock liquidity bank is required to hold a minimum stock of liquid assets sufficient to cover its agreed 'floor' and to ensure that its sterling stock liquidity ratio is at least 100 per cent, unless otherwise agreed with the FSA in writing.

The basic requirement for the sterling stock is:

(1) Net wholesale sterling outflow over the next five days;
(2) LESS any allowable sterling CDs;
(3) PLUS 5 per cent of sterling retail sight deposits;
(4) PLUS any time deposits falling due over the next five days.

'Net wholesale sterling outflow'

19.38 A sterling stock liquidity bank's wholesale sterling net outflow is obtained by subtracting wholesale sterling assets maturing over the next five working days from wholesale sterling liabilities falling due over the same period. For the purposes of this calculation, a bank should include as wholesale sterling liabilities:

(a) all sterling deposits from banks and building societies taken by its treasury division; and

(b) all other sterling deposits of £1mn or more taken on wholesale market terms (ie as part of treasury or other similar operations on the strength of the interest rate quoted on enquiry on each occasion that a deposit is made).

This test should be inverted in order to determine whether a deposit made by the bank is a wholesale deposit.

A sterling stock liquidity bank may offset its holdings of sterling certificates of deposit against up to 50 per cent of its wholesale sterling net outflow. When included in this way, sterling certificates of deposit are subject to a 15 per cent discount to reflect market risks on sale. For this purpose an arrangement can be a CD even if there is no CD—in circumstances where negotiable deposits are made on terms identical to those on which a sterling certificate of deposit would have been issued, but for which it is mutually convenient not to issue a certificate, the deposit may be treated as if it were a CD. CDs issued by the bank itself may be netted off. Any holdings of sterling certificates of deposit maturing within five working days may be included in the sterling liquidity stock ratio calculation. **19.39**

Sterling retail deposits

When calculating its sterling stock liquidity ratio, a bank should include its gross sterling retail deposits with a residual contractual maturity of five working days or less. For this purpose, retail deposits are defined as deposits which arise from customer acceptance of an advertised rate (including 0 per cent) for a particular product. Retail deposits include deposits taken in a sterling stock liquidity bank's branch network on the grounds of an existing or new customer relationship where the rates of interest are not directly linked to interbank rates, and are advertised or displayed at the branch counter or are part of standard tariff terms so that depositors can establish, without further enquiry, the rate applicable to each type of deposit. All deposits of under £1mn should be included as retail deposits, even if taken on wholesale terms. **19.40**

Retail deposits which are term deposits should be assumed to be withdrawn only on their technical maturity, unless the remaining term of the deposit is five days or less, or unless the deposit can be withdrawn early without penalty. **19.41**

In addition to the percentage requirement, a bank will also be subject to a 'floor' amount. This will be a minimum level of sterling stock which the bank is required to maintain at all times regardless of the basic requirement. The floor is imposed in order to ensure that an institution always maintains a credible level of sterling stock even if the basic requirement fluctuates to an artificially low level for a short period. **19.42**

Sterling liquid assets

19.43 For this purpose sterling liquid assets consists of:

(a) cash, ie Bank of England and other sterling notes and UK coin (including cash paid into another UK bank which has not yet been credited to the sterling stock liquidity bank's account in the books of the other UK bank, but not including gold sovereigns;

(b) operational balances with the Bank of England; including reserves held with the Bank of England's reserves scheme as part of the Bank of England's framework for its operations in the sterling money markets, of the type set out in Section V of the Bank of England's paper 'The Framework for the Bank of England's Operations in the Sterling Money Markets' (the 'Red Book'). Special deposits and cash ratio deposits are excluded;

(c) UK Treasury bills (including those denominated in Euro) and Bank of England Euro bills and notes;

(d) sterling international bonds ('bulldogs') where they have been issued into (and are held by) the CREST settlements system;

(e) sterling international bonds issued by certain EEA government and international financial institutions, where they have been issued into Euroclear or Clearstream settlement systems;

(f) Euro-denominated bonds issued by EEA governments or certain international financial institutions, where they have been issued into Euroclear or Clearstream settlement systems and where they are eligible for use in ESCB monetary policy operations;

(g) a range of Euro-denominated securities, where they are issued by the central governments and central banks of certain EEA countries, where they are eligible for use in ESCB monetary policy operations, and where the relevant central bank of a country participating in EMU has agreed to act as a bank's custodian under the Correspondent Central Banking Model (CCBM);

(Detailed lists of the bonds described in (d), (e),(f) and (g) above can be found on the Bank of England's website under 'Open Markets Operations' on the 'Eligible Securities' page.)[6]

(h) gilts; defined for this purpose as:
   (i) sterling and foreign currency denominated stock issued by HMG;
   (ii) stocks of nationalized industries guaranteed by HMG;
   (iii) the Irish land purchase stocks; and
   (iv) gilt strips;
      (other HMG guaranteed stocks are excluded);

---

[6] <http>//www.bankofengland.co.uk/markets/money/eligiblesecurities.htm>.

(i)   certificates of tax deposit; and

(j)   foreign currency debt securities issued by the Bank of England.

Sterling stock may frequently be lent or borrowed or used as collateral in other **19.44** transactions. Where sterling stock assets are acquired as a result of entering into a repo or reverse repo transaction, those assets may be included in the stock for the duration that they are held, and stock lent or charged may be included in the stock provided that title remains with the bank. For this latter reason, collateral taken in such transactions should not be included in the calculation by the collateral taker, since it is still being included by the collateral giver and it is important to avoid double counting. Stock taken as collateral under a charge should not be included in any circumstances, since it cannot be on-sold.

A sterling stock liquidity bank should monitor its liquidity position on an inter- **19.45** day basis. In normal circumstances, a bank's wholesale sterling actual net outflow should not exceed its wholesale sterling net outflow limit unless the bank concerned has enough surplus sterling stock liquidity, over and above that required to meet the sterling stock liquidity ratio.

Part V

BANK GROUP SUPERVISION

20

GROUP SUPERVISION

A. Introduction

At first glance the necessity for the supervision of banking groups—as opposed to banks themselves—is not obvious. There is no such thing as a creditor of a group—each creditor is a creditor of a particular legal entity, and in the case of depositors that legal entity is the relevant authorized bank. Provided that the capital rules are applied at the level of that authorized entity, it should have sufficient capital to ensure that those depositors are paid come what may, and no other group member will have any call on its assets until its own creditors are repaid. Thus, the classical analysis was that, provided that the bank itself was regulated, there was no necessity for the bank regulator to concern itself with any other member of that group. This argument works in theory but not in practice, and there are a variety of reasons which bank regulators need to be concerned with, bank groups as well as banks. **20.01**

The key principle is that banks are now known to be subject to contagion risk. In theory the failure of a company which is a member of a bank group has no effect on the regulated bank. In practice the failure of a company in a bank group will send a strong signal to the outside world that the group is in difficulty. It would in theory be possible to operate a group bank with such a degree of separation that the market as a whole believed that the bank would genuinely be unaffected by the failure of one of its subsidiaries. However, in practice the market believes that banks are closely connected with the groups of which they are members, and that failures elsewhere in a group will have important knock-on consequences for a **20.02** group bank. Thus a problem elsewhere in the group will set off a run on the group bank, with counterparties refusing to renew credit lines and creditors seeking early repayment of deposits. This will increase liquidity pressures on the bank and may eventually result in its failure.

20.03 It is also important that the exposure of a bank to members of its group varies according to the relationship between the bank and the group. In Figure 20.1, the failure of A would be fatal to confidence in the bank, whereas the failure of C would—in theory—be almost irrelevant to it.

The diagram can be used to illustrate the three different supervision concepts which need to be applied: solo, consolidated, and conglomerate supervision.

Solo supervision

20.04 The overriding priority remains to ensure that the bank itself remains solvent. However, for this purpose it is important to ensure that what is being supervised is the bank and only the bank—thus the bank's investment in D must be disregarded for this purpose.

Consolidated supervision

20.05 The bank is possibly most vulnerable to the failure of D. However, the primary issue here is whether D is engaged in the business of the bank (in a broader sense—for example as a booking vehicle, asset holding company, or SPV) or whether it is a separate commercial company unconnected with finance. The position here is that if D is a financial firm, then the bank should be supervised on a consolidated basis, with the balance sheets of bank and D consolidated together in order to establish whether the bank's capital is sufficient to support the combined

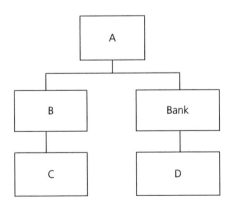

Fig. 20.1 Illustrative Bank Group Structure

undertaking. However, if D is a commercial company (unlikely but by no means impossible—banks sometimes do come to own significant stakes in commercial companies, either through private equity investment or for other reasons) then the consolidated figures should exclude it, and the bank's investment in D should be deducted.

Conglomerate supervision

For the purposes of financial supervision conglomerates come in two forms: **20.06** mixed-activity groups and financial conglomerates. For this purpose a mixed-activity group means a group which combines both financial and non-financial business, for example a bank owned by a car-maker. A financial conglomerate, by contrast, means a group which contains different types of financial businesses which are subject to different types of regulation—typically banks, insurance companies, and securities firms.

The basis of conglomerate supervision is the establishment of capital require- **20.07** ments at the parent company level. In general, the supervision of mixed-activity groups is not conducted on a consolidated basis, since consolidation across differ- ent forms of financial and non-financial businesses is unlikely to be helpful. This is likely to be the case even for financial conglomerates, since although consolida- tion across securities businesses and banks may be possible, consolidation across banks and insurance companies poses peculiar technical difficulties. Thus in gen- eral conglomerate supervision is conducted not through consolidation but by ensuring that the ultimate parent has at least sufficient capital to meet the capital requirements imposed on the regulated members of the group.

B. Consolidated Supervision

The mechanism by which regulators control this risk is by consolidated supervi- **20.08** sion. This, again, can best be explained diagrammatically, as shown in Figure 20.2.

What has happened here is that the 20 of equity investment in subsidiary has **20.09** disappeared (all intra-company balances—including equity investments—cancel out on consolidation). Thus, the remaining question is whether the equity of the parent company on its own is sufficient to support the risks of the combined balance sheet of all of the companies of the group.

C. Scope of Consolidation

Accounting consolidation includes all subsidiaries of an ultimate parent. **20.10** Regulatory consolidation is different—it includes only those subsidiaries of the

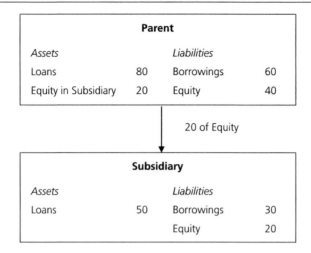

Fig. 20.2 **Illustration of Consolidation**

parent which are, in broad terms, financial businesses. This class is wider than that of authorized institutions—it includes a variety of businesses which do not require authorization—and some surprising omissions, but broadly the idea is to create within a larger group a consolidation of those businesses which are financial businesses. This limitation has effect in two ways. One is in the context of large conglomerates which have financial operations—the rule operates to exclude from the consolidation non-financial businesses. The other is in the context of financial firms which own non-financial businesses. If a bank, for example, were to own a chain of estate agents, the chain of estate agents would be excluded from the consolidated return of the bank. It is in this latter context that the rule is most commonly encountered, since almost all financial businesses own at least some non-financial subsidiaries.

20.11 Businesses which are not included in the consolidation are excluded from it. In practice what this means is that the investment which the group has made in the capital of the non-financial entity is deducted from the capital of the group. Thus, if a group with capital of 100 owns 100 per cent of an estate agency subsidiary which is being carried with a value of 10, the 10 will simply be deducted from the capital of the group, leaving a total group capital of 90. The working assumption behind this rule is that capital tied up in non-financial businesses cannot be liberated sufficiently rapidly to be of any use in the context of the financial business of the group.

It should be noted, however, that the fact that an entity is excluded from consolidation does not mean that it is ignored for all purposes. An entity which is excluded from consolidation may still be taken into account in determining whether certain financial entities are in the same group as each other, or are subject to consolidated supervision. Thus, if a bank owns a non-financial firm which owns a financial firm, the financial firm will be included in the bank's consolidated return, even though the entity which owns it is excluded from consolidation. **20.12**

What, then, is a financial business for this purpose? In the EU, the answer is: **20.13**

(1) an authorized bank;
(2) an authorized investment firm;
(3) a financial institution; meaning a firm whose purpose is to acquire holdings or to carry on one of any of the activities listed in Annex 1 to the CRD or MiFID. This broadly includes all of the following:
  (a) lending (including consumer credit, mortgage credit, factoring, and financing commercial transactions;
  (b) financial leasing;
  (c) money transmission;
  (d) issuing and administering credit cards, debit cards travellers cheques, bankers drafts and other means of payment;
  (e) guarantees and commitments;
  (f) trading in financial instruments,[1] whether for own account or on behalf of clients, along with the reception and transmission of orders;
  (g) investment advice;
  (h) participation in securities issues, including underwriting and placing (with or without commitment);
  (i) corporate finance advice;
  (j) money broking;
  (k) portfolio management and advice;[2]
  (l) safekeeping and administration of securities;
  (m) safe custody services;
  (n) credit reference services;

---

[1] As defined in Section C of Annex 1 of the Markets in Financial Instruments Directive (MiFID), Directive 2004/39/EC.
[2] But not the operation of collective investment schemes.

(o) operation of a multilateral trading facility;

(p) investment research.

For the purposes of this list, firms which are excluded from the scope of MiFID are included in the consolidation requirement, so otherwise exempt firms (such as firms which provide services exclusively to other group undertakings) are included in the consolidation.

(4) an asset management company;

(5) a financial holding company, defined as a company whose subsidiaries are either exclusively or mainly banks, investment firms or financial institutions; and

(6) an ancillary services undertaking; defined as an undertaking whose principal activity consists of holding property or providing services in a way which is ancillary to the principal activity of one of the banks or financial institutions contained in the group.

20.14 Where a firm has a majority holding of less than complete ownership (for example an 80 per cent equity stake) in a subsidiary, it must consolidate the subsidiary completely and treat the remaining minority holding as capital. However, where a firm holds between 20 per cent and 50 per cent of an entity, it must consolidate a proportionate share of the assets and liabilities of that entity equal to the proportion of its holding in the entity—thus, if it has a 30 per cent stake it must consolidate 30 per cent of the assets and 30 per cent of the liabilities.

20.15 In general a manager of regulated investment funds (a UCITS investment firm in EU-speak) only calculates its capital and concentration risk requirements in relation to its actual investment business, and does not calculate them with respect to scheme management activity. However, for the purposes of consolidated supervision the consolidation calculation includes the whole of the activities of a UCITS investment firm.

20.16 There is a *de minimis* level of consolidated supervision, in that a firm can exclude from consolidation any entity whose balance sheet is smaller than 1 per cent of the balance sheet total of the parent undertaking. However, in order to prevent exposures being excluded from consolidation through being held in multiple small vehicles, this exemption only applies where the total value of the exposures so excluded does not exceed 1 per cent of the parent balance sheet.

20.17 Regulators also have a discretion to permit regulated firms to exclude any entity from consolidation, which they may exercise if the inclusion would be misleading, or the entity is established in a jurisdiction which prohibits the entity obtaining relevant information, or otherwise if the inclusion would be of negligible interest. Regulators are in general very unwilling to agree that any non-trivial subsidiary should be excluded from consolidation.

D. Minority Interests

The inclusion of minority interests in group capital is an arcane subject, but an **20.18** important one. In a group which is structured in the ordinary way, with a parent company holding 100 per cent of the capital of subsidiaries which in turn hold 100 per cent of the capital of other subsidiaries and so on, minority interests will not arise. However, in practice it is unusual to encounter groups which do not have at least some members where the parent holding is less than 100 per cent, and external investors have, for one reason or another, come to own a proportion of the capital of the relevant subsidiary (this can happen through employee share schemes, earn-outs of newly acquired businesses or in a multitude of other ways). On consolidation, such interests appear as a non-distributable reserve labelled 'minority interests'.

If the ordinary accounting treatment were applied to minority interests, they **20.19** would all qualify as tier one at a group level, regardless of the terms, the duration or the degree of subordination of the instruments concerned. The regulatory system therefore does not follow the accounting treatment in this regard, but divided up minority interests according to the characteristics of the instruments by which that capital is raised. The capital is then allocated to the relevant tier in the consolidated capital calculation according to those characteristics. Thus, if a subsidiary has 20 per cent of its capital issued in a form which would qualify as lower tier two if the subsidiary were a regulated entity, that capital will qualify as lower tier two for the purpose of the consolidated capital calculation.

There is a different regime in place for capital issued by SPVs. The point here is **20.20** that on a consolidated basis such SPVs may be part of the consolidated group, and where this is the case the ordinary innovative tier one rules are amended such that capital which is issued by an SPV which is within the consolidated group will be treated in the same way as it would be in the accounts of a solo bank.

E. Solo Consolidation

Solo consolidation is an apparent contradiction in terms, in that banks are gener- **20.21** ally either supervised on a solo (stand-alone) or a consolidated (group) basis. The essence of solo consolidation is that it is a concessionary treatment whereby a group company is treated as not really existing. Where a bank solo-consolidates another entity, the process is that (a) the entity is consolidated into the bank in the normal fashion, and (b) the resulting consolidated balance sheet is treated as if it were the bank's own solo balance sheet. Solo consolidation is therefore a way of disregarding the separate corporate existence of a particular entity, and treating it as if it were a division of the relevant bank.

20.22 In general, solo consolidation is only available in circumstances where a bank has used a corporate vehicle for a particular purpose, and has such direct and immediate control over that vehicle that it can freely transfer assets and liabilities out of the vehicle and to itself. There are two ways in which this situation can arise; one being where the vehicle is wholly owned and controlled by the bank (this will be the case where the vehicle is used to hold assets for the bank) and the other being where the vehicle's assets consist wholly of claims on the bank (this will be the case where the vehicle is being used as a bond issuance vehicle for capital raising purposes). In either case the bank should be able to immediately close down the vehicle and access any capital which may be tied up in it.

F. Consolidated Capital

20.23 In principle consolidated supervision is exactly the same as solo supervision, in that the same rules are applied to the consolidated accounts as would be applied to solo accounts. Thus, the capital resources of the group are assessed in the same way as the capital resources of a single entity. Importantly, this means that the gearing restrictions which apply to individual types of capital (and the prohibition on using innovative tier one to meet Pillar one requirements) will apply on a consolidated basis. This may seem otiose, in that if the individual entities which compose the group comply with these limitations then it would seem obvious that the group will also comply with them. However, adjustments on consolidation (notably the writing off of goodwill) may result in group tier one being significantly less than the cumulative tier one component of the entities which comprise the group, and if this is the case then the gearing limits may reverberate all the way down the group capital structure. Where a group contains a bank it must calculate its group capital position using the rules applicable to banks, even if the ultimate parent company is an investment firm.

G. Consolidated Capital Resources Requirements

20.24 The calculation of the consolidated capital resources requirement of a firm's UK consolidation group or non-EEA sub-group involves taking the individual components that make up the capital resources requirement on a solo basis and applying them on a consolidated basis. Those components are:

- the capital charge for credit risk (the credit risk capital requirement),
- the capital charge for market risk (the market risk capital requirement),

- the capital charge for operational risk (the operational risk capital requirement).

The group must therefore calculate a group credit risk charge, a group market risk charge, and so on.

This calculation may be done in one of two ways. One is to pretend that the con- **20.25** solidated group is a single entity and to weight all of the group's exposures according to the requirements of the consolidated supervisor. This is known as the 'line by line' approach. This approach can, however, be exceptionally burdensome in cases where the consolidation includes subsidiary financial institutions incorporated in other jurisdictions which have already performed such calculations according to the rules of their local supervisors. Where this is the case, the group can reduce its burden by calculating a separate risk capital requirement for each group member (an aggregation approach) and summing those requirements. The FSA accepts certain regulators (for example the South African Reserve Bank, the Hong Kong regulator, and most of the US bank supervisors) as equivalent for this purpose, so that where a group headed by a UK bank has a US Federal Reserve regulated subsidiary, it may take the credit risk requirement reported to the Federal Reserve and use that figure as the credit risk capital requirement applicable to that business. An institution may mix the two approaches, adopting a line-by-line approach to some subsidiaries and an aggregation approach to others. A firm may also make the choice between an aggregation and a line by line approach differently for each consolidated requirement component. So, for example, a firm may decide to calculate the consolidated market risk requirement on an aggregation basis and the consolidated fixed overheads requirement on a line-by-line basis. The only exception to this rule is the calculation of the group large exposures charge—this must necessarily be calculated on a line-by-line basis, such that all of the exposures to the relevant counterparty across the group can be totalled.

The further problem which arises in this context is that where a group is composed **20.26** of a number of regulated banks in different jurisdictions, it may well be the case that some of them are on the standardized, some on the foundation, and some on the advanced IRB approaches. Combinations of approaches would generally not be permitted within a single institution, since once an institution has committed itself to adopting a particular approach it is required to aim to roll out that approach across the entire undertaking. However, there is no equivalent rule at a group level, and a group which combines different subsidiaries using different approaches may mix and match those approaches indefinitely in the calculation of its group capital requirement. However, a firm must not use both the financial collateral simple method and the financial collateral comprehensive method with respect to its UK consolidation group or non-EEA sub-group.

20.27 For the purposes of calculating the consolidated market risk requirement of a UK consolidation group or non-EEA sub-group, a firm must apply an aggregation method. The point here is that where a group has more than one regulated entity with a market making book, it is highly likely than the two books aggregated together will produce a lower capital requirement than the sum of the two requirements taken separately, since long positions in one will be offset by short positions in the other in at least some securities. The FSA's rules on this point are that the group requirement will be assessed by taking the sum of the requirements applied to the different books unless the institution can show that there is no material legal, regulatory, or contractual obstacle to the transfer of funds or to mutual financial support between the relevant undertakings, and that the market positions concerned are in fact monitored and managed on a co-ordinated basis.[3]

Operational risk

20.28 The calculation of operational risk is done through a variety of different approaches, and the same issues which arise with respect to the different approaches to credit risk also arise within groups in respect of the calculation of group operational risk requirements. Here again, firms have the issue in that where a basic indicator approach is used, the operational risk charge for individual subsidiaries, totalled together, may be larger than the charge which would be arrived at if the basic indicator approach were applied to the group as a whole, since at least some of the components of the basic indicator revenues will be intra-group charges which will be eliminated on consolidation. Groups have the choice between adopting an accounting consolidation approach, yielding the lower figure, or of simply aggregating the operational risk charges levied on each group member.

20.29 It is not, however, necessary to adopt a line-by-line approach to obtain the benefits of the elimination of intra-group balances, since the FSA permits the elimination of charges arising from intra-group balances and intra-group transactions regardless of the approach used.[4]

Advanced IRB approaches

20.30 The advanced IRB approach is intended to be unitary and to apply across the entire undertaking of an institution which uses it. A group which contains multiple banks in multiple jurisdictions may well have more than one advanced IRB approval. However, the firm is not permitted to aggregate the results of these two models. In practice the only way that an advanced IRB firm can use its advanced IRB model at group level is if it applies the model and the procedures approved by

---

[3] BIPRU 8.7.25.
[4] BIPRU 8.7.29.

the consolidating state supervisor to the entire group. The same is also true of the advanced measurement approach approved for the calculation of the operational risk charge—multiple AMAs may not be applied across different parts of the group[5] with the results being aggregated. Finally, the use of the advanced IRB method is conditional upon the adoption by the institution of governance and other practices as part of the implementation of the model, and in order to use the advanced IRB approach across multiple members of a group, it is necessary that these procedures be in place across all of the entities in respect of which the approach is intended to be used.

Large exposures

Large exposures restrictions are applied to consolidated groups in the same way in which they are applied to single institutions, and the group is limited in the same way to the total exposure which all of the institutions included in the consolidation may have to any one counterparty or group of counterparties. The slightly different definition of capital which is used for large exposures purposes is also applied on the consolidated level. Concentration risk is calculated using a single approach, that being a line-by-line consolidation subject to the rules of the consolidating regulator—there is no large exposures equivalent of the aggregation approach.   **20.31**

The rule exempting exposures within the group from large exposures restrictions continues to apply. This is clearly redundant where there is only one consolidated group, but may be relevant where the process of consolidation produces two or more consolidation groups within the overall group. For example, where a bank has a UK group and a worldwide group, the UK group may be able to exempt exposures between it and other members of the worldwide group on this basis. The same would apply between, for example, a UK consolidation group and an EREA sub-group.   **20.32**

The UK Integrated Groups and Wider Integrated Groups regimes apply on a consolidated level in the same way that they apply to a solo institution with minor amendments. The effect of these amendments is to permit consolidated groups to exclude in certain circumstances exposures to members of the wider group which are not members of the relevant consolidation group.   **20.33**

---

[5] Note that the AMA permits the recognition of insurance as a mitigant for operational risk. When an AMA is applied on a consolidated basis, insurance provided by captives and affiliates will not be recognized unless it is laid off to an independent undertaking outside the consolidated group which meets the eligibility criteria.

21

FINANCIAL CONGLOMERATES

A. Issues with Conglomerates

The Joint Forum on Financial Conglomerates released in 1999 a paper which sets **21.01** out the basis of the supervision of conglomerates,[1] and the basic principles set out in this paper remain the basis for conglomerate supervision. They are that supervisors should seek to assess the capital adequacy of financial conglomerates. In so doing, measurement techniques should be designed to:

I. detect and provide for situations of double or multiple gearing, ie where the same capital is used simultaneously as a buffer against risk in two or more legal entities;

II. detect and provide for situations where a parent issues debt and downstreams the proceeds in the form of equity, which can result in excessive leverage;

III. include a mechanism to detect and provide for the effects of double, multiple or excessive gearing through unregulated intermediate holding companies which have participations in dependants or affiliates engaged in financial activities;

IV. include a mechanism to address the risks being accepted by unregulated entities within a financial conglomerate that are carrying out activities similar to the activities of entities regulated for solvency purposes (eg leasing, factoring, reinsurance).

---

[1] Supervision of Financial Conglomerates, Papers prepared by the Joint Forum on Financial Conglomerates; February 1999, available on the BIS website.

V. address the issue of participations in regulated dependants (and in unregulated dependants covered by principle IV) and to ensure the treatment of minority and majority interests is prudentially sound.

Each of these merits a word of explanation.

Double or multiple gearing

21.02 Double gearing occurs when the same capital is counted twice. It is worth noting that the simplest form of double gearing would occur if banks were permitted to invest in each other's equity without restriction—thus, bank A could raise 100 of capital and invest it in the shares of bank B, on terms that bank B would re-invest in new shares of bank A. Within the banking system this problem is addressed by requiring banks to deduct equity holdings in other banks—thus if bank A raises 100 of new equity and invests that money in the capital of bank B, it will be required to deduct the holding in bank B from its total capital, and its position remains unchanged. Within a group, however, the position may be more complex—if a parent company raises equity and invests it in the shares of an insurance subsidiary, and that insurance subsidiary then acquires shares in a bank affiliate, then the same capital may be counted twice; once within the bank and once within the insurer. The point here is that it is only externally generated capital which can support the group as a whole, and to the extent that concerns arise as to the stability of the group, then it is the group's access to capital which will be relevant to external counterparties. The concern here is therefore that the capital position of the regulated entities within the group may be being artificially inflated at the expense of other group members.

Debt downstreamed as equity

21.03 It may not be immediately obvious to the observer why the bank regulator should care about the parent's capital levels. The answer may be seen from Figure 21.1.

The concern here is that investors are subscribing for what appears to be senior debt, whereas what is in fact being raised is subordinated bank capital. The reason that regulators find this concerning is the group itself may be increasing leverage and therefore reducing its financial stability. In addition, since the group as a whole is obliged to meet the obligations to the senior noteholders, and the group management will necessarily have significant influence over the board of the bank, the bank may in practice be obliged to treat the equity which it has received as being in effect on the terms of the senior debt raised. Ultimately this results in the suggestion that the equity is not 'true' equity, and that the bank's position is weaker than it appears.

Unregulated intermediate holding companies

21.04 An unregulated intermediate holding company may operate to break the chain of deductions. Thus, if a bank invests in another bank, the investment will be deducted

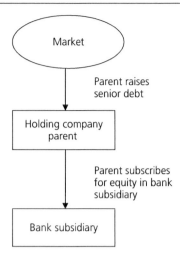

Fig. 21.1 Illustration of debt downstreamed as equity

from capital. However, if a bank invests in an unregulated holding company, that holding may not necessarily be deducted, particularly if it is a small holding. Thus intermediate unregulated holding companies may operate—deliberately or accidentally—to avoid the double-gearing rules.

Unregulated entities engaged in financial business

Where risk has been transferred by a regulated group member to an unregulated **21.05** member of the same group, the ordinary rules of risk transfer do not apply—the relevant risk is in many ways retained by the bank. This principle may be extended to the conduct of other activities. There are many activities—invoice discounting, factoring, holding assets—which may be engaged in by a bank as part of its ordinary activities, but which do not absolutely require a banking licence and may therefore equally well be engaged in by unregulated entities. As we have seen above (paras 20.11 to 20.14), when such entities are subsidiaries of a bank they are required to be included in the consolidation as financial entities rather than excluded from it as commercial entities. However, within a group such activities may be conducted by entities which have no direct linkage with the bank beyond a common ultimate parent.

Participations and minority interests in regulated entities

Where a group has neither control nor influence over a particular entity, that **21.06** entity should not be included in the supervised group. It is a generally established rule of thumb that the cut-off point for a holding which confers neither control nor influence is a holding of less than 20 per cent[2] in the voting equity of the relevant entity, although this presumption can be displaced if there is evidence that the holding does confer effective influence. Difficulties, however, arise where a group has a holding in an entity of between 20 per cent and 50 per cent. On ordinary corporate principles this means that the relevant entity is not a subsidiary of the group, but the holding is sufficiently large to ensure that the relevant entity can be used to further the interests of the group as a whole and, more importantly, may be perceived by the markets as sufficiently closely connected to the group that its failure would damage the creditworthiness of the group. If this is the case, then the entity will in practice have a claim on the financial resources of the group, and in assessing the stability of the group it must be taken into account.

21.07 However, an entity in which the group has a minority stake is clearly in a different position than an entity which the group wholly supports, and the position of the remaining shareholders cannot be completely disregarded in determining the appropriate regulatory approach. As a result, regulators in general deal with participations by including a pro rata share of the assets and liabilities of the regulated entity in the group supervision. As an exception to this approach; where the relevant entity has a shortfall in its regulatory capital position, the group will generally be treated as if it were solely liable to make good that shortfall. This reflects the fact that other shareholders are assumed to be more likely to refuse to support an undercapitalized group any further, whereas a regulated investor may be under a greater degree of moral pressure (including, of course, pressure from regulators) to stop the relevant entity failing.

B. Banks in Non-Financial Groups

21.08 There has been much discussion of the regulation of groups which combine financial and non-financial business, beginning with the question of whether they are desirable at all. Many jurisdictions have, or have had at some point, legislation prohibiting banks, insurance companies and securities firms from acquiring or being acquired by each other, and this is frequently defended as being in order to reduce systemic risks.

21.09 The reality is—of course—more complicated. It is generally accepted that the diversification of risk is broadly beneficial on systemic stability grounds, and there is no obvious reason why diversification between banking and insurance should not be at least as effective in this regard as diversification within different aspects

---

[2] In strict logic this figure might have been better set at 24 per cent, since in many corporate law systems a holding of 75 per cent of the equity of a company gives the holder absolute control.

of the business of banking—indeed it can plausibly be argued that a commercial bank which is grouped with an insurer is better diversified than a commercial bank which is grouped with a retail lender. However, you can take this one stage further and argue that a bank which is grouped with (say) an aerospace manufacturer is better diversified still, and it is at this point that bank and other financial supervisors become—justifiably—nervous.

There are some cases where financial groups exist within larger non-financial conglomerates. These may arise either because the non-financial conglomerate has expanded into financial business as part of its general business activities, or because a deliberate decision has been taken to expand into finance as a new business sector. Both of these are entirely legitimate business strategies, and regulators have in broad terms concluded that there is no policy reason for prohibiting non-financial corporate groups from owning financial businesses. **21.10**

This does, however, give rise to a concern regarding the pressures to which a group **21.11** financial firm (and in particular a group bank) may be subject. The key issue is that a bank is generally leveraged to a degree which would be unacceptable in an ordinary commercial company, and in some cases the management of a commercial company may seek to own a bank primarily for the purposes of creating an increase in group leverage. This increase may destabilize the group, and this in turn may destabilize the bank. Technically (as we have seen) a bank regulator has the power to regulate any entity which is the parent of a bank, regardless of the nature of that parent's activities. However, taken to extremes this would result in (say) the FSA seeking to exercise prudential capital supervision over (say) a Japanese car manufacturer merely because it happened to own a small bank in the UK. Such supervision would be redundant even if it were possible.

As a result, the regulatory system is constructed (in the EU at least) such that the **21.12** regulator supervises a sub-group within the main group. That sub-group is defined as the sub-group where not less than 40 per cent of the balance sheet value of the consolidated sub-group is composed of the balance sheets of any bank, insurance company or investment firm.[3] Capital adequacy supervision will be imposed on that sub-group as if it were an independent group, and it will be subjected to requirements on risk concentration, intra-group limits and internal control and risk management processes as if it were a free-standing group. This can frequently give rise to problems for such entities, since it will generally result in the financial group within a conglomerate being managed in a way which is very different from the management philosophy which applies across the conglomerate as a whole. However, regulators tend to be particularly concerned with such groups, and in reality the regulator will wish to be reassured that the degree of independence of

---

[3] CRD Art 3(1).

the management of the financial group within the conglomerate is sufficient to protect depositors and counterparties of the financial business of that conglomerate.

C. Mixed-Activity Groups

21.13 In addition to the issues raised where a non-financial entity owns a financial entity, a further stage of complexity arises where different types of financial business are combined within the same group. The European approach to this is to permit such combinations but to require group supervision to be applied across them. This means that mixed activity groups containing insurance, banking and investment banking activities along with—generally—other types of regulated financial activities are permitted.

21.14 Some specific issues arise with respect to such groups as a result of their inclusion of insurance companies. Regulators have spent many years grappling with the issues which arise where securities trading business is done within banks, and these two disciplines are now sufficiently interrelated that the preparation of consolidated accounts for a group which contains both banking and investment firm subsidiaries presents no very great difficulties, and such consolidation can (in theory) be accomplished on a 'line-by-line' basis. In general, however, an insurance company is prohibited from engaging in any business other than insurance business and ancillary activities. Consequently regulators have not generally had to deal with the issues involved in combining insurance and banking activities within the same entity and in practice supervision of these groups relied for many years on a firm-by-firm approach based on the regulator satisfying itself that the individual firms concerned had sufficient capital as measured by their appropriate standards.

21.15 There is, however, an interesting discontinuity in the regulation of the two firm types, in that a bank which owns an insurance company will (in general) be required to deduct its holding in the insurance company from capital on a solo basis. This means that it is effectively impossible for a bank which is at the head of a bank group to own a large insurance company directly. This problem can, however, be solved through the use of an unregulated holding company which holds the shares of both the bank and the insurer. Conversely, an insurance company which is the parent of a bank is not required to deduct the value of its stake in the bank from its capital, and structures where an insurance company is at the head of a mixed activity group are more common.

21.16 The vast majority of jurisdictions (and the EU) regulate such entities in different ways under different rules and through different supervisors, and the preparation of consolidated regulatory accounts is broadly outside the scope of any directly applicable piece of regulation. The EU has sought to address this through the financial groups directive regime, which amended the banking, investment and insurance regulatory regimes at the EU level in such a way as to provide in each of them for interlocking components designed to require consolidated reports at a group level reflecting the different provisions.

The basis of the supervision of financial conglomerates is broadly the same as the basis for the supervision of banking groups. The parent company of a conglomerate is very likely to be unregulated and outside the scope of the powers of the relevant regulator. Consequently, group capital requirements are imposed by requiring the regulated bank members of the group to ensure that the group as a whole maintains sufficient capital (calculated applying the basis which would apply to the relevant bank) to pass the relevant capital adequacy test if it were applied to it. This means in practice that if the group as a whole has insufficient capital, the regulated entity is itself required to have sufficient capital to make up the shortfall. Thus for a bank which is a member of a financial conglomerate, the practical effect of these rules is that it is required to maintain a level of capital which is the higher of: **21.17**

(a) the capital requirement applied to it on a stand-alone basis, and
(b) the difference between the actual capital of the remainder of the group and the amount of capital which the group would require were it a single regulated bank.

If the group does not satisfy this requirement then the bank's licence may be withdrawn, or administrative limitations may be placed on its ability to conduct regulated business until the position is regularized.

The basis of this approach is the rule of recognition for financial conglomerates. For these purposes any regulator may commence the process of determining whether a particular group is a financial conglomerate, or in some cases a member of the group may require the relevant authority to make that determination. The competent authority that would be coordinator will take the lead in establishing whether a group is a financial conglomerate once the process has been started. This process will normally involve discussions between the financial conglomerate and the competent authorities concerned.   **21.18**

A lead supervisor (called the coordinator) is appointed for each financial conglomerate. Article 10 of the Financial Groups Directive describes the criteria for deciding which competent authority is appointed as coordinator. Article 11 of the Financial Groups Directive sets out the tasks of the coordinator. A financial conglomerate means a consolidation group where: **21.19**

• the group contains at least one bank, investment firm or insurance company (a 'regulated entity');

- either the group is headed by a regulated entity, or regulated entities comprise more than 40 per cent of the of the balance sheet total of the group as a whole;

- the group contains both an insurance company and at least one of a bank or an investment firm, and the balance sheet totals of each should be more than 10 per cent of the balance sheet total of the financial sector entities in the group in total, or EUR 6bn.

Any subgroup of a group which satisfies these criteria will itself be a financial conglomerate. As a result a very large group may contain more than one financial conglomerate as well as possibly being itself a financial conglomerate.

21.20 Because the definition of a financial conglomerate is highly flexible, there is often scope for debate about whether a group is a financial conglomerate and whether it has, by reason of an acquisition, become one or not. As a result the rules on financial conglomerates do not apply as from the moment when a group actually becomes a conglomerate, but from the point at which a relevant regulator serves a notice that it considers the group to be a conglomerate. This raises the theoretical (and in some cases the actual) risk that of two identical groups, one may be treated as a conglomerate and the other not.

21.21 Once a financial conglomerate has become a financial conglomerate and subject to supervision in accordance with the Financial Groups Directive, it will only cease to be a financial conglomerate for this purpose if the total financial services sector activity in the group drops below 35 per cent of balance sheet total, or if the size of the smallest sector in the conglomerate drops below 8 per cent of balance sheet total or EUR 5bn. However, once a conglomerate has dropped below the original 40 per cent and 10 per cent levels, it will cease to be a financial conglomerate in any event three years after that.

21.22 For this purpose the comparison of balance sheets can produce some unusual results—for example, an insurance company will generally carry assets under management on its own balance sheet, whereas a bank will generally hold such assets in unconsolidated funds. It is therefore important to apply the percentage set out above intelligently and in consultation with the regulator, since the analysis is likely to require judgement as well as simple mathematics. Further, the Financial Groups Directive confers a remarkably wide degree of discretion on national regulators to flex the terms of the decision as to which groups will be caught by it. In particular, Articles 3(3) to 3(6), 5(4), and 6(5) permit regulators to:

(1) change the definition of financial conglomerate and the obligations applying with respect to a financial conglomerate;
(2) apply the scheme in the Financial Groups Directive to EEA regulated entities in specified kinds of group structures that do not come within the definition of financial conglomerate; and

(3) exclude a particular entity in the scope of capital adequacy requirements that apply with respect to a financial conglomerate.

D. Methods of Regulating Financial Conglomerates

The joint forum paper[4] classified the existing approaches to conglomerate regula- **21.23** tion into the 'building block prudential method', the 'risk based aggregation method', and the 'risk-based deduction method'. The building block prudential method essentially compares the fully consolidated capital of the conglomerate (as derived from its published financial accounts) to the sum of the regulatory capital requirements for each group member. The risk-based aggregation method sums the solo capital requirements for each regulated firm, and compares it with the capital of the group's parent. The risk-based deduction method takes the balance sheet of each company within the group and looks through to the net assets of each related company, making use of unconsolidated regulatory data. Under this method, the book value of each participation in a dependant company is replaced in the participating company's balance sheet by the difference between the relevant share of the dependant's capital surplus or deficit, and the adequacy of the capital of the group is measured against this yardstick.

The fact that the joint forum was unable to recommend a single method reflects **21.24** the fact that the effectiveness of these methods will vary according to the structure of the conglomerate. In particular, accounting requirements are unlikely to work well with groups headed by insurance companies, since such entities did not historically mark their investments in subsidiaries to market on a regular basis. Equally, the solvency requirement imposed on an insurance subsidiary may well be significantly less than the carrying value of the stake, but this will not reflect the double-counting involved in an insurer investing in the capital of other group entities.

As a result the EU Financial Groups Directive, although largely based on the work **21.25** of the Joint Forum, sets out three prescribed approaches to conglomerates which are similar but not identical to the Joint Forum categories. Those four methods are outlined below.

Method 1

This method calculates capital adequacy using accounting consolidation, and is **21.26** generally applied to bank groups. It operates by calculating the capital requirements which apply to each individual entity within the group and comparing

---

[4] See para 21.01.

them with accounting capital, and is broadly comparable to the building block prudential method. Since it is a good bet that each individual entity is compliant with its own minimum capital requirement (if it were not it would probably have been closed down by the relevant regulator), it may seem that the conglomerate capital resources requirement will necessarily always be satisfied, since if each entity has capital which exceeds its applicable requirement, then the total of the capital of the group as a whole must necessarily exceed the total of the capital requirements of the group as a whole. This would in fact be true if no group member had an equity interest in any other group member. However, in a group, by definition, at least one group member must have an equity interest in at least one other, and more commonly all (or almost all) of the capital of the subsidiaries in the group will be owned by the parent company of the group. There will therefore be some double-counting of capital within the group and the requirement in practice is that the group as a whole has sufficient capital, excluding intra-group investment, to support its balance sheet. For this purpose the capital of the group will constitute the capital of the parent company of the group plus any outside capital raised by any other member of the group.

21.27 The financial resources of a financial conglomerate are broadly calculated in accordance with the sectoral requirements which apply. However, where a conglomerate includes both insurance and non-insurance business (or in some cases investment businesses), the eligibility rules may be different. In particular, the gearing rules (which prescribe the proportion of capital which may be composed of any given type of capital) vary within business types. The issue is therefore whether capital which would be ineligible for a bank may count towards the group capital requirement. The rule here is that once the group capital requirement has been determined, it is then divided up into percentages based on the balance sheet size of the individual components, and the capital rules which apply to the appropriate component are used in respect of it. Thus, if 30 per cent of a conglomerate (measured by balance sheet size) is in the insurance sector, the insurance sector rules may be used in order to determine whether any particular element of group capital counts towards that requirement or not.

Method 2

21.28 This method calculates capital adequacy using a deduction and aggregation approach. This is generally applied to insurance groups. It is broadly comparable with the risk based aggregation method.

21.29 Under this approach, the capital requirement for the group is the sum of the capital requirements for each group member. The capital resources which are compared with this figure are the capital of the parent company plus, for each other group entity, its total capital less the book value of the parent's investment in it (which will usually be zero plus any retained profits not reflected in the parent's valuation of its holding).

Method 3

This method calculates capital adequacy using book values and the deduction of capital requirements. It is broadly comparable to the risk based deduction method. **21.30**

Under this method the capital requirement is the sum of the capital requirement of the group parent and, for each subsidiary, the higher of either its solo capital requirement or the book value of the parent's investment in it. What this approach effectively achieves is to go through the parent balance sheet, replacing each holding with the actual asset value of the entity concerned. Thus, where the parent is carrying a holding in a subsidiary at a value which is less than that subsidiary's capital requirement, the parent must in effect hold capital equal to the difference between the two over and above its holding in the subsidiary itself. **21.31**

Method 4

This is an approach based on a combination of Methods 1, 2 and 3, or a combination of two of those Methods. In general, Methods 1 and 3 will be combined for bank groups, and Methods 2 and 3 will be combined for insurance groups. **21.32**

E. Consolidating Unconnected Entities

It should be noted that the financial conglomerates regime permits the consolidated supervision of groups containing entities which have no capital ties between some of the members. This can arise, for example, where the group is deemed to exist because different EU members are ultimately owned by a non-EU non-financial parent company. This situation would arise if, for example, a Japanese motor company owned two small banks in the UK in circumstances where banking as a whole formed a trivial part of the overall balance sheet of the parent. In such a case Method 4 is the only practical method which can be applied due to the absence of a single financial parent company. **21.33**

One of the more important elements of bank group supervision is the application of limits on the size of individual risk concentrations and of intra-group transactions to the group itself. However, the application of such restrictions within financial conglomerates is exceptionally difficult, not least because these rules are not harmonized across the insurance and banking sectors. Where a group contains both banking and insurance business, the relevant rules are applied to the functional sub-group—thus the banks within a mixed group are subject to limits **21.34** on concentration and intra-group transfers as a whole as if they formed a banking group headed by the ultimate holding company. However, insurance firms within the group are not within this requirement. Technically the directive gives national supervisors the power to impose the rules of the dominant sector across the group as a whole—however, this has proved impossible in practice, and the FSA has chosen not to exercise this power.

21.35 It should be noted that asset management activity may for this purpose be classed either as investment or as insurance at the election of the group. Asset managers will be deemed to fall within the banking and investment group, but if this were an absolute rule it could have the effect that insurance groups with large independent asset management businesses could find themselves inadvertently falling into the conglomerate regime. As a result a group may make an election to treat its asset management activity generally as insurance business if it so desires.

F. Groups Headquartered Outside the EU

21.36 The directives permit groups to be exempted from the requirements of the conglomerates directive if they are subject to equivalent supervision in their home jurisdiction. The EU has concluded that the regimes which are formally equivalent for this purpose are the Swiss regimes (both the Swiss federal Banking Commission and the Federal Office of Private Insurance) and, in the US, the consolidated supervision rules of the Federal Reserve and the Office of the Comptroller of the Currency, the New York State Banking Department, and the Securities and Exchange Commission. Note, however, that groups headed by a US insurance company would not satisfy the equivalence test since US insurance regulation was not held to be compliant with the EU model.[5]

21.37 Where a group is headed by an entity which is not subject to equivalent rules, the relevant EU supervisor is, under the directive, given broad discretion to impose whatever measures he sees fit for the purpose of ensuring appropriate supervision. In practice this has tended to involve the imposition of high stand-alone capital ratios on the relevant regulated entity. However, regulators have the power (if they so choose) to impose on such entities the full weight of consolidated supervision at the group level.

---

[5] See Committee of European Banking Supervisors; Advice to the European Commission; CEBS/2008/04 (on the US) and CEBS/2008/05 on Switzerland.

22

CROSS-BORDER SUPERVISION OF BANK GROUPS

The cross-border supervision of banks is a topic which has ranked high on the list **22.01** of 'hot' banking regulatory topics over the last few years. In the modern financial markets banks tend to be international whilst regulators tend to remain national, and any suggestion of pooling of powers or competences between national regulators may soon lead to undesirable national political consequences. However, it is also generally accepted that this particular issue cannot safely be filed under 'too difficult' for the foreseeable future. Some of the most complex bank failures of recent years have been of cross-border institutions, and the failure of an international bank poses particular difficulties for any national government affected by that failure—not least because of the extreme political difficulty inherent in concerted intergovernmental action to rescue an international bank. The broad consensus at international level that something should be done about the issue has not, however, led to anything significant being done about it.

A. International Group Supervision

The current vogue is for 'colleges' of supervisors. The basic idea is that in order to **22.02** regulate an international bank you convene a meeting of all of the regulators who regulate different parts of that bank (in jurisdictions which have different regulators for different financial activities there may be several regulators present from one jurisdiction), and discuss in a concerted fashion the progress and performance of the bank as a whole.

The difficulties with the college of supervisors approach are well-known. The **22.03** Babel of conflicting views which the college of a large supervisor can engender is an alarming experience, and the primary conclusion to be drawn from any such convention is generally the unsurprising one that different regulators have different priorities, driven generally by national considerations. Attempts to slim down colleges of supervisors are also surprisingly difficult—how do you deal with the regulator in a small country where the bank's activities, although a few per cent of its total balance sheet, constitute a substantial part of that country's banking system. More importantly, there is the issue that the powers of financial regulators generally end where a bank gets into severe difficulties, and the powers of the courts and of court-appointed insolvency practitioners take over. It is sad but true that the primary role of a college of supervisors is to watch from the wings whilst things are going well, and to dissolve itself when they are not.

B. EU Group Supervision

22.04 The exception to this general principle is the European Union. As part of the EU regulatory architecture the EU has adopted a lead supervisor approach in which a single supervisor is appointed as responsible for overseeing the affairs of any group which straddles more than one member state. Since the EU architecture does not, by and large, give national supervisors any actual powers outside their home jurisdictions, the role of EU lead supervisor is broadly confined to consolidated supervision, although a lead supervisor does chair the meetings of the relevant college of supervisors, and the status of lead supervisor is believed in some quarters to give its holder some persuasive authority in dealing with other member state regulators. However, the complexities within the EU regime indicate that even the structuring of a set of rules to automatically determine which supervisor shall be the lead supervisor is a challenging and demanding task.

22.05 The basis of the EU approach is that where a bank is at the head of a group, its regulator is responsible for supervising the activities of that group on a consolidated basis. It is notable that although such credit institutions are required to provide disclosure on both a solo and a consolidated basis, significant subsidiaries of such groups are also required to provide Pillar three disclosures[1] as to their own activities, whether or not they are themselves regulated.

22.06 Where a bank is controlled by a parent which is both a financial holding company[2] and is established in the same member state as itself, it must perform

---

[1] BCD Art 72(1).

[2] A financial holding company for this purpose means a company whose primary purpose is either to conduct financial activities or to acquire holdings in entities whose purpose is to conduct financial activities. Thus, a company will only be a financial holding company if the majority of its activities—whether conducted directly or through subsidiaries—are themselves financial.

its prudential reporting from the perspective of its own holding company. This idea of 'upward consolidation' requires some explanation, since it is alien to the thinking of accountants and most financial professionals. The key point here is that the regulator's power to regulate is based on its power to authorize, and a regulator cannot therefore directly regulate an unauthorized company. In an arrangement where a regulator regulates a bank, but the shares of the bank are held through a holding company, the regulator cannot regulate the holding company if the holding company itself remains unauthorized. What it can do, however, is to say to the regulated bank, 'we will withdraw your authorization unless the group of which you are a part complies with certain requirements'. This is why the obligation to report on a consolidated basis rests on the group member and not on the group parent.

For these purposes the term 'group' has the old-fashioned meaning of a parent and **22.07** its full subsidiaries. As regards participations (that is, holdings of between 20 per cent and 50 per cent in the capital of another entity, the requirement is for proportional consolidation—that is, if an entity has 30 per cent of the capital of another, it must consolidate 30 per cent of the assets of that other, and 30 per cent of its liabilities.

For these purposes, an entity is also treated as a member of a group if it is 'closely **22.08** connected' with it. The notion of 'close connection' in this context dates back to the Seventh Company Law Directive,[3] which addressed (amongst other things) the fact identified in the aftermath of the BCCI collapse that institutions could in practice be inextricably connected without having any formal relationship of parent and subsidiary. Institutions are closely connected with each other for this purpose if:

(1) they are managed on a unified basis, pursuant to formal contract or provisions in their memorandum or articles of association; or
(2) the administrative, management or supervisory bodies of the undertakings consist of broadly the same persons.

This arrangement is known in the EU regime as an 'Article 12(1) relationship', since this definition is to be found in Article 12(1) of that directive.

Regulators have a broad discretion to require consolidation of entities which they **22.09** perceive to have 'capital ties' with a regulated group.[4] Provision is also made for regulators to be able to require consolidation in circumstances where one credit institution exercises 'significant influence' over another, whether by the existence of a common management or otherwise.[5]

---

[3] 83/349/EEC.
[4] This is made explicit in CRD Art 133(3).
[5] CRD Art 134.

22.10 In principle, consolidated supervision is applied within a group at the level of every bank within that group. Thus, where a group contains a parent bank which owns a subsidiary bank which in turn owns a subsidiary bank, there will be five regulatory submissions—three solo and two consolidated—and a sixth if the subsidiary bank itself owns subsidiaries. This is shown diagrammatically in Figure 22.1—each shaded box indicates a solo return, and each dotted box a consolidated return.

22.11 Within the EU, however, an exception is made where the entities are all established within a single jurisdiction. Thus, in the example given above, if all of the banks were in the UK, it would be permissible for the FSA to require only the parent to be consolidated. This permission is subject to conditions—in particular, there must be no foreseeable material obstacle to the transfer of assets within the group, the parent must control the subsidiary and so on. Where there is an ultimate parent holding company in the same jurisdiction, the regulator is also permitted to dispense with consolidated supervision at the subsidiary bank level.

22.12 EU regulators also retain, under the CRD, the right not to apply solo supervision to the parent bank of a group, provided that the parent reports on a consolidated basis. This is a controversial power, and few EU regulators avail themselves of it.[6]

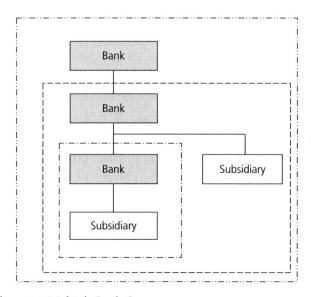

Fig. 22.1 Illustrative Multiple Bank Group

---

[6] CRD Art 69(3). According to the relevant CEBS website, only the French Regulator has availed itself of this right—see <http://www.c-ebs.org/sd/Rules.htm>.

The EU position is also complicated by a series of 'tie-break' provisions designed   **22.13**
to determine which amongst a number of competing national regulators should
be the EU consolidating regulator for a multi-national group with presences in a
number of EU markets. The EU consolidating supervisor functions as a sort of
referee amongst the EU supervisors who have jurisdiction over a particular bank
group, and is responsible for the co-ordination of the gathering and dissemination
of information relating to the group, and also for the planning and co-ordination of
supervisory activities relating to it,[7] and for dealing with emergencies in respect of
the group as a whole.[8] There has been some discussion as to whether, in the event
of a failure affecting a cross-border group within the EU, the consolidated supervisor could perform this role effectively, since the directive gives the co-ordinating
supervisor responsibility but little power. It is likely that the supervisor could use-
fully assist national regulators in reaching agreement, but unlikely that it could
achieve anything in the event of disagreement between those regulators.

These provisions are not straightforward even where the group holding company   **22.14**
is established in the EU, and rapidly become incomprehensible where the group
is ultimately headquartered outside the EU.

The basic EU principle is relatively straightforward.   **22.15**

(1) Where a bank established in a member state is itself the parent of a group, or
     is the parent institution within that member state (ie it is the ultimate holding
     company in that member state), the regulator in that member state is its con-
     solidated supervisor.[9]

(2) Where a bank has as its parent a holding company within the EU, the regula-
     tor which authorized that bank is the consolidated supervisor of that group,[10]
     regardless of the jurisdiction in which the holding company is established.

(3) Where a group contains more than one bank, and those banks are established
     in different EU member states, the supervisor of the bank in the jurisdiction
     in which the holding company is established is the consolidating supervisor.

(4) Where a group contains multiple banks established in different member
     states, but there is more than one parent within the EU (ie where the ultimate
     parent is outside the EU and the EU bank members of the group are
     held through different holding companies) and each parent is established in
     a different member state, the consolidated supervisor is the regulator in the
     jurisdiction containing the bank with the largest balance sheet.[11]

---

[7] CRD Art 129.
[8] CRD Art 130.
[9] CRD Art 125(1).
[10] CRD Art 125(2).
[11] Art 126(1).

(5) Where a group contains multiple banks established in different member states, and the parent company is established in a different jurisdiction from any of the banks, the bank with the largest balance sheet shall be deemed to be the parent bank in the EU and that bank's regulator will be the consolidated supervisor.[12]

(6) The relevant EU supervisors may agree amongst themselves that the consolidated supervisor should be any of them, and are not bound by the principles set out above.[13]

22.16 Where—as is common—an EU bank has a financial holding company, the consolidated supervisor is not required to play any part in the supervision of that holding company.[14]

22.17 Next, there is the effect of the Article 73(2) regime as it relates to cross-border subgroups. The effect of this is that where a UK group has a subsidiary in another non-EEA country, the credit institution which holds that subsidiary must report on a consolidated basis in respect of the group formed by the credit institution and the non-EEA subsidiary or subsidiaries. This rule is of no very great effect where the non-EEA subsidiary is held directly by the parent credit institution of the group, since in such a case the consolidated report will be similar. However, what it does mean is that if a non-EEA subsidiary is held at a lower level within a group, this may result in the inadvertent creation of a requirement to deliver a consolidated return at the level of the group entity which holds the position.

22.18 The next level of complexity arises where an EU bank is part of a group headquartered outside the EU. In this case the EU supervisor is required to ascertain whether the group as a whole is subjected by the regulator in the jurisdiction in which it is established to consolidated regulation which is 'equivalent' to that established under the directive. Somewhat oddly this determination is left to the regulator in the relevant member state concerned—thus it is open to the UK regulator to determine that Australian consolidated supervision is equivalent, whilst the French regulator determines that it is not—although national regulators must consult CEBS before making a final determination on the point. There is a process at the EU level which is intended to give EU-wide guidance on the point, but thus far it has considered and endorsed only the US and Switzerland and in both cases the endorsement is qualified rather than absolute.[15]

---

[12] Art 126(2).
[13] CRD Art 126(3).
[14] CRD Art 127(1).
[15] See <http://ec.europa.eu/internal_market/financial-conglomerates/docs/annex3swiss_en.pdf> for the position as regards Switzerland, and <http://ec.europa.eu/internal_market/financial-conglomerates/docs/annex4america_en.pdf> as regards the United States.

The difficulty, of course, arises where the supervision of the overseas entity is not **22.19** held to be equivalent to the EU regime. In this case supervisors face a situation in which they are permitted to do a wide variety of different things. The most extreme is to apply their own rules to the relevant group at the group level. This can result in the apparently absurd outcome that a group based in Brunei or Sudan is required to prepare a consolidated set of accounts for its worldwide activities and submit it to the relevant EU regulator. In practice, regulators resist this approach, since they would otherwise be deluged with irrelevant information, and the FSA states that it believes that this approach should only be used 'in response to very unusual group structures'.[16] In these circumstances the regulator and the group have a common interest in confining the scrutiny of the European regulator to the European activities of the group concerned, and supervision at the ultimate group level is done using what is known as 'supplementary supervision'—the conglomerates approach described in the previous chapter.

A firm that is a member of a UK consolidation group is required to comply with **22.20** the obligations relating to capital adequacy on the basis of the position if the group as a whole—in other words, if a subsidiary enters into a transaction which would be permissible for it on a standalone basis but which causes the group of which it is a member to contravene the regulatory capital restrictions to which it is subject, then that firm has committed a breach of the rules applicable to it.[17]

It should be noted that although consolidated supervision is generally applied **22.21** across the financial services industry, there is a potentially important exception for investment firms which either do not deal on account, or which deal on own account but are not permitted to hold client money or to maintain external customers in respect of the dealing services which they provide. Such firms (known as Article 22 firms, after Article 22 of the CAD) may be exempted by national regulators on a case-by-case basis from the consolidated supervision requirements otherwise imposed on investment firms.

---

[16] GENPRU 3.2.6.
[17] BIPRU 8.2.1.

23

PILLAR THREE—DISCLOSURE REQUIREMENTS

A. Introduction

23.01 Pillar three constitutes a disclosure regime for regulated banks. The aim is to provide sufficient transparency for investors so as to ensure that the price which banks pay to raise capital in the market reflects the level of risk undertaken by the bank.

23.02 The basis for the Pillar three approach is the idea that regulators can take advantage of market pricing as an aid to supervision. The idea is that the more information counterparties have about a bank, the better a position they are in to make decisions about the relative riskiness of exposures to that bank. If regulators can access information about the funding costs of various banks, they will therefore be able to see which institutions are regarded by the markets as relatively higher-risk than others, and use this information in the performance of their supervision function.

23.03 The problem which this creates is that not all banks have publicly traded bonds or equity, and although disclosure will still be useful to counterparties, the results of the assessments performed by counterparties will not be as accessible as market prices for traded securities. This has produced proposals (notably in the US) for all banks to be compelled to issue at least one tranche of subordinated debt to the public and to have that tranche listed on a stock exchange. The argument is that in this way the market's judgement on the creditworthiness of individual banks will be publicly available and will be improved by public scrutiny and market pricing. This proposal has not as yet found favour with any regulatory body, and there may be issues for many regulators as to whether they have the power to compel a private company to issue public debt.

23.04 The Pillar three framework is intended to complement bank accounts, and the proposals are intended to be supplementary to disclosure mandated by accounting standards. The disclosures are not required to be made as part of published financial accounts, and may be made in any way in which they are generally available. This has the important consequence that Pillar three disclosures are not required to be audited, and are not necessarily required to be presented at the same time as, or within, the relevant bank's financial statements.

23.05 Pillar three overlaps to a significant extent with IFRS 7, which requires reporting entities subject to it to provide disclosures in their accounts that enable users to evaluate the significance of financial instruments for the entities' financial position, and the nature and extent of the risks arising from financial instruments to which the entity is exposed during the period and how the entity manages those risks. These overlaps have created minor difficulties, but in general seem to be managed.

The Basel Pillar three requirements have been substantially incorporated into **23.06** chapter V and Annex XII of the EU Banking Directive.[1]

B. Scope of the Pillar Three Regime

In practice, the most difficult issue created by the Pillar three regime is its **23.07** scope. Basel provides that Pillar three is to apply at the top consolidated level of the relevant banking group, but goes on to say that certain summarized information (notably total and tier one capital ratios) should be disclosed separately for 'significant' subsidiaries. The EU provides much the same—in EU-speak, the requirement is imposed at the level of the EU Parent credit institution and any institution controlled by an EU parent holding company.[2] There is no formal guidance as to the meaning of the term 'significant' in this context, and practice appears to vary.

Within the EU, a bank which is at the head of an EU group may nonetheless be a **23.08** member of a larger banking group. Thus, where a non-EU parent bank which is subject to Pillar three has an EU subsidiary bank, the EU regime provides[3] that national regulators may exempt the EU bank from having to make separate Pillar three disclosure about their own affairs where the relevant information has already appeared within comparable disclosures.

Both Basel and the EU recognize that from time to time it may be necessary for a **23.09** bank not to disclose a particular piece of information for reasons of commercial confidentiality. However, there are no formal rules as to what will justify omission of information in this context, and in practice the issues are dealt with case by case by regulators.

Pillar three disclosures should be made at least annually. Regulators are entitled to **23.10** take the view that more frequent disclosure would be desirable (as, for that matter, are banks). However, practice within the market seems to have settled on an annual disclosure statement.

One of the consequences of the fact that Pillar three is a free-standing regulatory **23.11** obligation is that there is no formal receptacle for it—it is not required to be contained in the annual accounts, and is not required to be reported through a regulatory news service. As a result the Pillar three rules provide only that Pillar three disclosure should be made using an 'appropriate medium'. This has in practice meant the website of the bank concerned, and very few banks do not put this

---

[1] 2006/48/EC.
[2] Ibid, Art 72.1.
[3] Art 72(3).

information on their website. A logical approach would be to combine this information with the annual report; however, concerns have arisen both amongst banks and amongst regulators that numerical financial information presented in an annual report might be justifiably taken by investors to be audited, and since Pillar three information remains unaudited,[4] it is sometimes presented in a separate disclosure document.

23.12 Pillar three requires disclosure against 13 separate risk headings. For some reason the EU has diverged from the Basel requirements in some cases. For each Pillar three heading, both sets of requirements are set out below, with the Basel requirement followed by the EU equivalent.

C. Basic Requirements

Basel requirements

23.13	**Qualitative disclosures**	(a)	The name of the top corporate entity in the group to which the Capital Accord applies.
		(b)	An outline of differences in the basis of consolidation for accounting and regulatory purposes, with a brief description of the entities within the group: (a) that are fully consolidated; (b) that are pro-rata consolidated; (c) that are given a deduction treatment; and (d) from which surplus capital is recognized plus (e) that are neither consolidated nor deducted (eg where the investment is risk weighted).
		(c)	Any restrictions, or other major impediments, on transfer of funds or regulatory capital within the group.
		(d)	The aggregate amount of surplus capital of insurance subsidiaries (whether deducted or subjected to an alternative method) included in the capital of the consolidated group.
		(e)	The aggregate amount of capital deficiencies in all subsidiaries not included in the consolidation (ie that are deducted) and the name(s) of such subsidiaries.
	Quantitative disclosures	(f)	The aggregate amounts (eg current book value) of the firm's total interest in insurance entities, which are risk weighted rather than deducted from capital or subjected to an alternative group-wide method, as well as their name, their country of incorporation or residence, the proportion of ownership interest and, if different, the proportion of voting power in these entities. In addition indicated the quantitative impact on regulatory capital of using this method versus using the deduction or alternative group-wide method.

---

[4] The costs of doing so would be very significant.

EU requirements

The EU requirements are: **23.14**

(a) the name of the credit institution to which the requirements of this Directive
    apply;
(b) an outline of the differences in the basis of consolidation for accounting and
    prudential purposes, with a brief description of the entities that are:
     (i) fully consolidated;
    (ii) proportionally consolidated;
   (iii) deducted from own funds; or
    (iv) neither consolidated nor deducted;
(c) any current or foreseen material practical or legal impediment to the prompt
    transfer of own funds or repayment of liabilities among the parent undertak-
    ing and its subsidiaries;
(d) the aggregate amount by which the actual own funds are less than the required
    minimum in all subsidiaries not included in the consolidation, and the name
    or names of such subsidiaries; and
(e) if applicable, the circumstance of making use of any exemption from supervi-
    sion based on a group exemption[5] or solo-consolidation.[6]

D. Capital Structure

Basel requirements

Qualitative disclosures	(a)	Summary information on the terms and conditions of the main features of all capital instruments, especially in the case of innovative, complex or hybrid capital instruments.	**23.15**
Quantitative disclosures	(b)	The amount of Tier one capital, with separate disclosure of: • paid-up share capital/common stock; • reserves; • minority interests in the equity of subsidiaries; • innovative instruments; • other capital instruments; • surplus capital from insurance companies; and • goodwill and other amounts deducted from Tier one.	
	(c)	The total amount of Tier two and Tier three capital.	
	(d)	Deductions from Tier one and Tier two capital.	
	(e)	Total eligible capital.	

---

[5] BCD Art 69.
[6] BCD Art 70.

EU requirements

23.16 The following information must be disclosed by the credit institutions regarding their own funds:

(a) summary information on the terms and conditions of the main features of all regulatory capital ('own funds') items and components thereof;

(b) the amount of the original own funds, with separate disclosure of all positive items and deductions;

(c) the total amount of additional own funds, and own funds;

(d) deductions from original and additional own funds, with separate disclosure of expected loss items; and

(e) total eligible own funds, net of deductions and limits.

E. Capital Adequacy

Basel requirements

23.17 Qualitative disclosures	(a)	A summary discussion of the bank's approach to assessing the adequacy of its capital to support current and future activities.
Quantitative disclosures	(b)	Capital requirements for credit risk: • portfolio subject to standardized or simplified standardized approach; • portfolio subject to the IRB approaches; • corporate (including SL not subject to supervisory slotting criteria), sovereign and bank; • residential mortgage; • qualifying revolving retail; and • other retail; • securitization exposures.
	(c)	Capital requirements for equity risk in the IRB approach: • equity portfolios subject to the market-based approaches; • equity portfolios subject to simple risk weight method; and • equities in the banking book under the internal models approach (for banks using IMA for banking book equity exposures). • equity portfolios subject to PD/LGD approaches.
	(d)	Capital requirements for market risk: • standardized approach; and • internal models approach—trading book.
	(e)	Capital requirements for operational risk: • basic indicator approach; • standardized approach; and • advanced measurement approach (AMA).

(f)   Total and Tier one capital ratio:
- for the top consolidated group; and
- for significant bank subsidiaries (stand alone or sub-consolidation depending on how the Capital Accord is applied).

EU requirements

The following information must be disclosed regarding the compliance by the **23.18** credit institution with the requirements to maintain adequate capital:

(a)   a summary of the credit institution's approach to assessing the adequacy of its internal capital to support current and future activities;

(b)   for credit institutions calculating the risk-weighted exposure amounts in accordance with the standardized approach, 8 per cent of the risk-weighted exposure amounts for each of the exposure classes specified;

(c)   for credit institutions calculating risk-weighted exposure amounts in accordance with the IRB approach, 8 per cent of the risk-weighted exposure amounts for each of the exposure classes specified. For the retail exposure class, this requirement applies to SMEs, mortgage loans and qualifying revolving real estate exposures.[7] For the equity exposure class, this requirement applies to:
- (i)   the simple risk weight, PD/LGD and internal models approaches;
- (ii) exchange traded exposures, private equity exposures in sufficiently diversified portfolios, and other exposures;
- (iii) exposures subject to supervisory transition regarding capital requirements; and
- (iv) exposures subject to grandfathering provisions regarding capital requirements;

(d)   minimum capital requirements calculated in accordance with the trading book requirements, the foreign exchange and commodities risk requirements; and

(e)   minimum capital requirements calculated in accordance with the operational risk requirements, and disclosed separately.

F. Credit Risk: General Disclosures for All Banks

Both Basel and the EU impose a general disclosure requirement on all banks to **23.19** disclose risk management objectives and policies for each separate category of risk. Disclosure must include:

(a)   the strategies and processes to manage those risks;

---

[7] See Chapter 8 for these definitions.

(b) the structure and organization of the relevant risk management function or other appropriate arrangements;

(c) the scope and nature of risk reporting and measurement systems; and

(d) the policies for hedging and mitigating risk, and the strategies and processes for monitoring the continuing effectiveness of hedges and mitigants.

This is known as the general qualitative disclosure requirement.

Basel requirements

23.20	Qualitative disclosures	(a)	The general qualitative disclosures requirement (above) with respect to credit risk, including: <ul><li>definitions of past due and impaired (for accounting purposes);</li><li>description of approaches followed for specific and general allowances and statistical methods; and</li><li>discussion of the bank's credit risk management policy.</li></ul>
	Quantitative disclosures	(b)	Total gross credit risk exposures, plus average gross exposure over the period broken down by major types of credit exposure.
		(c)	Geographic distribution of exposures, broken down in significant areas by major types of credit exposure.
		(d)	Industry of counterparty type distribution of exposures, broken down by major types of credit exposure.
		(e)	Residual contractual maturity breakdown of the whole portfolio, broken down by major types of credit exposure.
		(f)	By major industry or counterparty type: <ul><li>amount of past due/impaired loans;</li><li>specific and general allowances; and</li><li>charges for specific allowances and charge-offs during the period.</li></ul>
		(g)	Amount of impaired loans and past due loans broken down by significant geographic areas including, if practical, the related amounts of specific and general allowance.
		(h)	Reconciliation of changes in the allowance for loan impairment.

EU requirements

23.21 The following information must be disclosed regarding the credit institution's exposure to credit risk and dilution risk:

(a) the definitions for accounting purposes of 'past due' and 'impaired';

(b) a description of the approaches and methods adopted for determining value adjustments and provisions;

(c) the total amount of exposures after accounting offsets and without taking into account the effects of credit risk mitigation, and the average amount of the exposures over the period broken down by different types of exposure classes;

(d) the geographic distribution of the exposures, broken down in significant areas by material exposure classes, and further detailed if appropriate;

(e) the distribution of the exposures by industry or counterparty type, broken down by exposure classes, and further detailed if appropriate;

(f) the residual maturity breakdown of all the exposures, broken down by exposure classes, and further detailed if appropriate;

(g) by significant industry or counterparty type, the amount of:
  (i) impaired exposures and past due exposures, provided separately;
  (ii) value adjustments and provisions; and
  (iii) charges for value adjustments and provisions during the period;

(h) the amount of the impaired exposures and past due exposures, provided separately, broken down by significant geographical areas including, if practical, the amounts of value adjustments and provisions related to each geographical area;

(i) the reconciliation of changes in the value adjustments and provisions for impaired exposures, shown separately.

The information must comprise:

  (i) a description of the type of value adjustments and provisions;
  (ii) the opening balances;
  (iii) the amounts taken against the provisions during the period;
  (iv) the amounts set aside or reversed for estimated probable losses on exposures during the period, any other adjustments including those determined by exchange rate differences, business combinations, acquisitions and disposals of subsidiaries, and transfers between provisions; and
  (v) the closing balances.

Value adjustments and recoveries recorded directly to the income statement shall be disclosed separately.

G. Credit Risk: Disclosure for Portfolio Subject to the Standardized Approach and Supervisory Risk Weights in the IRB Approaches

Basel requirements

Qualitative disclosures	(a)	For portfolios under the standardized approach: • names of credit assessment agencies used, plus reasons for any changes; • types of exposure for which each agency is used;	**23.22**

Qualitative disclosures (*cont.*)		• a description of the process used to transfer public issue ratings onto comparable assets in the banking book; and
		• the alignment of the alphanumerical scale of each agency used with risk buckets.
Quantitative disclosures	(b)	• For exposure amounts after risk mitigation subject to the standardized approach, amount of a bank's outstanding (rated and unrated) in each risk bucket as well as those that are deducted; and
		• for exposures subject to the supervisory risk weights in IRB (HVCRE and SL products subject to supervisory slotting criteria and equities under the simple risk-weighted method) amount of a bank's outstanding in each risk bucket.

EU requirements

23.23 For credit institutions calculating the risk-weighted exposure amounts in accordance with the standardized approach, the following information shall be disclosed for each of the exposure classes specified:

(a) the names of the nominated ECAIs and ECAs and the reasons for any changes;

(b) the exposure classes for which each ECAI or ECA is used;

(c) a description of the process used to transfer the issuer and issue credit assessments onto items not included in the trading book;

(d) the association of the external rating of each nominated ECAI or ECA with the credit quality steps, taking into account that this information need not be disclosed if the credit institution complies with the standard association published by the competent authority; and

(e) the exposure values and the exposure values after credit risk mitigation associated with each credit quality step, as well as those deducted from own funds.

H. Credit Risk: Disclosures for Portfolio Subject to IRB Approaches

Basel requirements

23.24	Qualitative disclosures	(a)	Supervisor's acceptance of approach/supervisory approved transition.
		(b)	Explanation and review of the:
			• structure of internal rating systems and relation between internal and external ratings;
			• use of internal estimates other than for IRB capital purposes;
			• process for managing and recognizing credit risk mitigation; and
			• control mechanisms for the rating system including discussion of independence, accountability, and rating systems review.

(c) Description of the internal ratings process, provided separately for five distinct portfolios:

- corporate (including SMEs, specialized lending and purchased corporate receivables), sovereign, and bank;
- equities;
- residential mortgage;
- qualifying revolving retail; and
- other retail.

The description should include, for each portfolio:

- the types of exposure included in the portfolio;
- the definitions, methods and data for estimation and validation of PD, and (for portfolios subject to the IRB advanced approach) LGD and/or EAD including assumptions employed in the derivation of these variables; and
- description of deviations as permitted under paragraph 418 and footnote 84 from the reference definition of default where determined to be material, including the board segments of the portfolio(s) affected by such deviations.

Quantitative disclosures: risk assessment

(d) Percentage of total credit exposures (drawn plus EAD on the undrawn) to which IRB approach disclosures relate.

(e) For each portfolio (as defined above) except retail:

- presentation of exposures (outstanding equities) across a sufficient number of PD grades (including default) to allow for a meaningful differentiation of credit risk;
- for banks on the IRB advanced approach, default-weighted average LGD (percentage) for each PD grade (as defined above); and
- for banks on the IRB advanced approach, amount of undrawn commitments and default-weighted average exposure at default ('ED').

For retail portfolios (as defined above), either:

- disclosures outlined above on a pool basis (ie same as for non-retail portfolios); or
- analysis of exposures on a pool basis (outstanding loans and EAD on commitments) against a sufficient number of expected loss ('EL') grades to allow for a meaningful differentiation of credit risk.

Quantitative disclosures: historical results

(f) Actual losses (eg charge-offs and specific provisions) in the preceding period for each portfolio (as defined above) and how this differs from past experience. A discussion of the factors that impacted on the loss experience in the preceding period—for example, has the bank experienced higher than average default rates, or higher than average LGDs and EADs?

(g) Banks' estimates against actual outcomes over a longer period. At a minimum, this should include information on estimates of losses against actual losses in each portfolio (as defined above) over a period sufficient to allow for a meaningful assessment of the performance of the internal rating processes for each portfolio. Where appropriate, banks should further decompose this to provide analysis of PD and, for banks on the advanced IRB approach, LGD and EAD outcomes against estimates provided in the quantitative risk assessment disclosures above.

EU requirements

23.25 The credit institutions calculating the risk-weighted exposure amounts in accordance with the IRB approach must disclose the following information:

(a) the competent authority's acceptance of approach or approved transition;

(b) an explanation and review of:
  (i) the structure of internal rating systems and relation between internal and external ratings;
  (ii) the use of internal estimates other than for calculating risk-weighted exposure amounts in accordance with Articles 84 to 89;
  (iii) the process for managing and recognizing credit risk mitigation; and
  (iv) the control mechanisms for rating systems including a description of independence, accountability, and rating systems review;

(c) a description of the internal ratings process, provided separately for the following exposure classes:
  (i) central governments and central banks;
  (ii) institutions;
  (iii) corporate, including SMEs, specialized lending and purchased corporate receivables;
  (iv) retail, for each of the categories of exposures to which the different correlations in Annex VII, Part 1, points 10 to 13 correspond; and
  (v) equities;

(d) the exposure values for each of the exposure classes specified in Article 86. Exposures to central governments and central banks, institutions and corporates where credit institutions use own estimates of LGDs or conversion factors for the calculation of risk-weighted exposure amounts must be disclosed separately from exposures for which the credit institutions do not use such estimates;

(e) for each of the exposure classes central governments and central banks, institutions, corporate and equity, and across a sufficient number of obligor grades (including default) to allow for a meaningful differentiation of credit risk, credit institutions must disclose:
  (i) the total exposures (for the exposure classes central governments and central banks, institutions and corporate, the sum of outstanding loans and exposure values for undrawn commitments; for equities, the outstanding amount);
  (ii) for the credit institutions using own LGD estimates for the calculation of risk-weighted exposure amounts, the exposure-weighted average LGD in percentage;

(iii)   the exposure-weighted average risk weight; and

(iv)   for the credit institutions using own estimates of conversion factors for the calculation of risk-weighted exposure amounts, the amount of undrawn commitments and exposure-weighted average exposure values for each exposure class;

(f)   for the retail exposure class and for each of the categories as defined under point (c)(iv), either the disclosures outlined under (e) above (if applicable, on a pooled basis), or an analysis of exposures (outstanding loans and exposure values for undrawn commitments) against a sufficient number of EL grades to allow for a meaningful differentiation of credit risk (if applicable, on a pooled basis);

(g)   the actual value adjustments in the preceding period for each exposure class (for retail, for each of the categories as defined under point (c)(iv) and how they differ from past experience;

(h)   a description of the factors that impacted on the loss experience in the preceding period (for example, has the credit institution experienced higher than average default rates, or higher than average LGDs and conversion factors); and

(i)   the credit institution's estimates against actual outcomes over a longer period. At a minimum, this must include information on estimates of losses against actual losses in each exposure class (for retail, for each of the categories as defined under point (c)(iv) over a period sufficient to allow for a meaningful assessment of the performance of the internal rating processes for each exposure class (for retail for each of the categories as defined under point (c)(iv). Where appropriate, the credit institutions must further decompose this to provide analysis of PD and, for the credit institutions using own estimates of LGDs and/or conversion factors, LGD and conversion factor outcomes against estimates provided in the quantitative risk assessment disclosures above.

For the purposes of point (c), the description must include the types of exposure included in the exposure class, the definitions, methods and data for estimation and validation of PD and, if applicable, LGD and conversion factors, including assumptions employed in the derivation of these variables, and the descriptions of material deviations from the definition of default as set out in Annex VII, Part 4, points 44 to 48, including the broad segments affected by such deviations.

I. Credit Risk Mitigation: Disclosures for Standardized and IRB Approaches

Basel requirements

23.26	**Qualitative disclosures** (a)	The general qualitative disclosures requirement (above) with respect to credit risk mitigation including:

- policies and processes for, and an indication of the extent to which the bank makes use of, on-and off-balance sheet netting;
- policies and processes for collateral valuation and management;
- a description of the main types of collateral taken by the bank;
- the main types of guarantor/credit derivative counterparty and their creditworthiness; and
- information about (market or credit) risk concentrations within the mitigation taken.

Quantitative disclosures (b) For each separately disclosed credit risk portfolio under the standardized and/or foundation IRB approach, the total exposure (after netting) that is covered by:

- eligible financial collateral; and
- other eligible IRB collateral;

before the application of haircuts.

(c) For each separately disclosed portfolio under the standardized and/or IRB approach, the total exposure (after netting) that is covered by guarantees/ credit derivatives.

EU requirements

23.27 The credit institutions applying credit risk mitigation techniques must disclose the following information:

(a) the policies and processes for, and an indication of the extent to which the entity makes use of, on- and off-balance sheet netting;

(b) the policies and processes for collateral valuation and management;

(c) a description of the main types of collateral taken by the credit institution;

(d) the main types of guarantor and credit derivative counterparty and their creditworthiness;

(e) information about market or credit risk concentrations within the credit mitigation taken;

(f) for credit institutions calculating risk-weighted exposure amounts in accordance with the standardized or foundation IRB, separately for each exposure class, the total exposure value (after, where applicable, on- or off-balance sheet netting) that is covered—after the application of volatility adjustments—by eligible financial collateral, and other eligible collateral; and

(g) separately for each exposure class, the total exposure (after, where applicable, on- or off-balance sheet netting) that is covered by guarantees or credit derivatives. For the equity exposure class, this requirement applies to SMEs, mortgage loans and qualifying revolving real estate exposures.

J. General Disclosure for Exposures Related to Counterparty Credit Risk

Basel requirements

Qualitative disclosures	(a)	The general qualitative disclosures requirement (above) with respect to derivatives and CCR including: • discussion of methodology used to assign economic capital and credit limits for counterparty credit exposures; • discussion of policies for securing collateral and establishing credit reserves; • discussion of policies with respect to wrong-way risk exposures; • discussion of the impact of the amount of collateral the bank would have to provide given a credit rating downgrade.	**23.28**
Quantitative disclosures	(b)	Gross positive fair value of contracts, netting benefits, netted current credit exposure, collateral held (including type eg cash, government securities, etc) and net derivatives credit exposure. Also report measures for exposure at default, or exposure amount, under the IMM, SM or CEM, whichever is applicable. The notional values of credit derivative hedges and the distribution of current credit exposure by types of credit exposure.	
	(c)	Credit derivative transactions that create exposures to CRR (notional value), segregated between use for the institutions own credit portfolio. As well as in its intermediation activities, including the distribution of the credit derivatives products used, broken down further by protection bought and sold within each product group.	
	(d)	The estimate of alpha if the bank has received supervisory approval to estimate alpha.	

EU requirements

The following information must be disclosed regarding the credit institution's exposure to counterparty credit risk: **23.29**

(a) a discussion of the methodology used to assign internal capital and credit limits for counterparty credit exposures;

(b) a discussion of policies for securing collateral and establishing credit reserves;

(c) a discussion of policies with respect to wrong-way risk exposures;

(d) a discussion of the impact of the amount of collateral the credit institution would have to provide given a downgrade in its credit rating;

(e) gross positive fair value of contracts, netting benefits, netted current credit exposure, collateral held and net derivatives credit exposure. Net derivatives credit exposure is the credit exposure on derivatives transactions after considering both the benefits from legally enforceable netting agreements and collateral arrangements;

(f) measures for exposure value under the mark-to-market, original exposure, standardized and internal models methods of calculating counterparty risk;

(g) the notional value of credit derivative hedges, and the distribution of current credit exposure by types of credit exposure;

(h) credit derivative transactions (notional), segregated between use for the credit institution's own credit portfolio, as well as in its intermediation activities, including the distribution of the credit derivatives products used, broken down further by protection bought and sold within each product group; and

(i) the estimate of α^8 if the credit institution has received the approval of the competent authorities to estimate α.

K. Securitization: Disclosure for Standardized and IRB Approaches

Basel requirements

23.30 Qualitative disclosures	(a)	The general qualitative disclosure requirement (above) with respect to securitization (including synthetics), includes a discussion of: • the bank's objectives in relation to securitization activity; and • the roles played by the bank in the securitization process and an indication of the extent of the bank's involvement in each of them.
	(b)	Summarize the bank's accounting policies for securitization activities, including: • whether the transactions are treated as sales or financing; • recognition of gain on sale; • key assumption for valuing retained interests; and • treatment of synthetic securitizations if this is not covered by other accounting policies (eg on derivatives).
	(c)	Names of ECAIs used for securitizations and the types of securitization exposure for which each agency is used.

---

[8] The internal models method estimate of exposure value: see para 15.33.

Qualitative disclosures	(d)	The total outstanding exposures securitized by the bank and subject to the securitization framework (broken down into traditional/synthetic), by exposure type.
	(e)	For exposure securitized by the bank and subject to the securitization framework: • amount of impaired/past due assets securitized; and • losses recognized by the bank during the current period broken down by exposure type.
	(f)	Aggregate amount of securitization exposures retained or purchased broken down by exposure type.
	(g)	Aggregate amount of securitization exposures retained or purchased and the associated IRB capital charges for these exposures broken down into a meaningful number of risk weight bands. Exposures that have been deducted entirely from Tier one capital, credit enhancing I/Os deducted from Total Capital, and other exposures deducted from total capital should be disclosed separately by type of underlying asset.
	(h)	For securitizations subject to the early amortization treatment, the following items by underlying asset type for securitized facilities: • the aggregate drawn exposures attributed to the seller's and investors' interests; • the aggregate IRB capital charges incurred by the bank against its retained (ie the seller's) shares of the drawn balances and undrawn lines; and • the aggregate IRB capital charges incurred by the bank against the investor's shares of drawn balances and undrawn lines.
	(i)	Banks using the standardized approach are also subject to disclosures (g) and (h), but should use the capital charges for the standardized approach.
	(j)	Summary of current year's securitization activity, including the amount of exposures securitized (by exposure type), and recognized gain or loss on sale by asset type.

EU requirements

The credit institutions calculating risk-weighted exposure amounts in accordance **23.31** with the securitization regime shall disclose the following information:

(a) a description of the credit institution's objectives in relation to securitization activity;

(b) the roles played by the credit institution in the securitization process;

(c) an indication of the extent of the credit institution's involvement in each of them;

(d) the approaches to calculating risk-weighted exposure amounts that the credit institution follows for its securitization activities;

(e) a summary of the credit institution's accounting policies for securitization activities, including:
   (i) whether the transactions are treated as sales or financings;
   (ii) the recognition of gains on sales;

     (iii) the key assumptions for valuing retained interests; and

     (iv) the treatment of synthetic securitizations if this is not covered by other accounting policies;

(f) the names of the ECAIs used for securitizations and the types of exposure for which each agency is used;

(g) the total outstanding amount of exposures securitized by the credit institution and subject to the securitization framework (broken down into traditional and synthetic), by exposure type;

(h) for exposures securitized by the credit institution and subject to the securitization framework, a breakdown by exposure type of the amount of impaired and past due exposures securitized, and the losses recognized by the credit institution during the period;

(i) the aggregate amount of securitization positions retained or purchased, broken down by exposure type;

(j) the aggregate amount of securitization positions retained or purchased, broken down into a meaningful number of risk weight bands. Positions that have been risk weighted at 1250 per cent or deducted must be disclosed separately;

(k) the aggregate outstanding amount of securitized revolving exposures segregated by the originator's interest and the investors' interest; and

(l) a summary of the securitization activity in the period, including the amount of exposures securitized (by exposure type), and recognized gain or loss on sale by exposure type.

L. Market Risk: Disclosures for Banks using the Standardized Approach

Basel requirements

23.32	Qualitative disclosures	(a) The general qualitative disclosure requirement (above) for market risk including the portfolios covered by the standardized approach.
	Quantitative disclosures	(b) The capital requirements for: • interest rate risk; • equity position risk; • foreign exchange risk; and • commodity risk.

EU requirements

The credit institutions calculating their capital requirements in accordance with **23.33** the trading book regime must disclose those requirements separately for each risk referred to in those provisions.

M. Market Risk: Disclosures for Banks using the Internal Models Approach (IMA) for Trading Portfolios

Basel requirements

Qualitative disclosures	(a)	The general qualitative disclosure requirement (above) for market risk including the portfolios covered by the IMA.	**23.34**
	(b)	For each portfolio covered by the IMA: • the characteristics of the models used; • a description of stress testing applied to the portfolio; and • a description of the approach used for backtesting/validating the accuracy and consistency of the internal models and modelling processes.	
	(c)	The scope of acceptance by the supervisor.	
Quantitative disclosures	(d)	For trading portfolios under the IMA: • The high, mean and low VaR values over the reporting period and period-end; and • A comparison of VaR estimates with actual outcomes, with analysis of important 'outliers' in backtest results.	

EU requirements

The following information must be disclosed by each credit institution which uses **23.35** internal models to calculate capital requirements for any portfolio:

(a) for each sub-portfolio covered:
   (i) the characteristics of the models used;
   (ii) a description of stress testing applied to the sub-portfolio;
   (iii) a description of the approaches used for back-testing and validating the accuracy and consistency of the internal models and modelling processes;
(b) the scope of acceptance by the competent authority; and
(c) a description of the extent and methodologies for compliance with the systems and controls requirements for the use of models.

N. Operational Risk

Basel requirements

23.36 **Qualitative disclosures**	(a)	In addition to the general qualitative disclosure requirement (above), the approach(es) for operational risk capital assessment for which the bank qualifies.
	(b)	Description of the AMA, if used by the bank, including a discussion of relevant internal and external factors considered in the bank's measurement approach. In the case of partial use, the scope and coverage of the different approaches used.
Quantitative disclosures	(c)	For banks using the AMA, the operational risk charge before and after any reduction in capital resulting from the use of insurance.

EU requirements

23.37 The following information must be disclosed on operational risk:

(a) the approaches for the assessment of own funds requirements for operational risk that the credit institution qualifies for; and

(b) a description of the methodology set out in Article 105, if used by the credit institution, including a discussion of relevant internal and external factors considered in the credit institution's measurement approach. In the case of partial use, the scope and coverage of the different methodologies used.

The credit institutions using the advanced measurement approach for calculating operational risk requirements must disclose a description of the use of insurance for the purpose of mitigating the risk.

O. Equities: Disclosures for Banking Book Positions

Basel requirements

23.38 **Qualitative disclosures**	(a)	The general qualitative disclosure requirement (above) with respect to equity risk, including: • differentiation between holdings on which capital gains are expected and those taken under other objectives including for relationship and strategic reasons; and • discussion of important policies covering the valuation and accounting of equity holdings in the banking book. This includes the accounting techniques and valuation methodologies used, including key assumptions and practices affecting valuation as well as significant changes in these practices.

Qualitative disclosures	(b)	Value disclosed in the balance sheet of investments, as well as the fair value of those investments; for quoted securities, a comparison to publicly quoted share values where the share price is materially different from fair value.
	(c)	The types and nature of investments, including the amount that can be classified as: • Publicly traded; and • Privately held.
	(d)	The cumulative realized gains (losses) arising from sales and liquidations in the reporting period.
	(e)	Total unrealized or latent revaluation gains (losses) and any amounts included in Tier one and/or Tier two capital.
	(f)	Capital requirements broken down by appropriate equity groupings, consistent with the bank's methodology, as well as the aggregate amounts and the type of equity investments subject to any supervisory transition or grandfathering provisions regarding regulatory capital requirements.

EU requirements

The following information must be disclosed regarding the exposures in equities **23.39** not included in the trading book:

(a) the differentiation between exposures based on their objectives, including for capital gains relationship and strategic reasons, and an overview of the accounting techniques and valuation methodologies used, including key assumptions and practices affecting valuation and any significant changes in these practices;

(b) the balance sheet value, the fair value and, for those exchange-traded, a comparison to the market price where it is materially different from the fair value;

(c) the types, nature and amounts of exchange-traded exposures, private equity exposures in sufficiently diversified portfolios, and other exposures;

(d) the cumulative realized gains or losses arising from sales and liquidations in the period; and

(e) the total unrealized gains or losses, the total latent revaluation gains or losses, and any of these amounts included in the original or additional own funds.

P. Interest Rate Risk in the Banking Book

Basel requirements

| **Qualitative disclosures** | (a) | The general qualitative disclosure requirement (above), including the nature of IRRBB and key assumptions regarding loan prepayments and behaviour of non-maturity deposits, and frequency of IRRBB measurement. | **23.40** |

Quantitative disclosures	(b)	The increase (decline) in earnings or economic value (or relevant measure used by management) for upward and downward rate shocks according to management's method for measuring IRRBB, broken down by currency (as relevant).

EU requirements

23.41 The following information must be disclosed by credit institutions on their exposure to interest rate risk on positions not included in the trading book:

(a) the nature of the interest rate risk and the key assumptions (including assumptions regarding loan prepayments and behaviour of non-maturity deposits), and frequency of measurement of the interest rate risk; and

(b) the variation in earnings, economic value or other relevant measure used by the management for upward and downward rate shocks according to management's method for measuring the interest rate risk, broken down by currency.

INDEX